D0353898

Explorer
Germany

 Publishing

Front cover (a): *traditional Bavarian dress* (b) *interior of the redesigned Reichstag in Berlin* (c) *the medieval town of Rothenburg-ob-der-Tauber, Northern Bavaria* Spine: *decorated beer mug, Upper Bavaria* Back cover: *brass band playing in Berlin* Page 3: *the Gothic Rathaus and the Marienplatz, Munich* Page 4: *Dinkelsbühl, a pretty walled town in Northern Bavaria* Page 5: *decorated maypole in the food market* Page 6: *Bamberg's Rathaus, built on an island between two rival parts of the city* Page 7 (a): *bronze statue, Munich* Page 7 (b): *enjoying a drink in Munich's famous Hofbräuhaus* Page 8: *the resort of Oberstdorf, near the Allgäuer Alps* Page 9: *half-timbered houses in the medieval town of Bad Wimpfen*

Written by John Ardagh, Lindsay Hunt, Michael Ivory, Tim Locke, Michael Kallenbach, Stephen Locke, Colin and Fleur Speakman
Additional writing and research by Tony Evans, Audrey Horne
Revision verifier: Robert Tilley
Cover design by Carroll Associates
Revised fourth edition 2000
Revised third edition 1996
First published 1993

Edited, designed, produced by AA Publishing 1993, 1995, 1996, 2000
© The Automobile Association 1993, 1995, 1996, 2000
Maps © The Automobile Association 1993, 1995, 1996, 2000

Distributed in the United Kingdom by AA Publishing, Norfolk House, Priestley Road, Basingstoke, Hampshire, RG24 9NY.

The contents of this publication are believed correct at the time of printing. Nevertheless, the publishers cannot be held responsible for any errors or omissions or for changes in the details given in this guide or for the consequences of any reliance on the information provided by the same. Assessments of attractions, hotels, restaurants and so forth are based upon the author's own personal experience and, therefore, descriptions given in this guide necessarily contain an element of subjective opinion which may not reflect the publishers' opinion or dictate a reader's own experiences on another occasion.
We have tried to ensure accuracy in this guide, but things do change and we would be grateful if readers would advise us of any inaccuracies they may encounter.

© The Automobile Association 1993, 1995, 1996, 2000

A CIP catalogue record for this book is available from the British Library.

ISBN 0 7495 2281 X

Published by AA Publishing (a trading name of Automobile Association Developments Limited whose registered office is Norfolk House, Priestley Road, Basingstoke, Hampshire, RG24 9NY. Registered number 1878835).

Titles in the Explorer series:
Australia • Boston & New England • Britain • Brittany California • Caribbean • China • Costa Rica • Crete • Cuba Cyprus • Egypt • Florence & Tuscany • Florida • France Greek Islands • Hawaii • India • Indonesia • Ireland • Israel Italy • Japan • London • Mallorca • Mexico • Moscow & St Petersburg • New York • New Zealand • Paris • Portugal Provence • Rome • San Francisco • Scotland • Singapore & Malaysia • South Africa • Spain • Tenerife • Thailand • Tunisia Turkey • Turkish Coast• Venice • Vietnam

AA World Travel Guides publish nearly 300 guidebooks to a full range of cities, countries and regions across the world. Find out more about AA Publishing and the wide range of services the AA provides by visiting our Web site at www.theaa.co.uk

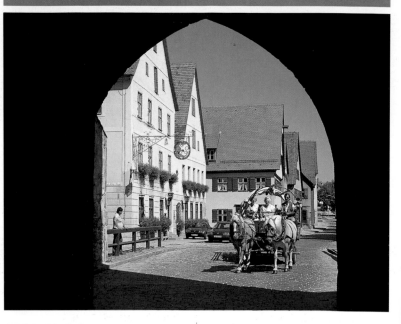

ORGANISATION

Germany Is, Germany Was
Discusses aspects of life and culture in contemporary Germany and explores significant periods in its history.

A–Z
Breaks down the country into regional chapters, and covers places to visit, including walks and drives. Within this section fall the Focus On articles, which consider a variety of subjects in greater detail.

Travel Facts
Contains the strictly practical information vital for a successful trip.

Hotels and Restaurants
Lists recommended establishments throughout Germany, giving a brief summary of their attractions.

ABOUT THE RATINGS
Most places described in this book have been given a separate rating. These are as follows:

► ► ►   **Do not miss**

► ►   **Highly recommended**

►   **Worth seeing**

MAPS
To make each particular location easier to find, every main entry in this book has a map reference to the right of its name. This comprises a number, followed by a letter, followed by another number, such as 176B3. The first number (176) refers to the page on which the map can be found, the letter (B) and the second number (3) pinpoint the square in which the main entry is located. The maps on the inside front cover and inside back cover are referred to as IFC and IBC respectively.

Contents

6

Robert Tilley has lived in Germany for more than 30 years, where he writes (mostly film-scripts, travel articles, and books) and produces English-language programmes for German television. He commutes between homes in Munich, the Bavarian Alps and Mallorca.

My Germany

Visitors may encounter only a few of the facets of this surprisingly diverse country – certainly too few to form a complete picture of present-day Germany and its people. But just a handful would be sufficient to supply a positive picture to add to the collection of snapshots from a holiday tour. First impressions are of course provided by the landscape and the people within it. Germans are uncharacteristically reticent about the often astounding beauty and variety of their country, probably because it would take the lifetime of the average German to discover them all. From the deserted beaches and dunes of the North Sea and Baltic coastlines, the country rises through regions of vast forests and thick woodland, hauntingly romantic river valleys, wild upland and on to the towering Bavarian Alps. Punctuating this map are cities and towns of outstanding beauty and cultural energy and villages where time stands still – each community a living tribute to its people.

And so to the people – the Germans themselves. In general, they are scrupulously correct, friendly and helpful, but that doesn't mean the Germans are unable to relax and just have fun. Only the Spanish can rival the Germans in seizing on any opportunity for a party – it's significant that Spain and Germany have more public holidays than any other European country. And nowhere in Europe is it easier to stock up for a party – the beer is Europe's best and cheapest, and the wine is by no means Europe's worst. A Bavarian lakeside beer bash, a Rhineland wine festival, Berlin's annual 'Love Parade', Hamburg's 'Dom' festivities, Carnival in Mainz and Cologne, Fasching in Munich – the opportunities for celebration are endless. Other benefits of life in Germany include a public transport system that's the envy of other European countries; moderate prices; and a wide range of accessible cultural activities in even the most provincial towns. The only drawback can be the weather!
Robert Tilley

Germany Is
Germany Was

For centuries, Germany consisted of small, independent units. The differences between the peoples were – and still are – very great. Asked to sum up Germany as a country, some foreigners claim that it still doesn't exist. Yet, as a current political controversy shows, when the concept of nationhood is under threat, the Germans close ranks and demonstrate a solid front.

The controversy over government proposals to allow non-German residents to take out dual citizenship threw a new light on a dilemma that caused even the 19th-century German philosopher Friedrich Nietsche some bother. He said: 'The Germans are characterised by the fact that they never cease asking themselves what is German'.

Germany's new left-wing coalition government of Social Democrats and Greens maintained that the measure would ease the integration of the country's minorities, particularly the Turks. Bavaria's right-wing Christian Social Union, which dominates political life in that *Land* (State), argued that dual citizenship would have the reverse effect, creating a two-nation society.

The major opposition party in Bonn, the Christian Democratic Union, expanded the Bavarian campaign into a Germany-wide popular plebiscite, with staggering results. Half a million opponents of the proposed dual citizenship legislation signed the plebiscite within its first two weeks. The plebiscite, now a hot political potato, was cited as a chief cause for the defeat suffered by the Bonn coalition parties in the first popularity test of their reign, in an election for the State legislature of Hessen in February, 1999.

The dual-citizenship issue touches a sensitive German nerve and highlights another central paradox of German nationhood. No other European country can claim to have

GERMANY

11

A paradox

The tourist's Germany: an Augsburg café

done more to shelter refugees from the slaughter in former Yugoslavia, while Germany's geographical location also makes the country a natural destination for other migrants from the East. Yet the idea of actually sharing German nationality with these fellow residents is anathema to a large number of Germans. On this central issue, regional, cultural, historical and language differences are forgotten – and a large slice of society, from north to south, west to east, finds unity in the fact of 'being German'. As Nietsche said 100 years ago, the debate has no end ...

Sausage, sauerkraut, beer, coffee and enormous cakes come to mind as typical German fare. And, yes...sausages do come in hundreds of different varieties, while cabbage is consumed quite frequently, along with large quantities of potatoes. These stereotypical images are, as you might expect, only a small part of the picture. The reality is actually much more varied and adventurous...

There are some staple menu items: *Kaffee und Kuchen* – coffee and cake – is a favourite afternoon snack, with rich cakes, usually topped with mounds of whipped cream. Beer is found in a variety of forms, from Pilsner to Berlin's *Weisse*, a beer with a sweet syrup added to it. Local wine is a welcome addition to a hearty German meal.

QUALITY AND VARIETY Visitors are often surprised at how well prepared German food is – and at its variety. A visit to the food halls in Berlin's giant KaDeWe department store or the elegant Alois Dallmayr store in Munich will bear this out.

❏ In KaDeWe's seventh-floor food hall, with its special high-speed elevator that stops nowhere else, there are over a thousand varieties of German sausage – overwhelming to the uninitiated sausage buyer! ❏

German cooking is reputedly heavy, but the country's restaurant scene has recently been invaded by *neue deutsche Küche – nouvelle cuisine* German style – featuring creative and tasty dishes using traditional German ingredients.

EATING THROUGH THE DAY For most Germans, breakfast may include a boiled egg, cereal and yoghurt, but more probably bread with cheese, jam and/or cold meats.

Lunch, the main meal of the day, could include a juicy *Schnitzel* (cutlet) – usually pork – roasted potatoes and a salad. Dinner is often a cold and lighter meal of bread, a larger variety of meats and cheeses than at breakfast, and, in colder weather, perhaps a soup or small stew. A popular stew is a combination of lentils and local varieties of sausage. German desserts are almost always fruit- or cream-based dishes.

The amount of bread consumed by most Germans will astound visitors, and the variety and amount of textured, heavy, dark brown breads in the bakery is amazing. Try them all and decide which you like most.

Bread is an important ingredient in German cuisine

The homeland of Bach, Beethoven, Brahms, Wagner and Stockhausen, among many other of the world's musical geniuses, Germany has a reputation for nurturing musicians and composers – a tradition centuries old that survives today. Visitors will find a wealth of musical events, from the historic and classical to modern, up-to-the-minute rock.

Among the joys of a trip to Germany are evenings at the Berlin Philharmonic, the Staatsoper of east Berlin, the Hamburg Opera and Munich's National Theatre (home of the Bavarian State Opera), which offer some of the best orchestral sounds and operatic productions to be heard and seen anywhere in the world.

14

❑ The Berlin Philharmonic – the best orchestra in the country and one of the best in the world – has had Claudio Abbado as its chief conductor. ❑

A BRIEF HISTORY The German love of music and traditional folk songs can be traced back to pre-Christian tribal times. By the end of the 15th century, with the widespread use of the newly developed organ in churches, national interest and support for classical music had blossomed. In the 16th and 17th centuries, with the Reformation and the flowering of the Lutheran chorale, musical excellence was associated with churches. At this time vocalists, choristers, organists, instrumentalists, and their directors worked as professional musicians.

By the 18th century, court patronage was an important source of employment for musicians. German Baroque music began to flower in such geniuses as Handel, Telemann, and Bach. At the same time, musical theatre was developing in Vienna, and the German singspiel became the rage. At the peak of the singspiel's popularity, Mozart wrote his last opera, *The Magic Flute*, and German opera came of age. Beethoven

Above: Ludwig Van Beethoven
Top: the Munich Oktoberfest

produced his major romantic symphonies and his only opera, *Fidelio*, soon after this time.

Romanticism was in the air in Germany in the 19th century. After Beethoven came Schumann and Mendelssohn, then Brahms, Liszt, and Wagner, who transformed German national folk tales into powerful Romantic operas.

German music suffered a setback in the mid-20th century, under Nazism, when all 'Jewish' music was banned. However, since the war the avant-garde – headed by Karlheinz Stockhausen – has pioneered new musical forms.

THE MUSIC SCENE TODAY The numerous choirs founded earlier in Germany are still the springboard for much of the country's musical talent. Thanks to the nation's generous tax system, which includes a levy for churches, choirs are found in many small communities. At city, state, and national levels, huge subsidies for the performing arts and symphony orchestras help keep standards extremely high, and the cost of tickets for performances exceptionally low. Thus classical music is enjoyed by a greater segment of society in Germany than almost anywhere else, though this has the drawback that tickets are hard to come by.

Visitors are always advised to plan ahead and reserve seats well in advance. However, as in most major cities, the concierge in the bigger hotels invariably has his own excellent contacts and will generally be able to meet your last-minute wishes – encouraged, of course, by a generous tip.

During the 1950s, jazz – totally suppressed by the Third Reich – was effectively a copy of the American scene. By the 1960s foreign jazz musicians had lost their appeal to German youth, and the embryonic rock groups flourishing in Britain, most notably the Beatles, were invited to play in new clubs in Hamburg,

Hannover, and West Berlin. Their popularity quickly spawned imitators such as the Rattles, who enjoyed great domestic success, but their lack of confidence and rock tradition meant that any songs for foreign markets were sung in English.

Particularly popular was the heavier, more introspective end of the rock spectrum, represented by Amon Duul and Tangerine Dream. The enormous drama of German reunification gave performers such as Udo Lindenberg and the Scorpions ample material for politically-rooted numbers, and the Scorpions 'internationalised' the euphoric mood with their hit 'Winds of Change', Germany's own Bruce Springsteen, the rocker Peter Maffei, caught the mood well and kept pace with changes through the 1990s with compositions that pleaded for social harmony in the face of the challenges presented by the painful process of reunification.

Music in all forms flourishes in Germany. Below: jazz in Hamburg; top: the Berlin Philharmonic Orchestra

Health in Germany is a national obsession. Foreigners living in the country remark at how often they are told by Germans that certain foods, certain activities and many prescribed drugs are 'not good for you'. But the German view of health is not usually negative. Good health is seen as an attainable goal, and Germans tend to take a positive, active approach to staying healthy.

Even a dentist will try to talk you out of having an injection of anaesthetic during a filling because of its poisonous content. Germans, it seems, prefer to endure the pain!

With doctors and pharmacists prescribing homeopathic drugs, and people cycling to work on specially designated pathways during the week or enjoying long hikes in the woods and forests during weekends, it is no wonder that the average life expectancy in Germany is one of the highest in Europe.

THE SPA The best place to study this pursuit of good health is at the *Kurort*, or spa town. Spas are dotted all over Germany, from seaside towns to the Bavarian Alps. Usually, they have a giant bathhouse where anyone can take the healing waters.

In most other countries in Europe, spa towns have become relics of the 19th century, but German spas are

Baden-Baden (below and top): a popular spa in the southwest

> ❑ Until recently German medical students were required, as part of their qualifying studies, to take a course in *Balneologie*, the science of taking the waters. ❑

kept alive by medical aid schemes that provide for periodic stays of between three and six weeks in spa clinics and hotels. Cuts in government expenditure on health and welfare have trimmed spa benefits considerably in recent years, although anyone with a history of illness can normally spend a few weeks at a spa every three or four years, with most of the cost covered by medical aid. Some of the spas are very luxurious indeed, with 'grand hotel' accommodation and sports facilities ranging from archery, golf and tennis to riding and boating. Many have gambling casinos and glittering nightclubs. Besides the baths, today's modern spa resorts offer such amenities as golf, tennis, horse racing, casinos, boating, and skiing – something for every taste. A typical spa treatment might include a mud bath or hydrotherapy, saunas and steam treatments, all followed by a wrap in warm blankets and a compulsory rest.

A trip to some of the large bathing and swimming centres in spa resorts can be a treat for all family members. Amenities often include wave pools, pools with currents, lap pools, and whirlpools. These giant complexes provide enormous fun whatever the weather, as they often have adjoining outdoor bathing areas.

THE SPORTING LIFE Nearly half of all Germans between the ages of ten and 40 engage regularly in active sport, and no less than six million Germans belong to soccer clubs. Soccer is still the national sport, despite the poor showing of the national side in the 1998 World Cup. If they are not playing soccer, active Germans ski in the winter and play tennis in the summer. Visitors to Germany will find ample opportunity to enjoy both sports.

Tennis bounced into fashion in the late 1980s with the successes on the

Skiing is one of the three national favourite sports and has become widely popular

❑ The German airline Lufthansa tried to ban smoking on domestic flights, but this caused such an angry response from the tobacco industry that the airline quickly caved in and changed its mind. Given that the longest domestic flight lasts less than two hours, this was rather fainthearted of Lufthansa. ❑

Steffi Graf, victorious once again, at the 1999 French Open Championship

international circuit by Steffi Graf, Boris Becker and Michael Stich. While Stich has all but retired from the scene, Graf and Becker still enjoy popularity in Germany, rivaling racing car driver Michael Schumacher, whose 1999 victories in

San Marino and Monte Carlo gave Germany a hero to replace the soccer professionals who so let the country down in the World Cup.

THE SMOKING PARADOX Given that Germans are so keen on good health and fitness, it is ironic that many are also smokers. The no-smoking lobby has no influence, and a campaign to ban smoking in public places has had little effect. Cinemas depend heavily on cigarette advertising.However, more and more restaurants now have no-smoking sections and surveys indicate that young people now smoke less than their elders.

The Federal Republic of Germany came into being in 1949 and has proved remarkably durable, being responsible for bringing the West German people from a state of near ruin to their present prosperous condition. It has seen the collapse of the Communist system in the former GDR, has absorbed that state, and is now struggling to bring equal prosperity and democracy to the whole of Germany.

The German political structure is based on its constitution – the *Grundgesetz* (basic law), which includes human rights guarantees. It is often used as an excuse for inactivity by politicians, although it has been amended more than 30 times.

THE BUNDESTAG The German parliament has two chambers. The Bundestag, the lower chamber, carries more weight in decision-making. It is directly elected to a four-year term, though the government can call an election earlier after referring to the federal constitutional court.

In the 1998 general election, the Social Democratic Party won the most votes and formed a left-wing coalition government with the minority Greens, replacing the conservative-liberal coalition headed by Chancellor Helmut Kohl. Kohl was replaced by Social Democrat Gerhard Schröder, and a leader of the Greens, Oskar Fischer, became Foreign Minister. It was an uneasy coalition

partnership from the start, and Schröder clashed not only with his 'Green' Environment Minister but also with Finance Minister Oscar Lafontaine, who resigned in total frustration, putting severe strains on the coalition. Schröder was later put under pressure to maintain party and coalition unity when NATO launched its air war against Serbia. The Chancellor threw the full weight of his government behind the NATO action, secure in the knowledge that most Germans supported him, but as the war dragged on there were disgruntled noises from pacifist members of the Social Democrats and of the Greens. Two other minority parties, the liberal Free Democratic Party, and the Party of Democratic Socialism, the revamped Communists of eastern Germany, could wield influence if Schröder's coalition starts to disintegrate.

THE BUNDESRAT The upper house represents all 16 German Länder. Delegates are chosen by the Länder and include state prime ministers. The Bundesrat approves all laws that affect the states. Leadership of the Bundesrat is currently in the hands of the Social Democrats.

TOP JOBS The German chancellor is not directly elected but holds the office as leader of the majority party in the Bundestag. The post of federal president is mostly ceremonial; the president is elected for five years.

THE CONSTITUTIONAL COURT Germany's judicial system is led by the *Bundesverfassungsgericht*

18

The Bundestag in Bonn

(constitutional court), which has two chambers, one for individual liberties, the other for political issues. Each court has eight judges, elected by the Bundestag and Bundesrat. In 1994 the court ruled that Germany had the right to use troops abroad, for UN or other Missions, exactly like other NATO members, but in each case Parliament had to approve.

EXTREMISTS OUT In Germany, the system of proportional representation allows every voter two votes, one for a constituency candidate and another for a political party. Any political party is excluded from the Bundestag if it polls less than 5 per cent of a party list vote – effectively keeping out the extremist groups.

THE ECONOMIC MIRACLE The rapid development of the economy after near total collapse at the end of World War II – the *Wirtschafts- wunder* – transformed West Germany and gave its citizens some of the highest living standards in the European Union (EU). This was despite strong bureaucratic controls that seemed to discourage private enterprise, minimal emphasis on customer service, and relatively little use of high-tech equipment. Economic success was helped along by America's Marshall Plan and other aid programs. However, it was probably due above all to the Germans' hard work, and their desire to forget the past and rebuild their country.

SLOWDOWN With the absorption of 17 million people from the former GDR and the world recession in the early 1990s, the miracle began to fade. As the economy stagnated unemployment climbed – particularly in eastern Germany as it moved from a 'command' to a market economy. As the 1990s drew to a close there were signs that the steadily rising unemployment rate had hit its peak, but there was little hope of a rapid turnaround for the more than four million jobless.

THE BUNDESBANK Central to the German economy, the bank controls interest rates – and so inflation. The bank, an independent body, often opposes the economic policies of the

Where the decisions are made: the Bundestag, or lower chamber

federal government. Its national independence is balanced now in the wider European sphere by the dictates of the new European Central Bank, particularly relating to the European monetary unit, the Euro.

The West Germans have for many years been in the forefront of the environmental or 'Green' movement. 'Green' politics have been much more central to events in Germany than, for example, in Britain where the issues have been largely peripheral. The term 'environmentally friendly' was invented here in the mouthful umweltfreundlich. *An aversion to atomic power provided the motivating force for 10 years of student and youth activism. Habits that have become second nature to environment-conscious people – such as the separation of glass, paper and other waste for recycling – began here.*

20

NUCLEAR POWER At the height of the German environment debate, the apparently impossible occurred: the Greens entered government in 1998 and a Green activist, Trittin, became Environment Minister. But Trittin's efforts to introduce radical environmental policies, particularly the abolition of nuclear power, clashed with political realities. The Greens' proposals to shut down nuclear power stations became hopelessly entangled

with legal complications and international commitments, and the Red-Green coalition government was forced to retreat to a position not far from that of the previous administration – namely, a vague commitment to phase out nuclear power.

INDUSTRIAL POLLUTION Another central plank of Green policy, a proposed tax on harmful power sources, particularly gasoline, also had to be watered down to meet pragmatic

considerations. Nevertheless, some progress is being made on the environmental front, if not at the speed set in Green party manifestos. Chancellor Kohl's government inherited industrial pollution of an appalling magnitude when the two Germanies were united in 1989. For decades, East German industry placed environmental concerns at the very bottom of its list of priorities in meeting Communist-regime targets. The effects of this short-sightedness were visible to anyone travelling from the West to Berlin: the industrial town of Bitterfeld, on the main line from Bavaria, was constantly swathed in a choking yellow haze, much of it caused by two huge factories manufacturing pesticides, herbicides, and paints. The factories have been closed down, but environmentalists say the pollution they caused will live on for decades.

ALTERNATIVE ENERGY Kohl's own Environment Ministry tackled the environmental problems of the East with commendable energy and

---

❑ West Germans are particularly avid ecologists: they recycle 59 per cent of their wastepaper and reprocess 71 per cent of their glass bottles and about 70 per cent of their tyres. ❑

introduced at the same time proposals to promote the use of alternative sources of power, such as solar energy. At least in this area, the Kohl government handed over to the Red-Green coalition an intact programme for the future, and Germany is likely to remain in the vanguard of environmental protection into the next century.

THE CAR IS KING The traditional German love of the great outdoors, and the almost mystical relationship to the forests that cover a third of the country – these are important factors that will guarantee Germany's leading role in environmental protection. Nature-loving Germans discuss in hushed tones the statistics showing that almost half the country's trees are terminally ill, victims of 'acid rain' and car-exhaust pollution. But their concern is compromised by the place they reserve in their lives for the very cause of much of the problem: the car. If anything at all is sacrosanct in changing Germany, it is the car. Supported by motoring organisations, car manufacturers and political lobbies, Germans assert their right to drive where and when they please and with no limit on the speed of their vehicles (Germany is one of the few countries in Europe without any official speed limit on its motorways). The same German heart that bleeds to see a tree die pounds with excitement when tearing down the autobahn at 200 kph.

HOPE FOR THE FUTURE Western conservationists have rediscovered a forgotten landscape in the Lower Oder Valley National Park, near the Polish border. The River Oder flows through the middle, with Poland on one bank and Germany on the other. Several projects are being set up to conserve the diverse flora and fauna that have been discovered, including ospreys, sea eagles and beavers.

The German film industry does not operate on the Hollywood scale and has not achieved the same worldwide success. Nevertheless, film is a respected art form. It enjoyed a golden creative age in the 1970s and 1980s, but in the 1990s has again been in the doldrums, producing very few notable films.

Hopes that the German film industry would receive a boost with reunification and the reopening of the old Babelsberg studios in east Berlin failed to materialise in the following ten years, and most German film-makers entered the 21st century in a cloud of gloom. The golden years of the 1920s and the Fassbinder-led renaissance of the 1970s and 1980s seemed very far away as studios struggled to find a new, financially viable and internationally recognised identity.

THE INDUSTRY'S MALAISE Film-makers watched with frustration as cinemas reported record box-office figures. In 1998, 1.6 billion Deutschmarks were grossed by an ever-growing number of cinemas, yet less than ten percent of the films shown were German – most were American. Particularly galling was to see home-grown actors, directors, and camera men on the credits of American-made films, and reports that German public funding had been absorbed by American studios fuelled the frustration even more. Efforts by German studios to break into the American market, or at least to collect an Oscar nomination, were dismissed by the cynics as a naive waste of time. The German film

Jenseits der Stille was short-listed for the Oscar for best foreign film in 1998, but Germany's 1999 nomination, *Lola Rennt*, failed even the nomination test, and German studios were totally shut out of the Oscar awards.

STATE SUPPORT The irony is that the German film industry receives State and central government support that is the envy of other countries. The subsidies are allocated on a regional basis by the country's *Länder* (States), and critics say this is at the heart of the malaise within the film industry. Regional rivalry rules over nationwide cooperation, so that Munich's Bavaria Film Studios is in direct competition with Berlin's Babelsberg studios, in a contest where neither can win. Twenty years ago, directors such as Ingmar Bergmann and Norman Jewison worked on box-office successes at the Bavaria studios. Now, the studios are engaged mostly in the production of German soaps – and in taking visitors on guided tours of the fading film lots where *Das Boot* and *Cabaret* were produced.

A scene from Der Himmel über Berlin (Wings of Desire)

Some aspects of German culture, such as classical music, are internationally known; others are confined within the country's borders. Open any German television magazine, read about the trials and tribulations of the media stars, and marvel – you won't have heard of most of them.

Although Germany has its share of blue-blooded nobility (notably the descendants of the Hohenzollern and Wittelsbach rulers), it is the lives and exploits of foreign 'royals' that make headlines in the popular press.

The famous in sports (Boris Becker, top) and in politics (Helmut Schmidt, above left, and Helmut Kohl)

ROYALTY WATCHING Even in death, Britain's Princess Diana still commands faithful albeit morbid attention, while one member or other of the British royal family is almost daily in the news. The Grimaldis of Monaco are also monitored faithfully by Germany's society reporters, while readers are constantly reminded that they, too, have a European royal – Sweden's Queen, who was a Stuttgart commoner before King Gustav fell under her spell at the Olympic Games in Munich in 1972. Germany's resident royals keep a low profile, even though the head of the House of Wittelsbach, Prinz Franz von Bayern, as direct descendant of the last of the Stuarts, is Pretender to the throne of Scotland. With typical diffidence, he renounced all claim to the Scottish throne in a speech in the presence of

the heir to the British throne, Prince Charles! Germany is more likely to hang royal titles on sports stars than on the princes, counts, viscounts, and barons (and their female equivalents), who are an unobtrusive part of the German social fabric. It is nearly 90 years since Germany had a real Kaiser, yet that is the title bestowed on the country's popular soccer star, Franz (the 'Kaiser') Beckenbauer, while tennis star Steffi Graf was frequently called the 'princess' of the Centre Court.

POLITICAL GIANTS In politics, the departure from the world scene of Germany's heavyweight Chancellor, Helmut Kohl, did not diminish the country's image in the international arena, for he was followed by a leader in the charismatic mold of Willy Brandt and Helmut Schmidt – the handsome Gerhard Schröder. Schröder brought more than a whiff of glamour to Bonn and Berlin, for he was accompanied by a young, pretty (and blonde) wife who writes for the country's leading news magazine.

The first identifiable permanent settlers in the area that is now Germany were Celtic tribes in the 8th century BC; the Rhineland was a key area of production in their industrial society. But new forces were developing in Europe. The Roman Empire was expanding, and Germanic peoples were on the move from Scandinavia.

Germanic tribes moved to lands east of the Rhine and north of the Black Sea, and their invasions and periodic uprisings created instability within the Roman Empire. Roman attempts to push across the Rhine failed to establish permanent occupation. These ended in AD 9; after reaching the Elbe the Romans were pushed back by German tribes under the leadership of Arminius, who destroyed three legions.

Charlemagne's coronation as Holy Roman Emperor marked a new era

In the 16th century Germany was suffering under a greedy and powerful aristocracy that appropriated land and held the oppressed peasantry in serfdom. This, alongside an equally grasping and cynical church trading in 'indulgences', led to the religious upheaval of the Reformation in the 16th century.

Discontent with the church authorities increased. Martin Luther led accusations over corruption, nailing his '95 theses', an attack against papal abuses, to the door of Wittenberg church in 1517. Luther was excommunicated by the church, but politically powerful German princes were able to protect him from sentence of death.

CENTURY OF CONFLICT After publication of Luther's translation of the Bible, the oppressed in Germany were ready to revolt. The Peasants' Rebellion of 1524–5 brought destruction of church properties but was put down by princely armies.

The period of the Reformation and Counter-Reformation created more than a century of strife between Catholics and Protestants, and by the early 17th century, Europe was embroiled in the Thirty Years' War. Many battles were fought on German lands, bringing about extensive destruction. Negotiations to end the war began in 1643, culminating in the Peace of Westphalia in 1648. The treaty ended the conflict, reduced the status of Holy Roman Emperor and began the decline of the House of Habsburg, while giving power to more than 300 principalities and other territories.

❏ In the 16th century, German mercenaries led the way in high fashion. The style of 'slashing' clothes – cutting slits in the material and pulling the lining through for display – started with battlefield booty used to patch clothes and found its way to the French and English courts. ❏

THE RISE OF BRANDENBURG-PRUSSIA By the end of the 17th century, a power in the area of Brandenburg-Prussia emerged. The Hohenzollern family, who held the Electorate of Brandenburg, defied the laws of the Holy Roman Empire and assumed the title of kings of Prussia. Frederick William, the Great Elector, was the first; the dynasty consolidated itself in the early 18th century. Under Frederick the Great, the third Hohenzollern king, Prussia rose to be one of the dominant European powers in the middle of that century.

Despite liberal laws at home, Frederick asserted Prussia's military authority and, after going to battle with Austria over Silesia, engaged in the Seven Years' War (1756–63). Frederick annexed much of Poland and established Prussia as a counter power to Austria. Prussia's power was tested during the Napoleonic Wars of the early 19th century, but in the Battle of Waterloo in 1815 Napoleon was defeated by the armies of Britain, Hannover, and Prussia. The Congress of Vienna, which met that same year and created the Deutscher Bund (German Confederation), established Prussian dominance among some 40 states in the German world, alongside neighbouring Austria.

GERMAN UNIFICATION Now Germany began to experience the pains of the industrial revolution. Economic reforms and customs unions were introduced to ease the strain caused by the many protective borders in the German region. Also, a wage-earning class as well as a bourgeoisie emerged. Uprisings in 1848 demonstrated how serious the demands for the dissolution of an older political order in Germany were becoming. In 1862, Prussia's Wilhelm I chose Otto von Bismarck as his chancellor. Within a decade Bismarck united Germany under Prussian leadership. After a war with Denmark over Schleswig-Holstein in 1864, and the Bohemian War with Austria in 1866, all the German states north of the River Main were united.

To gain the support of German southern states (Bavaria, Baden and Württemberg), Bismarck provoked a war with France; after the Franco-Prussian War ended in 1871, Germany was united as the Second Reich, with King Wilhelm of Prussia

Below: the Rüdesheim Niederwald Monument celebrates German unification in 1871

Above: the Peasants' Rebellion, 1524–5
Below: Bismarck

as kaiser. Bismarck then embarked on a number of liberal domestic reforms, as well as creating alliances with Austria and Russia.

WORLD WAR I France sought revenge for 1871 and, together with Russia, feared the strength of the German army. Britain for its part was worried by the threatening expansion of the German navy. These three powers, therefore, stood against the alliance of Germany and Austria in 1914, when World War I broke out over Habsburg claims in the Balkans. Germany's defeat came in 1918, hastened by the entry of the United States into the war the year before.

Germany's defeat in World War I was followed in 1919 by the founding of the Weimar Republic, based on a democratic constitution. The same year, Germany's new leaders were forced to sign the Treaty of Versailles, marking a radical shift in the European balance of power. It called for enormous war reparations as well as the confiscation of and withdrawal from territories that Germany had controlled, in some cases, for centuries.

28

Unemployment and inflation hit Europe after World War I, and in almost every country political movements on the extreme left and right began to gather strength and make themselves heard.

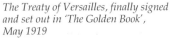

The Treaty of Versailles, finally signed and set out in 'The Golden Book', May 1919

THE RISE OF THE NAZIS During the 1920s and early 1930s, Germany suffered galloping inflation. Due to the lack of central political strength in Germany, elections in 1930 allowed extremist parties to gain prominence, most noticeably the Nazi Party, led by Adolf Hitler. This attracted the unemployed and destitute, and industrialists and other wealthy groups who saw the party's authoritarian policies as a return to the order that the country had known under the last kaiser. Adolf Hitler gained

more power and was made chancellor by the republic's president, Paul von Hindenburg, in January 1933. On 27 February, 1933, the Reichstag, the nation's parliament building, was set on fire, an incident orchestrated by the Nazis. Hindenburg declared a state of emergency.

THE ROAD TO WAR The Nazi Party became the only legal party in the country, and Hitler became president as well as chancellor. Democracy was suppressed under Joseph Goebbels's propaganda ministry. Many horrors occurred during Hitler's Third Reich. Jews were persecuted and murdered. The government and education systems were perverted. Many of the nation's most talented people – many of Jewish origin – emigrated, and gradually the terms of the Treaty of Versailles were nullified. Hitler's plan for Europe became well understood, but the West was not ready to stand up to him until 1 September, 1939, when Germany invaded Poland. Two days later, Britain and France declared war.

WORLD WAR II AND ITS AFTERMATH The war and the vicious activities of Nazis against Jews, Slavs, and others are well documented. At first the war went well for the Nazis, but their invasion of Russia in 1941 proved a turning point. Defeats in North Africa and at Stalingrad followed in 1942 and 1943. A German resistance movement developed among the top army leadership and attempts were made on Hitler's life. Germany was totally defeated, and in 1945 Hitler

❏ An estimated 6 million Jews were murdered in the Holocaust, the programme known as the 'Final Solution'. This was drawn up by Nazi leaders at the Wannsee Conference near Berlin on 20 January, 1942. The participants, under the chairmanship of Reinhard Heydrich but acting on Hitler's direct orders, extended Germany's death camps to occupied territories in Eastern Europe, sealing the fate of Jews throughout Europe. Today Wannsee is a pleasant suburb, and associations with the 'Final Solution' are just a ghastly memory. ❏

committed suicide. The legacy of the Third Reich and World War II will be a burden to Germany for decades to come. Six million Jews murdered in concentration camps cannot, nor should not, be forgotten by the world. Those leaders held responsible were put on trial for war crimes and crimes against humanity.

The victorious Allies divided Germany into four occupied zones under Soviet, US, British, and French control. Two separate political systems emerged; in May 1949 the territories occupied by the British, Americans, and French combined to form the Federal Republic of Germany. Four months later, the Russians created the German Democratic Republic. The two Germanys rivalled each other for more than 40 years, each trying to rebuild a nation out of the ruins and rubble of World War II. They came to represent the cold-war division of Europe, formalised by the erection of the Berlin Wall in 1961.

THE YEARS OF DIVISION Throughout the cold-war period, West Germany's economy became Europe's strongest while East Germany's industriousness made it the most prosperous country in Comecon, the Eastern bloc's economic alliance. By the 1970s, many Germans accepted the division, though they still hoped that Germany would be reunited. Unofficial recognition of the division developed in the Ostpolitik policies of Willy Brandt, when he became chancellor from 1969. Nevertheless, West German political parties, while attempting to work with the leaders of the GDR on some economic and social programmes, still insisted that unification was the ultimate aim.

Adolf Hitler at the Nazis' Parteitag in Nürnberg, 1933
Top: a Nazi parade

On November 9, 1989, the momentous decision to open up the Berlin Wall was made. East Germans had spent days and nights peacefully demonstrating for political rights. The communist East German regime no longer had the steadfast military support of its closest ally, the former Soviet Union. The government of the GDR finally gave way and opened up points on the wall, allowing its citizens to flood over into West Germany.

Some had never seen the west in their lifetime, but most had conjured up a picture in their minds from television programmes that had been beamed across the barbed wire.

ONE GERMANY Within months, a new democratically elected federal government had been set up, with the task of uniting East and West Germany. At first, people thought the process would take several years, but the government moved quickly to merge the two economies, providing East Germans with Deutschmarks on 1 July, 1990. East Germany's economy began to deteriorate as a result of the inability of its industries to compete with western production standards. The Federal Republic's ruling coalition was compelled to move very quickly and absorb the territory of the former East Germany into the republic much faster than had been expected. On 3 October, 1990, after more than four decades of division following Germany's defeat in World War II, a dream came true for many Germans when the country was finally reunited.

AFTER EUPHORIA The political leaders in east and west called on the nation to work together and to avoid treating the former East Germans as second-class citizens. Sadly, the wall still exists in many people's minds. Those from the east continue to complain that their country was simply annexed by the west, and accuse the West Germans of arrogance, while many West Germans are angry that their taxes have been increased to

pay for reunification (despite repeated assurances by Chancellor Helmut Kohl that this would not happen).

In the early 1990s, high unemployment, especially in eastern Germany, led to a wave of resentment against immigrants. Many East Germans, unused to people of colour, reacted with a xenophobia bred of fear and ignorance, and racist incidents grew. This mood was exploited by groups of neo-Nazi thugs both in east and west, who attacked and killed a number of Turks. Germany's politicians were at first slow to react, and in view of Germany's past, fears grew abroad of a revival of Nazism.

But in fact the neo-Nazis are only a tiny minority, and most Germans abhor the violence. The killers of five Turks near Köln in 1993 were finally tried and jailed in 1995. Even so, social unrest seems likely to continue in Germany until the economy becomes stabilised.

RETURN TO BERLIN With unification, the federal government was faced with the important question: should the seat of government remain in Bonn, the former capital of western Germany, or return to Berlin, the historical seat of the German government? Parliament was besieged with concerns about the costs, and fears that a return to Berlin could rekindle old German militaristic attitudes about German leadership in Europe.

Finally, Parliament voted narrowly in favour of a return to Berlin, despite the heavy costs, and the move was due to be completed by the end of the year 2000. In the meantime, infra-structure developments – roads, telephones, electricity, and economic integration of the east – have become the main focus of the federal government's policy. Special federal taxes have been introduced to pay for the very costly work.

THE EUROPEAN GOAL Since the Federal Republic of Germany (West Germany) was founded in 1949, German national policy has passionately supported European integration. At first through common agricultural and trade policies, and now through economic and political integration, German politicians have used the banner of the European Union as a standard for the next generation. This policy is often at odds with the other European countries, particularly Britain – and some opponents fear German dominance of the Union. Others argue that tight European integration is needed to curb a rise of German nationalism. But though Germans want a politically unified Europe, many remain dubious about the wisdom of relinquishing the historically strong Deutschmark in favour of the common European currency, the Euro, due to become the only legal tender in Germany and other members of the currency union by the year 2002.

Top right: souvenir pieces of the Wall go on sale
Below: the Brandenburg Gate, an accessible meeting point once again

A strong tradition of stories and poetry undoubtedly existed in the German language long before written literature. The one tantalising glimpse of this that was written down is the 'Hildebrandslied' (The Lay of Hildebrand), a 9th-century fragment of an alliterative heroic poem. Otherwise, the earliest German manuscripts were of a religious nature, written and preserved as part of the Christian monastic tradition of learning.

32

By the 12th century, literature had passed from the monasteries to the courts. German versions of French romances, such as the tale of Tristan and Isolde and the Arthurian stories, were written; in about 1200, tales of the hero Siegfried took form in the anonymous *Nibelungenlied*. *Minnesang* (lyrical love songs) also flourished in the 12th century.

THE LITERARY RENAISSANCE
Martin Luther's translation of the Bible (1534) is generally regarded as the first great modern German work of literature, but it was not until the 18th century that German writings – notably those of Johann von Goethe and Friedrich von Schiller – reached a level comparable with that of the Middle Ages. A meeting between Herder and Goethe led to the Sturm und Drang (Storm and Stress) movement. Weimar, where Goethe

Luther, father of the Reformation

❏ Philosopher and mathematician Gottfried von Leibniz (1646–1716) is remembered for the development of differential calculus, for which his notation is still used. His ideas of expressing 'all truth' in terms of simple statements using symbols was a forerunner of modern mathematical logic. ❏

and Schiller spent much of their lives, became synonymous with their writings – Schiller's poetry and many dramas, and Goethe's dramas (notably *Faust*), novels, poetry, and philosophical works.

FROM ROMANTICISM TO NATURALISM The German Romantic movement started around 1790. It had a profound effect throughout the whole of Europe, and Romantic ideas

❏ Philosopher Georg Wilhelm Friedrich Hegel (1770–1831) put forward the theory that history, which he called the *Weltgeist* (world spirit), was a developing process of 'consciousness of freedom', from the 'Oriental' through the 'Greek' to the 'Christian–German' period. He saw the process paralleled in three stages of awareness, from 'awareness of objects' through 'awareness of self' to 'awareness of reason.' ❏

OMMENDANS. EX HAC MORTALI VITA E
ÆTATIS SVÆ. LXIII. CUM ECCLESIAM DEI IN
MELIIUS XXX. PIE ❦ FELICITER TSXVISS ET. CORPO VE
M EST.

Ésaiæ LII.
Quiam Speciosj pedæ
gelj ᵶ antium Pacem

❏ The philosopher Immanuel Kant (1724–1804) greatly influenced the 18th-century Weimar literary school with his emphasis on moral duty and aesthetics. ❏

dominated German literature up to the mid-19th century, with 'folk' poetry and traditional tales (such as those of the Brothers Grimm) being an important element.

TRANSITION The poet and political radical Heinrich Heine marks a transition from Romanticism to realism. Contemporary life became the theme of writers at the end of the 19th century, as in the stories of Gottfried Keller and Theodor Storm, and the plays of Gerhart Hauptmann.

THE 20TH CENTURY At the turn of the century there was a reaction to naturalism in the Nietzsche-inspired poetry of Richard Dehmel and the

aestheticism of Stefan George. The greatest German poet of the 20th century was undoubtedly Czech-born Rainer Maria Rilke, whose intense poetic world was spun almost entirely out of his own psyche. Another Czech-born 20th-century giant was Franz Kafka, whose novels shed a grotesque and often absurd light on human experiences. The novelist Thomas Mann explored the contrast between solid bourgeois insensitivity and the fragile world of the artist.

In 1947 Gruppe 47, a group of politically left-wing writers, was formed. Some of its members have gained international status, including Heinrich Böll (Nobel Prize winner for Literature in 1972) and Günter Grass, known for *The Tin Drum.*

Martin Heidegger (1889–1976) espoused a philosophy that was a form of early existentialism. His ideas had influence in Germany in the first half of this century.

Notable among writers of the former GDR are the innovative dramatist Bertolt Brecht, who died in East Berlin in 1956, and the novelist Christa Wolf.

33

❏ The reputation of Friedrich Wilhelm Nietzsche (1844–1900) has suffered as a result of Nazi enthusiasm for his philosophy. His concept of the *Übermensch* (superman) is to blame for this, though it was not connected to the Aryan myth. For Nietzsche the basic motive of human action was the will to have power (he despised Christian morality based on humility). He saw the superman as one who succeeds in overcoming himself. ❏

The cover of Hansel and Gretel *by the Brothers Grimm, 1892*

The first architectural style to emerge in medieval Germany – the Romanesque – owed much to the traditions of Rome. The Rhineland has relics of Roman buildings, notably at Trier, where the great Porta Nigra, a gateway in the Roman city walls, still stands. The Roman basilica (meeting hall) inspired many Romanesque churches and cathedrals.

ROMANESQUE AND GOTHIC Fine cathedrals arose during the 11th to 15th centuries: Romanesque Speyer, Mainz, and Worms, then the soaring Gothic splendours of Bamberg, Cologne, Ulm, and Freiburg. Sculpture in stone and wood was used to complement architecture. Painting, often done anonymously, can be seen in altarpiece panels and manuscript illuminations.

34

❑ The rococo style – a kind of ultra-baroque – emerged in Germany in the mid-18th century. A French invention, it is characterised by dainty and irregular 'Louis Quinze' motifs. Sanssouci Palace at Potsdam and Cuvillié's Amalienburg in Munich are examples of the style. ❑

The Roman Porta Nigra, Trier

❑ The sculptor Tilman Riemenschneider – the 'Master of Wurzburg' bridged the Gothic and Renaissance in Germany. He was one of the first German sculptors not to use gilding or colour in his work. ❑

RENAISSANCE In the late 15th to early 17th centuries, architecture took a backseat as the influence of the church waned and the wealthy middle classes asserted themselves. Many notable buildings show Italian

influence. Some of the great names of German art belong to this time, including the Renaissance painter, draftsman and engraver Albrecht Dürer and the mystical painter Matthias Grünewald. In this period Lucas Cranach the Elder painted the portraits of the leaders of the Reformation, and the two Holbeins, Elder and Younger, were prominent.

BAROQUE AND NEO-CLASSICAL The 17th and 18th centuries arguably produced very few distinguished German artists, but saw a brilliant age of Baroque architecture by Lukas von Hildebrandt, Balthasar Neumann, Andreas Schlüter and others. During the Age of Enlightenment, Frederick the Great employed Georg Wenzeslaus von Knobelsdorff to help design official buildings for Berlin, and the Prussian capital continued its prominence as an architectural center into the 19th century, as the neo-classicism of Karl Friedrich Schinkel made its mark.

ROMANTICISM As in music and literature, the trend toward Romanticism is seen in art and architecture in the 19th century. Otto Runge and Caspar David Friedrich, who worked in

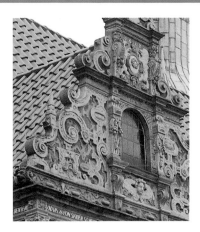

Rathaus detail, Lemgo

After World War I, the Bauhaus (literally, Building House) movement developed. Its founder in Weimar, Walter Gropius, envisaged cooperation between art and industry, and the name Bauhaus became synonymous with austere functionalism. Nazi hostility led to the dissolution of the Movement in 1933. Members of the Movement settled in other countries, where they continued to have an important influence on architectural developments.

35

THE CONTEMPORARY SCENE
Today, German painters are again prominent figures in the international art world. The current German movement, influenced by

Above: The Garden Café, *by Ludwig Kirchner (1880–1938)*
Top: People by the Pool, *by August Macke (1887–1914)*

Dresden, were the finest of the German Romantic painters. In architecture, Romanticism is found to an almost absurd degree in castles built for King Ludwig II of Bavaria: the Baroque-style Linderhof, the mini-Versailles of Herrenchiemsee and the 'Disneyland' Neuschwanstein.

THE MODERN AGE At the end of the last century, many German painters adopted the Impressionist style of France, and painters such as Max Liebermann had strong support from the emerging German bourgeoisie. Jugendstil, the German form of Art Nouveau, was emerging.

By the beginning of the 20th century, the Expressionist school was in full swing with the founding in Dresden and Munich of Die Brücke (The Bridge) and later Der Blaue Reiter (The Blue Rider) groups. This historic era inspired many powerful and important works.

the flourishing avant-garde interpretations of social and cultural life in a prosperous modern society, has been referred to as Neo-Expressionism. Postwar Germany's best-known artists include Georg Baselitz and the sculptor Joseph Beuys.

Since the Berlin Wall began to crumble on that extraordinary night in November 1989, the city's two halves have slowly, sometimes painfully, but inevitably fused into something like the fascinating capital city of old. Berlin is now just as fascinating for a visitor as it ever was in the midst of the cold war. The minor thrill of crossing Checkpoint Charlie (and wondering if you would ever return) has vanished, and you can now drive unhindered across the Glienicke Bridge (where once only spies set foot), but Berlin remains a compelling city. Now again the capital of a reunited and restrengthened Germany, Berlin is perhaps a litmus test for relations between East and West. Berlin has always been a place on the fringe, bursting with avant-garde ideas and sometimes subversive culture. Its reputation for decadence, even vice, is not unfounded – mostly a legacy from the Weimar years of the 1920s. It's a city of youth, and a cosmopolitan one. In the late 1960s and 1970s, young people flocked here to study on government grants, or to avoid military service, from which Berliners were exempt. A large number of foreigners have settled here – many of them guest workers. This has enriched Berlin's culture, but has sometimes led to racial tension.

Berlin is vast in area – Munich, Frankfurt, and Hamburg could all fit within it. Its population is 3.5 million, but huge tracts of the city consist of forests, villages

TURKISH WORKERS
More Turks live in Berlin
than in any other city outside Turkey. Many arrived
originally as Gastarbeiter,
to do the jobs that few
Berliners wanted to do.
Now many of them are
second- and third-
generation citizens who
want their fair share of
the city's resources. A
high proportion live in
Kreuzberg. They were at
the centre in 1999 of a
heated debate over
government plans to offer
them and other foreign
long-time residents of
Germany double-citizen-
ship, German and that of
their native country.
Conservative opposition
parties forced the government to retreat and trim
the proposed law allowing
the children of foreigners
to hold double-citzenship
until old enough to decide
in favour of one.

and lakes, even farmland, contrasting oddly with the
intense urbanisation of other areas. The west, all but
razed by the Allies during Hitler's last stand in 1945, is
almost entirely modern. The best of postwar West Berlin
is a tour de force, studded with startling examples of art,
architecture, and design. East Berlin, also badly mauled
by the bombs, has been reconstructed in two bizarrely
conflicting styles: drab, Stalinist functionalism on one
hand and a painstakingly accurate reproduction of
grandiose monuments on the other. Two former working-class districts with some intact (or carefully
renovated) architecture give a more realistic picture of
prewar Berlin: Kreuzberg in the west and Prenzlauer Berg
in the east both display a volatile mixture of bohemian
lifestyles and 'alternative' culture.

Berlin gives visitors a sense of double vision. Most cultural venues are duplicated on the other side of the city
(two national galleries, two Egyptian museums, etc.).
Sometimes an extra one is added for good measure (*three*
symphony orchestras, universities, etc.). The city has
about 60 museums, and some are world-class.

The former No Man's Land astride the Wall in the very
heart of the city, empty and sinister, was still a hive of
construction activity when the German parliament, chancellery, and most government ministries moved there
from Bonn in 1999. New ministries and a new Chancellor's office are being built. The Potsdamer Platz – once
a wasteland – is now the largest building site in Europe
with a massive new complex of offices, stores and housing, and a tunnel for traffic carved out beneath the
Tiergarten park. However, the mental scars left by the
divided city will take longer to heal than the physical
ones; attitudes and lifestyle in east and west remain quite
different, and suspicions linger.

▶▶ Ägyptisches (Egyptian) Museum   *36A2*
Schlossstrasse 70
Open: Mon–Fri 9–5, Sat and Sun 10–5
This collection is in an officers' barracks and the Old
Royal Stables opposite the Charlottenburg Palace. The
star exhibit is a bust of Nefertiti; other fine pieces include
smiling mummies, a carving of the priest Tenti and his
wife holding hands, a flying scarab, and a strange blue
hedgehog. The 2,000-year-old Kalabscha Gate was a gift
from the Egyptian government in 1973.

▶▶ Alexanderplatz   *37E3*
Before World War II, 'Alex' was the hub of the Mitte district, the historic core of old Berlin. After the war, many of
its buildings were replaced by truly ghastly architecture.
The Alexander-Haus and Berolina-Haus are examples of
an earlier 'objective' style, dating from the late 1920s.
Since the wall came down, the square's antiseptic dreari-
ness has been exchanged for a patina of graffiti and litter,
though street musicians and artists add a human touch.
One focal point in the square is the Weltzeituhr (world
clock) which gives the times in various cities around the
world. The high office buildings on the north side are due
to be pulled down and replaced.

The square has several times seen revolutionary hap-
penings, including the pro-democracy rallies of 1989. The

*Fabrics at the Turkish
market, Maybachufer*

Berlin

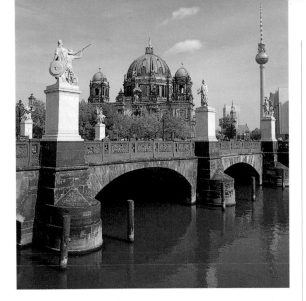

The dome of the Protestant cathedral beside the River Spree

history of the square is depicted in eight panels in a pedestrian underpass near the Hotel Stadt Berlin. East Berlin's television tower, the Fernsehturm, Europe's second highest structure, dominates the centre of the square. It totally dwarfs Berlin's second-oldest parish church, the Marienkirche, restored in 1950. Its best feature is a dance of death fresco near the organ.

Southwest of Alexanderplatz is the Rotes Rathaus (Red Town Hall), so named for its bricks, not its politics! A 74m tower dominates this neo-Renaissance building, decorated by 36 lively terracotta reliefs depicting Berlin's history. Near its entrance is the bronze Neptunbrunnen (Neptune Fountain).

▶ Bauhaus-Archiv 36C2

Klingelhöferstrasse 13
Open: Wed–Mon 10–5
This distinctive building beside the Landwehrkanal holds a variety of exhibits showing how widely the Bauhaus movement influenced 20th-century design, from architecture to typography. Plans and models of Mies van der Rohe's boxlike buildings, period coffee services and desk lamps, paintings by Kandinsky and Klee, and Marcel Breuer's famously uncomfortable-looking chair are all on display. Computerised information (in English) summarises the ideas and achievements of the Bauhaus artists. (See also **Dessau**, page 135.)

▶ Berliner Dom 37D3

Museumsinsel
Open: Mon–Sat 9–5.30, Sun 12–6. Admission charge to some parts of the cathedral
The Protestant cathedral (Dom) is one of the landmarks of eastern Berlin. Built at the turn of the century by Julius Carl Raschdorff, in heavy neo-Baroque it is surmounted by an imposing dome. Massive restoration has recently been completed. Inside are tombs of the Hohenzollerns and the Imperial Staircase leading to the parish church, where there is an exhibition.

TV TOWN
Alexanderplatz's most unmissable structure is the 365m-high Fernsehturm (TV tower), like a baseball stuck on a skewer. The Berliners call it Telespargel (Tele-asparagus). An elevator takes visitors to a viewing platform at the top (40km views on a clear day) and a revolving restaurant. At its base there is a useful tourist information centre.

QUEEN NEFERTITI
The famous limestone bust in the Ägyptisches Museum of Queen Nefertiti shows her as a remarkably beautiful woman by today's Western standards (best seen in profile). She was the wife of the unorthodox Pharaoh Akhenaton, who ruled Egypt from 1375 to 1358 BC. The first thing you notice is that she has only one eye. Some historians believe Nefertiti may have suffered from a cataract, a common disease in ancient Egypt. The bust was unearthed by a German archeologist in 1912, during excavations of Akhenaton's royal capital. It was removed from the Neues-Museum on Museumsinsel toward the end of World War II to keep it out of Soviet hands. Other Egyptian antiquities are displayed in the Bode-Museum in eastern Berlin.

39

Brandenburger Tor from the east side

DÖBLIN'S NOVEL
Alfred Döblin drew on his experiences as a doctor in one of Berlin's districts for his novel *Berlin Alexanderplatz*. A pioneer stream-of-consciousness novel, it tells the grim story of an ex-convict released from prison after being wrongly convicted of murdering a prostitute. Trying to build a new life in the Berlin of the 1920s, he winds up in a lunatic asylum, then, eventually, in a bottom-of-the-heap job as a porter.

QUADRIGA CHARIOT
Sculptor Gottfried Schadow's *Quadriga*, the four-horse chariot that crowns the Brandenburger Tor was seized by Napoleon as war booty in one of his Prussian campaigns, but within 10 years the Prussians had recaptured it. Recast in copper after the original was destroyed in World War II, it was vandalised at the end of 1989 as crowds marked the peaceful revolution in East Germany. The *Quadriga* was fit again by August 1991 – just in time for the gate's 200th anniversary.

▶▶ **Berlin-Museum** 37D2
Lindenstrasse 14
This major museum of Jewish history in Berlin is due to be opened in October 2000. Its gleaming, labyrinth-like design is the work of the Polish, Berlin-based architect Daniel Libeskind, who designed the futuristic extension to London's Victoria and Albert Museum.

▶▶ **Berlin Wall** 37E2
You can still see two sizable chunks of the old Berlin Wall. The longest section, just over 2km long, at Mühlenstrasse, has been declared an historic monument. One year after the fall of the Wall, more than 100 artists from all over the world decorated it with their work, and this section is now known as the 'East Side Gallery'. Sadly, the art work is falling victim to decay and graffiti, but it is still worth seeing.

Other sections of the Wall, some 180m long, are in Stresemannstrasse and neighbouring Niederkirchnerstrasse, alongside a plot of land where the Berlin Gestapo once had its headquarters.

▶ **Berlinische Galerie** 37D2
Stresemannstrasse 110
Open: Tue–Sun 10–8
This museum of modern art, photography, and architecture is in the famous Martin-Gropius-Bau.

▶▶▶ **Brandenburger Tor** 37D2
After the erection of the Berlin Wall, the Brandenburg Gate – stranded in no-man's-land – symbolised the division of Germany. It was built in 1788–91 as a triumphal arch for Friedrich Wilhelm II of Prussia by Langhans the Elder. Six tall Doric columns, front and back, form five passages. Under the Prussian empire, the gate made a spectacular theatre for military parades. Draped in swastikas, it also became a symbol of Nazi Germany.

▶▶ **Charlottenburg Museums** 36A2
Antikenmuseum (Schlossstrasse 1. *Open* Mon–Thu 9–5, Sat and Sun, 10–5. *Admission charge.*) An excellent display of antiquities contains objects of great aesthetic appeal as well as scholarly interest.

Bröhan Museum (Schlossstrasse 1a. *Open* Tue–Sun 10–6, until 8 on Thu. *Admission charge*.) In this museum, next to the Antikenmuseum, you can see a collection of art-nouveau and art-deco objets d'art: ceramics and glass, silver, paintings and furniture.

Museum für Vor- und Frühgeschichte (Langhans [West] Wing, Schloss Charlottenburg, Spandauer Damm 22; *Open* Mon–Thu 9–5, Sat and Sun 10–5. *Admission charge*) An excellently organised collection of material from early Paleolithic cultures through the Bronze and Iron ages. Though depleted after World War II, the collection of Schliemann's Trojan finds is still remarkable. There are other Trojan finds displayed in the Bode-Museum (see page 42).

Gendarmenmarkt 37D2

The two churches that frame this lovely square, just south of Unter den Linden, sum up the cosmopolitan openness of Berlin under the rule of Frederick the Great. Both churches, the Französischer Dom (French Cathedral) and the Deutscher Dom (German Cathedral) were built by Protestant Huguenot refugees from France, given refuge by Prussia. A third side of the cobbled square is taken up by Schinkel's neo-classical Schauspielhaus (theatre).

▶▶ Haus am Checkpoint Charlie 37D2

Friedrichstrasse 44
Open: daily 9–10. Admission charge
Checkpoint Charlie – the former crossing point for foreigners – is now mostly a memory, although one of the control-towers still stands as a silent sentinel. A replica of the sign warning travellers they were leaving the American sector and entering the Soviet zone has been erected at the crossing. The original and other memorabilia are found in the nearby museum 'House at Checkpoint Charlie', which details many of the most dramatic escapes through the heavily-guarded crossing.

▶▶▶ Kurfürstendamm 36A1

The famous Kurfürstendamm (Elector's Causeway) dates to the 16th century, when it was a bridleway used by the Prussian kings to reach their hunting lodges in the Grunewald. It became a favoured address for Berlin's high society and was remodelled in 1871 by Bismarck, who had been impressed by the Champs Elysées. In World War II virtually all its great houses were destroyed and its 3.6km length became a parade of bars and shops. The most striking landmark is the ruined tower of the Kaiser Wilhelm Gedächtniskirche (memorial church), bombed in 1943 but left as a reminder of the war. An exhibition inside refers to such cities as Coventry (in England), which suffered similarly. Don't overlook the box-like modern church standing alongside. It's not much from the outside, but the interior is bathed with the light streaming through rich blue glazing, a gift of reconciliation from France.

The tall, black plate-glass slab, the Europa-Center is nearby (see page 46), surmounted by a whirling Mercedes logo. The area at this top end of the Ku'damm can be seedy at night, a haunt of homeless youngsters and loitering prostitutes.

DIE BRÜKE ARTISTS The eight-year association of the artists who called themselves Die Brücke (The Bridge) was unusually coherent. Four young artists, Kirchner, Heckel, Schmidt-Rottluff, and Bleyl, founded the group in Dresden in 1905. They wanted to get away from the dull, imitative German art of the 19th century, and painted in a crude style using distortion and clashing colors in order to express emotions rather than verisimilitude. The name of this school of art: is Expressionism.

41

TRANSPORT MUSEUM
The Museum für Verkehr und Technik (Museum of Transport and Technology), at Trebbinerstrasse 9, Kreuzberg, explains the history of aviation, railroads, cars, shipbuilding, printing, computers, and much more. It is housed in market buildings and old workshops of the Anhalter Bahnhof. There is a remarkable Klaus Buscher mural on one external wall (*Open* Tue–Fri 9–5.30, Sat and Sun 10–6. *Admission charge*).

►►► Museen-Dahlem (Dahlem Museums) 36A1

Arnimallee 23–27
Open: Tue–Sun 9–5, Sat and Sun 10–5. Admission charge (all Dahlem museums)
Dahlem, home of the Free University and a residential area, is known for its important group of museums. The **Gemäldegalerie** (Picture Gallery) houses a huge range of European paintings from the Middle Ages to the end of the 18th century. The German section includes works by Dürer, Altdorfer, Cranach, and Holbein the Younger. The Dutch section has works by Rembrandt and Bosch. There is also a fine collection of Islamic art. In the **Skulpturengalerie** (Sculpture Gallery) is work by the 15th-century master wood-carver Riemenschneider. The **Museum für Indische Kunst** (Museum of Indian Art) has one of Europe's largest collections, with bronzes, wood carving and early Sanskrit manuscripts. The **Museum für Völkerkunde** (Ethnographic Museum), near the main complex, covers cultures from around the world.

The Museum für Verkehr und Technik includes old German warplanes from World War I

►►► Museumsinsel 37D3

Friedrich Wilhelm IV of Prussia in 1841 designated Museumsinsel (Museum Island) 'an open space for art and science'. This complex of museums stands on an island in the River Spree. If you only have time to visit one museum, make it the Pergamon.

The **Altes Museum►**, on Lustgarten, was built in 1824–30 by Schinkel. Completely destroyed during World War II and rebuilt in 1966, it houses the National Gallery's 20th-century collection and the Kupferstichkabinett (print cabinet), which contains illustrations by Botticelli for Dante's *Divina Commedia*. The museum is closed until further notice for extensive renovations.

The **Bode-Museum►►**, formerly the Kaiser Friedrich Museum, was the final addition to the Museumsinsel. Renamed in 1956 after its founder, the great art-historian Wilhelm von Bode, it is in reality two museums in one: the Agyptisches Museum (Egyptian Museum), with a sphynx from 1,500 BC among its treasures, and the Museum fur Ur-und Fruhgeschichte (Museum of Pre- and Early History). The museum is closed for extensive renovations until 2004.

The restored German Reichstag in central Berlin is again the home of Germany's Bundestag, or Parliament

NIKOLAIVIERTEL
This area southwest of Alexanderplatz and centred on Berlin's oldest recorded building, the 13th-century Nikolaikirche, is a creation of the postwar planners of East Berlin. Destroyed in 1944, it is now a renovated quarter with restaurants and shops, masquerading as medieval Berlin. Some buildings are replicas of originals; others, modern in style, were designed to blend with the surroundings. East Berliners disdainfully referred to the area as Honecker's Disneyland, a reference to the former Communist Party chief, who poured scarce funding into the dubious project.

There are three great wonders of the ancient world in the **Pergamonmuseum▶▶▶** *Open* daily 9–5. Only major exhibits are open on Mon and Tue. *Admission charge*), which had to be constructed around them. The colossal Pergamon Altar is a temple of Zeus and Athena from Asia Minor and dates from 180–160 BC. Marble steps ascend to a wide colonnade; gods and giants writhe around the plinths. Next is the huge Roman Market Gate from Miletus. Third is the most startling exhibit of all – Nebuchadnezzar's Ishtar Gate and Processional Way from Babylon, with lions striding towering walls of azure tiles. Upstairs is the Pergamon's Islamic collection. Don't miss the Mshatta Gate from Jordan and the panelled Aleppo Room.

▶▶ Neue Nationalgalerie 36C2
Potsdamer Strasse 50
Open: Tue–Fri 9–5, Sat and Sun, 10–5. Admission charge
The glass-and-steel New National Gallery was designed by Mies van der Rohe and completed in 1968. The collection of paintings, drawings and sculpture from the 19th and 20th centuries includes works by Kokoschka, Klee, Picasso, Beckmann, von Menzel, Corot and Courbet.

▶ Potsdamer Platz 37D2
For more than 30 years a no-man's-land straddling the Berlin Wall, the Potsdamer Platz will become one of the showpiece plazas of the world. Two developments, the Sony Centre and the Daimler-Benz ensemble of buildings, illustrate the kind of cityscape it will present.

▶▶ Reichstag 37D2
Platz der Republik
Built in 1884–94 for the all-German Parliament, the Reichstag was burnt out in 1933. The building was further damaged in World War II, and then was forgotten in its corner of west Berlin, close to the Wall, for more than 50 years. Now it has been completely refurbished and redesigned internally as the home of the German Parliament, the Bundestag. The British architect Sir Norman Foster designed the changes, adding to the building a glass dome, symbolic of the transparency of democratic government.

MUSIC MUSEUM
A bright and cheerful museum, the Musikinstrumenten Museum (Museum of Musical Instruments), at Tiergartenstrasse 1, is right next door to the Philharmonic (Philharmonic Hall). It features instruments and their manufacture from the 16th century to the present day, from an ancient set of bagpipes to synthesisers. There are occasional demonstrations of instruments and special tours at 11 on Saturday mornings (*Open:* Tue–Fri 9–5, Sat and Sun 10–5. *Admission charge*).

HELL IN SUBURBIA
Sachsenhausen is a former Nazi concentration camp that stands in the middle of an otherwise pleasant Berlin suburb. Now the place is oddly peaceful and birds sing, but during the war thousands of 'undesirables', or *Untermenschen*, were herded here – liberals, pacifists, communists, homosexuals, as well as Jews and captured Allies. Sachsenhausen charts a period of Berlin's history that should never be forgotten.

44

The head of a dying warrior at the former Zeughaus

►► Sachsenhausen · · · · · · · · · · · · · 132 B3

Strasse der Nationen, Oranienburg (take S-Bahn to Oranienburg).
Open: Tue–Sun. Admission free
Sachsenhausen Concentration Camp was opened as a memorial after 45 years in East German hands. First you see the boot-testing track, where prisoners were forced to run on different surfaces carrying heavy weights until they dropped (at which point they would be shot where they lay); then the accommodation blocks, the cell blocks in which prisoners languished in darkness for months until they died; and the 'hospital' where the most horrific experiments were carried out on inmates. The displays consist mostly of photographs and information boards charting the sombre history of the place.

►► Schloss Charlottenburg · · · · · · · · 36A3

Luisenplatz
Open: Tue–Fri 9–5, Sat and Sun 10–5. Admission charge
This vast palace began life in 1695 as a home for Sophie-Charlotte, wife of the future Friedrich I of Prussia. Eventually it became a summer residence for the Prussian kings. The rococo-style Neuer Flügel (New – or Knobelsdorff – Wing) was built for Frederick the Great.

The gardens first laid out in 1697 in the French style were transformed into an English-style garden in the early 19th century. Be sure to see the Schinkel Pavilion, the Mausoleum and the Belvedere, with its fine collection of porcelain (Meissen and Berlin's homegrown KPM, or Königliche Porzellan Manufaktur).

►►► Unter den Linden · · · · · · · · · · · 37D2

Berlin's famous thoroughfare – the name means 'under the Linden trees' – was once a royal mall. Frederick the Great's bronze equestrian statue, backed by the Brandenburger Tor, looks down on the swirling traffic from the centre of his great avenue. The statue was turned around by the former communist authorities so that Frederick appears to ride eastward, rather than bearing down on the Brandenburger Tor. The 'Linden' runs from the Brandenburg Gate to the river. The immense former embassy of the Soviet Union (now used by the Russian Federation), dominates the western end of the avenue and still flourishes Communist hammer-and-sickle emblems but is now minus the front-garden bust of Lenin. It will be joined by new American and French Embassy buildings in an ensemble recapturing the former elegance of this area adjacent to the Brandenburger Tor. If you follow it east you will reach, on the left, the neo-classical palace of the **Humboldt University** building. The former **Zeughaus** ►► (Arsenal), is situated near the eastern end, and houses the Deutsches Historisches Museum (*Closed* until farther notice for renovation). The sculptor Andreas Schlüter designed and cast the 22 heads of dying warriors in the inner courtyard; they are outstanding examples of German monumental sculpture.

Other buildings worth looking out for are Schinkel's neo-classical **Neue Wache** (New Guardhouse), the restored baroque **Alte Bibliothek**, and the **Deutsche Staatsoper** (opera house), a splendid example of neo-classical architecture.

Excursion

▶▶▶ Potsdam 132B3

Public transportation and organised bus tours allow easy access to Potsdam. Its main claim to fame is **Schloss Sanssouci**▶▶ (*Closed* Mon), summer home of Frederick the Great of Prussia, whose aim was to indulge in cultural pursuits sans souci – 'without care'. This example of German architecture is widely recognised as the finest example of rococo in Europe. Below it are broad south-facing terraces where Frederick the Great planted vines: their rows of green-framed protective glass screens are a curious sight.

In 1945 the town's **Cecilienhof**▶ (*Closed* Mon) – an English-looking, 1916 mock-Tudor building – hosted the Potsdam Conference, when Churchill (and then Attlee), Truman, and Stalin met to decide Germany's future. Part of the building is now used as a hotel; some of the rooms can be visited.

The ostentatious **Neues Palais** (New Palace) is open once more (same times as Schloss Sanssouci.) Look for the huge Marble Hall and, beneath it, a fine indoor grotto encrusted with shells and minerals. In the park is the 18th-century **Chinesisches Teehaus** (Chinese Teahouse). Additionally there is the restored 18th-century theatre, and the lovely **Belvedere** (*Closed* Fri), shelled by the Russians in 1945 but restored in time for Potsdam's 1,000th anniversary, in 1993.

In the town Try to see the fine classical **Nikolaikirche** (St Nicholas Church) by Schinkel and Persius, restored after war damage, and the 18th-century **Holländisches Viertel** (Dutch Quarter).

ROYAL REBURIAL
Thanks to reunification, Frederick the Great's family was able, in 1991, to carry out the king's wishes and rebury his remains, which had lain at Burg Hohenzollern near Stuttgart, at Sanssouci, next to his 13 greyhounds. Frederick wrote: 'Let me be taken by the light of a single lantern, with no cortege, to Sanssouci, and buried simply on the right-hand side of the terrace'. His wishes were not carried out at the time of his death, since his family was appalled at the prospect of his lying in unconsecrated ground. The evocative reinterment ceremony on the 205th anniversary of Frederick's death, on 18 August, 1991, caused controversy as it was seen by some as a revival of Prussian-style nationalism.

45

Potsdam: Frederick the Great's rococo summer palace is surprisingly small and intimate

Berlin

WEEKEND ITINERARY

SATURDAY

Morning: Breakfast at a Ku'damm café and board the S-Bahn at the Zoologischergarten station for Hackischer Tor. Cross the Museumsinsel and devote an hour to the exhibits in the Pergamonmuseum. Take a look in the nearby Berliner Dom (Cathedral). Turn down Unter den Linden, take a left opposite the Humboldt University, cross the square where the Nazis ceremonially burnt the books, and then enter one of Europe's most beautiful piazzas, the Gendarmenmarkt. There are several good restaurants in the area

Afternoon: Retrace your steps to Unter den Linden, turn left and there before you is the Brandenburger Tor. Tour the nearby Reichstag, then board the S-Bahn at nearby Pariserplatz for Potsdamer Platz. Wander down Stresemannstrasse, take a left into Niederkirchnerstrasse, where you'll find a remnant of the Berlin Wall. Continue into Friedrichstrasse and you're on 'Checkpoint Charlie'.

Evening: Try for seats at the Staatsoper Unter den Linden; tickets at the Friedrichstadtpalast, Europe's biggest revue theatre; or at any of the smaller cabarets.

SUNDAY

Morning: 20 bus from the Zoologischergarten railway station to the Reichstag. Walk west along the Strasse des 17 Juni to the market. Lunch at one of the stalls selling German or ethnic dishes.

Afternoon: Stroll back to central Breitscheidplatz for coffee and delicious cakes at the fine old Café Einstein. Spend the rest of the afternoon visiting either the Charlottenburg palace or Potsdam.

Shopping

There is only one store that is an absolute must – the famous **KaDeWe** (Kaufhaus des Westens – Store of the West), which claims to be Europe's biggest department store, larger even than London's Harrods and – many shoppers say – with a greater variety of high-class goods. You could spend all day shopping here, but don't miss a

visit to the Feinschmecker Etage (Gourmet Floor), where there are delicacies from all over the world.

Not far from the KaDeWe, on Tauentzienstrasse, is the **Europa-Center**. Although it has more than 70 shops and restaurants, there is little of interest to the tourist. Shop owners have the reputation of being abrupt and unfriendly; you may want to pass it up.

For fashion, the area to frequent is the Kurfürstendamm and its side streets, particularly Uhlandstrasse and Fasanenstrasse, where exclusive shops sell the latest creations of Berlin's top designers. Fashion of yesteryear is also a Berlin speciality, in the form of stylish secondhand clothing on sale in flea markets and in many other shops in the Kreuzberg, Schöneberg, Charlottenburg and Prenzlauer Berg districts. Around Savignyplatz are a wealth of antiques and specialised shops.

Elegant Friedrichstrasse, the prewar shopping mecca of the well-heeled, is again developing into an exciting area for shoppers, with new stores opening all the time. The stylishly French Galeries Lafayette is worth a visit just for its amazing interior. The same applies to the revived old centre of Spandau, a select residential suburb. Rather than the inevitable bear, you might choose Berlin porcelain as a souvenir of your visit; attractive, if pricey, it is available from the Ku'damm showroom. If you prefer the 'opposition', try the Meissen showroom on Unter den Linden.

Markets Local markets abound in Berlin. For bric-a-brac, **Trödelmarkt** in Prenzlauer Berg can produce a bargain, as can the **Nollendorf flea market**, under cover in the old Nollendorf S-Bahn (not Tue), or the colourful weekend **Strasse des 17 Juni flea market** which sells former Soviet Union trinkets and military souvenirs. For a taste of the Orient, visit the **Turkish market** on Maybachufer, in Neukölln (Tue and Fri afternoons).

Food and drink

Where to eat German food is frequently somewhat heavy, but with a degree of Austrian influence and a dash of German creativity, a new generation of chefs have come up with *neue Deutsche Küche* – Germany's version of *nouvelle cuisine* (not cheap).

Highly recommended is **Trio** at Klausenerplatz 14 (*Closed* Wed and Thu); The **Spree-Atken** in Charlottenburg offers music from old Berlin and six-course meals. If money is no object, the **Bamberger Reiter**, Regensburgerstrasse 7, is your best bet. At the **Opernpalais unter der Linden**, Fridericus specialises in a variety of fish dishes.

Die Alte Pumpe, Lützsowstrasse, 42 Schonberg, with an enormous restored water pump as centrepiece, is a three-storey restaurant with traditional Berlin specialities, and a superb array of sweet and savory pancakes. Also recommended is its Sunday breakfast, 'Pumpenfrühstück'.

The eastern part of the city, a culinary desert until reunification, is now able to match the West in range and quality of restaurants, and prices are often significantly lower. The Prenzlauer Berg district is particularly worth exploring, and on Kastanienallee (Nr. 7–9) you'll find one of the city's most atmospheric taverns, the **Prater Garten**, which has Berlin's oldest beer garden.

In the ancient heart of the city, also in the eastern part, is the tavern-restaurant where Mikhail Gorbachev dined shortly before writing off the German Democratic Republic, the suitably gloomy **Zur Letzen Instanz** (Waisenstrasse 14–16).

Berlin, with its large expanses of lakes and open countryside, has many charming country restaurants within its boundaries: the **Alter Dorfkrug Lubars** in the village of Lubars (Alt Lubars 8) and the **Blockhaus Nikolskoe** in the wooded depths of Glienecker Park are both worth the drive or taxi ride. **Café Einstein** (Kurfürstenstrasse 58) is a popular (and crowded) re-creation of Viennese coffee-house culture, with gardens at the back.

The department store **KaDeWe** has a number of counters where you can enjoy a typical Berliner lunch that won't break the bank. **Restaurant Hardtke** in Meinekestrasse offers traditional, robust food with wurst and various cuts of meat for those with very healthy appetites. Try their homemade sausages or Eisbein, or their amazing selection of fresh meats.

47

WIESSE MIT SCHUSS
A popular summer drink is Berliner Weisse mit Schuss – light beer with a shot of raspberry syrup or liqueur, which turns it pink, or extract of the plant woodruff, which makes it green. This 'champagne of the north' was concocted by Huguenots in the 17th century, when they found the local beer too bitter.

The cafés along Berlin's Kurfürstendamm, popularly known as the Ku'damm, have a touch of Parisian flair

WEEK'S ITINERARY

MONDAY
Morning: Ku'damm and Kaiser Wilhelm Gedächtniskirche; explore side-street shops.
Afternoon: Bus tour to Potsdam (but check opening times).

TUESDAY
Morning: Dahlem museums, with lunch in museum café.
Afternoon: Finish Dahlem museums or wander around Dahlem village and its small church.

WEDNESDAY
Morning: Zoo; Neue Nationalgalerie; Musikinstrumenten-Museum; Kunstgewerbemuseum.
Afternoon: Martin-Gropius-Bau (Stresemannstrasse, Kreuzberg, tea at café), and walk along the Schöneberger Ufer.

THURSDAY
Morning: Schloss Charlottenburg; walk through the gardens at the back of the castle.
Afternoon: Ägyptisches Museum and Bröhan Museum.

FRIDAY
Morning: Tour the Reichstag; Brandenburger Tor; Alexanderplatz; Nikolaiviertel.
Afternoon: Shopping/leisure or, if stamina allows, Museumsinsel.

SATURDAY
Morning: Coffee on the Ku'damm, then on to the open-air market at Winterfelderplatz.
Afternoon: Walk in the Tiergarten; market on Strasse des 17 Juni.

SUNDAY
Morning: Breakfast at Savignyplatz; visit to an art gallery or museum (e.g., Bauhaus-Archiv).
Afternoon: Walk around Englischer Garten, part of the grounds of the Schloss Bellevue; alternatively, look out from the train window on the S-Bahn line to Sachsenhausen, getting off for a wander.

Nightlife

Like New York, Berlin is a city that never sleeps, and certainly not at night. The nightlife starts in the early hours of the morning, so if you' need a good night's rest, you'll probably miss out on the more exciting aspects of the city. Nothing ever gets going before midnight, and while prowling around the discos at 11pm will get you an entrance ticket, you'll find you're alone. Young Germans living in Hamburg or Munich come to Berlin for a weekend of clubbing; there are no laws for closing hours, and many bars and discos stay open until 6am. You might consider the **Friedrichstadt Palast** (Friedrichstrasse 107), highly recommended for all sorts of night shows and revues.

For night bars, discos and cabarets, the liveliest youth scene is now in the Scheunenviertel ('barn quarter') in the east, near the restored New Synagogue: very trendy is the **Tacheles** counter culture centre, and the Hackischer Markt area. If your German is limited you could choose from one of several international cabaret or revue theaters; they're relatively expensive but offer world-class entertainment. Among the best are the **Friedrichstadt Palais** (Friedrichstrasse 107), the **Winter Garten** (Potsdamerstrasse 96), the **Chamäleon Variete**, (Rosenthaler Strasse 40–1) and the legendary **Bar jeder Vernunft**, at Schaperstrasse 24.

The touristy Ku'damm is by day a fashionable shopping street; by night it is the haunt of prostitutes. In Kreuzberg there are a variety of leather bars, discos, and strip joints, making up the city's 'alternative' scene.

Cabaret, folk music, and dance clubs are scattered throughout the city. For jazz lovers, the **Quasimodo Club** on Kantstrasse is a must. Magazines such as *Checkpoint*, *Berlin-Program*, *Tip*, and *Zitty*, provide details on what's on where. On a different level, there are three opera houses, four symphony orchestras and enough cabaret and theatre to keep you occupied for months on end. In the summer, the **Waldbühne**, the city's open-air arena in the shadow of the Olympic stadium, plays host to classical concerts and performances by international pop stars.

T-shirts for sale

Accommodation

Reunification restored to Berlin some of its finest and most famous hotels, which had been left to decay by the Communist regime. One, the Adlon, Berlin's most historic and best-loved hotel, named after its self-made hotelier owner, was literally stranded for more than 30 years in the no-man's-land at the junction of Unter den Linden and the Brandenburger Tor. Now it is restored to all its former glory. The equally palatial Grand Hotel gleams again in its central location just off Friedrichstrasse, while Berlin's Hilton has made its home in the restored shell of the old Dom Hotel in Mohrenstrasse. The lingering squabbles over property ownership in east Berlin mean that the range of hotel accommodation there is by no means as extensive as in the West and rates are usually higher, although some small pensions, particularly in the Penzlauerberg district, offer excellent value for money. Berlin hotels have become very expensive since the Wall fell. Increasingly, tourists find themselves using small

pensions and bed-and-breakfast accommodation, or staying some distance out of town. Since public transport is so efficient, the last is quite feasible if you have the time and don't mind quiet evenings or travelling to the centre at night; there are several peaceful hotels in the Grunewald area near the Wannsee. Other options for budget travellers are a number of youth hostels and hotels designed with students in mind. The tourist office provides a free list. Accommodations are basic, possibly without a private bath or shower, but civilised.

If you like more idiosyncratic accommodation, try a pension or small hotel on or just off the Ku'damm in the older houses that escaped bombings. Many are family-run, with characterful rooms, often retaining original art deco or Jugendstil (art nouveau) features. There are several in Wielandstrasse, others in Meinikestrasse. Most hotels lie clustered around the Europa-Center, and are a bit dull. Though generally in good condition, with most facilities and sparklingly clean, they now look quite passé.

If you are a non smoker it's as well to note that a surprising number of 'health-conscious' Germans smoke (see page 17), and hotel bedrooms may smell of stale tobacco. Ask for nonsmoking rooms, if they are available.

(see page 17)

BEDROOMS DEBUGGED

Following the collapse of the Communist regime, many hard-currency hotels were closed for several days so that corridor cameras could be taken out, bedrooms debugged and secret-police rooms converted to hotel use.

WHERE THE RICH AND FAMOUS GO

The best place to observe the rich and famous is at the Deutsche Oper on Bismarckstrasse – spend the intervals celebrity-spotting in the bars. Between January and March the fashionable world takes to the dance floor in balls, including the Press Ball, usually attended by the chancellor and foreign minister. The most sought-after and elegant ball is organised by the wealthy business community. The top shopping spot is along the western end of the Ku'damm, while top people dine at the Grand Slam restaurant in Zehlendorf or in the heart of the Grunewald at the Landhaus Bott.

Housefronts and terrace cafés give style to the mighty Ku'damm boulevard

Berlin

*The trains may not be
new, but are fast and
frequent*

Transport

There are few areas in Berlin that you cannot reach by
public transport. Compared with many European cities,
traffic congestion is low; buses move at a reasonable
speed and keep to timetables. Since reunification the
city's twin transport networks (formerly impeded by the
Wall) have been merged, and many of the old subway
lines and stations reopened. Berlin has an underground
rail U-Bahn system (11 lines, excellent for the central
areas), an S-Bahn system (10 lines) serving outlying areas,
and a conventional rail network for the distant suburbs.

An excellent bus system operates throughout the city,
with night services too. There are some ferries, and the

**Map labels:**

Bernau S4
Birkenwerder S10
U2
Pankow
Blankenburg S8
Pankow-Heinersdorf
Vinetastraße
Bornholmerstr.
B
Greifswalder Straße
Schönhauser Allee
Prenzlauer Allee
Landsberger Allee
Voltastraße
Eberswalder Straße
Bernauer Straße
Senefelderplatz
Storkower Str.
Rosenthaler Platz
Rosa-Luxemburg-Platz
Weinmeisterstr.
A
Frankfurter Allee
Schillingstr.
Weberwiese
Samariterstr.
Hackescher Markt
Strausberger Platz
Frankfurter Tor
Hönow U5
Alexander-platz
Jannowitzbrücke
Klosterstr.
U5
Strausberg Nord S75
Wartenburg
Märkisches Museum
Ostbahnhof
Spittelmarkt
Hausvogteiplatz
S6 U15
U1 U12
Stadtmitte
Warschauer Straße
Kochstraße
Heinrich-Heine-Straße
Moritzplatz
Ostkreuz
S3 Erkner
Ahrensfeld
Hallesches Tor
Kottbusser Tor
Prinzenstr.
Schlesisches Tor
Gorlitzer Bahnhof
Görlitzer Bahnhof
Treptower Park
Mehringdamm
Schönleinstr.
Hermannplatz
Gneisenaustr.
Südstern
Rathaus Neukölln
Sonnenallee
Boddinstraße
Karl-Marx-Str.
Platz der Luftbrücke
Paradestr.
Leinestraße
Plänterwald
Neukölln
Tempelhof
U6 Hermannstr.
Köllnische Heide
Grenzallee
Alt-Tempelhof
Blaschkoallee
Parchimer Allee
Baumschulenweg
Kaiserin-Augusta-Str.
Britz-Süd
Schöneweide
Ullsteinstraße
Johannisthaler Chaussee
Lipschitzallee
Grünau
Westphalweg
Wutzkyallee
S8 Zeuthen
Zwickauer Damm
S10 Spindlersfeld
S9 S45 Flughafen Schönefeld
Alt-Mariendorf U6
U7 Rudow
S46 Königs Wusterhausen

©TCS 9C02117/exp/uk UDN.4

BUS NO 100

One bus route of particular interest to visitors is Bus No 100, from outside the tourist office past many of Berlin's sights to Alexanderplatz. With a pass, you can get on and off as you like and see much of the city. Several companies offer city bus tours and excursions to Potsdam or Dresden; in summer boats ply the lakes and canals. Private cars are as unwelcome in central Berlin as in most major cities.

TOURIST OFFICES

There is a local Verkehrsamt (tourist office) in the Europa-Center, with its entrance on Budapesterstrasse (tel: 262–6031), which is near to the main train station and KaDeWe. Amerika Haus and the British Council are both nearby, on Hardenberger-strasse, if you want to inquire about English-lan-guage events in town. The local tourist offices are open 8am–11pm.

Official red-starred caps of the old GDR are now collectors' items

east has a few trams. This network is now being improved. Standard fares operate for buses, U-Bahn and S-Bahn (cheaper for short hops, or *Kurzstrecke*, and children). Tickets are valid for two hours and can be used on any system within that time. Before your journey, validate each ticket by punching it into a machine to stamp the time. For visitors planning to explore Berlin extensively, it is worth buying a 'Welcome Card': this gives free travel on public transport for three days, plus reductions on entry to many museums, theaters, and tours.

Ask for details of inclusive or family tickets at main transport offices (the companies serving the two halves of the city are BVG and BVB), for example outside Zoo Station or at Alexanderplatz S-Bahn.

THE NORTHWEST

52

Nordsee

Nordfriesische Inseln

Deutsche Bucht

Helgoländer Bucht

Ostfriesische Inseln

Wattenmeer

Sylt
Kampen
Keitum
Westerland
Nolde-Museum
Schloss Glücksburg
Niebüll
Leck
Flensburg
Föhr
Amrum
Bredstedt
A7
Halligen
Silberstedt
Peilworm
Dannewerk
Nordstrand
Husum
Eiderstedt
Friedrichstadt
St.Peter-Ording
Tönning
Heide
Büsum
Meldorf
A23
Wilster
Itzeh
Brunsbüttel
Cuxhaven
Otterndorf
Glückstadt
Hemmoor
Bederkesa
Stade
Bremerhaven
Bremervörde
Altes
Wilhelmshaven
A27
Osterholz-Scharmbeck
Zeven
Brake
Oste
A1
Varel
Elsfleth
Tarmstedt
Westerstede
Worpswede
A29
Rastede
A28
Hunte
Weser
Leer
Bad Zwischenahn
Oldenburg
Delmenhorst
BREMEN
Rotenbur
Wümme
Papenburg
Ganderkesee
Weyhe
Achim
Verden
A27
Friesoythe
Grossenkneten
Wildeshausen
Syke
A31
Werlte
Essen
Bassum
Sögel
Cloppenburg
Visbek
Twistringen
Rethem
Rodewald
Haren
Löningen
Vechta
Barnstorf
Sulingen
Nienburg
Quakenbrück
A1
Meppen
Haselünne
Lohne
Barenburg
Emlichheim
Bersenbrück
Steinfeld
Diepholz
Uelsen
Neuenhaus
Lingen
Wagenfeld
Uchte
Steinhuder Meer
Nordhorn
Freren
Fürstenau
Damme
Rahden
Espelkamp
Bramsche
Levern
Stadthagen
Recke
Hörstel
Bad Bentheim
Ibbenbüren
Osnabrück
Lübbecke
Buckeburg
Rhelne
Tecklenburg
Melle
Minden
A2
Gronau
Ochtrup
Enger
A30
Rinteln
Springe
Fischbeck
Lengerich
Bad Iburg
Herford
Hameln
Ahaus
Burgsteinfurt
Ostbevern
BIELEFELD
Bad Salzuflen
Lemgo
MÜNSTER
Telgte
Lage
Bad Pyrmon
Coesfeld
A31
Warendorf
Gütersloh
Detmold

Helgoland

Norderney
Langeoog
Spiekeroog
Wangerooge
Juist
Baltrum
Borkum
Memmert
Esens
Norden
Wittmund
Jever
Greetsiel
Jade-Kanal
Auuich
Schloss Gödens
Emden
Wiesmoor
A31

NL

Teutoburger Wald
Wiehengebirge

Mittellandkanal
Dortmund-Ems-Kanal
Küsten-Kanal

Northwest Germany

53

▶▶▶ REGION HIGHLIGHTS

Northwest Germany

THE GUELPH PRINCES
The powerful Welfen (Guelph) family were a thorn in the side of the imperial family, challenging their power and policy. Heinrich der Löwe (Henry the Lion) was a powerful imperial prince, but was forced to retire to Brunswick by his cousin the emperor – a close childhood friend who became a rival in adulthood.

*Katharinenkirche
(St Catherine's Church)
in Braunschweig*

The northwest includes the two seaports of **Hamburg** and **Bremen**, each a semiautonomous Land (state) on its own, as well as the whole of the Land of Schleswig-Holstein and nearly all of Niedersachsen (Lower Saxony). The area lacks the scenic wonders of the south, but it has its own quiet beauties, such as the **Lüneburg Heath**, the windswept North Sea and Baltic beaches and islands and many historic and picturesque towns with buildings of mellow red brick, half-timbers and stepped gables.

Some areas carry on the Hanseatic merchant tradition (see page 75); others are influenced by the great princely houses of the past, such as the Guelphs and Brunswicks. The farms on the rolling plains tend to be large, rich, and modern. **Schleswig**, long fought over between Germany and Denmark, did not become part of Prussia until 1864, and still has some Danish character. In 1945 the two former dukedoms of Schleswig and Holstein merged to form one *Land* with its capital at **Kiel**. The coastlines of the two *Länder* are very different; the Baltic coast is gently pastoral, cut by low fjords and backed by wooded hills, while the North Sea coast is more flat and stark, buffeted by winds and storms that erode the coast. Major holiday resorts include the offshore island of **Sylt**.

Lower Saxony is misleadingly named, for its Saxon tribes emigrated in the Dark Ages and today it has no connection with true Saxony around Leipzig (see page 148). It has handsome old towns, such as **Celle**, **Lüneburg** and **Stade**, and modern industry, mostly around its capital, **Hannover**. In coastal area **Friesland**, which extends up into Schleswig, people keep their own culture and dialect.

▶ Braunschweig (Brunswick) 53D1
A historic city with royal connections: in the 12th century it was the seat of Germany's most powerful ruler, the Guelph prince Henry the Lion. His symbol, a bronze, rampant lion, was erected on the Burgplatz in 1166 and later was adopted as the city's crest. The lion that now stands in the square is a copy; the original, badly corroded by industrial pollution, was removed 20 years ago and is in the **Herzog Anton Ulrich Museum** (*Closed* Mon), where you will also find some fine works by Rembrandt, Rubens and Cranach. Later (1753–1918) the dukes of Brunswick lived here. The city was heavily bombed and then rebuilt. Today it is mainly industrial (trucks, machinery, etc.), but some fine buildings survive – notably the half-timbered Gothic and Renaissance houses on the Altstadtmarkt, and Henry's Romanesque cathedral. The latter contains his gift of a big seven-branch candelabra, the splendid Imervard Crucifix (1150), and the tomb of Henry and his English wife, Mathilda.

▶▶ Bremen 52C2
Germany's largest port after Hamburg is a fascinating old Hanseatic city with a quirky, individualist personality. Like its bigger rival, it has a long history of independence. Its people are maritime, outwards-looking and liberal-minded. Its port expanded in the 19th century as a centre for coffee and cotton imports. Although it is 60km upstream from the mouth of the Weser, it can take ocean-going ships and still handles much of the German intake of raw materials (it is well worth seeing).

Sadly, like Hamburg, the port is today in trouble. Its shipyards have declined and, despite the arrival of new modern industries (notably aerospace and electronics), many people are out of work. The new university began life in the 1970s, in a blaze of radical leftism. It has now grown milder but remains innovative.

Despite being a northern city, Bremen is full of colourful outdoor life – markets, street musicians, festivals. In the **Marktplatz▶** (Market Square) you might find men in sailors' outfits singing sea chantys, or see a man in top hat and tails sweeping rubbish from the cathedral steps (it's a local custom that a man still unwed on his 30th birthday is expected to do this, then marry the first girl who kisses him). The buildings are varied – tall mansions in Weser Renaissance style (see page 119), newer Jugendstil villas with oddly shaped gables, even a windmill on a grassy hill made from part of the old ramparts that enclose the Altstadt (Old Town).

Rebuilt after World War II, much of the Altstadt is traffic-free and best toured on foot. The twin-towered cathedral is a Romanesque/Gothic mix and has a 13th-century bronze font. The arcaded **Rathaus▶▶** (town hall), also Gothic, with a rich Renaissance, has a noble banqueting hall. Its *Ratskeller* (cellar restaurant) serves no French wines, only German (a custom kept from Napoleonic days), and has 17th-century cubicles for private parties (a woman and a man dining alone must keep the door open). Outside stand two famous statues. One, built in 1404 as a symbol of independence, is a 10m figure of Charlemagne's nephew, Roland. The other is modern: a bronze pyramid of a cock, a cat, a dog and a donkey – the town musicians of Grimm's folktale.

The **Böttcherstrasse▶**, leading off the Marktplatz, is a Jugendstil alleyway designed in the 1920s by the offbeat Worpswede (see page 77) architect Bernhard Hoetger. Its gabled houses form a shopping arcade with stylish

The statue of the Knight Roland (1404), in the stately Markplatz, bears the sword of justice

55

The Renaissance façade of the majestic Rathaus. Inside is a sumptuous Guildhall

HELGOLAND
In the North Sea, 90km northwest of Bremerhaven, Helgoland is an unspectacular small sandstone island. Its strategic position, however, commanding the sea-lanes to the North Sea ports, made it a valuable possession. Germany eventually gained possession in 1890 by swapping it with Britain for the island of Zanzibar.

Celle's town crest derives from the mighty Guelph princes who ruled the town from 1378 to 1705

boutiques. There are also two small museums, one of medieval art, the Roselius-Haus (*Closed* Mon), one devoted to Paula Modersohn-Becker and other Worpswede artists (*Closed* Mon). The nearby Schnoor district is a 'village' of narrow streets lined with old fishermen's cottages. It is now a popular tourist resort, full of crafts stores, cafés and boutiques, but still engaging.

The main museums are outside the Altstadt. The large **Focke Museum▶** (*Closed* Mon) gives a wonderful idea of Bremen's history, with maps, paintings, photos, model ships and much else, set in parkland, the Übersee-museum is Germany's leading ethnological museum. The excellent Kunsthalle's varied paintings range from Cranach and Altdorfer via Brueghel and Delacroix to the Worpswede school (*Closed* Mon).

▶ Bremerhaven   52C3
This big workaday port, 60km downstream from Bremen at the mouth of the Weser, was created in 1827 as Bremen's deep-sea port. It is still busy, but the Columbuskaje (quay), where ocean liners used to berth, is now used only by ferries and cruise ships. This is also Germany's leading fishing port and has several museums: an aquarium and fishing museum, an outdoor museum with 17th-century peasant houses, and the Deutsches Schiffahrtsmuseum (*Closed* Mon), a big museum of maritime history with models of old boats and harbours, plus a genuine Hanseatic trading vessel of 1380, found in Bremen harbour in 196.

▶▶ Celle   53D2
This is a stately old town, one of north Germany's finest, with a princely history. It has a neat, gridlike Altstadt of 16th- to 18th-century red and white gabled, half-timbered houses, some with upper floors overhanging. In the Celle region, horses are bred – the parade of stallions through Celle in early autumn is well worth seeing.

The Lüneburg branch of the Guelph dynasty, distantly related to the British royal family, ruled here from 1378 to 1705. Their handsome white **Schloss▶**, enclosed by a swan-filled moat, has a 17th-century theatre that is still used for staging classic plays. The lovely vaulted 15th-century chapel has rich Renaissance decor, while the state rooms are Italian baroque. Nearby, note the biblical quotes on the decorated façade of the Lateinschule (1602), a former college, and the trompe-l'oeil – of the old grey Rathaus (1579). Every day at 7.30am and 6.30pm the town's bugler mounts the 235 steps of the Gothic Stadtkirche to blow his horn. Southeast of Celle is a true marvel – the big 13th-century Cistercian abbey of **Wienhausen**, warmly evocative of medieval times. Since the Reformation it has been a kind of retirement home for elderly lay Protestant women, who will escort you around. The stunning medieval tapestries are on display only around Whitsun (late May until late June), but you can see the 14th-century murals in the chapel, and other curiosities – above all the tiny museum containing 15th-century scissors, knives, nail files, spectacles, notebooks, etc., all found under the chapel floorboards in 1953 and supposed to have been hidden or dropped there by the nuns before the Reformation!

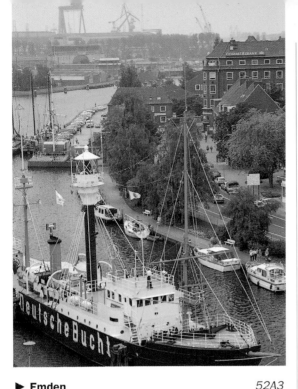

The harbour at Emden, from the viewing deck of the Rathaus tower

WORKING WINDMILLS
The Grossefehn area is known for its five handsome 19th-century windmills. Two have recently been restored to working order and are again grinding corn. This brings in some money, but the main purpose is to attract tourists. The friendly owner of the Dutch-type mill at Spezterfehn will show visitors around on the weekends and take them up to the gallery to inspect the metal sails. The other restored mill is at Bagland. These are the only working windmills left in the region.

▶ Emden   52A3

Emden is situated on the Ems estuary and is a herring-fishing centre and industrial port for the Ruhr via the Ems-Dortmund canal. The Landesmuseum has displays of weapons and of local history (*Open* daily). The windy Friesland plain is mainly dull, but **Greetsiel** is a pretty fishing village. To the east is the quiet and attractive **Grossefehn** area, where wooden bridges span canals.

▶ Flensburg   52C5

Set on a fjord by the Danish border, this handsome old port was long part of Denmark and still has a Danish look and ambience. Its fine buildings include the 15th-century Gothic Nikolaikirche and the 16th-century Nordertor (north gate). For local history visit the Städtisches Museum. Flensburg used to be a wealthy merchant centre based on Caribbean sugar imports. The town's history is documented in the **Schiffahrtsmuseum** (*Closed* Mon) with exhibits that date from the 16th century.

Out on an islet in the fjord to the northeast is majestic, white-walled **Glücksburg Castle▶**, a northern Renaissance jewel. It contains mementos of its former owners, relatives of the Danish royal family, as well as Gobelin tapestries and a richly decorated banqueting hall (*Open* Apr–Oct daily, Nov to Mar weekends only. *Admission charge*). The coastal route leads east to the old port of **Kappeln**. From here in the 5th and 6th centuries the Angles, who gave their name to England, went colonising under their leaders Hengist and Horsa.

West of Flensburg is the former **home of Emil Nolde▶** (*Open* Mar–Nov daily. *Closed* Dec–Feb), the Expressionist artist. It is now a museum of his colourful, anguished work – powerful, but maybe not to all tastes.

EMIL NOLDE
Although he joined the Nazis in 1920, the painter Emil Hanse (called Emil Nolde after his birthplace) was forced into internal exile by the Third Reich. His Expressionistic style of painting was considered to be degenerate by the Nazis.

HAMBURG

▶▶▶ **Hamburg**   *53D3*

Germany's second-largest city and major port (and Europe's second busiest) is the proud heir of a great merchant-seafaring tradition dating from Hanseatic days. A cultured as well as an industrial city, Hamburg is an unusually spacious and civilised place. For centuries it was a Free Imperial City and today is a *Land* on its own, an autonomous city-state; its most famous son in postwar times is ex-Chancellor Helmut Schmidt, a former city senator. His Socialist party (SPD) has ruled this city almost without a break since the war.

Set by the broad Elbe some 100km upstream from the sea, it's a town of water – the river, the huge port, the many canals (it has more bridges than any other world city, 2,195 against Venice's 400), and the big and beautiful Alster Lake, at its very heart. As it was never a royal or episcopal town but a merchant one, it has few grand or distinguished buildings compared with, say, Munich. Overall, though it is harmonious and after massive wartime destruction has been tactfully rebuilt, mostly in local redbrick style, avoiding the concrete harshness of so many German towns. There are no skyscrapers to spoil the elegant skyline of green-copper spires by the Alster. In the suburbs are charming Jugendstil wrought-iron balconies, parks and gardens, even old timbered farmsteads and leafy lanes within the city's wide borders. Some streets retain odd names, such as Ole Hoop.

Many North American and British visitors feel instantly at home in Hamburg. They advance various reasons – the trim, red-brick appearance of its better-off suburbs (reminiscent even of some parts of Boston and certainly of London), the matter-of-fact, reserved character of its people, and the matching coolness of its weather for much of the year. Reserved and even distant they may be, but the people of Hamburg are correct and polite and display that openness to foreigners so typical of port cities. Hamburg is a liberal city – liberal in its politics as well as in its social life. It may lack the exuberance and rough charm of Munich at the other end of the country with which is so often compared, but it is no less appealing for that.

MEDIA CAPITAL
Since World War II, Hamburg has been the press and media capital of Germany. The national TV news programmes are edited here, as are most of the big weekly magazines, such as *Der Speigel* and *Stern*. These days a few national daily newspapers (such as *Die Welt*) are shifting back to Berlin, but Hamburg is still home to the weekly *Die Zeit*, intellectual symbol of the city's liberal, free-thinking tradition.

FERRY-HOUSE CEREMONY

Hamburg-bound ships are greeted at the entrance to the Elbe estuary leading to the harbour with an elaborate ceremony enacted at the Schulauer Fährhaus (ferry-house). During daylight hours every ship over 500 BRT is welcomed with the formal raising of the flag of its registered country and the respective national anthem. Captains and crews of arriving ships are also hailed with a welcome message in their own language. You can experience the ceremony from the terrace of the ferry-house, which also has a restaurant. In the ferry-house cellar is a collection of ships in bottles. You can reach the ferry-house on the S-1 metropolitan line (to the Wedel terminus).

Hamburg has long been a major commercial centre. First established as a port in 1189, then a leader of the Hanseatic League, it created Germany's first stock exchange in 1558 and was a Free Imperial City from 1618. Wrecked by a fire in 1842, it was rebuilt on the spacious scale it still enjoys. Its growth came in the late 1800s due to sea trade with America. Later, this free-thinking town was less welcoming to Hitler than other towns were, and the Nazis never held major rallies here – but it was to suffer badly from British RAF fire raids in 1943.

Since the war, although it has shared in the economic miracle, Hamburg is no longer Germany's richest city, overtaken by others as German industry shifted south. This huge port suffered as a result of Rotterdam's better situation for the Atlantic trade. Although new modern industry has arrived, notably in electronics (Philips, etc.) and aeronautics (huge Lufthansa repair yards, MBB factories working on Airbus, etc.), unemployment remains high. After 1945 Hamburg was cut off from its natural markets in the GDR and Poland, but today it is eagerly reclaiming them, and its prospects have improved.

Despite the decline of the old merchant firms, there is still much wealth in Hamburg. With its musical tradition – it's the hometown of Brahms, and the first German opera house opened here in 1678 – there's a wealth of culture here as well. Since World War II Hamburg opera and ballet have been as good as any in Germany, the former under the great Rolf Libermann (now retired), the latter

The city of Hamburg, viewed from the harbour

under John Neumeier. Theatre has shone under Peter Zadek and Michael Bogdanov. Since its merchant rulers were less concerned with collecting art treasures than were the aristocrats of south Germany, Hamburg has few major art museums. But it is a key German centre for modern popular music: many big record companies are here. The Beatles played here regularly before going on to fabulous fame in Britain and the United States. Placido Domingo began his career at the Hamburg opera house.

THE FREE PORT

Hamburg's wealth is based on trade and commerce. One important source of earnings is the *Freihafen* (free port), which is a customs-exempt area where goods can be stored in transit or processed for re-export without incurring duty.

The port and city centre With annual traffic of some 60 million metric tons, this is Europe's fourth-biggest port, taking vessels of up to 110,000 tons. Its terminals can load or unload rapidly, using few workers. This has put many dockers out of work, but it suits the owners of the contaiers, as port dues are high.

A good way to start a city visit is a guided **boat tour of the port**▶ (starting from, the Landungsbrücken in the suburb of St Pauli). You'll be shown the 68km of Kohlbrand quays, the 4km bridge (1975), and the protective walls built after the 1962 floods, that caused 350 deaths. Near the eastern side of the port, Speicherstadt is an impressive group of high gabled brick warehouses by canals. Built in the 1880s, they are still used for storing spices, tobacco, etc.

Nearby is what remains of the Altstadt after the 1842 and 1943 fires. Here St Catherine's Church is Gothic with a baroque tower; St Nicholas's, with its slim spire, has been left partly in ruins as a war memorial. Attractive gabled warehouses line the Nikolai fleet canal, and many of the 17th-century merchants' houses off the narrow Deichstrasse are now atmospheric restaurants. To the west, the baroque church of St Michael, the finest in northern Germany, has a famous tall green tower (with a good view from its platform). The nearby **Krameramtswohnungen▶**, an alley of 17th-century almshouses, is a most picturesque surviving corner of old Hamburg.

Glance at the high-pedestalled statue of an arrogant Bismarck with sword and spiked helmet, in a park by St Pauli. Move on to the Hamburg history museum, which has photos and models of city and port, and a large model railway (*Closed* Mon). Farther along the broad inner ringway you'll come to the rebuilt Opera House, then to an area of new shopping arcades, wonderfully stylish and luxurious, with startling window displays – Hanse Viertel and Galleria are the best. The massive Rathaus, with its heavy, lavish interiors built in 1897 in the neo-Renaissance style seems symbolic of the city's proud heyday. The broad square and the canal beside it are attractive with smart restaurants and cafés beneath the arcades. Nearby are St Jacob's late Gothic hall-church, and St Peter's with its high 14th-century tower. Beyond

A boat tour around the harbour at Hamburg offers interesting views

Hamburg's massive neo-Renaissance Rathaus is still the seat of the city's government, the Senate

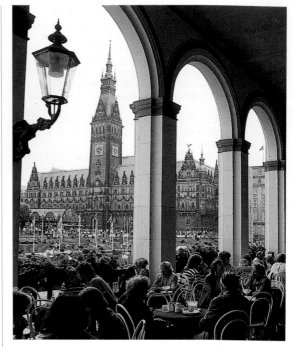

LOCAL BEER
Hamburg beer is known for being cold, with a good head (like its citizens, some would say) – and it's also strong. A speciality of the harbour district is *Lütt um Lütt*, beer fortified with schnapps – not a drink for the fainthearted.

Flowers that bloom in the Planten und Blomen flower park

the ringway looms the glass-vaulted roof of the Hauptbahnhof (station), next to the Museum für Kunst und Gewerbe (arts and crafts), which has Renaissance furniture, Jugendstil ornaments, etc., and even offers authentic Japanese tea ceremonies in a real teahouse (*Closed* Mon). The **Kunsthalle▶** (*Closed* Mon), the city's main art museum, offers a huge but confusingly presented array, from north German primitives via European masters to the Romantic Caspar David Friedrich, Dix and Klee. A wing for contemporary art was added in 1999.

Alster and the north side The **Aussenalster▶**, the larger outer lake, is a focus of the city's life used for recreation. Against a setting of spires, handsome villas and weeping willows, sails glide and Hamburgers stride the shore paths with their dogs. There are outdoor cafés for summer; in winter the lake often freezes so hard that, despite police warnings, stalls selling *Glühwein* (mulled wine) are set up on the ice.

The up-market residential district of Harvestehude, on the lake's west side, contains the charming village of Pöseldorf, with bistros and bars frequented by media folk and the trendy set. At the Museum für Völkerkunde (ethnology) do not miss the Javanese shadow puppets among the displays of Developing World folk art brought to Hamburg by past explorers. Nearby is the huge university, founded in 1919; further on are the attractive Planten und Blomen flower park, the Botanical Garden (illuminated fountains on summer nights), and the 271m TV tower (with a fine view from its top). To the north, the Hagenbeck Zoo pioneered the civilised trend of letting zoo animals live outdoors in some freedom (*Open* daily).

St Pauli and Altona The suburb of St Pauli, a former fishing village, is best known for its garish main street, the notorious **Reeperbahn▶**, which has thrice changed its tone. It began in the 19th century as a fairly respectable amusement district for the new transatlantic passenger trade, full of terrace cafés with live orchestras; the sailors' brothels were in side alleys. After the war, as the liner age waned, it slid downmarket into sex and voyeurism for tourists and businessmen. Today, owing in part to AIDS, the Reeperbahn is moving back to 'decency' – the biggest brothel has closed hotels and even chic restaurants are opening – but if you wish you can still spot the women in the pink-lit windows of the Herbertstrasse. St Pauli also has a new Museum of Erotic Art (*Open* daily), with some 500 works on show. The Star Club, where the Beatles first won fame, is no more.

On the quayside below, the traditional St Pauli Fischmarkt (fish market) is held every Sunday from 5 to 10am. It is now mainly a flea-market, with food stalls, but does sell some fish. Go afterwards to the exuberant Fischerhaus restaurant for a Hamburg breakfast of eel-and-plum soup, herring and beer.

The big suburb of Altona, Danish until 1864, still feels like a separate town. It has white patrician houses and a fine view of the river from the Altonaer Balkon (Altona Balcony). Its **Nord-Deutsches Landesmuseum▶** (*Closed* Mon), rebuilt after a recent fire, is Hamburg's nicest museum, with splendid old ships' figureheads and fishing boats, local costumes, rural interiors and paintings of Schleswig scenes. Beyond Altona, you can stroll under trees by the river at idyllic Övelgönne, where some old boats now form a 'museum harbour' (*Open* daily). Visit the neo-classical Villa Jenisch (with superbly furnished interiors) and the Ernst-Barlach Haus (works by the sculptor), both in a pretty park (*Closed* Mon). Finally you reach the former fishing village of Blankenese, with its steep alleys lined with old houses clinging to the slopes.

THE FISH MARKET
All life meets at St Pauli's Fischmarkt between 5 and 10 every Sunday morning. Revellers partying into the small hours mix with market workers digging into a hearty breakfast in the bars and restaurants, and early, morning shoppers buying fish, fruit and vegetables or browsing in the flea market.

SPRINGE'S FAMOUS SON
The bright lights of Hamburg (and elsewhere) owe their existence to the inventive efforts of a north German clockmaker who embarked here for a new life in the United States in 1848. The town of Springe, south of Hamburg, claims that Heinrich Göbel invented the electric lamp 25 years before Thomas Edison. A 1m-high electric lamp, a statue and a museum commemorate Springe's most famous son, and an eternal lamp burns in the house where he lived. American visitors smile indulgently, but Springe takes its (disputed) claim to fame very seriously.

63

Some girlie 'live-shows' still survive along the once-so-garish Reeperbahn

►► Hannover

Worldwide attention focused on this dynamic city in the year 2000, when it hosted the huge international fair Expo 2000. The city was given a major overhaul and clean-up for the occasion and even a new train station was opened for the fair site. Hannover is Germany's major trade fair city and a natural choice of venue for Expo 2000. It is a place of great historic importance, with much worth seeing. It was the princely seat of the House of Brunswick from the 17th century, and the House of Hanover inherited the British throne in 1714 through a Stuart connection. Hannover became a kingdom itself until its absorption by Prussia in 1866. Its people, with a reputation for being reserved, speak the most precise and accentless German.

The modern central area, situated around the broad Kröpcke square and the imposing opera house, is affluent and spacious. From here you can stroll through the rebuilt and picturesque Altstadt, full of interest; the half-timbered Ballhof (1650), now a theatre; the historical museum, with old maps and four state coaches; the busy taverns of the narrow Krämerstrasse; the high gabled façade of the 15th-century Altes Rathaus; and the Gothic Marktkirche with its superb stained glass. On the banks of the little River Leine, opposite the neo-classical Leineschloss (now housing the Landtag), are three insouciant pop-art sculptures, the 'Nanas' (meaning wench in French), by the French artist Niki de St-Phalle. The Gothic Aegidienkirche with its blue tower has been deliberately kept half-ruined after the bombing, as a memorial.

The grandiose neo-Gothic Neues Rathaus (1913), across the ringway, has scale models of what the city was like before the bombing. The adjacent **Kestner Museum►** (*Closed* Mon), covered in an odd honeycomb of concrete, contains Greco-Roman antiquities and much medieval art. Further on, close to the Maschsee (an artificial lake used for water sports), are two other major museums: the **Landesmuseum►** (*Closed* Mon) (with paintings of many

ROYAL CULTURE
Hannover's golden age began in the mid-17th century when a branch of the House of Brunswick built a royal palace. Under the ambitious Elector Ernst August and his cultured wife, Princess Sophie, the city saw a flowering of the arts. Handel gave concerts and the philospher Gottfried Leibnitz was court librarian for 40 years.

64

The ornate Herren-hausen gardens contain a fountain with Europe's highest jet and are per-haps the finest baroque gardens in Germany

periods, notably German late 19th century) and the Sprengel Museum (*Closed* Mon), excellent for 20th-century art (e.g., Klee, Picasso, lots of Germans such as Dix and Beckmann, and the Hannover-born surrealist Kurt Schwitters).

In the western suburbs you can see the famous and masterly baroque **Herrenhausen**▶ ▶ (*Closed* Mon), the former royal gardens of the Brunswicks. The main one, the Grosser Garten, is formal and French, with a maze, statues, and fountains which are sometimes lit up (one jet rises 269 feet). This is a wonderful setting for the concerts and plays performed here in summer. The Georgengarten contains a museum devoted to the hugely popular cartoonist and poet Wilhelm Busch (1832–1908). The smaller botanical Berggarten has a wealth of interesting tropical plants and flowers. Nearby was the royal palace of the House of Hannover, largely destroyed in the war. But the royal mausoleum, with the tomb of George I, survives.

THE BRITISH THRONE
The Hannoverian King George III watched helplessly from his throne in London as Britain lost its American colonies in the War of Independence. He encouraged friendly German states to send troops to help the British forces in North America, but to no avail. Many American families trace their ancestry to these German mercenaries.

The Michaeliskirche, one of Hildesheim's two restored Romanesque churches, dates from the 11th century

▶ ▶ **Hildesheim**   *53D1*

Apart from the 15th-century Templarhaus, few of the many old buildings of this distinguished town survived the war. Some have been well restored, notably the Gothic Rathaus and two Romanesque churches: the Michaeliskirche and the **cathedral**▶, where there is an 11th-century carved bronze column, with biblical scenes. A rose bush in the cathedral's finely arched and columned cloisters plays a central role in Hildesheim history. The bush is said to be more than 1,000 years old and appeared to have been destroyed in an air-raid in early 1945. But when peace came in May, 1945, it revived and bloomed— confirming a centuries-old belief that Hildesheim will live as long as its celebrated rose bush!

NORDSTRAND ISLAND

The island of Nordstrand, connected to the mainland near Husum by a man-made isthmus, provides a stark reminder of the constant threat posed to this stretch of coast by the North Sea. Nordstrand is part of a much larger island that was torn apart by disastrous sea-flooding in 1362 and 1634. One large piece of the former island, Pellworm, is now a 8km ferry-ride away, while other islets, called the Halligen, are distributed along the coast of Nordfriedland, like the front line of a defence wall in face of the unpredictable North Sea.

▶ Holsteinische Schweiz   53D4

This is a gentle region of woods and low hills that are good for walking, and lakes for sailing and swimming. Its nickname, Holstein Switzerland, was given it locally in the last century to attract tourism. Its a misnomer, for none of the hills is higher than 168m. You can tour the lakes by excursion boat from Plön, an old town with a big white baroque hilltop castle that formerly housed a Prussian army college.

At Eutin, a pleasant town of 18th-century brick buildings, there's another baroque castle, with a moat and bronze cupola. In summer, its pink courtyard hosts the operas of Carl Maria von Weber (1786–1826), born in Eutin. Malente, nearby, is a little lakeside resort where water galas are held. Hohwacht is the best of the nearby Baltic seaside resorts.

▶ Husum   52C5

This graceful old North Sea fishing port and market town is close to a region of polders. The history of these reclaimed tracts of land and the age-old battle against sea and storm is well recorded in the Nissenhaus Museum (*Open* Apr–Oct daily. *Closed* Nov–Mar Sat, Mon). Another museum is in the home of Theodor Storm (1817–88), a suitably named poet and novelist whose work movingly evokes the life of this strange, flat, melancholy region (*Open* Apr–Oct daily; Nov–Mar Tue, Thu, Sat pm only). Friedrichstadt, to the south, was built in the 17th century by Dutch Protestant refugees. It's a picturesque little Dutch-looking town of stepped gables, canals, and cobbled streets. St Peter Ordning, a resort with good sandy beaches, known for its sulphur cures is on the long peninsula to the west.

▶ Jever   52B3

This brewery town is known for its pilsner beer and for its pink hunting **Schloss▶** set in a moated park. This once belonged to the Russian czars, hence the portraits of Catherine the Great, alongside local costumes, toys, furniture, etc., in its museum.

On the wall of the café by its gates is an old Glockenspiel (musical clock) where figurines of Catherine and others do an hourly dance. In the Marktplatz, note the Renaissance sarcophagus with marble statues, situated in the belfry next to a modern church.

▶ Kiel   53D4

At the head of a broad fjord, always lively with shipping, stands Schleswig-Holstein's capital, formerly the leading German naval base. Badly bombed in World War II, it has been gracelessly rebuilt and has few notable buildings except for the restored Jugendstil Rathaus (1911). Shipping

THE POLDERS
Northwest of Husum, around Bredstedt, you can explore some of the polders – areas of low-lying land reclaimed from the sea – known here as *Köge* (singular *Koog*); typical examples are St Cecilien and Sonke-Nissen. The people tend to be taciturn and dour, due maybe to the incessant howling winds. They live in houses with flat green tin roofs and breed sheep, which sometimes even graze on the seawards side of the dykes.

The Olympiahafen (harbour) at Kiel

is still a major activity. The 100km **Kiel Canal**, which links the Baltic with the North Sea, is the world's busiest, with 50,000 ships a year – ahead of Panama or Suez.

There's a bracing sea walk along the Hindenburgufer (quay) to the Holtenau locks, where the passage of ships between canal and sound is an impressive sight. At **Laboe**, the high brick tower shaped like a ship's stern is Germany's main naval war memorial (climb to its roof for a fine view). The museum inside includes a model of the 1916 Battle of Jutland (*Open* daily).

To the southwest, at Molfsee, the Schleswig-Holsteinisches **Freilichtmuseum▶** is one of the best of the new German outdoor museums of rural life. About 60 old buildings, half-timbered and redbrick in the regional style – including three windmills, a watermill, a 16th-century vicarage, and an 18th-century manor (note its 1817 school timetable) – are set in a pleasant park; bakers, carvers, and potters work here and sell their products.

KIEL REGATTA
Kiel is a mecca for watersports enthusiasts. Since 1882 the Kieler Wache (sailing regatta) has been an annual event (in late June, early July). Kiel has also been the watersports centre for two Olympics – 1936 (Berlin) and 1972 (Munich).

▶▶▶ Lübeck
53E4

This Baltic river port and onetime leader of the Hanseatic League is a stately old city with tremendous local pride and a lovely relaxed, civilised ambience. Although the city was badly bombed and then rebuilt, its main streets still evoke its wealthy merchant heyday. Here you will see those high zigzag gabled façades often mistakenly thought of as Dutch. In fact the old builders of Lübeck invented this style, which the Dutch later copied. Some old houses also have the unusual Lübeck brickwork which uses alternating strips of red unglazed and black glazed brick. Behind the brick street fronts you'll find many small houses amid greenery, for this is secretly a very verdant city, full of enclosed gardens.

In the Middle Ages this 'Queen of the Hanse' was the main business centre of northern Europe, and Germany's largest town after Köln (Cologne). Later it lost ground to Bremen and Hamburg, but it still handles a great volume of cargo, and has some big industries. Its position on the old GDR border was once a handicap, but today it is reforging links with its natural Mecklenburg hinterland.

Some of the old merchant families still flourish today. One leading family, the Manns, wealthy grain dealers, produced two great writers, Thomas and Heinrich (see panel, left). The family's old home Mengstrasse 4, where they lived from 1841 to 1891, was the model for Thomas Mann's novel *Buddenbrooks*. It has been rebuilt since World War II bombing and now houses a museum of the Manns' life and work (*Open* daily).

THOMAS MANN
Thomas Mann's family left Lübeck for Munich in 1891, when Thomas was 16 years old. He recorded his youth in his masterly novel *Buddenbrooks* (1901), which first made him famous. It gives a vividly detailed picture of the city's upper-crust society and is a poignant study of human frailty. Its central characters were based on real people and this did not please Lübeck. Mann had won the Nobel Prize for Literature in 1929.

Lübeck's Altstadt (old town) is famous for its decorative brickwork and façade decoration

Lübeck's medieval centre lies between two arms of the River Trave and is best visited on foot. The grander quarter, with fine old houses, is west of the central Breitstrasse; the artisan quarter is to the east. To make a circular tour, enter by the **Holstentor▶**, an imposing red twin-towered gateway housing a museum of history. Here there are some 16th- to 17th-century gabled warehouses by the river, used to store salt in transit from the Lüneburg mines to Sweden. Cross the river and you can visit the Gothic Petrikirche and the beautiful Music Academy, converted from 22 merchant homes (concerts are often held here). In the narrow street called simply Kolk, the marionette theatre and puppet museum have a

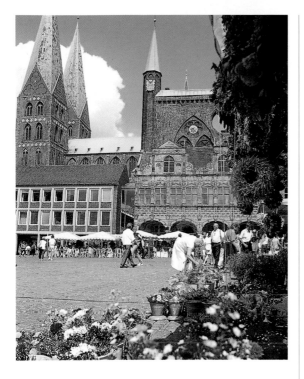

The Marktplatz at Lübeck, with the impressive Marienkirche in the background

RATZEBURG AND MÖLLN
South of Lübeck are two charming old towns. Ratzeburg, on a lake, has a tall redbrick Romanesque cathedral on its outskirts. Mölln, with its 14th-century Rathaus, is where the folk hero Till Eulenspiegel is said to have died of the plague in 1350. Touching the thumb of his statue (in the market) is supposed to bring good luck. Before reunification Ratzeburg was the archetypal frontier town. Until recently the eastern shore of the lake near the town (which is built on an island) was fenced off, forming the border between West and East Germany.

splendid and intriguing collection of exotic oriental puppets (*Open* daily).

To the southeast, the double-towered cathedral (1173) is Romanesque with a Gothic chancel; the nearby St Annen museum contains relics of old Lübeck. Just to the north, in an area of mewslike alleys, are two fine 17th-century almshouses, Füchtingshof and Glandorpshof, built for the widows of merchants and craftsmen and still used as homes for the elderly. On the 14th-century façade of the Katharinenkirche (now a museum; *Open* Apr–Sep Tue–Sun) are fine modern statues, three of them by Barlach. The nearby Behnhaus and Drägerhaus are elegant houses, now small museums showing Mann souvenirs and paintings by Munch (*Closed* Mon).

The Heiligen-Geist-Hospital, built in the 13th century as an old people's home, has a superb vaulted Gothic chapel with old frescoes. In the Gothic Jakobkirche are 17th-century organ lofts. Just opposite, the tall step-gabled Fischergesellschaft, a Renaissance mansion built for the Fishermen's Guild, today serves as a tavern, very popular with tourists, and atmospheric. The lofty Marienkirche, with the highest brick nave in the world, was the main church of the merchant rulers. Badly bombed, it has been skillfully restored to its original style.

The handsome Gothic/Renaissance **Rathaus**▶ should be seen for its council chamber and the memorial to eight citizens shot for their resistance to the Nazis.

Lübeck is famous for its marzipan, the rich almond paste that Germans love. The famous Niederegger store sells marzipan in all kinds of shapes (including realistic-looking oranges, apples and a selection of other fruits).

TRAVEMÜNDE
Officially a district of Lübeck, Travemünde is Germany's oldest seaside resort. Bathing huts appeared on its long sandy beach as early as 1802, and the new health fad of seawater dips and sea-air inhalation cures attracted not only the Lübeck bourgeoisie (captured in Thomas Mann's *Die Buddenbrooks*) but also titled visitors from much further afield. Today's Travemünde has lost much of its glitter, although it has a casino and a couple of fine old hotels.

▶▶ Lüneburg   53D3

This is a distinguished old town on the edge of the heath that bears its name, the Lüneburger Heide. In the Middle Ages it grew prosperous from its salt deposits, which were sold to Scandinavia and the Baltic towns. Tall houses with oddly shaped stepped gables line the broad street called Am Sande; some, as in Holland, still have the iron bars near the roof that were used for pulling up furniture from the street.

The big yellowish **Rathaus**▶ (13th to 16th century) has a superbly ornate interior: a Renaissance council chamber with detailed wood carvings, and a Gothic Fürstensaal (princes' chamber) with lamps made from stags' antlers. Close by is the highly picturesque **Wasserviertel**▶, the old river port, with a gabled Renaissance brewery, a half-timbered millhouse by the water, and an 18th-century crane.

At **Ebstorf**, to the south, little remains of its 14th-century Benedictine abbey save a Gothic gallery and cloister. Its main attraction is a copy of a 13th-century map of the world: the original was destroyed in the war.

Lüneburg's large and elegant Rathaus has a sumptuous interior. In the council chamber are delicate wood sculptures by Albert Von Soest (1566)

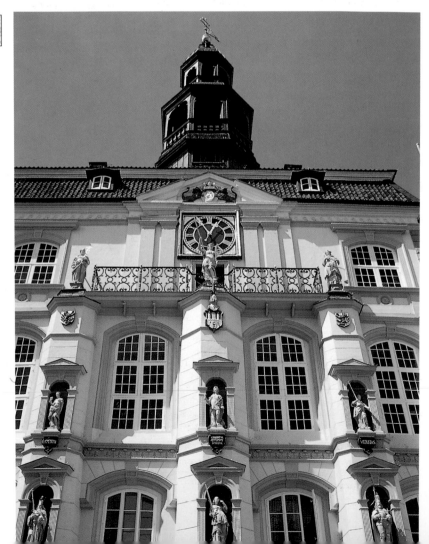

►► Lüneburger Heide (Lüneburg Heath)   53D3

The famous Lüneburger Heide, not flat but gently undulating, is a large and subtly beautiful area stretching from the Elbe down to the River Aller, near Celle. It is best visited in August or September, when the juniper shrubs are in leaf and the vast tracts of heather are in bloom – but in any season this varied landscape is well worth visiting. You'll find low valleys, marshy ponds, pastures full of sheep, and forests rich in game.

In the three big nature reserves cars must stay on the main road, but you can rent a horse and cart, horse, or bicycle and go meandering down quiet, clearly signposted paths. In some places, cross-country skiing is possible when snow falls in winter. The sheep that browse on the juniper and heather yield a delicious fragrant mutton, known as *Heidschnucken*, which is found on the menus of many local restaurants.

The main nature reserve is just west of the Hannover-Hamburg Autobahn and has several entry points. Among them are Undeloh to the north and Döhle to the east, two pretty villages reachable by car. From either you can hike or ride to the Wilseder Berg, a 169m hill that offers a wide view of the heath – even as far as the spires of Hamburg on a clear day (with binoculars). The rolling heathland is covered with oaks, pines, birches, red-berried junipers, and above all with heather. Here and there are large, thatched, smelly sheepfolds where the animals spend the night.

There is heather everywhere. The villages have stalls selling heather bouquets (in season) and kitschy heather ornaments of all kinds.

At Egestorf, a picturesque village east of Undeloh, heather is used to decorate the altar of the Protestant Heidekirche, an unusual half-timbered structure that – from the outside –

One of Nazi Germany's most notorious concentration camps, Bergen-Belsen, on the southern edge of the Lüneburger Heide, was burnt to the ground after British forces liberated it in 1945, but today there is a memorial to the 50,000 prisoners who died there and a small museum documenting their suffering. The British armed forces still have a sizable presence in the area, which is dotted with military maneuver grounds. The cruelty inflicted on the Bergen-Belsen prisoners, most of them Jewish, was particularly hideous, and the camp's bestial commander, Josef Kramer, and ten guards, including three women, were hanged for their crimes. The memorial and the museum, accessible by bus from Bergen and Belsen, are open daily.

71

looks less like a church than a dwelling. Several churches in the area have curious-looking wooden belfries.

The poet Hermann Löns sentimentally extolled the glories of the Heide. His memorial tomb stands alone in an area of cairns and ancient chamber tombs near Fallingbostel, southwest of Soltau. Further west is the huge **Vogelpark Walsrode►** (*Open* daily. *Admission charge*), a bird sanctuary where parrots, flamingos, cranes and ostriches are among the huge variety of species of birds from the world over that live and fly freely here. There's a playground for children at the sanctuary.

The huge Lüneburg Heath has wide expanses of birch and pine trees, as well as its famous heather (Heide) and juniper bushes

SHOWY SYLT

In the 1960s the island of Sylt became 'the St Tropez of the north' – a much publicised haunt of German film stars and wealthy playboys, many of whom flew in regularly in private planes for week-end beach parties. In the 1990s Sylt lost some of its glamour as Germany's jet set rediscovered the Mediterranean island of Mallorca, although the big mansions behind the North Sea dunes still often resound to the noise of parties.

▶ Minden   52C1

This busy junction town on the Weser has a huge *Schachtschleuse* (lock), 85m long, that links the river with the Mittelland canal; a small museum describes the lock's workings and the Weser area. The cathedral has a Romanesque façade and a striking 11th-century crucifix. At the Porta Westfalica, a scenic spot to the south, the River Weser has forced its way between two wooded hills. On each stands an unlovely memorial: a tower dedicated to Wilhelm I, and a statue of Bismarck.

▶▶ Nordfriesische Inseln
(North Friesian Islands)   52B5

This low-lying archipelago off the west coast of Schleswig is popular with holidaymakers. There are hotels on Amrum and Fohr – islands served by ferry – but the biggest and by far the best-known island is **Sylt▶▶**, a long strip of land linked to the mainland by a causeway that bears a railway but no road. Cars must board the train shuttle at Niebüll, and fares are high.

Sylt is a legend in Germany for showy jet-set tourism. Its windy but bracing climate made it a fashionable resort since the 19th century; Thomas Mann and Marlene Dietrich used to vacation here. Today its heyday is past, but Sylt remains a haunt of senior tycoons, politicians, editors and others seeking privacy. Sylt's history far predates tourism: witness the 12th-century church at Keitum, and the Altfriesisches Haus, an old farmhouse that is now a museum of local lore and history.

The remorseless wind from the North Sea whips the clouds into odd shapes, causing shifting patterns of light, and this lends Sylt a special beauty. The North Sea coast has high dunes in the form of reddish cliffs, above a long and broad sandy beach. Coastal erosion is a serious problem, but Sylt is a paradise for bathing and surfing, as well as for cycling, riding and jogging. It attracts huge numbers of sport lovers and health freaks from all social classes – almost all of them Germans. Sylt has nine separate resorts. Westerland is the biggest, but not the trendiest. Of the others, Keitum is the prettiest, a showpiece full of boutiques, galleries, and thatched cottages. The trendiest is Kampern, where bars and nightclubs try to keep alive the glory of the sixties. One short street, Stron Wai, is known as Whisky Strasse, its neat modern thatched villas bizarrely constructed into bistros and boutiques. Kupferkanne, a former wartime bunker on the cliffs, is a popular disco and bistro, with a garden café.

▶ Oldenburg   52B3

A modern, spacious town with a new university and a river port linked to the North Sea by a tributary of the Weser, Oldenburg is also the market centre of a rich farming region noted for horse and cattle breeding. In the small Altstadt, agreeably closed to traffic, some handsome older buildings remain, notably the Gothic Lambertikirche and the 15th-century Lappan tower. The nearby Schlossgarten has splendid ancient oaks and beeches. Of the three museums, the Augusteum has paintings from the Worpswede colony (*Closed* Mon); the Landesmuseum, in the former ducal palace, contains works by Tischbein and reconstructed farmhouse interiors (*Closed* Mon); and the natural history museum (*Closed* Mon) has displays of 2,400-year-old corpses that were preserved over the centuries in nearby peat bogs.

Bad Zwischenahn▶, to the west, is one of the most fashionable of North German spas and a large summer resort, beside a big lake much used for water sports. The Johanniskirche is an exceptionally lovely church, with charming paintings on its wooden gallery, 16th-century frescoes on its wooden ceiling, and a fine painted altar. The well-kept lakeside gardens contain an outdoor **rural museum▶** (*Open* Apr–Oct daily. *Closed* Nov–Mar) with a real windmill, old cottages and a superbly restored 17th-century redbrick farmhouse from the plain nearby: humans and animals used to live together in its one huge room. At Ocholt village, to the west, is the picturesque old Howieker water mill.

▶ Osnabrück   *52B1*

Today heavily industrial, producing paper, textiles and metalwork, this town of 150,000 people is also strongly historical, having been a bishopric since 785. Here, and in Münster, the 1648 Peace of Westphalia was negotiated – in a room in the Rathaus that is now called the Friedenssaal (peace hall). The room bears portraits of the signatories of the peace treaty. The town has three fine old churches but the rest of the buildings are mostly modern. Curiously, its daily paper, the *Osnabrücker Nachrichten*, is renowned in Germany for its high-level political interviews and scoops from Bonn.

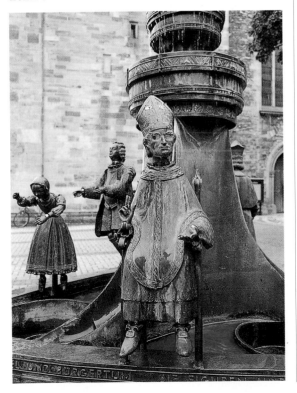

Beside this modern fountain in Osnabrück is a satirical new sculpture (of bishop and townsfolk) in a style common in German towns today

BRONZE-AGE CEMETERY
South of Oldenburg, just east of the A-1 autobahn leading to Osnabrück (take the Ahlhorn exit) is a bronze-age cemetery known as the 'classical square mile of prehistory'. the Pestruper Gräberfeld. Within an area of less than 2.5 sq km are packed more than 500 bronze-age graves, a somber landscape of small hillocks. Their bronze-age treasures are guarded in several North German museums.

73

PEACE OF WESTPHALIA
The Treaty of Osnabrück (1648) was part of the Peace of Westphalia, which ended the civil war of religion, the Thirty Years' War. Among the treaty's provisions was one that the bishopric of Osnabrück should be administered alternately by a Catholic bishop and a Protestant appointed by the Guelph family.

THE FRIESIANS

The Friesians first settled in the Netherlands and on Germany's west coast in prehistoric times, driving out their Celtic predecessors. They were eventually conquered and converted to Christianity by Charlemagne.

74

OPEN-AIR MUSEUMS

Northwest Germany, like other areas, has a number of open-air museums (*Frerlichtmuseen*) of rural life. Old farmhouses and other buildings have been collected and reassembled, complete with old furniture and farm implements. It is a key aspect of modern Germany's new concern with tradition and ecology.

► Ostfriesische Inseln (East Friesian Islands)   *52A4*

This is the eastern half of a long string of offshore islands that extends into Holland. Not surprisingly, this part of Friesland is quite like Holland, with windmills, dykes, and black-and-white Friesian cows.

The seven German islands, all inhabited and reachable by ferry, are popular for summer holidays, thanks to their bracing climate and broad sandy beaches backed by high dunes. Langeoog has an important bird sanctuary; the old church on Spiekeroog has mementos of the Spanish Armada; and Borkum and Juist are lively family resorts, good for horseback riding and sailing. The most populous island and biggest resort is Norderney, 12km long. It is reached by regular ferries from Norddeich, which will take cars. To discourage motorists, auto fares are set high and so for a short stay, it might be best to park at Norddeich and travel by foot or taxi on the island.

Norderney is not a fashionable resort, but it has an elegant-looking casino and lots of amenities. The little Fischerhaus museum gives details of the history and folklore of the island, a resort since 1797. The town and hotels are at its western end and the rest is rolling dune, much of it covered with wild grass. The interior seems like desolate moorland, with the sea out of sight behind the dunes, but the long sandy beaches are excellent. The insistent wind is a problem, as in other North Sea resorts; the beaches are neatly dotted with big hooded wicker chairs that give protection. As on Sylt, coastal erosion is a menace, and breakwaters are being built to check it.

►► Schleswig   *52C5*

Starting life as a Viking trade centre, this attractive old seaport stands at the head of the Schlei, a long, low fjord filled with small boats. Just to the south is a new museum of Viking culture and history, the **Haithabu** (*Open* daily). The town's towering redbrick Gothic cathedral contains the beautiful Bordesholm Altar (1521). In the nearby Holm district you'll find little streets of old fishermen's cottages that are a bit too neatly restored.

Continued on page 76.

In the Schleswig region, many cottages are whitewashed – in contrast to the red-brick and half-timbering so common in north Germany

At a time when Germany had yet to become a single political unit, its cities and merchant groups, benefiting from lively international trade, formed a wealthy and influential sector of medieval society. When these groups joined they became an impressive force. The Hanseatic League was a union of 150 mainly north German towns, and the most powerful economic and political power of the region.

Having started in the mid-14th century as a loose association for the protection of German tradesmen, the league created a single market that covered all trade between the North and Baltic seas, a market that it fully controlled under the leadership of the town of Lübeck.

Top: The league's ships
Above: Merchant ships unloading their cargo at Danzig in the 16th century

Member cities followed the decisions of the Hansetag, the league's representative assembly. Any breaches of these decisions by a city would bring on the process of *Verhansung*, the boycott of the city by all others. No trade would take place with the boycotted city, nor could it use the league's common facilities abroad

until it was brought back into line. By using such measures, the league managed to influence the economic and political development of each city as it wished. But this defect in the system – a loss of individual sovereignty – was compensated for by the enormous advantages of membership: no customs duties, common protection against competition, harmonised units of measurement, to name but a few. The parallels with the modern European Union and its Single Market, together with the possibility of introducing a single currency, are remarkable.

By 1370 the league was so strong it could afford to wage war against Denmark in order to gain free access to the Baltic Sea. However, with the development in the 16th century of nation-states such as Sweden and Russia, the influence of the Hanseatic League began to wane and by the time of the Thirty Years' War (1618–48), its useful life had ended.

Lübeck (above) and Danzig were both chief cities within the league

VIKING SETTLEMENT
Close to Schleswig, the 8th- to 9th-century Viking settlement of Haithabu was a major trading centre. Trade in Scandinavian furs and marine ivory and slaves from east of the Baltic passed through the settlement on the way to Western Europe and Arab territories.

ELM WINDMILL
Windmills played a major role in the economic life of this breezy part of northern Germany before the arrival of gas and electricity. One of the last windmills to serve Hamburg was dismantled a century ago and re-erected in the village of Elm, southwest of Stade. It is a handsome 18th-century Dutch model, thatched with specially prepared reeds.

76

Continued on page 74.

Schleswig's main glory is the moated white **Schloss Gottorf**►► (16th to 18th century), former home of the Holstein-Gottorf family, who acceded to the Russian throne in 1762. It is full of riches – an ornate Gothic hall with a painted ceiling, a Renaissance chapel with a carved ducal gallery and a Schleswig regional museum (*Open* daily). Next door is the **Nyddam Boat**►►, one of the world's oldest surviving vessels, dating from the 4th century. This elegant 23m oaken craft, built to be manned by 36 oarsmen, was found, well preserved, in the Danish marshes in 1863. In another room are the gruesome and unforgettable 'moor corpses' – skeletons of those who, 2,000 years ago, were tied up, blindfolded and left to die on the marshes, perhaps as a punishment for crimes.

► **Stade**   *52C3*
This is a restored old Hanseatic port near the Elbe west of Hamburg. An unusual wooden crane, formerly used for unloading grain, stands by the narrow curving harbour. It is bordered with handsome old houses – best of these is the white-and-pink Renaissance one, number 23. Upstream is the Altes Land, a picturesque, district of cherry and apple orchards, best seen at blossom time. The old brick farmhouses, many thatched and timbered, are also attractive.

► **Visbek**   *52B2*
Down a woodland path near this village south of Oldenburg are some strange megaliths that Stone Age man created from granite boulders left by the Ice Age. One long double line of stones, forming a funeral chamber with adjacent sacrificial table, is known as the Visbeker Bräutigam (bridegroom). Similar but smaller is the Visbeker Braut (bride). To the west, at Cloppenburg, the **Niedersächsiches Freilichtmuseum**► (*Open* daily) is an excellent example of the many museums of traditional rural life, so popular in Germany today. In a big park, farmhouses and other old buildings from all over the *Land* have been rebuilt and arranged to look like a real old village. There's a tiny school, a church, a manor, live ducks and sheep in a pen, plus an old pub.

►► **Wolfenbüttel**   *53D1*
A dignified old town which, for three centuries, was the residence of the dukes of Brunswick. Chief relic of that time is the great white Schloss, with its fine Renaissance tower and baroque additions. Handsome old half-timbered houses line the Stadtmarkt and Holzmarkt.
  The Herzog-August-Bibliothek, Europe's leading library in the 17th century, includes among its 6 million volumes precious medieval illuminated manuscripts. The playwright Ephraim Lessing Ephraim was its librarian from 1770 to 1781 – his home next door is now a museum of his life and work (*Closed* Mon).

► **Wolfsburg**   *53E1*
The principal factory of the Volkswagen car company is located here, founded by Hitler in 1938 to produce the 'people's car'. Today the firm employs 45,000 people in this town of 130,000 – a true 'company town'. The factory

pioneered industrial robots and you can go on a guided tour to watch these orange creatures perform precise balletic steps as they assemble the latest models.

►► Worpswede   52C3

In the 1880s Worpswede was colonised by a group of gifted young artists and writers from Berlin and Munich, who were drawn by the melancholy beauty of the moorlands. When they left, the odd houses they built began to crumble; these have now been restored, and several contain private galleries of pictures painted by the Worpswede colony. The most interesting is in the former home of one of the colony's most talented founder-artists, Otto Modersohn, the **Museum-am-Otto Modersohn-Haus**► (*Open* daily. *Admission charge*). It has works by the Worpswede artists, whose ideas were close to the Pre-Raphaelites: Fritz Mackensen, Otto Modersohn, Paula Modersohn-Becker, and the eccentric Romantic Heinrich Vogeler are represented. The architect Bernhard Hoetger has left several offbeat buildings and sculptures.

The picturesque old harbour of Stade is no longer in use. A museum tells the story of the town's remarkable history

77

RHINELAND

NL

78

F

0   20   40   60   80 km

0   10   20   30   40   50 miles

This westernmost part of Germany focuses on the mighty Rhine and its tributaries, some of them scenic rivers in their own right – the Mosel, Lahn and Ahr. Other tributaries – the Saar and above all the Ruhr – have given their name to great industrial conurbations.

This is a region of contrasts. The Ruhr cities, comparatively new, have their own identity and high cultural status, but none compares with the richness of 2,000-year-old Köln (Cologne), one of the great cities of Europe. Sophisticated Düsseldorf is the capital of the Land of Nordrhein-Westfalen, relaxed Mainz of the Land of Rheinland Pfalz, while Bonn will soon lose most, but not all, of its role as Germany's capital.

To the west, the Eifel and the Hunsrück have some of Germany's loneliest and most rugged landscapes. To the southeast, the Palatinate wears a kindlier air, perhaps due to the warm red sandstone from which many of its buildings are made. Beyond the deep trench of the Rhine Gorge are farther uplands, of which the most extensive is the Sauerland, its rivers and woods a haven for the crowded populations of nearby cities.

To the north, the hills give way to the rich agricultural countryside of the North German Plain, where riverside poplars take the place of beech and spruce forests.

The region's vineyards are the world's northernmost, with delightful wine villages and cheerful cellars and taverns. Life is taken less seriously here than in other parts of Germany, particularly in the Catholic cities of Köln (Cologne) and Mainz, where exuberance knows no bounds during the pre-Lenten carnival.

This was the most Romanised part of Germany, with the Rhine forming the frontier of the empire for centuries. Potent reminders of the Roman presence exist in Trier, with the greatest concentration of Roman monuments north of the Alps. French influence has been felt constantly, as successive kings, revolutionaries, emperors, and republican governments all sought to push France's frontier eastwards.

Today, no other part of Germany is so intimately tied to its neighbours across the unguarded frontiers, in links aptly symbolised by the joint administration of the nature parks that lie along the Belgian and Luxembourg borders and by a park that straddles a border on the edge of Saarbrücken, the Deutsch-Französischer Garten (Franco-German Park).

Rüdesheim, seen from the Niederwald Monument

HOTTEST SPA
The spa in Aachen's suburb of Burtscheid, with a water temperature of 76°C, is the hottest in Central Europe. Most of the hotels in Burtscheid offer health treatments using the hot water, which has a high concentration of important minerals.

Aachen's splendid Rathaus is built on the site of Charlemagne's palace, of which two towers survive

►► **Aachen**   78A4

Germany's westernmost city, the country's gateway to many visitors from Great Britain and Belgium, Aachen deserves more than passing attention.

The city limits extend to the frontiers of both Belgium and Holland; a popular excursion is to the Dreiländereck, the wooded hills where the three countries meet. In the late 9th century, Aachen's location attracted Charlemagne (Karl der Grosse, or Charles the Great), who built a fine palace here from which to rule the Frankish Empire, which extended over most of Western Europe. Aachen's hot springs may have influenced the emperor's choice: he was a notable bather. Though Aachen is still a spa town, with a good reputation in the treatment of rheumatism and similar afflictions, empire and palace have long since crumbled away, save for the Imperial Chapel. But what a fantastic chapel!

Forming the centrepiece of the city's *Dom* (cathedral), **Charlemagne's** octagonal **chapel**►►► is one of the key monuments of early Christian Europe. It has a two-story arcaded gallery and is embellished with marble brought from Italy. The huge 12th-century chandelier hanging from its dome is one of the many treasures that make the cathedral such a storehouse of ecclesiastical art. In the light and airy 14th-century Gothic chancel is the Ambo, an extraordinarily ornate pulpit, as well as the gorgeous altar front known as the Pala d'Oro and the golden shrine containing Charlemagne's mortal remains. In the gallery is the imposing stone throne on which some 30 German kings were crowned. An incomparable array of precious objects – crucifixes, chasubles, and reliquaries – fills the **Schatzkammer**►► (cathedral treasury) (*Open* daily).

The first German city to be taken by the Americans in late 1944, Aachen sustained severe damage, but enough of the Altstadt remains to remind us that this is an ancient and lived-in place. Appropriately for a spa town, water features prominently in the townscape; the lighthearted Puppenbrunnen (Dolls' Fountain) has figures with movable limbs, while the thermal springs themselves are housed in neo-classical pavilions designed by the great Prussian architect Schinkel.

Dominating the marketplace is the fortresslike Rathaus; its splendid Kaisersaal (Kaiser's Hall) is decorated with 19th-century paintings of episodes in Charlemagne's career and also houses reproductions of the crown jewels (the Habsburgs having made off with the original jewels to Vienna).

Museums The city's museums are varied; the Suermondt-Ludwig-Museum (*Closed* Mon) has old masters as well as a medley of medieval sculpture, while the Ludwig Forum (*Closed* Mon) specialises in more modern work. The Couven Museum has well-appointed interiors showing how the comfortable classes lived in the 18th and 19th century. More unusual is the Internationales Zeitungsmuseum (International Newspaper Museum), (*Closed* Mon), commemorating Paul Julius von Reuter's early days, when his news service depended on carrier pigeons; the intriguing displays reveal how the news has been reported – or misreported – over the years.

▶ Bocholt 78A5

This cotton town close to the Dutch border is graced by two architectural landmarks. Dedicated to St George, the late Gothic hall church has a spectacular west window and a high altar with a fine 15th-century depiction of the Crucifixion by a Cologne master. The gabled and arcaded Renaissance Rathaus is one of the best preserved of its kind in the country.

Wasserburg Anholt stands right on the frontier with Holland, 16km west of the town. The origins of this moated stronghold go back to the 13th century, when the squat tower known as the Dicker Turm was built. The castle now houses the local museum.

▶▶ Bonn 78B4

For centuries, Bonn languished in pleasant provincial obscurity on the west bank of the Rhine at the point where the great river flows past the Seven Mountains into the flatlands around Cologne. In 1949, the committee assembled here to draft the constitution of the new West German state decided that the city should be made the capital of the Federal Republic. Far from the East German border and with no metropolitan pretensions of its own that might upset more obvious candidates, such as Frankfurt, Bonn had the advantage of being a short ferry ride across the Rhine from the Königswinter home of Konrad Adenauer, the elderly but immensely shrewd chancellor of the newborn state.

Express trains were persuaded to stop in Bonn, rather than steaming straight through, and an influx of civil servants and diplomats helped double the population. The notion that one day Berlin would resume its rightful place as the nation's capital inhibited grandiloquent government building; parliament was housed in a teachers' college, the chancellor was in the 19th-century Villa

Aachen's little squares are full of outdoor cafés and statue fountains – one fountain is made of bronze dolls

BEETHOVEN'S BONN
Bonn's most famous son, Ludwig van Beethoven (1770–1827), left the place at the age of 22 for Vienna, never to return. He is commemorated in Bonn by a statue, the Beethovenhalle (a modern concert hall) and an annual international festival. His birthplace contains an exemplary display of memorabilia, including, most poignantly, the ear trumpets that failed to breach the barrier of the composer's advancing deafness (*Open* daily).

Hammerschmidt. By the 1970s, hopes for reunification were fading, and lumpy modern 'official' buildings began to transform the townscape. By the year 2000 the German Parliament, government offices, the Chancellery and most ministries moved to Berlin. There was no shortage of tenants for the vacated buildings, and several ministries and government agencies remained in Bonn. Nevertheless, the Rhineside area that once hummed with government activity has lost its old 'buzz', leaving few frissons of surprise to be had from sighting a famous face in one of the bars favoured by the political elite.

Look for the spectacular complexes housing the City Art Museum (*Closed* Mon) and the National Art and Exhibition Centre, the latter's 16 rusty columns symbolising the German *Länder*. Much damaged in the last war, Bonn's old core still contains plenty of evidence of its long past. Prehistoric, Roman and Frankish remains are in the Landesmuseum (*Closed* for renovations until 2001), where the star exhibit is the skull of Neanderthal Man, found near Düsseldorf in 1856 (see panel page 83). The late Romanesque/early Gothic *Münster* (minster), with its tall central tower, airy interior and splendid cloisters, is one of the finest of many such churches in the Rhineland. The prince-bishops of Cologne preferred to reside in backwater Bonn rather than among the more rowdy citizens of their cathedral city; their contributions to the urban scene include the pink rococo Rathaus, as well as the Residenz and the Poppelsdorfer Schloss, both part of the university.

One of Bonn's great assets is its setting (its humid climate less so). The vast new Rheinauen Park links the city to the river and gives fine views of Drachenfels peak and the Seven Mountains (see page 100). Southwards lies the old spa of Bad Godesberg, with a pleasant riverside promenade, while the terrace of the Godesburg, the ruined castle high above the town, offers a fine panorama.

▶ Düsseldorf 78B4

Capital of Nordrhein-Westfalen, Germany's most populous *Land*, money-conscious Düsseldorf is the showcase in which the country's wealth is dazzlingly displayed. The city's skyline is dominated less by its numerous old churches than by such monuments of modern commerce as the coldly elegant Thyssen skyscraper. As well as the headquarters of many of the great Ruhr industrial concerns, Düsseldorf has also attracted numerous Japanese firms, which have made it the base of their overseas operations; the city's Japanese community is now the largest in Europe.

Private affluence is balanced by a strong sense of civic pride dating back to the city's rule by its electors, the most notable of whom was Johann Wilhelm (1679–1716). Known affectionately as Jan Wellem, he laid out the spacious new districts beyond the Altstadt and attracted artists to the city; he is commemorated by a statue in front of the Renaissance Rathaus. Modern Düsseldorf is well endowed with parks, gardens and landscaped pedestrian areas, so that one can stroll free of traffic.

Theatre, music, opera and cabaret all thrive here, and the city's galleries are outstanding; the collection of Paul Klee paintings in the Kunstsammlung Nordrhein-Westfalen (*Closed* Mon) is the biggest in the country.

Excursions

Schloss Benrath (*Closed* Mon), a sumptuous rococo palace in a fine park, is a favorite local outing. It was built in the mid-18th century by a French architect for one of Jan Wellem's successors.

The **River Wupper** snakes through a steep-sided valley to the east of Düsseldorf. Wuppertal is a string of industrial towns that form a linear city. Birthplace of Freidrich Engels, the city has an outstanding collection of 19th- and 20th-century German and French art in the Von der Heydt Museum, and is the home of Germany's leading modern dance company, created and run by the great Pina Bausch.

Wuppertal is also known for its Schwebebahn, the overhead railway that has stitched its disparate communities together since 1901. The railway lost its reputation as Germany's safest and most reliable transport system in 1999 when one of the cars jumped of the line and plunged into the shallow river below, killing five passengers. Downstream, the valley is crossed by a more conventional railway line, carried 107m above the river on the Müngstenerbrücke, Europe's highest railway bridge. This links the timber-framed and slate-roofed town of Remscheid with Solingen, where the Klingen-museum displays every possible kind of cutlery, a traditional centre of steel production. Farther downstream still, high above the river, is the spectacularly sited castle of Burg an der Wupper, housing the local history museum.

▶▶ The Eifel   78A3

Bounded by the Rhine, the Mosel, and the country's border with Belgium and Luxembourg, the rugged Eifel is the northwesternmost of Germany's upland massifs. In spite of its proximity to great centres of population, its sweeping heights, vast forests and deep valleys offer endless opportunities for escaping the crowds.

The area's core is formed by the Hohe Eifel, composed of ancient volcanoes. Its highest point is the Hohe Acht, a basalt peak of 747m. The hills are pitted with strange

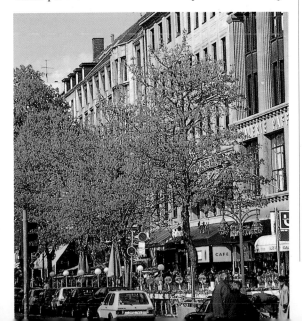

BRAHMS TO BEUYS
Writers, artists and musicians have been associated with Düsseldorf. The poet Heine was born here. Brahms, Mendelssohn and Schumann all found the atmosphere congenial, as did the ex-Messerschmitt pilot and postwar *enfant terrible* Josef Beuys (d.1986), whose felt-and-fat sculptures won international attention, if not always complete approval.

LIVELY ALTSTADT
Düsseldorf brews an unusual beer, 'Alt', not unlike a pale ale, consumed in large quantities in the Altstadt. Echoes of the days when the city was no more than a riverside fishing village can still be picked up among the many bars, pubs, restaurants and discos, which pack Germany's most crowded restaurant and bar scene, an Altstadt zone just 1 sq km in area.

NEANDERTHAL MAN
The valley of the little Düssel River was a favourite retreat of the poet Joachim Neander, who gave it his name. The site of the cave where the skeletal remains of Neanderthal Man were found in 1856 is marked by a plaque. The skull is now in the Landesmuseum in Bonn (*Closed* for renovations until 2001), but there is a small museum at the cave with displays on life 60,000 years ago.

Düsseldorf's Königsallee, known as the 'Kö', is lined with some of Europe's most stylish cafés

The Rhineland

The Ahr Valley, home of some of Germany's best red wines

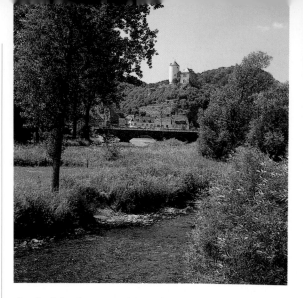

BAD NEUENAHR
While ancient Ahrweiler has kept its town wall, with towers and gates, the spa town of Bad Neuenahr is a 19th-century creation, dating from the discovery of medicinal springs here in 1852. Parks and gardens provide a manicured setting for visitors taking their cure. On the Silberberg hill, a patrician Roman villa now houses the Museum Roemervilla (*Closed* Mon).

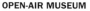

OPEN-AIR MUSEUM
In a wooded setting on the edge of Mechernich-Kommern, the Rheinisches Freilichtmuseum (Rhineland Open-Air Museum) is an extensive collection of carefully re-erected traditional buildings of the countryside, including wind and water mills and workshops, as well as cottages and farmsteads (*Closed* Mon).

circular lakes known as *Maare*, formed by violent volcanic explosions that also left other curiosities in the shape of 'bombs', like the one near the little spa town of Daun. Perhaps the loneliest part of the Eifel is the Schnee-Eifel, to the west, where cross-border nature parks merge with the Belgian and Luxembourg Ardennes. To the north is a 'Lake District', formed by the damming of the Rur and Erft rivers, and very popular with holidaymakers from across the Dutch and Belgian borders. More popular still is the valley of the River Ahr, descending eastwards through a series of picturesque wine villages to the Rhine. An entire holiday could easily be spent in these attractive uplands, particularly by lovers of fresh air and exercise. Some of the Eifel's characteristic landscapes and little towns can be visited as an alternative to the autobahn on the way southeast.

Monschau► Overlooked by its medieval castle, and generally agreed to be the prettiest place in the Eifel, Monschau winds along the steep-sided valley of the River Rur. Among its black-and-white houses stands the grand redbrick residence known as the Rotes Haus (*Closed* Mon); its interior is evocative of the comfortable lifestyle of its 18th-century proprietor, a dealer in the cloth for which the town was famous.

Bad Münstereifel With its walls still enclosing an intricate web of cobbled streets and alleyways, this is one of Germany's best-preserved medieval small towns. The River Erft chatters alongside the main street, while the castle stands guard over one side of the valley, the buildings of the town's renowned spa on the other. The best townscape is to be seen in the Orchheimer Strasse, where the high-gabled and intriguingly carved Windeckhaus forms a perfect composition with its neighbours. On the lonely plateau to the east of the town is a great surprise – the utterly unmedieval structure of the Eifelsberg radio telescope, the largest in the world. The country road to the east drops down into the romantic valley of the River Ahr, a delightful miniature version of the Rhine Gorge.

Altenahr A pretty little place, dominated by its castle ruin and with many inviting wine cellars where you can taste the local wines, Altenahr marks the western end of Germany's northernmost wine-growing area. Sheltered by the Hohe Eifel, the slatey slopes rising precipitously from the twisting river provide excellent growing conditions for vines. The local Spätburgunder, a 'velvety, noble wine', is considered by many connoisseurs to be easily the best of the country's otherwise rather undistinguished reds.

Maria Laach▶ This splendid Benedictine abbey stands in what was once a remote setting beside the largest of all the volcanic lakes in the Eifel, the Laacher See. Founded in 1093, the great six-towered abbey church is one of the grandest and most harmonious Romanesque buildings in Germany. After the dissolution of the country's monasteries in 1802, the abbey's numerous art treasures disappeared, leaving the interior looking rather bare but still very dignified.

SCHLOSS BÜRRESHEIM
The castle, southwest of Maria Laach, owes its exceptionally picturesque appearance to successive waves of building and rebuilding from the 12th to the 19th century. The interior, unusually for Germany, is well furnished, and there is an attractive formal garden with high hedges (*Open* Apr–Nov daily. *Closed* Dec–Mar).

ANNE OF CLEVES
Daughter of one of
Kleve's dukes, Anne of
Cleves (1515–57)
became Henry VIII's
fourth wife in 1539.
Their marriage was intended to
consolidate an alliance of
Protestant rulers, but
Henry took a dislike to the
meek and unprepossess-
ing 'Mare of Flanders' and
had their unconsummated
union annulled after six
months.

CRAZY CARNIVAL
Of German pre-Lenten
carnivals, the biggest and
most boisterous is
Cologne's and it fits well
with the city's spirit of
fun-loving whimsy. First a
Carnival Prince is elected
along with his two hench-
men, the Peasant and the
Virgin (she has always
been a man, save under
the Nazis who hated
transvestism). They 'rule'
the city during the *Tolle
Tage* (Crazy Days). On
Thursday vengeful women
cut off the tie of any male
(very Freudian?). Sunday
is devoted to satiric floats,
and on Monday a million
people line the route for
the main parade, full of
pirouetting majorettes.
Karneval is one merry
booze-up of local pub
parties and street parties.

▶ **Kleve (Cleves)** 78A5

The last substantial place on the west bank of the Rhine before the Dutch border, Kleve is an ancient ducal residence whose *Oberstadt* (upper town) is built on the low hills rising over the floodplain of the great river. To the southwest is the vast forest tract known as the Reichswald, the scene of bitter fighting as the Allied armies prepared to cross the Rhine early in 1945. To the northeast stretch watery flatlands where the Rhine once wandered at will before being confined behind its present high embankments.

The medieval counts of Kleve eventually rose to the rank of duke, though their bid for even more enhanced status by marrying into the English royal family came to nothing (see panel). Though virtually destroyed in World War II, the town is still marked by their castle, the Schwanenburg, and by the fine parks and gardens they laid out.

Excursions
Emmerich, 8km east, is reached from Kleve by the country's longest suspension bridge. The brick-built port of Emmerich makes its living from the river, and celebrates this long-standing connection in its Rheinmuseum (*Closed* Sat).

Kalkar, 12km southeast, was famous in the late Middle Ages for its talented wood-carvers. This small town boasts a brick church with an astonishing array of fine altarpieces, as well as a number of houses with stepped gables and a 15th-century Rathaus.

Xanten, 27km southeast, was rebuilt after its near-destruction in early 1945. This is a neat little town that has conserved stretches of medieval fortifications (including the picturesque Kleve Gate) and a cathedral crammed with splendid artwork. The town lies between two Roman settlements, civilian Colonia Trojana to the north and military Castra Vetera to the south. The civilian town is now an archeological park, with thorough reconstructions of fortifications and buildings that attempt to bring the days of Roman occupation back to life.

▶▶▶ **Köln (Cologne)** 78B4

With the twin spires of its glorious cathedral visible far away across the surrounding plain, this is one of Germany's great metropolitan cities, a centre of culture and learning as well as industry and commerce.

First founded by the Romans in 33 BC, 'Colonia' achieved city status under Emperor Claudius in AD 40. Its importance at this time is reflected in the superb Dionysus Mosaic forming the centrepiece of the splendid modern Römisch-Germanisches Museum (*Closed* Mon) in the city's heart. By the Middle Ages, Cologne had become the largest city in Germany, with no fewer than 150 churches. The Altstadt is consequently huge, extending to the semicircular Ring, a boulevard laid out along the line of fortifications demolished in the 19th century but still punctuated at intervals by the surviving city gates (Eigelstein Tor, Hahnentor, St Severin's Tor).

The city suffered the first allied 1,000-bomber raid in 1942, and in the course of the war nine-tenths of the buildings in the centre of town were destroyed. Their replacements may not always be of the highest architectural quality, but planners' retention of the ancient street pattern has helped maintain something of the spirit of the city's 2,000 years of history. Konrad Adenauer, later to be Germany's Chancellor, was the city's mayor in 1917–33. Another distinguished son of Cologne in this century was the novelist Heinrich Böll, who spent most of his life and set many of his books here. His satirical humour and Catholic humanism were typical of the Rhineland.

Cologne's atmosphere is that of a city-state, its strong local patriotism expressed in its own impenetrable *Kölsch* (dialect). Kölsch also happens to be the name of Cologne's excellent beer, served in small glasses which have been

EAU DE COLOGNE
In the 18th century an Italian resident distilled an astringent liquid from flower blossoms. Intended originally as an aphrodisiac, the famous Kölnisch Wasser (Cologne water, or eau de Cologne) is more commonly used as toilet water.

87

The towers and spires of Köln cathedral (right) and the Romanesque Gross St Martin dominate the city's riverside landscape

ST URSULA
Daughter of a 4th-century British king, the virginal St Ursula is reputed to have been murdered in Cologne by rampaging Huns, along with 11,000 other Christian maidens. This spectacular end led to her beatification and commemoration in the city's coat of arms, as well as in the church that bears her name.

known to prompt revolt among Bavarian visitors used to seeing it served in litre mugs. The number and variety of Cologne breweries rivals even Munich's, and the Rhinelanders claim their beers are stronger and better than anything brewed in Bavaria. Cologne's beer taverns also rival Bavaria's, and Cologne waiters have an almost gallic charm that contrasts with the brusqueness of the buxom Munich beerhall waitresses. The Rhinelander is probably the friendliest, most hospitable and amusing German you'll meet, and nowhere is this friendliness more evident than in Cologne.

Most visitors probably get their first glimpse of Cologne from the hall of the main train station, whose high windows frame the clifflike side of the cathedral. Walk out along the railway bridge (Höhenzollernbrücke) to savour the city's silhouette rising over the bustle of traffic on and alongside the Rhine.

The **Dom►►►** (cathedral) is one of the world's great Gothic structures. Begun in the 13th century, it was completed only in the 19th, still in faithful accord with the intentions of its medieval architects, whose original drawings had miraculously survived. Externally its sheer mass is relieved by the lacelike delicacy of its masonry, while the vast interior contains such incomparable works of art as the majestic golden shrine of the Magi, the 9th-century Gero Crucifix, the glorious 15th-century Cologne School altarpiece painted by Stefan Lochner, and superb stained glass. If you make the stiff climb up the south tower you will be rewarded by a fine panorama over the city centre.

The well-designed pedestrian spaces characteristic of so many German cities invite exploration. Southeast of the Dom is the **Romisch-Germanisches Museum►** (*Closed* Mon), with its wonderful collection of Roman art found locally (notably the Dionysus Mosaic) as well as items such as toys and clothes that illustrate daily Roman life. Nearby is a modern complex housing the Philharmonie, the central concert hall, as well as the **Wallraf-Richartz and Ludwig museums►** (*Closed* Mon), with their major collections of German and international art. Not to be missed are the exquisite late medieval paintings of the Cologne School or the works by such early 20th-century masters as Dix, Beckmann, Kirchner, and Barlach. This is also a good place to ponder the Americana of the postwar Pop Artists – Roy Lichtenstein and Andy Warhol.

Leading southwards is the Hohe Strasse, the city's main shopping street. Other streets and passageways penetrate the core of the Altstadt, centred on the Alter Markt and the 14th-century Gothic Rathaus, with its Renaissance loggia. Before the completion of the Dom, the distinctive four-turreted tower of the Romanesque church of Gross St Martin dominated the skyline; completed in 1172, this is one of the city's several **pre-Gothic churches▶** (a grouping unique in Europe), each with its own special features. St Pantaleon, from the 10th century, is the oldest; St Gereon is the most spectacular, with a superb delicately ribbed, 10-sided tower, the Decagon; while St Maria im Kapitol is richly furnished, with remarkable 11th-century carved doors. The best place to see religious art and furnishings is in the deconsecrated church housing the Schnütgen Museum (*Closed* Mon); the squeamish should avoid the exquisitely carved *memento mori* (corpses in the last stages of decay).

Cologne continues to be a churchy place. Many striking places of worship have been built this century, notably St Gertrud, north of the Ring, or Neu St Alban, to the west, with a dimly lit, highly atmospheric interior. Nearby is the Fernmeldeturm (telecommunications tower), 242m high, offering a vast panorama. The large Imhoff-Stollwerck Museum (*Closed* Mon), entirely devoted to the history of the production of chocolate, stands on an island in the Rhine.

On the far bank, use the cable-car to reach the Rheinpark; its centrepiece is the Tanzbrunnen, a vast fountain above a canopied dance floor.

Excursion

Altenberger Dom is about 16km northeast of Cologne among the woodlands of the hilly countryside known as the Bergisches Länd. This is no cathedral but a former Cistercian monastery, one of the finest examples of Gothic architecture in Germany, restored in the last century. Both Catholics and Protestants worship here.

NIGHT TRAIN
'The Express feels its way and pushes the darkness along....Then suddenly the ground roars like a sea: we are flying, suspended, royally through air seized from the night, high above the current ...Rushing like torches.'– Ernst Stadler, *Journey over the Rhine Bridge at Cologne by Night.*

89

SCHLOSS AUGUSTUSBURG
Brühl, 15km southwest of Cologne, has Germany's largest theme park, Phantasie-land, as well as the pleasure gardens from an earlier time that surround Schloss Augustusburg, the sumptuous rococo palace of the archbishops of Cologne. Often used for state receptions (and consequently liable to be closed to the public), this echo of Bavarian light-heartedness has an ornate staircase by the great south German architect Balthasar Neumann.

Cafés in Cologne

GOETHE'S LOVE
Goethe came to Wetzlar as a young man and fell for a local girl, Charlotte Buff, who was already betrothed to another man, who subsequently killed himself. The experience of this tragedy was distilled by Goethe into *The Sorrows of Young Werther*, a key work of German Romanticism. Charlotte's house (Lottehaus) is now a museum devoted to the sad affair (*Closed* Mon).

Top: Bad Ems
Below: Limburg

► **Lahn Valley**   *78C4*

Rising in the Rothaargebirge nature park (see page 102) and flowing for much of its length through a wooded gorge, the River Lahn winds past picturesquely sited castles, ruined like Balduinstein or romantically rebuilt like Schaumburg and Braunfels, before joining the Rhine near Koblenz. The valley can be explored by car – but also along riverside foot and cycle paths, by pleasure-boat, canoe and raft, or by railway, which often hugs the river more closely than the road.

Each of the Lahn towns has a highly individual character. The classic spa town of **Bad Ems** was the favoured resort of Kaiser Wilhelm I; his statue stands in the immaculate riverside gardens. As well as haughty hotels, aristocratic Ems has a casino, an onion-domed Russian Orthodox church, and a cable-hauled railway to hoist health seekers up to the modern spa installations on the heights above the narrow valley. Both **Nassau** and **Diez**, the latter with a high-walled castle, are associated with the Orange-Nassau dynasty which was involved in European national rivalries and royal intrigues in the 17th and 18th centuries (*Closed* Mon).

Limburg►, in a more open part of the valley, has won a number of prizes for its careful conservation work, and the results can be enjoyed among the picturesque timber-framed houses of the medieval centre. Alleyways lead up to Limburg's cathedral, on a rocky spur overlooking the river. With its exterior repainted in the bright orange and white livery of medieval times, the cathedral is a fine example of the transition from Romanesque to Gothic. The cool interior has unique 12th-century paintings, while the Diocesan Museum and Treasury house ecclesiastical art objects.

The medieval Burg at **Runkel** was once the biggest castle along the Lahn; its rugged walls still rise imposingly over the old village with its bridge and weir.

The stronghold at **Weilburg** is different altogether – an elegant Renaissance residence built by the counts of Nassau. Ornate interiors are complemented by terraced gardens stepping down to the river, which almost encircles the spur on which the castle and its dependent little baroque town are built. Boat traffic can take a shortcut through the promontory via a 235m tunnel, the longest of its kind in Germany.

Wetzlar's industries make an array of products, of which Leica cameras may be the most famous. But this is a historic town, too, for over 100 years the seat of the law courts of the Holy Roman Empire. Towering over the old houses that step down to the seven-arched bridge over the Lahn is the unfinished cathedral, a strange amalgam of Romanesque and Gothic.

▶ Mainz   78C2

Seat of the government of Rheinland-Pfalz, 2,000-year-old Mainz is endowed with most of the good things to be expected of a lively provincial capital: a cathedral, an archbishop's palace, an ancient university, museums, an attractive Altstadt. Its position on the banks of the Rhine and its exceptionally mild climate may explain its cheerful atmosphere; its great pre-Lenten Karneval is second only to Cologne's for high spirits, and there are more jollifications – like Johannisnacht in March and a big wine festival in August/September.

The great red sandstone cathedral, with its six towers, looms over the largely pedestrianised city centre. Essentially Romanesque, though with many later additions, it has a spacious interior containing the splendid tombs of its powerful prince-bishops. The Diocesan Museum off the Gothic cloisters (*Closed* Mon) houses some of the wonderfully sensitive sculpture of the mysterious medieval mason the Master of Naumburg.

A short walk from the cathedral, the banks of the Rhine hold a medley of public buildings ancient and modern, including the exuberant Renaissance-baroque Schloss housing the Römisch-Germanisches Zentralmuseum (*Closed* Mon). There are more spectacular Roman artifacts in the Landesmuseum nearby (*Closed* Mon).

Start a stroll 'inland', through the Altstadt with its half timbered houses and wine taverns, at the Marktbrunnen, the delightful Renaissance fountain. Perhaps the outstanding work of modern art in Mainz is to be found in the Stefanskirche; because the church's **stained glass▶**, which glows with visionary intensity, is the work of the great Russian artist Marc Chagall, who took as his theme 'Reconciliation'.

▶▶ Marburg   78C4

With half-timbered houses clustering around the castle high above the river Lahn, a great **church▶** dedicated to St Elisabeth, and a venerable university, Marburg seems to represent the essence of medieval Germany.

The focal point of Marburg's Altstadt, particularly in university semesters, is the Marktplatz, with its late-Gothic Rathaus and St George fountain. In this part of town, the steep streets are supplemented by stairways. One leads up to the Schloss, the residence of Elisabeth's descendants, the Landgraves. Built from about 1260 on, it has a three-story Rittersaal (Knights' Hall) and houses part of the outstanding collections of the Universitätsmuseum (University Museum) (*Closed* Mon).

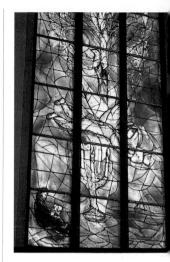

A window by Chagall in Stefanskirche, Mainz

GUTENBERG, PRINTER
A native of Mainz, Johannes Gutenberg revolutionised communications by elaborating the idea of printing using movable metal type, rendering the painstaking work of the medieval scribe obsolete at a stroke. Between 1452 and 1455 he printed some 200 Bibles, one of which can be seen in the fascinating Gutenberg Museum. Housed in the Renaissance mansion known as the Römischer Kaiser, the museum includes a replica of his original workshop with an operating press. Hounded by a grasping partner, Gutenberg made no money from his extraordinary achievements, though in later life he was elevated to the petty nobility and given a pension by the elector of Nassau. Mainz celebrates the 600th anniversary of Gutenberg's birth in the year 2000, and the newly-renovated museum (*Closed* Mon) is the centre of celebrations.

BOAT TRIPS

While it's possible to drive the whole length of the signposted Mosel-weinstrasse, it's more fun to do at least part of the trip by steamer. Various permutations of car, boat, and even train travel are possible and can be investigated locally (a good one: train from Cochem to Traben-Trarbach and return by steamer). You can also choose to walk up to the viewpoints offered by the many castles – intact or in ruins – along the route. Though extremely popular, the Mosel is less commercialised than its counterpart, the Rhine Gorge. River traffic is less intense, and the railway runs along only one bank, often wandering off altogether. You can always get away from the crowds by taking to the footpaths or coming out of season – vineyards in winter have a special charm!

Opposite page: Cochem, with its romantic castle overlooking the Mosel River

The river Mosel at Zell, a charming wine-town whose round tower was part of its defences in medieval times

THE MOSEL

The 514km Mosel River rises in eastern France. For 34km it forms the border between Luxembourg and Germany; it then travels 242km in Germany, ending in the Rhine at Koblenz.

▶▶▶ Mosel (Moselle) Valley   78B3

Rising high up in France's Vosges Mountains, the Mosel forms the boundary between Germany and Luxembourg before reaching the ancient city of Trier. From here to its confluence with the Rhine at Koblenz, the river cuts through the Hunsrück and Eifel uplands in a series of extraordinary loops and bends lined by vineyards that produce the famous Mosel wines. Every square metre of steep slope able to catch the sun is completely covered with a forest of poles to hold the vines steady in the rather slatey soil. The white wines that are yielded range from crisp, young vintages to sweeter, late-harvested ones, all of them sold in distinctive slim green bottles.

It was the Romans who brought the vine to this north-eastern extremity of their empire. A replica of the famous Roman Wine Ship (the original is in the Landesmuseum in Trier) stands in the Peterskapelle in Neumagen, the town where it was found. Downstream is the charming double town of **Bernkastel-Kues▶**, renowned for its Doktor vineyard. Colourful Renaissance houses line the sloping market square with its fountain, while the odd-shaped Spitzgielbelhaus ('the house of the pointed gables') nearby comes straight out of a picture book. Among the vines above the town stand the ruins of Landshut castle. On the far bank, Kues has a Gothic almshouse still serving its original purpose; in the chapel is a fine 15th-century altarpiece.

Another double town spanning the river is the resort of **Traben-Trarbach**, not particularly attractive, but a useful centre for touring the area. In the square at **Zell** is a curious statue of a black grimacing cat, subject of a local legend (*Schwarz Katz* is one local wine). Fortified **Beilstein** is dominated by the massive ruined castle once owned by Metternich. **Cochem's** picturesque setting, with its romantically rebuilt castle crowning a vine-clad knoll, has inevitably made it one of the most-visited places along the river. Equally popular is **Burg Eltz▶**, a short distance up a deeply wooded side valley. This is one of Germany's dream castles (built between the 13th and 16th centuries), its sheer walls rising spectacularly through the trees and capped by steep-pitched slate roofs and an array of turrets. The interior is relatively intimate – a succession of small courtyards with half-timbered façades. A tour includes the hall of banners, the 'treasure chamber,' and a fascinating collection of old weapons. The castle is open only from April through October (daily), but even in the winter months the walk up to its rampants is captivating.

More castles follow, one at **Thurant** and two at **Kobern-Gondorf**, before the river makes the last of its sinuous turns at Winningen, a charming vineyard village with Germany's oldest (1320) half-timbered house, at Church Street 1, and then flows beneath the great autobahn bridge that marks the approach to Koblenz and the river's junction with the Rhine.

▶ Münster 78B5

The historic capital of Westphalia, Münster is a prosperous university city, proud of its Catholic identity in a largely Protestant province. Its varied architectural heritage suffered badly in World War II, but local pride has expressed itself in loving restoration and reconstruction.

The bustle on the Domplatz (Cathedral Square) is presided over by the handsome, twin-towered **cathedral▶**, built in the early 13th century in the transitional style between Romanesque and Gothic. The interior is richly endowed with statuary, tombs, and altars, and has a remarkable astronomical clock of 1540, with automata that bestir themselves daily at noon for the benefit of the assembled crowds. The foundations of the present building's 8th-century predecessor can be seen in the cloisters; beyond is the treasury, which has an 11th-century jewel-studded reliquary of St Paul.

As well as the cathedral, Münster has other remarkable churches, including the 14th-century Überwasserkirche, with an elaborately decorated tower, and the Gothic Lambertikirche. The three cages hanging from the latter's tower once held the corpses of leading Anabaptists, Protestant extremists, who in the 16th century unwisely overthrew church rule and proclaimed the millennium. This rash act precipitated the massacre of the townsfolk and the Anabaptists' own execution by mercenaries in the pay of the bishop. From the Lambertikirche, the city's

The Rhineland

PFÄLZER WALD (PALATINATE FOREST)

The splendid stretches of forest of this upland country, much of it protected as a nature park, forms the most extensive area of continuous woodland in the whole of Germany. To the east rises the Haardt, a high ridge that then falls steeply to the vineyards lining the Weinstrasse (see page 107). To the south, linking with the Vosges Mountains in Alsace, are the sandstone hills of the Wasgau, weirdly weathered into castle-crowned cones, cliffs, and spikes.

With its timber-framed houses and millstream, the little town of Annweiler is a good centre for exploring the southern part of the forest. Within easy reach is a clutch of castles. Overlooking the town itself is 11th-century Trifels, where Richard the Lion-Hearted was imprisoned in 1193. Splendid views from the chapel tower include the lesser castles of Anebos and Scharfenberg. To the southwest is Berwartstein, typifying the 19th-century Romantic view of what a crag-top castle should look like. Nearby Drachenfels, now a ruin, had no need of walls, so sheer were its natural defenses. Dahn is the best place to investigate the effects of wind and weather on the soft local sandstone. Eroded into strange shapes, it formed the building material for Dahn's three castles, all of them erected within the same perimeter wall.

main thoroughfare, the Prinzipalmarkt, is lined with the arcaded and gabled Renaissance town houses (mostly rebuilt) of prosperous merchants. At the far end is the superb Rathaus, with a wonderful panelled chamber (*Open* daily, Sun am only) – the Friedenssaal (Hall of Peace); this is where the Peace of Westphalia was signed in 1648, bringing to an end the Thirty Years' War.

Less flamboyant than its south German equivalent, the baroque style evolved by the local architect Johann Schlaun resulted in a number of notable buildings, such as the aristocratic mansion called the Erbdrostenhof, the unusual circular Clemenskirche and, above all, the huge palace of the prince-bishops (1767–73), now the main building of the university.

Two museums merit mention. Medieval sculpture and old masters feature in the Landesmuseum. Rural Westphalia has been re-created on the banks of the Aasee, the city's big recreational lake, at the Mühlenhof museum – one of the longest established of Germany's open-air museums, with a fascinating collection of old buildings, water mills, windmills, timber-framed farmsteads, and more (*Open* daily).

The agriculturally rich and rather damp area around Münster – the **Münsterland▶** – is famous for its country houses, most of them moated. Ranging from the grandiose 'Westphalian Versailles' at Nordkirchen to the more homey Haus Rüschhaus just outside Münster, these delightful *Wasserburgen* (water castles) could hold your interest for days. Start at the 700-year-old Burg Vischering (near Lüddenhausen), which conveniently houses an informative Münsterland museum (*Closed* Mon). Rüschhaus was from 1826 to 1846 the home of the great poetess Annette von Droste-Hülshoff, who was born nearby at the lovely **Hülshoff water-castle▶**. Its Renaissance and neo-Gothic buildings are on two tiny islands, within a moat where swans glide.

Nahe Valley and the Hunsrück   78B2

The idyllic valley of the River Nahe runs northeastwards through a series of gorges to join the Rhine at **Bingen**. The picturesque vineyards along its course are among Germany's smallest wine-producing areas, but the Nahe white wine is highly prized among connoisseurs. It has a fresh yet full flavour that approaches the best of the Rhinegau wines. Farther north is the rugged Hunsrück, a high plateau of upland farms and extensive forests of beech and spruce. Quaint old houses stand on the bridge at **Bad Kreuznach**, a good starting point for a tour of the Nahe. This pleasant spa town comes complete with casino and strange timber structures known as 'salinas' in which brine is vaporised for the benefit of health seekers.

Bad Münster is another spa, located south of Bad Kreuznach on the B48. It is overlooked by the lofty castle called the Ebernburg. To the west of Bad Münster on the riverside road, and shouldering the river aside, is the mighty cliff known as the **Rotenfels**. Vines flourish in the narrow strip of soil at its base, as they do on the slopes around the villages that succeed one another upstream.

At **Odernheim** the valley of the River Glan leads to medieval **Meisenheim**, which has an array of picturesque old houses and a fine stone church. The road along the

Nahe valley can then be rejoined if you wish, near the abbey ruins at Disibodenberg.

Beyond the health resort of **Sobernheim**, the village of **Monzingen** has particularly fine half-timbered houses, among them the Altes Haus of 1589. Off the main valley to the north the castle ruin of **Dhaun** affords a splendid panoramic viewpoint, while **Kirn** is dominated by another ruin, the **Kyrburg**.

The steep rock face at the jewellery town of **Idar-Oberstein** is also crowned with fragments of old fortress, but the real curiosity here is the Gothic church set into the cliff itself and reached via 214 steep steps from the town's market square. Much is made of Idar-Oberstein's history of mining, cutting and polishing precious stones; after visiting the Heimatmuseum (local history museum), both open daily, the **Edelsteinmuseum▶** (Museum of Precious Stones) and the Steinkaulenberg mine (*Open* mid-Mar–mid-Nov daily. *Closed* mid-Nov–mid-Mar), you should know more about gemology than most!

A half-hour drive north from Idar-Oberstein will bring you onto the Hunsrück Höhenstrasse. This fine highway was built in the interwar period to relieve unemployment and help open up this inhospitable area, then one of Germany's poorest and most isolated regions. More prosperous today, the Hunsrück is still a lonely place, drawing city dwellers in search of rural peace and quiet.

The Nahe River flows along the southern side of the Hunsrück plateau. Here Edgar Reitz, born nearby, at Morbach, set and filmed his masterly 15-hour epic Heimat *(1984), the saga of a local family from 1919 until 1982*

95

From the Niederwald memorial high above the Rhine, a chairlift (top) descends to Rüdesheim, where the tourist-filled Drosselgasse (above) is lined with picturesque 18th-century taverns

▶▶▶ Rheintal (The Rhine Valley)   78C1

The Rhine invariably conjures up a string of clichés: a rocky gorge with a robber baron's castle clinging to each crag, vineyards growing precariously on the steep slopes, passengers waving at each other from the decks of white steamers, unbridled merriment in the cobbled streets of cheerful wine villages. Accurate enough, like all clichés, yet really only applicable to the Rhine Gorge, the relatively short Bingen–Koblenz stretch of the 1,320km river. A mountain torrent near its source in the Swiss Alps, and still pretty untamed at the great falls near Schaffhausen, the Rhine is for most of its length the watery equivalent of a many-laned highway, a traffic artery tying together the canal and river systems of most of Europe. Below Lake Constance the river forms most of the boundary between Germany and Switzerland, turning north at Basel to flow across the broad plain between the French Vosges Mountains and the Black Forest. Its erratic past, when it wandered freely over its floodplain, means that most cities are built on one bank only, or even a fair distance away, like Strasbourg and Karlsruhe. Fed from the east by its tributaries the Main and Neckar, the Rhine near Mainz is up to 800m wide, a dimension it attains again only well below its gorge. Downstream from Bonn the river matures, carrying the heavy traffic of the industrial Ruhr region across the flatlands linking northwest Germany and Holland to its ocean outlet at Rotterdam's Europoort.

Places of interest along the river (L = left bank, looking downstream; R = right bank) are described from south to north (i.e., downstream), from Wiesbaden to Bonn.

Between Wiesbaden and Mainz the vines of the **Rheingau** (R) extend to the very top of the high south-facing slopes. Sheltered from the north by the wooded Taunus hills, this is one of Germany's most renowned wine regions. It has its own scenic highway, the Rheingau-Riesling-Route, which hops up and down among the slopes taking in such pretty places as Kiedrich, with a Gothic church full of fine furnishings. Eberbach Abbey has a splendid collection of winepresses and prvided the setting for the film *The Name of the Rose*. Johannisberg Castle has a panoramic view.

TRAVEL OPTIONS

There are many ways of getting acquainted with the Rhine Valley's spectacular landscape. Even the hurried traveller should consider leaving the autobahn and driving along one of the riverside roads. There are railway lines along both banks of the river, offering two choices of landscape – and speed. Those in a hurry should opt for the western route, travelled by InterCity and EuroCity expresses connecting Köln, Bonn, Koblenz, Bingen and Mainz. The eastern route is served by the slower, regional trains which stop at all of the resorts on that side of the river. For the best views of the Lorelei rock take the western route. Drivers with time to spare can try the signposted scenic routes on either bank (Rheingoldstrasse on the left bank, Lorelei-Burgenstrasse on the right), which link minor roads together to give some of the best views down into the gorge. There's a high-level route for ramblers, too – the Rheinhöhenweg – while cyclists can ride along sections of the old towpath. Remember that there are no bridges between Koblenz and Bingen, though there are plenty of ferries (some for foot passengers only).

Perhaps the most relaxing and time-efficient mode of transportation is to go one way by boat (possibly downstream) and return by train (combined tickets available; see the helpful leaflet in English published by German Rhine Line).

The Rhineland

LORELEI ROCK

A particularly rugged section of the gorge leads to the high Lorelei rock, around which the river makes one of its more tortured twists. This legendary haunt of troglodytic dwarfs may be the place where the treasure of the Nibelungs lies buried, but it is known above all as the place from which a flaxen-haired temptress (the Lorelei herself) lured sailors to a watery grave with her seductive song (definitive version by the Romantic poet Heine). The danger to shipping is real enough: the river is forced by the rock to squeeze itself through a gap only a third of its normal width, and here it reaches its greatest depth of 20m.

98

The Rheingau's 'capital' is Rüdesheim; the tavern-lined Drosselgasse alleyway does its best to contain the high tide of tourists washing up from the landing stage. Genuine picturesqueness fights it out with the tackiness of takeaway joints and souvenir shops. High above the town stands the Niederwald memorial. Its massive figure of Germania celebrating the German unification after victory over the French in 1871 is in better shape than the crumbling remains of Ehrenfeld castle nearby.

At the railway town of **Bingen** (L) the Rhine narrows and turns north to enter the gorge. This turbulent section is known as the Binger Loch (Bingen Hole) and still presents some difficulties to navigation, though the reefs of hard quartzite that once gave rise to dangerous rapids have long since been blown up.

A succession of strongholds now follows (L): Rheinstein, Reichenstein, Sooneck. Tiny fiefdoms, good defensive sites and the chance of extorting tolls from traffic on the river help explain the building of so many castles. Many now stand in ruins, while most others were overzealously restored in the 19th-century rush to re-create a more than medieval Middle Ages, a mania that went to the lengths of embellishing railway tunnels with turrets and battlements.

Boppard, a large and very lively resort, especially at wine-festival time, has outdoor dancing in many of its Rhineside cafés

MOUSE TOWER

Standing guard in the stream at Bingen is the 13th-century Mouse Tower. Legend has it that this is where Bishop Hatto of Mainz was eaten alive by mice in just retribution for a variety of misdeeds (hoarding grain in time of famine, burning bands of beggars to death...).

Attractive, slate-roofed **Bacharach** (L) has its fortress, too, Burg Stahleck, now a youth hostel. Towers and ramparts still protect this attractive little town; its main enemy is now the railway trains roaring past on its embankment. It's touristy, to be sure, but there's lots to see along its cobbled streets and around the pretty marketplace.

Kaub (R) is overlooked by Gutenfels Castle, where the lords continued to exact tribute from passing traffic until well into the 19th century. Their instrument for doing so was the 14th-century Pfalz, the extraordinary white toll-castle standing shiplike amid the stream. **Oberwesel** (L) is dominated by verticals – the Ochsenturm near the waterfront, the red tower and slate steeple of the Liebfrauenkirche (Church of Our Lady), and the keeps and ramparts of Burg Schönburg high above.

St Goar (L) is overlooked by **Rheinfels▶**, a city-sized castle that French Revolutionaries did their best to demolish, without quite succeeding. Burg Katz (Cat Castle) above **St Goarshausen** (R) can't match Rheinfels for sheer size; it was built in the late 14th century by the count of Katzenelnbogen to outface his territorial rival, the bishop of Trier, whose fortress downstream the count disdainfully nicknamed Burg Maus (Mouse Tower; see panel page 98). Beyond are two more castles, Sterrenberg and Liebenstein (R), named 'the Warring Brothers' after a 14th-century family feud.

As befits its origins – it was founded by the Romans – **Boppard** (L) is the most substantial place along the gorge, with two fine churches, remains of Roman and medieval defenses, and a Heimatmuseum in the Archbishop's Castle (*Closed* Mon). The town turns an attractive face to the Rhine and its long promenade dates from the 19th century, when it first became popular as a place of retirement and refined tourism. Hotels abound, together with taverns dispensing the produce of the big Bopparder Hamm vineyard. Boppard is a good starting point for river trips and for excursions inland as well; a branch railway winds up through the woods to the rugged Hunsrück region (see page 95), or there is a chairlift up to the famous Vierseenblick viewpoint.

Old-fashioned **Rhens** (L) and **Braubach** (R) are both worth a visit. High above the latter is the imposing silhouette of **Marksburg▶**, the only medieval castle to have escaped ruin or wholesale restoration, and consequently able to give a truly authentic feel of life along the medieval Rhine. **Stolzenfels** (L), opposite Marksburg, is one of the more thoroughgoing efforts at making a ruined castle better than new.

The city of **Koblenz▶** has made the most of its position at the confluence of the Rhine and Mosel since Roman times. Four-fifths flattened in World War II, the town is still worth a stroll, starting perhaps at the Deutsches Eck, the promontory between the rivers. A massive masonry plinth bears a statue of Kaiser Wilhelm I, a controversial symbol of German nationhood. The original statue was blown up by American forces in the last days of World War II, but a replacement was erected on the site after

Burg Stahleck, a typical Rhine castle, stands above the quaint old wine town of Bacharach, its narrow streets lined with wine bars and craft shops in half-timbered houses

The Rhineland

100

REMAGEN BRIDGE

In early 1945, the Ludendorff railway bridge at Remagen was the only bridge to survive the German defenders' attempts to blow up all the Rhine crossings. Secured by a company of infantry from the American 9th Armored Division, the bridge resisted bombing, shelling, and attack by V2 rocket and frogmen for 10 days before dropping into the river. By this time it had enabled several Allied divisions to establish a bridgehead on the far bank of Germany's last natural barrier to invasion. It has not been rebuilt, though the abutment on the left bank houses a small Peace Museum.

DRACHENFELS

Legend has it that Siegfried, hero of the Ring saga (*Nibelungenlied*), killed a dragon that lived on the Drachenfelsrock, and bathed in its blood. This made him invincible, except for an area between his shoulders where a leaf had fallen while he bathed.

Koblenz, where the River Rhine and the River Mosel meet

German reunification. The riverside promenades enfold the old town, with its two fine twin-towered churches, Romanesque St Kastor and the Liebfrauenkirche. On the heights on the far side of the Rhine is the vast fortress of Ehrenbreitstein, an impressive setting for the August fireworks extravaganza 'The Rhine in Flames'.

Between Koblenz and Bonn the riverside scenery remains varied and interesting. Attractive towns include **Andernach** (L), Roman and medieval; and **Linz** (R), whose Schloss contains two unusual museums, one of musical instruments, the other of medieval tortures. **Sinzig** (L), has a perfect example of a Rhineland Romanesque church. High above **Remagen** (famous for its bridge – see panel) stands a virtual scale model of Cologne Cathedral, the pilgrimage church dedicated to St Apollinaris.

Downstream, the river divides to flow past Nonnenwörth (Nuns Island), overlooked by the ruins of **Rolandsbogen** (L) – supposedly built by the paladin Roland to give him an occasional glimpse of his fiancée, who became a nun on the (false) news of his death. It commands a fine panorama of the old volcanic hills on the far bank, collectively called the Siebengebirge (Seven Mountains). These myth-encrusted heights have long furnished the stuff of fairy tales and legends, the most potent story (see panel) being that of the dragon that met its end at the hands of Siegfried on the 'castled crag of **Drachenfels'**▶ (Byron) – today Europe's most popular summit, climbed by 3 million visitors every year (on foot or by rack railway).

Walkers can try to escape the crowds among the lovely woodlands of these miniature mountains with their 30-odd (not seven) peaks, many of them topped by castle ruins. At their base lie the riverside resorts of **Bad Honnef** and **Königswinter**, the latter with the **Konrad Adenauer Museum**▶ (*Closed* Mon). This is housed in the former residence of federal Germany's first and perhaps greatest chancellor, whose liking for his home ground seems to have influenced the choice of Bonn – just downstream – as the country's provisional capital.

Germany's 11 main wine-growing areas follow the valleys of the Rhine and its tributaries the Mosel, Main, Nahe and Neckar; the former GDR has some little-known vineyards around Naumburg and Dresden. The mild climate and 2,000 years' expertise (the Romans introduced the vine to these parts) mean that these vineyards – further north than any other major vineyard – yield some of the world's greatest (and most expensive) wines.

Most German wine is light, largely from the white-wine-producing Riesling, Müller-Thurgau, and Silvaner grapes, but about one-eighth of the total production is red, little known abroad but much appreciated at home. Wine production has created some spectacular landscapes. The need to capture as much sunshine as possible explains the remarkable terracing on the steep sides of the valleys, where even the most inaccessible south- or west-facing slope is cultivated. Wines are best tasted where they are made, but nowhere more so than in Germany.

New tastes German wines are traditionally sweet, but the recent hankering after a more 'sophisticated' taste has encouraged a range of *trocken* (dry) or *halb-trocken* (medium-dry) wines. Categorisation and labelling are strictly regulated, producing useful information about the area of origin and standard of a particular bottle. A *Deutscher Tafelwein* (German table wine) is a pleasant, unpretentious product from one of five main areas. A *Qualitätswein* (quality wine), of a higher standard, must be characteristic of both grape type and one of the 11 main regions. A *Qualitätswein mit Prädikat* (quality wine with distinctive features) has special attributes: the grapes must be fully mature and the wine have a certain percentage of alcohol without added sugar. All wines within this category (beginning with those designated *Kabinett*) come from one district. The very best wines are those made with ripe and overripe grapes, selected specially, either in the vineyard (*Spätlese, Auslese*) or in the vat room (*Beerenauslese, Trockenbeerenauslese*). Trockenberrenauslese is the summit of German wine culture, made from raisinlike grapes affected by the mould known as 'noble rot' and picked as autumn expires.

Even as the first winter frosts take hold in the vineyards the vintners are still busy, producing the country's great rarity: Eiswein. This is made from specially selected grapes left to mature still further on the vine and deliberately allowed to freeze. The wine from these frozen grapes is an aromatic delicacy, so rare and expensive that it's normally only obtainable in half-bottles.

Germany's sparkling wines, known as Sekt, are not in the champagne league, but many brands – produced by the champagne method – are of very high quality, and one producer takes great pride in supplying at least one (anonymous) royal house.

Below: Only a fraction of Germany's wines are produced by the red grape

101

SAUERLAND AND ROTHAARGEBIRGE

Little known abroad, these green hills make a wonderful playground for the cities of the Rhine and Ruhr. Consisting of forested ridges broken by sometimes gorgelike valleys, the area is an important water-gathering ground, with many reservoirs providing endless opportunities for watersports. Outdoor life isn't confined to one season: the chief resort, Winterberg, has probably the best winter-sports facilities north of the Alps.

The hills are attractive rather than spectacular, with more or less continuous forest cover. The most comprehensive view is from the bare summit of the Kahler Asten (841m) in the Rothaargebirge (Redhead Heights), the easternmost of the four nature parks making up the area. With abundant ores and minerals beneath the surface, wood for fuel and rushing streams for power, the valleys attracted metalworkers long before the Ruhr was industrialised. Some spots have the dismal air of a workplace past its prime, but elsewhere the long-standing industrial tradition has been used to advantage, with good examples of industrial archaeology. The building tradition is a distinctive one, with many fine old timber-framed and whitewashed houses under steep slate roofs making a harmonious picture against the invariably green background. There are sturdy upland villages around the Kahler Asten (Nordenau, Oberkirchen, Grafschaft...), and most of the towns have some features of interest, such as Altena, dominated by its massive castle.

▶ The Ruhr   78C5

Named after the river running along its southern boundary to join the Rhine near Duisburg, Germany's 'Kohlenpott', or Black Country, is still Europe's greatest industrial agglomeration, though coal and steel are no longer as important as they once were. Population, though still an impressive 5.5 million, has declined – spread over a combination of varied settlements ranging from such great cities as **Essen** and **Dortmund** to picturesque riverside places like **Kettwig** and **Herdecke**.

The Ruhr was never a continuously urbanised area, and sensible planning has ensured that the whole conurbation is now interspersed with green spaces threaded by footpaths and cycleways that connect city centres with splendid new parks (like Essen's Grugapark) and with the open countryside. Ruhr tourist authorities have mapped out four new routes for holidaymakers. One of them takes visitors back into the early industrial age, incorporating a series of preserved pitheads and technological curiosities.

It is still industry that characterises the scene, and most visitors are here for business rather than pleasure. Urban pleasures are plentiful, however. Each city proclaims its own identity and boasts an enviable array of cultural facilities. Galleries abound, foremost among them the **Museum Folk-wang▶** in Essen, with superb collections of 19th- and 20th-century painting (*Closed* Mon), and the Ruhrland Museum with its dour souvenirs of the life of 19th-century miners and steelworkers (*Closed* Mon). **Recklinghausen** has a rarity, a museum devoted almost entirely to icons (*Closed* Mon). **Bochum**'s modern Städtisches Schauspielhaus (City Theater) enjoys an international reputation for its classical and avant-garde productions. At Hagen is a remarkable open-air museum, the Westfälishes Freilichtmuseum, devoted not to rural life but to the early technology of the region (*Open* Mar–Nov Tue–Sun. *Closed* Dec–Feb).

Bochum's **Bergbaumuseum▶** (Mining Museum), with its excellent displays and underground galleries, is outstanding, and the city also has an Eisenbahnmuseum (Railway Museum) (*Open* Wed and Fri). Industrial history can be enjoyed in the open air, too – notably in the Muttental, near **Witten**, where the Bergbauhistorischer Rundwanderweg (Mining Heritage Trail) features horse-operated pithead gear and the chapel where the miners gathered to pray and be counted before descending.

With the digging of coal went the drinking of beer, and brews evolved to quench the miners' thirst taste just as good today, with a more distinctive character than their Bavarian counterparts. Some, like Dortmunder Union, travel the world, while others of no less quality remain a local secret (willingly shared with visitors!).

▶ Saarland   78A1

Like the Mosel, the Saar rises in the Vosges Mountains in France, joining the larger river just above **Trier**. It has given its name to Germany's second smallest *Land*. Long disputed between Germany and France, and still with a Gallic air about it, the **Saarland** and its capital, Saarbrücken, look to the future rather than back to their grimy past of rust-belt industries based on coal and steel. Thus, while Saarbrücken makes the most of its definitely limited architectural heritage (18th-century Schloss and Rathaus), it promotes itself as a business and cultural centre, and cultivates a 'green' image.

Industry extends downriver to **Saarlouis**, founded by Louis XIV as one of the fortresses consolidating his hold on France's eastern frontier and the town's market square still has the air of a parade ground.

Below **Merzig** the valley narrows and begins to run through a wild, spectacular defile. **Mettlach** is an important centre of the ceramics industry, and here Germany's leading commercial ceramics manufacturer, Villeroy-Boch, is based, with headquarters in an 18th century Benedictine abbey. The nearby Schloss Ziegelberg, formerly the palatial home of the Boch family, contains an interesting history of German ceramics, spanning more than two centuries (*Closed* Sun. *Admission charge*). The viewpoint at **Cloef** overlooks the great loop in the river – the Saarschleife. Downstream from **Serrig**, scrub and woodland give way to vines, and from here the valley takes on an attractive Mosel-like character: vineyards climb the steep slopes, yielding lively wines that are dispensed in the taverns of such villages as Ayl and Ockfen, Wavern and Wiltingen. Centre of this little wine region is 1,000-year-old **Saarburg**, with a castle and a stream dropping precipitously past houses and vineyards.

The countryside between the Saar and the Mosel was favoured by the Romans. Among the 50 or so villas that have been excavated, the one at **Nennig** has the largest mosaic floor north of the Alps, with scenes of the hunt and of the gladiators. Other Roman remains, with reconstructions of original buildings, can be seen in the **Römisches Freilichtmuseum Schwarzenacker**, an open-air museum near Homburg east of Saarbrücken. To the north, **Ottweiler** has a carefully conserved Altstadt and St Wendel, a three-towered church, while near **Nonnweiler** is the Hunnenring, the spectacular remains of a Celtic fortified settlement.

Modern industrial Saarbrücken, by the French border, has not only a Franco-German Park but a bilingual Franco-German Lycée/Gymnasium – a practical example of the new entente

THE RURAL RUHR
The Ruhr is not only industrial but idyllically rural too, at least on its southern side. Here disused mineheads and steelworks have been cleared away, to give the river valley back to nature. Close to Bochum's factories you'll find winding country lanes, glens where deer graze, and the romantic castle of Blankenstein. There are new pleasure-marinas, and old villages with quaint cobbled paths and streams.

Route north from steelmaking Siegen to medieval Soest

The old core of Siegen, with its Schloss, overlooks the River Sieg. Rubens was born here, and there are several of his paintings in the castle's Siegerland museum.

To the northwest Freudenberg's black-and-white houses step harmoniously up the hill. Beyond Olpe is the largest of the region's lakes, the Biggesee. The landscape varies from rocky (at Attendorn) to industrial

(around Rönkhausen) to grandiose (in the Lenne Mountains).

To the west of the Sorpe dam is the Luisenhütte, Germany's oldest blast furnace, dating from 1732. Arnsberg, an ancient centre of administration, rises in tiers over the River Ruhr. Like the Sorpe and Eder dams, the Möhne dam was attacked by Britain's Royal Air Force in 1943. After five attempts, the masonry wall of the dam, 34m thick at its base, was breached, flooding a vast area and disrupting water supplies to the armament industries of the Ruhr. Long since repaired, the dam holds back a 10km lake used by water-sports enthusiasts (north shore) and birds (south shore).

Soest is approached from the south across the Kassel–Ruhr Autobahn.

The Rhineland

BERTELSMANN
In decentralised Germany, many institutions are scattered in various cities. Thus the world's largest publishing firm, Bertelsmann, has its headquarters in modest Gütersloh – a true company town, swarming with editors and printers. The Bertelsmann world empire embraces other publishing giants such as Doubleday, Random House, Bantam Books, a Berlin daily newspaper, a leading magazine group, and a book club with 6.5 million members.

In Soest, many red-roofed and half-timbered houses line the streets within the ramparts

---

105

▶▶ Soest   78C5

In the Middle Ages Soest was the most important city in Westphalia, making good use of its position on the Hellweg (the ancient highway running right across northern Germany) to trade with Novgorod and Milan, Bruges and London. Having escaped the industrialisation that befell Dortmund, its old rival, Soest still wears an attractive medieval air.

Near the baroque Rathaus stands a sturdy pair of Romanesque churches, each with an impressive westwork, topped, in the case of the St Patrokli-Münster, by a formidable tower. The Petrikirche has frescos attributed to a local master of medieval times, Konrad von Soest, who also painted the altar in the nearby chapel dedicated to St Nicholas.

Reflected in the waters of the pretty little lake – the Grosser Teich – are the twin spires of the Gothic Wiesenkirche (Our Lady of the Meadows). The stained glass of the splendidly light interior includes a depiction of the Last Supper with typical Westphalian refreshments on the table – ham, beer, and pumpernickel, along with some Steinhäger, the local schnapps. On rising ground nearby is St Maria zur Höhe (Our Lady of the Heights), with original Romanesque paintings.

Soest's attractive ambience has drawn artists; works by two local men, Heinrich Aldegrever (a follower of Dürer) and Wilhelm Morgner (a contemporary of the Expressionist Emil Nolde), are shown in the modern Wilhelm-Morgner Haus (*Closed* Mon). The municipal museum is in the 16th-century Burghof, next to a town house dating back to the 12th century.

To the south, the river Möhne, a tributary of the Ruhr, has been broadened to form the Möhnesee, whose dam is famous: in 1943 a squadron of RAF Lancaster bombers of Britain's Royal Air Force – the 'Dambusters' – successfully bombed it, and 125 factories were wrecked by the the subsequent flooding.

►►► Trier

78A2

Trier, among the vineyards of the Mosel Valley, is probably the oldest city in Germany. Its heritage of buildings spanning two millennia makes it irresistible for visitors.

Start exploring Trier's compact centre at the massive **Porta Nigra►►**, the biggest and best-preserved Roman gateway in Europe, so named for the blackened appearance of the huge blocks of limestone from which it is made. In the Middle Ages it was converted into a church in honor of St Simeon; the nearby monastery bearing his name has a delightful courtyard with two-storey cloisters.

The traffic-free Simeonsstrasse leads to the Hauptmarkt, with its ornate Renaissance fountain. On the rise to the east is the huge **cathedral►**, begun by Constantine but predominantly Romanesque with a baroquified interior.

Part of Constantine's great imperial palace, the brick Konstantinsbasilika survives as a Protestant church; apart from the Pantheon in Rome, it is the biggest enclosed space to survive from the days of antiquity. Next door, in total contrast, is the lighthearted strawberry-and-vanilla façade of the rococo Prince-Bishop's Palace; its formal garden extends south to Trier's third great Roman monument, the **Kaiserthermen►** (Imperial Baths). The excavated remains of the baths can be visited Tue–Fri 9:30–5; weekends and public holidays 10:30–5 (*Admission charge*). Other Roman remains and artifacts are on show in the Landesmuseum. This is Germany's largest collection of Roman antiquities, with a 3rd-century stone relief of a Roman wine ship as its world-famous highlight.

Trier's further delights include a 20,000-seat Roman amphitheater, the piers of a bridge over the Mosel, the **Bischöfliches** (Episcopal) **Museum►** (*Open* Apr–Oct Mon 1–6, Tue–Sun 10–6; Nov–Mar Mon 3–6, Tue–Sun 10–1, 3–6. *Admission charge*), the medieval interior of St Matthias Church, St Paulin Church by Balthasar Neumann, and modern Karl Marx Haus.

ROMAN CITY
First established by the Celtic Treveri peoples, Trier was called Augusta Treverorum in 15 BC, becoming one of the most important Roman cities north of the Alps. With a population of 80,000 – close to today's total – it flourished as an imperial residence and capital of the western part of the empire. Emperor Constantine made it Germany's first bishopric. By the Middle Ages, Trier's prince-bishops were powerful rulers. But the city's most influential son was Karl Marx: the house where he was born in 1818 is now a fascinating museum of his life and work. (*Open* Mon–Sat 9–5, Sun 1–5. *Admission charge*.)

Modern Trier, once the Roman Empire's northern capital

At the foot of the Haardt Mountains, forming the eastern rim of the vast Palatinate Forest, lies a cheerful, sun-drenched countryside that produced fine wines for the Romans. Today the delightful wine towns and villages of the Rheinpfalz are linked by one of Germany's best-known touring routes, the Deutsche Weinstrasse, or Wine Road. Some 80km long, it links Bockenheim in the north to the border with Alsace in the south.

Pfalz wines are made from a variety of grapes; the whites span the whole quality range from everyday table wines to the most exquisite Trockenbeerenauslese. Reds account for only one-tenth of total production. No one should miss tasting the wines offered in traditional vintners' houses opening off cobbled village streets. Every place has something special to offer: charming half-timbered or mellow red sandstone houses; the remains of medieval fortifications; a ruined castle on a hill… The landscape gives continual pleasure, too, with ever-changing views of hills and broad plains. The benevolent climate means that not only vines but other southern plants thrive, such as fig, almond and chestnut trees, tobacco and maize. Kallstadt is proud of its local speciality, *Saumagen* literally 'sow's belly', but actually a delicately-spiced and delicious meatloaf-type speciality – former Chancellor Helmut Kohl always served it to his State guests.

Bad Dürkheim celebrates the vintage with Germany's biggest wine festival, the Wurstmarkt. Deidesheim has one of the best arrays of restaurants and inns, including the oldest tavern in the Palatinate. Medieval Neustadt, with its viticultural institute, is the region's miniature metropolis, while nearby Hambach Castle is where Germany's black-red-gold tricolour was raised by patriots for the first time in 1832. There are stunning panoramas from the Kalmit summit (673m), a short way into the hills, or from Bavarian King Ludwig I's summer residence, Schloss Ludwigshohe. The fantastic turrets and ramparts of another castle, Madenburg, loom over Eschbach. Beyond the resort of Bad Bergzabern, the route's terminus is marked by the huge Weintor gateway.

107

Weinstrasse vineyards

The Germans tend to keep the charms of Central Germany to themselves. Only a handful of towns, such as **Hameln** (Hamelin), with its Pied Piper fable and spectacular Weser Renaissance houses (see page 119), are on the international tourist circuit. Although it has none of the drama of the Alps, it can be rewarding making your own discoveries in the numerous attractive small towns and rolling, forested uplands. The State of **Hessen** (Hesse) is crossed by the River Main and **Frankfurt** is its chief city. Frankfurt was used by the Americans as an administrative centre after World War II and is very much the centre of Germany. It did, however, exist long before the Americans came along, although fragmented along geographic and religious lines. In 1866 Hesse was incorporated in the Kingdom of

Prussia, and five years later became part of the Greater German Reich. While Frankfurt, the banking capital of Germany and seat of the European Central Bank, remains the heart of the country's economic wealth, other towns, notably **Kassel** in north Hesse, generate wealth from industrial output. Not far away from the urban landscapes of the 20th century are reminders of slower-moving times in such old towns as **Marburg** and **Alsfeld**.

For lovers of the countryside, the **Vogelsberg**, a plateau created by a volcanic eruption approximately 30 million years ago, is a little-developed area of hills and forests. The unspoilt rural landscape embraces sleepy medieval towns studded with romantic castles and evokes the tales of the Brothers Grimm, who lived and worked in the region. The region stretches from **Göttingen** up into the **Weserbergland**, whose green hills (which rise to 500m) flank the Weser, one of the loveliest rivers in Germany. Attractive little towns with entire streets of half-timbered buildings flank this sinuous river and have given rise to their own recognised class of architecture: Weser Renaissance. Today it's literally fairy-tale country, traversed by one of Germany's most enchanting holiday routes, the Deutsche Märchenstrasse (German Fairy Tale Road). The path into the traditional fairy-tale past begins in Hanau, an unlovely town famous in this context only because it is the birthplace of the Grimm Brothers. The route winds lazily on, through the little hilltop town of Steinau an der Strasse, where the two Grimms grew up, crossing half the length of Germany before ending at the coast, at Bremerhaven. The **Harz Mountains,** which comprise the highest ground in the region, once were divided by the East–West German border. Now they offer opportunities for discovering the lesser-known Germany.

Alsfeld's town square, with the Rathaus in the background

Central Germany

This door is typical of the ornate architecture of Alsfeld, a key centre of folk tradition

JUGENDSTIL
Darmstadt was a centre of the Jugendstil – German art nouveau. The style began as quite floral and naturalistic, but after the 1900s it took on an increasingly abstract form. The architect Peter Behrens, who built a house for himself in the Mathilden-höhe, was an enthusiastic exponent of the late Jugendstil.

▶▶ **Alsfeld** *108B2*

Set amid the rolling, wooded Vögelsberg hills on the pretty Schwalm river, Alsfeld is a picturesque old town with some fine half-timbered Renaissance buildings. The folk traditions here inspired the Grimm brothers and at summer festivals the girls still wear the local red folk costumes. Outside the Walpurgiskirche is a fountain with a figure of a goose girl in the style of costume worn by Little Red Riding Hood.

In the Marktplatz the tiny, quaint 1516 *Rathaus* (town hall) stands above arcades where markets were once held. Opposite is the Renaissance-style Hochzeithaus, built for weddings, as its name implies. Fine examples of baroque architecture can be seen in the Rittergasse, notably the Neurath Haus at number 3 and the Minnigerode Haus at number 5. In Hersfelderstrasse, numbers 10 and 12 are among Germany's oldest half-timbered buildings.

Bielefeld *108A4*

This big industrial town has manufactured linen since the 16th century. Today it is also a centre for engineering, electronics, and food-processing. It has an interesting art gallery, the Kunsthalle (*Closed* Mon), which has some German Expressionist works (Beckmann, etc.), and sculptures by Rodin, Moore, and others.

Herford, an old Hanseatic town nearby, has a late Romanesque Münster and a number of Gothic churches; of these, the Johanniskirche has notable 17th-century woodwork and stained-glass windows.

▶ **Darmstadt** *108A1*

This otherwise dullish industrial town is best known as the heartland of the Jugendstil (art nouveau) movement of the early 1900s. An artists' colony was established on the low hill of Mathildenhöhe, and their **Jugendstil buildings**▶ still stand there (see panel): the Ernst-Ludwig-Haus with its Adam and Eve figures on the portal, the Behrens Haus, and the Hochzeitturm (wedding tower), designed for the wedding of Grand Duke Ernst Ludwig in 1905. The spectacular Russian Orthodox chapel with its gilded domes dates from the 1890s. A collection of Jugendstil artifacts is displayed in the Landesmuseum near the reconstructed 18th-century Schloss. The rococo Prinz Georg Palais holds a notable collection of porcelain given by members of various European royal families.

▶ **Detmold** *108A4*

Until 1918 this town was capital of the principality of Lippe, and it still has a strong sense of its own identity. Its noble 16th-century castle has Brussels tapestries and souvenirs of the family of Prince Bernhard of the Netherlands, whose seat was here. There are British Army barracks in the town, nicknamed 'Little London'.

To the south is the Teutoburger Wald, a long, narrow range of wooded hills with two interesting sights on its crest. One is the Hermannsdenkmal, an 26m green-copper statue of Arminius, the local chieftain who in about AD 9 rallied the Germanic tribes to oppose Rome's rule and defeated its legions near this spot. Erected under Bismarck, the memorial became a focus for German nationalism since the Nazis sometimes held rallies here.

PERSUASIVE MAYOR
During World War II
Einbeck would have been
levelled to the ground had
it not been for the persuasive skills of one Heinrich
Keim, who talked a Nazi
officer out of destroying
this medieval gem. Keim
later became Bürger-
meister of the town.

*Duderstadt, a small
town right beside the
former GDR border, has
over 500 half-timbered
buildings. This one is the
town hall*

111

The **Externsteine▶** nearby is a cluster of high rocks
in strange, toothy shapes, which were once used as a place
of worship by pagan tribes, and later by Christians.
Carved on one rock is a 12th-century bas-relief depicting
the Descent from the Cross. Also hewn from the rock are
a tomb and a pulpit. The summer solstice used to be celebrated here, as the sun rose between the rocks.

If you want to take a closer view, you can climb up the
new stairways carved into the rock. On the plain below
there is a large ornithological park, as well as the
Westfälisches Freilichtsmuseum, an open-air museum
that has a display of nearly 100 reassembled farm
buildings from the region.

▶ Duderstadt   108C3

Only 21km east of the university town of Göttingen,
Duderstadt has a successful blend of Renaissance and
Gothic architecture, which can be seen both on
Hinterstrasse and in the Rathaus. The Westertorturm
(gate tower) is notable for its twisted narrow roof.

The town contains two worthwhile churches: the Gothic
St Cyriakuskirche, decorated in ostentatious baroque
style, and St Servatiuskirche, refurbished in the art nouveau manner after a fire in 1915.

▶ Einbeck   108B4

A small town with a population of 29,000, Einbeck was
known in the Middle Ages for its beer. There were no
fewer than 700 breweries at that time, but only one of
them survives, producing a well-known strong beer, the
Einbecker Bockbier. The brewery gives guided tours
Monday to Friday.

Around the cobbled Marktplatz and in the Tidexer-
strasse are half-timbered Gothic and Renaissance houses.
The oldest choir stall in Germany (1288) is in the
Stiftskirche St Alexandri.

Central Germany

A PROUD HISTORY

Barbarossa and other early German kings were elected in Frankfurt, and from 1562 to 1806 the Holy Roman Emperors were crowned here. Goethe, born in the city, called it 'Germany's secret capital' (perhaps it still is?), and the first pan-German parliament met here in 1848–9. The city began to mint its own money in the 16th century; then in the 19th century local financiers, such as Rothschild, made it into a key world centre of banking. After 1945 it was proposed as the new federal capital, but Adenauer insisted on Bonn – a pity, very many people think. Today, together with Hannover, it is Germany's major trade-fair venue, and it has the country's leading international airport. Industry includes machine tools and chemicals.

Excursion boats pass
Frankfurt cathedral

▶▶ Frankfurt-am-Main   108A1

Urban American visitors smile indulgently at the name Germans sometimes give to Frankfurt-am-Main – 'Mainhattan', a word-play incorporating the name of the river on which it stands and the cluster of skyscrapers that form its downtown skyline, unique in Germany. Compared to Manhattan itself Frankfurt is small town stuff. Yet by German standards its assembly of tall office buildings is impressive – The 'Wolkenkratzer' (literally 'cloud-scrapers') include mainland Europe's largest office building, the 299m Commerzbank tower, designed by Britain's Sir Norman Foster, and the new European Central Bank headquarters. Frankfurt is also the home of the still-powerful German Central Bank, the Bundesbank, and has branches of nearly 400 world banks. The German Stock Exchange is also based here. Despite its position as the German – and now European – financial capital, Frankfurt is by no means just a money-spinning metropolis. Visitors arriving at its huge international airport are well advised to spend a day or two getting to know Frankfurt's other face.

There's a great deal for the tourist to see, including some of Germany's best museums. Because the city is rich, it has the money to spend on culture, such as high-class opera, and at its annual Book Fair – the world's largest – literature and commerce join hands. Many other international trade fairs are also held in Frankfurt.

Frankfurt has a metropolitan, outward-looking ambience, largely due to all the high-profile international activity. It is also a city of tensions, with relatively high levels of crime and drug abuse and a large immigrant population, nearly 30 percent of the total. Politically, it

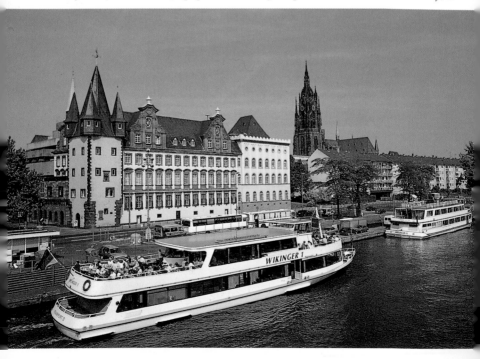

has a history of left-wing activism, possibly because of its visible symbols of capitalism. By 1999, however, the right-wing Christian Democrats had become the major party in the city council, forming a 'Platform' (an informal coalition) with the Social Democrats. A Christian Democrat Lady Mayoress ruled the city.

One local hotbed of Leftism has been the famous university (45,000 students), where radical philosophers such as Habermas and Adorno once propounded new ideas. This city of money is also a lively centre of the alternative avant-garde, with many fringe theatres and a big jazz scene. The controversial film director Rainer Werner Fassbinder once worked here.

The opera house (left), built in the 1880s, is now used for conventions, while operas are staged in the city theatre. The high Gothic cathedral (below) is a local landmark, even if dwarfed by some of the skyscrapers

The main sights are central, and many can be toured on foot. Near the Messegelände (exhibition centre) and the central station is the financial district, where the 24-storey Deutsche Bank building is the most graceful of the city's skyscrapers (the Bundesbank itself is out in the suburbs). Much of this central area was gracelessly rebuilt after wartime bombing, but some older buildings have been well restored, notably the big neo-classical opera house (though operas are now staged elsewhere). The 15th-century Eschenheimer Turm is one of the 42 towers that used to encircle the city. The Börse (stock exchange) is nearby and the 18th-century *Hauptwache* (guard room). The Goethehaus, an adjacent museum opened in 1997, is the family home where the poet was brought up. It has been well restored (*Open* daily; Sun am only).

Frankfurt before the bombing had the biggest medieval Altstadt in Germany. Little now survives save for a carefully restored sector around the cathedral and the Römerberg, a cobbled square lined with fine half-timbered houses. The **Römer▶**, a group of 15th-century houses that once formed the Rathaus, has a Renaissance stairway leading to the stately Kaisersaal. Across the square is the tiny Gothic Nikolaikirche and the History Museum. Just to the east is a fascinating zone where new modernistic buildings have purposely been put up next to ancient ones. The new glass-walled Kultur-Schirn, an arts centre, overlooks the ruins of a Carolingian palace and a Roman bath (around AD 100) beside **St Bartholomew's**

Once the setting for royal ceremonies: Frankfurt's cobbled square, Römerberg

GOETHE THE GREAT
Born in Frankfurt-am-Main in 1749, Goethe is undoubtedly Germany's greatest literary figure – and a lifelong lover of women. The young Johann reluctantly studied law in Leipzig, where he met his first love, Kätchen Schönkopf. He continued his law studies in Strasbourg, where he had another love affair and met the German writer and thinker Herder. With Herder's help, Goethe became part of the Sturm und Drang (Storm and Stress) movement. In 1771 he returned to Frankfurt and became a newspaper critic.

Cathedral►, with its lofty Gothic tower (there is a commanding view from the top). The emperors were crowned in this austere reddish church, which has medieval murals and choir stalls. In the adjacent Wahlkapelle the Holy Roman Empire's seven electors chose their king, and the cathedral's little museum displays the adornments they wore (*Closed* Mon). The nearby 15th-century St Leonard's Church has impressive stained glass.

Frankfurt prides itself on its impressive collection of museums, most of them grouped together in conveniently accessible form along the Main river. Berlin has its 'museum island' – Frankfurt its 'museum river bank', a riverside complex of no less than seven museums. From west to east they are: (1) the Liebieg museum of sculpture, ranging from ancient Egypt to the baroque; (2) the important **Städel Museum of art►**, with a collection of works by Holbein, Cranach, Tintoretto, Rembrandt, Renoir, Monet, and a rich array of German painting, including Tischbein's portrait of Goethe sitting pensively near Rome, and works by Liebermann, Thoma, Beckmann, Kirchner, and Nolde; (3) the Postal Museum, with details of stamps, mail coaches, and telephones; (4) the Deutsches-Architectur-Museum, offering a tour of world architecture in a house constructed within a house; (5) the Film Museum, mostly technical and scientific; (6) the Museum of Ethnography, with objects from native tribes; (7) the Museum of Applied Art, with a collection of glass, porcelain, Jugendstil furniture, a good Asian and Islamic section, and more, all in a lovely new building.

On the other river bank is Germany's most interesting museum of Jewish history, the Jüdisches Museum (Jewish Museum), housed in the former Rothschild palace (*Closed* Mon). The museum is divided into two sections: one illustrating the Jewish contribution to Frankfurt's cultural life, the other documenting the history of Frankfurt's Jewish community, from the Middle Ages to the present day.

Frankfurt's reputation as a cultural and financial metropolis leaves first-time visitors unprepared for the bohemian charm of its Sachsenhausen quarter, south of the river. It's Frankfurt's 'Chelsea' or 'Greenwich Village' – a leafy, residential district, with some old city mansions and cider taverns unique to Germany. They serve up cider (Apfelwein or 'Appelwoi') comparable to the best of France or Britain (see panel).

If zoos are your thing, Frankfurt has one of Germany's best, with a spectacular aquarium of rare fish and a special section on nocturnal creatures. Dead or extinct animals, such as dinosaurs, can be studied in the Senckenberg natural history museum, which is near the university and the large Grüneburg Park, containing botanical and tropical gardens.

Two towns near Frankfurt are well worth a visit. **Offenbach**, Germany's chief leather-making centre, has a big museum devoted to the subject (*Open* daily). **Höchst**, home of the giant Hoechst chemicals firm, has a charming undamaged Altstadt and several fine old buildings. One is the Justiniuskirche of Carolingian origin; another is the baroque Bolongaro palace, former home of Italian snuff makers. Hochst was a famous porcelain-producing centre in the 18th century; this industry is now being revived.

POWERFUL CIDER
Frankfurters cross the river to let their hair down in the cider houses of Sachsenhausen. *Apfelwein* is the local speciality, but if you're not used to this cider the first quaff could take your breath away – it's dry, almost vinegary, and very strong.

SCHLOSS FASANERIE
If you haven't yet had your fill of baroque, visit Schloss Fasanerie (guided tours Apr–Oct, closed Mon), built for the 18th-century prince-bishops of Fulda. Its sumptuous décor and size are almost over-powering, but the park offers a relaxing respite. (You get there on the bus 3 or 4 from Fulda.) Near the town is the Kirche auf dem Petersberg (Petersberg Church), built on a 400m-high rock and visible from afar.

The tall 14th-century Adolpsturm overlooks the old streets of the 'dual' town of Friedberg

► **Friedberg**   *108A1*

Few Jewish bathhouses remain in Germany but Friedberg has one of them. The Judenbad here is a particularly fine example of this type of ritual bathing place. Built in the 13th century, it descends 25m below ground level – reached by 74 steps. The Burg (Imperial Town) was built by the emperor Frederick Barbarossa in 1180 and today remains a district community, as in medieval times. The separation of church and state is apparent, with the other main part of town being focussed on the Stadtkirche, dating from the 13th and 14th centuries.

►► **Fulda**   *108B2*

Ever since the 8th century, Fulda has been one of the most important centres for Catholic religious instruction in Germany. It all began when a Benedictine abbey was founded here by St Boniface, an English missionary to the pagan Germanic tribes. The abbey became a famous centre for culture and learning throughout the whole Christian world.

Today the town contains a variety of architectural styles. Above all there is a wealth of baroque, a style that extends to the huge palace (now a museum, *Closed* Mon) and even the former police station. The main *Dom* (cathedral) was rebuilt by Johann Dientzenhofer (one of a noted family of architects) at the beginning of the 18th century, having been inspired by Italian baroque architecture – in fact, he worked from a model copy of St Peter's in Rome. The Michaelskirche is one of the oldest churches in Germany, with a crypt dating from 822.

The Hanauisches Amtshaus at **Steinau**, about 24km southwest of Fulda, was the boyhood home of the Brothers Grimm and today a puppet theatre re-enacts their fairy tales. The much-fortified Schloss contains a museum that is devoted to the Grimm brothers (*Closed* Mon, Fri and Jan).

► **Gelnhausen**   *108B1*

This town of Gelnhausen is said to have been founded by Emperor Frederick Barbarossa in 1170 (it is sometimes called Barbarossa Stadt). It stands on a slope of the Kinzig Valley (close to the Naturpark Hessischer Spessart, which is good walking country with its forested hills). The town was built as a military foundation and is still partly sur-rounded by fortifications.

The Marienkirche (St Mary's) is a multitowered Romanesque church that looks over Gelnhausen from above. The chancel is the best feature of the interior, with its high altar and a shrine depicting the Madonna with four saints. The unusual choir stalls are ornately deco-rated, and there are two well-preserved tapestries. Barbarossa's castle, the Kaiserpfalz, stands on an island in the River Kinzig, but now only ruins remain of the former stronghold (*Open* daily except Mon).

Büdingen, about 10km north of Gelnhausen, possesses an intact town wall that dates from the 15th and 16th centuries and is distinguished by squat towers and pierced by elaborate Gothic gateways. You can take guided tours of the Schloss (Mar–Oct Tue to Sun, 11.30–4) over a still-inhabited 12th- to 17th-century building ranged around a courtyard.

Many of the older houses in Goslar are half-timbered, like these lining a stream in the heart of town

▶▶ Goslar   108C4

One of the loveliest towns in north Germany, Goslar is also a winter-sports resort that is very popular with Berliners. It was a seat of the Salian emperors in the 11th century, then a Free Imperial City. In the Middle Ages it became a centre of silver and lead mining. Merchants began to pour in, lead and silver were increasingly mined and refined, and this led to a building boom around the 16th century, the peak of Goslar's prosperity. This explains its legacy of fine buildings from different epochs – Gothic, Renaissance, baroque. Many are half-timbered or of stone, rather than the usual north German red brick. The mines, in the hills south of the town, ultimately went bankrupt and the last one closed in 1992. By the 19th century, Goslar was prospering again under Prussian domination.

The Altstadt is full of interest for the visitor. The traffic-free, cobbled Marktplatz, surrounded by dignified stone and half-timbered houses with elaborate slate roofs, has a quaint chiming clock (modern) on the treasurer's building, which performs four times a day – at 9 am, noon, 3pm and 6pm – with scenes outlining the mining history of the town dating back to the Middle Ages.

In the old arcaded Rathaus, a fine Gothic building, the **Huldigungsaal▶▶** is covered from floor to ceiling with splendid coloured frescoes from around 1500; it also holds the Goslar Gospel (1230). Across the square, the 15th-century Kaiserworth, once a guildhouse, is now a hotel: on the lefthand-side corner gable is a impudent statue of a boy ejecting a coin from his backside (symbolic of Goslar's former right to mint coins). The square also has a fountain with two large bronze basins surmounted by an imperial eagle. Many of the houses in the streets off the square are half-timbered (*Fachwerkhäuser*).

The Siemenshaus (Schreiberstrasse 12, daily guided tours by arrangement) was built in 1693 by Hans Siemens, an ancestor of the Berlin industrialist who created the Siemens empire. The Goslarer Museum (Königstrasse 1) contains a detailed outline of the artistic and cultural history of the Harz region, as well as models of the town. The Mönchehaus (Mönchestrasse 3) contains a modest collection of modern art. The terrace by the Bismark statue near the station offers a good view of the town and its encircling hills.

117

FRANKFURT FUROR
The ongoing Left/Right feud in Frankfurt came to a head in 1981, when work began on a new runway for the airport, Germany's largest. Greens, anarchists and others staged sit-ins, to protest that farms and forests would be damaged and the runway would benefit only the US Air Force. There were violent clashes with the police, some of whom overreacted brutally. Local opinion was polarised and everyone took sides. Finally the runway *was* completed – the environmentalists had lost.

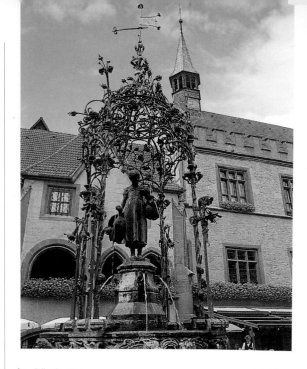

FRIEDLAND CAMP
At Friedland, near the former GDR border south of Göttingen, there used to be a large transit camp for political refugees arriving not from the GDR but from other east European countries. Here they stayed while their papers were processed, before moving on to a new life in some West German town.

The Gänselieselbrunnen at Göttingen (top right) and (below) the door of the city's 16th-century pharmacy

▶ **Göttingen**   *108B3*

Göttingen is first and foremost a university town. The university, named after its founder, the elector of Hannover, who was also George II, king of Great Britain and Ireland, has given the town a hallowed reputation as a leading place of learning. The university has produced several Nobel Prize winners, and is the headquarters of the Max Planck-Institut, which groups some 50 high-level scientific research bodies all over Germany. Max Planck, creator of the quantum theory in physics, spent his final years in the town and is buried here.

The 30,000 university students and 2,500 teachers and professors bring added life and colour to the town, which prides itself on its Gothic churches and neo-classical buildings, such as the Aula, or Great Hall, scattered about the campus. The students have made the town hall area and its Ratskeller the hub of activity. Even during vacations you will find throngs of young people milling about. Nightlife is always interesting. A famous music festival devoted to Handel is held in June. There is a tradition for students to visit the *Gänselieselbrunnen* ('Goose Lizzie's fountain') in the centre of town in front of the Rathaus, once they've completed their examinations, and to kiss the bronze statue of a graceful young girl.

The Vierkirchenblick (viewpoint of four churches) is a particularly memorable sight. Stand at the southeast corner of the Markt and you will see, to the east, the 15th-century St Albanus; to the south, St Michael; to the west, the two octagonal towers of the Johanniskirche; and to the north, St Jakobi, the tallest, which stands at 72m. There are half-timbered houses in the old quarter of the town – one dating from 1563, northeast of the Markt, houses the old pharmacy and is also elaborately and attractively decorated.

►► Hameln (Hamelin) 108B4

There is more to Hameln than just the legend of a man in a strange costume and a plague of rats. There are many attractive half-timbered buildings left, despite severe damage done during the 1618–48 Thirty Years' War (World War II fortunately had less impact).

The town is a treasure house of immaculately restored buildings in the so-called Weser Renaissance style of the 16th and 17th centuries. Typically this makes use of scroll decorations and pinnacles on gables, carved-stone banding and large bay windows. The **Rattenfängerhaus►** (Rat Catcher's House), at Osterstrasse 28, dates back to 1603 and is a good example. Its carved stonework is embellished with busts and heads, and there is an inscription about the Pied Piper on the side – the house was actually built for a councillor.

The Hochzeitshaus (Wedding House), at Osterstrasse 2, was built between 1610 and 1617 and was used for burghers' weddings. You will easily recognise it, since today it is the town hall and library. On the side facing the Marktplatz, the Pied Piper clock features mechanical figures, which appear three times a day – at 1:05, 3.35 and 5.35 pm precisely.

A stroll through the streets will reveal other beautiful old buildings. Two in Osterstrasse house the Museum Hameln (*Open* Tue–Sun), with a collection of religious art, local history, and Pied Piper lore.

Excursion

Hämelschenburg, about 16km south of Hameln, is a magnificent example of the Weser Renaissance style. The castle (guided tours Apr–Oct; *Closed* Mon) was built between 1588 and 1618 in a horseshoe shape.

North of Hameln is **Fischbeck** (8km), where there is a convent dating from the 10th century. The church is 12th-century and has a fine Romanesque crypt.

119

'Rat pastries'

Local children play the part of rats, lured away by the Piper's music

THE BROTHERS GRIMM

Northern Hessen, around Kassel, is the heartland of the folk tales collected by Jacob and Wilhelm Grimm. Born near Frankfurt, they spent their early careers (1805–30) as court librarians at Kassel, where they concieved a passion for folklore and spent many years collecting their material orally from country people. Jacob was the scholar, Wilhelm the poet who put the tales into readable form. After their death, other writers tried to make the tales less frightening to children.

HARZ WITCHES

The Harz is famed for its witch legends. The eve of 1 May is believed to be the Walpurgisnacht, the night of the witches' sabbath on the Brocken (1,142m), the highest mountain in the region; this occasion is an episode in Goethe's famous play, *Faust*.

There is a strange mixture of the comic and the tragic in German folklore – the piper of Hameln who charmed the rats away, then, because he was not properly paid, took the children with him, too and Tannhäuser, the knight who abandoned his vows and went into a strange mountain to spend the rest of his days in the company of Venus. The most celebrated mountain in Germany is the Kyffhauser, east of Göttingen, where the emperor Frederick Barbarossa slumbers in a hidden cavern, radiant with gold and jewels. His great red beard has grown almost three times around the stone table at which he sits. A shepherd once strayed into the cavern and spoke to the emperor, who told him that he must remain there until the ravens cease to fly around the peak outside.

Traditionally, the 16th-century Dr. Johann Faust, a mountebank who travelled throughout Germany but who is particularly associated with the city of Erfurt, sold his soul to the devil in return for knowledge of science and alchemy, and died with his neck being wrung by an archdemon. The devil was, however, outwitted at Cologne, for the great cathedral was built there supposedly according to a plan drafted by him as a lure to gain the soul of the architect. The clever architect came to a rendezvous carrying a crucifix, which kept the devil at bay while he snatched the document.

In many parts of the country there are traditions of the *Wilde Jagd* (wild hunt), a ghostly cavalry crashing through the forests to the accompaniment of trumpets and shouts. This is a survival of the cult of the great Teutonic deity Odin.

The transfer from paganism to Christianity, too, is represented in various legends, such as that of the Drachenfels, a mountain near Bonn, where it is said that a wicked fire-breathing dragon tried to seize a beautiful Christian maiden but was hurled by the girl's prayers into the river below.

The Rhine is the most venerable of European rivers. According to legend, a treasure trove lies hidden in it and the secret was known only to the last two Nibelung heroes, who refused to divulge it despite torture and death. When the sun shines on the Rhine, the reflection of this treasure can be seen, but none of it can be found. Old lore also tells of Charlemagne, who was especially

Figures from German
folklore: Red Riding
Hood (opposite page);
the Valiant Tailor and
Giant (left); and the
Goose Girl (above)

partial to a castle that he had at Ingelheim. When he
noticed that the snow melted quickly on the hills of
Rüdesheim, west of Mainz, he established fine vineyards
there, and now his spirit can be seen on spring nights,
blessing the vines. A predilection for wine was also
shown by the 14th-century emperor Wenzel, who once
feasted in a beautiful meadow at Rhens, south of
Koblenz, and was so impressed with a cask of fiery wine
from Bacharach that he sold his realm for it.

At Bingen, in the 10th century, lived Hatto, a bishop
who was so rapacious that in time of famine he refused
food to the starving multitude. By divine punishment his
palace was infested with mice. To escape the pests, he
retired to a tower in the Rhine, but he was pursued there
by the mice and devoured by them. More fortunate was a
prisoner in Frankfurt long ago, who was offered his freedom if he could hit a weathercock on a wall tower with
nine consecutive shots from his musket. He succeeded,
leaving holes in the weathercock in the perfect shape of
the figure 9.

At Darmstadt, a story is told of a poor and inept knight
stopping to pray at a roadside statue of the Virgin Mary.
He fell into a faint, and while he remained there, the
Virgin took on his appearance and won the laurels at a
great tournament.

A fine deed was performed by the women of Weisberg,
north of Stuttgart, whose town was besieged during the
civil wars of the 12th century. They begged to be allowed
to depart in safety with whatever they could carry with
them. This request was granted, and they walked unmol-
ested through the enemy lines, each lady carrying her
husband on her back!

BROCKEN SORCERY
Goethe in Faust describes
the sorcery associated
with the Brocken in folk-
lore: 'And when we sail
around the top, first skim
the ground, then fill it up,
that all the Brocken height
may be smothered in
swarms of witchery.'

HARZ

Langelsheim · Vienenburg · Osterwieck · Badersleben · Groningen
GOSLAR · A395 · Heudeber · Wegeleben
Seesen · Oker · Bad Harzburg · Halberstadt
Lautenthal · Ilsenburg · Derenburg · Harsleben
Bockswiese · Hahnenklee · Wildemann · Wernigerode
Torfhaus · Brocken 1142m
Bad Grund
Clausthal-Zellerfeld · Altenau · Oderteich · Elbingerode · Blankenburg · Quedlinburg
Riefenbeek · Schierke · Thale
Osterode · Rappbode-Stausee · Bad Suderode · Gernrode
Sankt Andreasberg · Ellend · Braunlage · Ballenstedt
Sieber · Tanne · Hasselfelde · Friedrichsbrunn · Selke
Herzberg · Hohegeiss · Benneckenstein · Stiege · Harzgerode
Oder · Zorge · Güntersberge
Rhume · Gieboldehausen · Bad Lauterberg · 600m · Unterharz · Wipper
Bad Sachsa · Walkenried · Stolberg · Wippra
Ellrich · Morungen
Duderstadt · Helme · Rottleberode
Nordhausen · Sangerhausen

The neat spa town of Bad Harzburg

►► Harz   108C3

Straddling the old East–West German border, the Harz Mountains, the highest land in northern and central Germany, are a rewarding area for exploration. Summits rise to over 1,000m and although the 'Little Switzerland' nickname may be an exaggeration, it contrasts strikingly with the surrounding plains.

On the west side, hotels are efficiently run, restaurants and cafés plentiful, buildings well restored and neat pine forests crossed by well-signposted paths and skiing routes. In the east, everything is catching up fast, and now there is virtually little difference between the two.

The Harz region comprises two distinct areas – the **Oberharz** (Upper Harz) in the west, containing vast areas of delightful forests and valleys suitable for long refreshing walks, and the **Unterharz** (Lower Harz) in the east, which has more open land scattered with beech forests. The Brocken was situated just east of the boundary between the former German Democratic Republic and the Federal Republic. It is still possible to spot the old border posts but difficult to discern where the border once was.

Because it is relatively easy to get to the Harz from several German cities, it has become a popular tourist destination, in both summer and winter. An unpredictable climate, often damp and cold, does not deter the visitors who come for the walking, skiing, and spas. They follow in the footsteps of 19th-century Romantics, who saw the Harz Mountains as the epitome of poetic, landscape.

Since reunification, you can visit this area without constraint. **Wernigerode▶**, a well-preserved 14th-century town with its very beautiful Rathaus and other half-timbered houses with ornate façades, is packed every weekend, even when the weather is not good. An enormous amount of careful renovation has been achieved in a short time, and more will follow. **Stolberg** also has some superb streets of half-timbered houses. **Quedlinburg▶** with its UNESCO World Heritage status has a superb collection of timber-framed buildings. The spa and health resort of Bad **Harzburg**, a short drive from Goslar, is a good base from which to explore the Harz region.

The highest point of the Harz, the **Brocken▶** (1,142m), was in the old forbidden zone close to the border, but now it can be visited again, either on foot or by Brockenbahn to the scene that features in Goethe's *Faust*. You can go up by cable-car to the Hexentanzplatz in the lovely **Bode** Valley south of Thale, or visit the giant caves at **Rübeland** with their stalagmites and stalactites, which are also worth exploring.

The Romerkalle waterfall, in the Harz, lies close to the high rocky cliffs of the Bode gorge

123

Goslar to Hahnenklee (11km)

Hahnenklee is one of the leading Harz ski resorts.

Start at the parking lot at the Forsthaus Königsberg, on the western edge of Goslar. Follow the blue circle marked route, passing the Glockenberg on the right and then the Hohekehl on the left. Follow the Alte Harzstrasse to the Auerhahn. Scale the final 300m to the Bocksberg (726m) or follow the path to Hahnenklee, from where a bus will take you back to Goslar.

Bad Harzburg to the Brocken to Hahnenklee (about 16km)

The Brocken (1,142m) is the highest point of the Harz region – not quite alpine standard, but still a demanding hike. Make sure that you are wearing good walking shoes or boots, and take a change of clothing, a

snack, and a drink in a knapsack. Set out from the tourist information office at the Haus der Natur on the southern edge of Bad Harzburg (where you can pick up a hikers' map). A few hundred metres on the left (opposite a car parking lot) head off on the upwards trail marked by a blue cross, following it to the Ecker-stausee dam. Below the dam, take the trail marked by a blue line on a white background, which will lead you to the Brocken. It is a long, upwards slog, but you can relax on the journey home by taking the mountain railway down the valley and a bus back to Bad Harzburg.

► Kassel

Badly bombed in 1943 and rebuilt in a dull style, the principal city of north Hesse is today an industrial centre for engineering, chemicals, etc., and has little charm (its Altstadt has vanished). But its setting amid wooded hills is pleasant, and it is worth visiting for the extravagantly Romantic **Wilhelmshöhe park**► ► and for its excellent museums – the city has the largest number of leading museums in Central Germany.

The *Landgraves* (counts) of Hesse developed Kassel in the 17th and 18th centuries, creating the great park and encouraging industry. They were avid art collectors – a tradition kept alive today with the famous avant-garde and multimedia Dokumenta exhibition, held every five years since 1955 (next in 2000). One of its patrons was the late Joseph Beuys, who planted 7,000 oak trees in Kassel as an action sculpture. In the town centre is the Dokumenta's main venue, the opera house and the curiously shaped Ottoneum, Germany's oldest theatre (1606). Best of the nearby museums is the Landesmuseum (*Closed* Mon) with its early astronomical and scientific instruments, prehistory and an unusual display of wallpapers dating from the 16th century. A small museum nearby (*Closed* Mon) is devoted to the Brothers Grimm, who lived and worked in Kassel. The Neue Galerie (*Closed* Mon) has 19th- and 20th-century paintings, few of them notable, but there are some attractive canvases by Tischbein, who was born near Kassel.

In the western suburbs is the pink granite **Schloss Hohenlohe**, where the Westphalian king Jerome Bonaparte held lavish court (1807–13). The Schloss contains a large and excellent **museum**► ► (*Closed* Mon), notable less for its Egyptian, Greek, and Roman antiquities than for its excellent paintings, especially Italian, Flemish, and Dutch (note Teniers's *Peasants' Dance*). Napoleon III was interned here in 1870: as he passed through Aachen the crowd jeered, '*Ab nach Kassel!*' – which means 'Off we go!'

WILHELMSHÖHE PARK
From the rear of Schloss Hohenlohe there's a fine view over the Wilhelmshöhe Schlosspark, as splendid a Romantic landscape park as any in Europe, begun soon after 1700. It is crowned by a vast Hercules statue (copy of the Farnese Hercules in Naples) atop a towering 70m grey granite monument. Below it are waterfalls and fountains (activated Wed, Sun, and public holidays mid-May to Oct) and some charming 18th-century follies – Pluto's Grotto, Devil's Bridge, baroque temples, and the startling grey-pinnacled castle of Löwenburg, which may look medieval but is pure Romantic fake.

SCHLOSS WILHELMSTHAL
Just north of Kassel, the pretty rococo Schloss Wilhelmsthal is worth a visit: its ornate interior, designed by Cuvilliés, contains Tischbein portraits of ladies (*Closed* Mon).

Kassel's Hesse Museum

►► Lemgo   108A4

One of the best-preserved towns in northern and central Germany and formerly a member of the Hanseatic League, Lemgo was once known as the Leipzig of Westphalia because of its printing presses (Leipzig was the publishing capital of Germany). In the 15th and 16th centuries trade with Flanders and England brought wealth to Lemgo. Today signs of this early prosperity are much in evidence, particularly as the town escaped damage in World War II. The unusual old Rathaus consists of eight adjacent buildings dating from different periods. You'll find many half-timbered houses with a rich variety of façades in Breitestrasse, the town's main street. At number 19 there is the **Hexenbürgermeisterhaus►** (House of the Witches' Mayor), completed in 1568, is a famous example of the Weser Renaissance style with characteristic oriel windows. The house gets its name from Hermann Cothmann, who sentenced 90 women to death for witchcraft when he was mayor of Lemgo, from 1666 to 1681. It houses a Heimatmuseum (local history museum) which is closed for renovations in 2000. When it reopens it will have a display relating to law and punishment as they were applied to witchcraft, including a macabre display of instruments of torture.

The Marienkirche is a Gothic hall church with a Renaissance organ still in excellent shape, both in sound and appearance. Take advantage of any concert being performed in the church. The 13th-century Nickolai-kirche, with its two dissimilar towers, shows both Romanesque and Gothic work.

► Münden (Hannoversch Münden)   108B3

A delightful old town of narrow streets and black-and-white half-timbered houses, Münden stands, in the words of a well-known poem, 'where Werra and Fulda kiss each other', for these rivers meet here, and the

FINE REMBRANDTS
The Staatliche Kunstsammlungen in Kassel has an outstanding collection of paintings by Rembrandt. The gallery once boasted 17 canvases by the artist, but the origins of six of these are now in dispute. An undisputed masterpiece is *Jacob Blessing the Sons of Joseph*, a late work of remarkable tenderness.

DR EISENBART
Münden's most famous son, Johann Andreas Eisenbart, was an 18th-century doctor with allegedly miraculous powers. A costume play commemorating his life is performed outdoors on Sundays from mid-May to the end of August.

Scrollwork, pyramids and statues adorn Münden's Rathaus (right), in a town rich in old half-timbered houses

Weserstein, a monumental stone, marks the spot. The bridge over the Werra behind the Schloss dates from no later than the 14th century.

In the Marktplatz there are buildings in Weser Renaissance style, including the very handsome gabled Rathaus. The St Blasiuskirche is a Gothic hall church with a late-14th-century bronze font.

▶ Münzenberg   *108A2*
You can visit Schloss Münzenberg, about 19 miles north of Frankfurt-am-Main, all year round. (*Open* Apr–Oct Tue–Sun 10–noon, 2–6; Nov–Mar 10–noon, 2–4). You will be able to visit the grounds and the fortifications and living quarters. The latter are heavily decorated in the Romanesque style, especially apparent in the rounded arches of the windows and the gallery. There is a keep at each end of the complex. The well-maintained grounds are pleasant for a leisurely stroll, and there is a magnificent view from the top of the east tower, which takes in the low-lying Welterau, a region between two upland massifs, the Taunus and the Vogelberg.

Paderborn 108A3

This ancient Westphalian town (pop. 123,000) is an active commercial and industrial centre. It entered history in 799, when Charlemagne had an important meeting here with Pope Leo III, reaching an agreement that led the following year to the creation of the Holy Roman Empire. The site of the palace where the meeting took place came to light during the rebuilding of the city after World War II. Paderborn's main landmark is its **cathedral►**, which dates mainly from the 13th century: its Romanesque tower has become the city's emblem. The Bartolomäuskapelle (St Bartholomew's Chapel), a separate structure north of the cathedral, was Germany's first hall church (11th century). On the exterior of the cathedral, note the Paradiesportal, a 13th-century porch on the south side. Another porch, the Brautportal, bears sculpted scenes from the life of Christ. Just below the church of the Abdinghof monastery are more than 200 warm springs, the source of the little River Pader.

► Taunus 108A1

The rolling hills of the Taunus, densely clothed in forests, are Germany's richest region of mineral springs. These springs have resulted in the opening up of several famous spas. The region's proximity to Wiesbaden, Mainz, and Frankfurt-am-Main has helped in its development. There are several good roads giving easy access to the peaks – the highest is the **Grosser Feldberg**, an important telecommunications centre at 880m. You can drive near the summit, then climb the tower on top (167 steps) for a grand view, as far as Frankfurt to the south and Westerwald to the north.

The little town of **Königstein im Taunus** is situated high up, well away from the main slope. Its most interesting feature is Burg Königstein, a mighty ruined castle with 16th-century bastions and 17th-century projecting defenses. Built around 1200, the castle was finally destroyed in 1796.

Bad Homburg►, in the foothills of the Taunus, used to be one of Europe's most fashionable spas, visited by Kaiser Wilhelm II, the prince of Wales, and other prominent guests (Dostoevsky set *The Gambler* here). Today it has moved somewhat downmarket, but the big Kurpark is still attractive, with a Russian chapel and a Thai temple, gifts from royal visitors from those lands. In the centre are the medicinal springs and lawns and walks. The stately white high-towered 17th-century Schloss was the residence of the Landgraves of Hesse-Homburg and subsequently summer palace of the kings of Prussia. Concerts take place in the Schlosskirche.

North of Bad Homburg, amid pleasant forests, is the *in situ* reconstruction of **Saalburg Roman Camp►** (*Open* daily), originally guarding the adjacent Limes fortifications, marking the northern extent of Roman occupation (still visible, to varying degrees).

Just outside the village of Neu Anspach is the **Freilicht Museum Hessenpark**, with reconstructed Hessian buildings, including a functioning bakery, and workshops that produce crafts. (Museum *Open* Mar–Oct daily. Central market, square, with reconstructed village tavern *Open* daily all year).

127

Paderborn's massive 13th-century cathedral exemplifies, in its interior, the transition from Romanesque to Gothic

▶ **Waldeck** *108B3*

Thanks largely to the spa resort of Bad Wildungen, the Waldeck region, just southwest of Kassel, has become one of the most popular tourist areas of central Germany. The countryside is attractive, with dense forests and gentle hills cut through by the course of the River Eder. The most spectacular feature of the locality is the great lake formed behind the Edertalsperre (Eder Dam).

The waters of **Bad Wildungen** are used mainly to treat kidney and gallbladder complaints, as well as problems of hypertension and metabolism. Peaceful walks cross the Kurpark to the Georg Viktor spring. The Evangelische Stadtkirche (Protestant church), which is famed for its altarpiece of 1403 by Konrad von Soest, has a 14th-century tower that overlooks the rest of the town. Farther east, the fortified town of **Fritzlar** occupies a site above the River Eder. Dom St Petri, founded by St Boniface in 724, is

Right and below: Burg Waldeck has a Witches' Tower, with three prison cells. It stands above the Eder Dam, which was blown up by a 4-ton RAF bomb in 1943, causing severe flooding

essentially late Romanesque with baroque additions. Huge crypts are the main feature of the cathedral and pre-date its reconstruction in 1180. The Marktplatz is also interesting, containing an appealing range of half-timbered buildings.

In the town of **Waldeck** itself, part of the castle of the Waldeck princes (Burg Waldeck) is now a hotel, and there is a museum in the vaults that relate the colourful history of the House of Waldeck (*Open* daily). One of Germany's largest feudal castles, **Burg Waldeck▶** was built in the late 12th century and much added to in subsequent centuries. It was abandoned by the House of Waldeck in the 17th century. The view from the castle terrace is particularly impressive. Spread out below the castle you can see the Eder Dam with its artificial lake, surrounded by wooded shores.

About an hour's drive away is **Korbach**, with its many old timber houses. The town was formed after two fortified settlements, Altstadt and Neustadt (Old Town and New Town), amalgamated.

North of Korbach is **Arolsen**, its regular plan very much the creation of the Waldeck princes who lived here. Their baroque-styled Schloss, which hosts concerts and theatre evenings, is at the eastern end of the main street. Built between 1714 and 1724, the palace was inspired by Versailles; but some of the rooms were not decorated until almost a hundred years later, in 1811.

A view from Waldeck's castle towards Eder Dam

Weserbergland

WESERBERGLAND

HAMELN

Kirchohsen

Hünenschloss   Hämelschenburg
                Grohnde

Humme

Emmer

Weser

Bad Pyrmont
Lügde   Hehlen
          Ottenstein   Bodenwerder
          Brevörde
Rischenau   Polle

Köterberg
496m

                    Bevern

          Holzminden
Höxter   Kloster
              Corvey
     Boffzen
                    Neuhaus
          Fürstenberg

                Schönhagen
Beverungen   **Uslar**
Bad Karlshafen   Wahlsburg
                      Lippoldsberg
Helmarshausen   Gewissenruh
Trendelburg   Gieselwerder
              Gottsbüren
                        Bursfelde
          Sababurg
Hofgeismar   Bramwald
     Grebenstein   Veckerhagen

Reinhardswald
Weser
Esse

                    Mollenfelde
          Münden

0 ____ 10 km
0 ____ 5 miles

A7

▶▶ **Weserbergland**   *108B4*

The Weserbergland is a region of green hills lining both banks of the River Weser. This is one of Germany's most picturesque river valleys, and it is well worth taking four or five days to follow the river's course north. You can either take the passenger boats that glide downstream, or drive along one of two roads. Take either the Wesertalstrasse (Weser Valley Road) or, on the other side of the river, the B80, part of the Deutsche Märchenstrasse (Fairy Tale Road) route the Brothers Grimm took when they gathered their famous fairy tales. The towns and villages along the way are characterised by the Weser Renaissance style of architecture.

A good route starts at the old town of **Münden** (see page 125), founded in 1170 by Henry the Lion. From there, go through the beautiful Kaufunger Wald, a forest south of Münden, part of which is a nature park, and on to **Mollenfelde**, with its unique bread museum, the Zentrum von Korn zum Brot (*Open* Mar–Oct daily. *Closed* Nov–Feb), where you can trace the history of bread from ancient Egyptian days to the present. Now go north to the romantic 14th-century **Schloss Sababurg**, where the Brothers Grimm used to attend hunting parties. It is said to be the model for the castle in *The Sleeping Beauty*, and is now a hotel. The nearby zoo, with bears, penguins, etc., is Germany's oldest (1571).

Further on, **Bad Karlshafen** is a beautiful Weser-harbour town, founded in 1699 for French Huguenot settlers, while **Höxter**▶ has a townscape of elaborately painted and carved façades, and a magnificent Renaissance alabaster pulpit in the twin-towered Kilianikirche. The Dechanei (Deanery) and Rathaus are two of the most eye-catching buildings, and busy Westerbachstrasse is perhaps the finest street. Nearby, at **Corvey**, you can see the Imperial Abbey (822), with a rare example of an original Carolingian west end. The poet Hoffmann von Fallersleben composed the German national anthem in the abbey (now converted to secular use).

Continuing north, the Rathaus at **Bodenwerder**▶ was once the home of Baron Münchhausen, famous for tall stories about his unbelievable feats (he did actually live, but his true exploits were somewhat tamer than the tales).

The building houses a small museum that commemorates the Baron and his exploits. At **Hämelschenburg**, you can visit the splendid Weser Renaissance castle (1588–1610) (see page 119), while the nearby town of **Hameln** is famous for its story of the Pied Piper (see page 119). At the Porta Westfalica, the Weser breaks through the mountains into the north German lowlands and continues north through Bremen and Bremerhaven (see pages 54–6) before flowing into the North Sea.

► **Wiesbaden**   *108A1*

The capital of Hesse and an important spa, Wiesbaden lies between the Rheingau wine region and the Taunus Mountains. The Romans first used its healing waters and built a forum – one arch now survives from their time. The spa's 26 hot springs have long attracted visitors; today it is popular with the rich and famous, artists, and businesspeople. Many thermal baths are inside hotels, but two can be visited without an overnight stay: the Kaiser Friedrich Bad in Langgasse and the Thermalbad Wiesbaden in Leibniz-strasse.

There are countless literary and musical associations. Goethe came here, as did the Russian writers Turgenev and Dostoevsky. Brahms, Wagner, and Robert and Clara Schumann were also visitors.Wiesbaden hosts a series of annual events, ranging from horse-riding competitions to wine tastings. In May an important festival attracts top foreign theatre companies.

Other sights in the town include the Stadtschloss, which became a royal castle in 1866 and is used today as the seat of the Hesse state parliament. There is an old town hall and the Städtisches Museum (town museum) (*Closed Mon*). It contains many important paintings including works by the Expressionist artist Alexei von Jawlensky, who worked with the Russian artist Kandinsky in Munich and later settled in Wiesbaden, where he died in 1941.

TAKING THE CURE
Wiesbaden's Neoclassical Kurhaus was built in 1906. It houses the Spielbank casino (note the portico with six Ionic columns).

Be warned that saunas in Germany are often unisex, so if you are not used to this, check with the facility beforehand. Make an appointment for a massage in advance if possible, as the masseurs tend to be booked up.

131

Wiesbaden's stately Kurhaus, today housing a concert hall, casino, and congress centre, has an amazing interior dating from 1907 – a mix of neo-byzantine, neo-classical, neo-baroque and art nouveau

In the days when it was the German Democratic Republic (GDR), visitors to Eastern Germany were hedged about with visas and customs checks, and controlled on where they could go. But all that has changed totally since the Berlin Wall fell. The east, now fully part of Germany, can be toured freely and is mostly well equipped for tourism.

It richly rewards a visit. There is the great city of Dresden, horribly bombed but still full of culture and history and its rival, Leipzig, is equally interesting. There are many fine historic smaller towns, such as Schwerin and Stralsund, Quedlinburg and Erfurt. Weimar, home of Goethe, Schiller and Herder, is a major world literary centre, at the heart of Germany and in 1999 was Europe's 'Cultural City'. The region has many superb museums and fine old palaces and castles, notably the Wartburg at Eisenach, where Martin Luther translated the Bible. In fact, the east produced many of Germany's leading writers, thinkers and musicians, such as Dürer, Holbein, Bach, Handel and Wagner.

In the south there is some beautiful scenery, hilly and wooded – the Thüringer Wald, the Harz mountains and the Erzgebirge. The north is flat, but not without charm – such as the great woods, lakes and rivers of the Spreewald and Mecklenburg, and the wide beaches of the Baltic.

In many ways the east now looks much like the west: yet below the surface lie differences. Many people are poorer than in the west and unemployment (more than 20 per cent in some areas) is far higher than the national average, and many town centres have been renovated, but in some suburbs you will still find dereliction and neglect. Nearly all the roads are now up to western standards, and new gas stations are plentiful. As for hotels, there are many large new modern ones, or well-renovated older ones, in the more expensive brackets. Good medium-priced hotels are still less frequent but family pensions are appearing. And you can always find rooms in private homes, at low prices – these can be booked through a tourist office. Restaurants of all kinds are now plentiful, but food is seldom as good as in the west. Lots of lively bars, pubs, and cabarets have sprung up in the towns.

Sadly, pockets of ultra-right-wing fanaticism remain entrenched in some outlying towns and villages, and if you are obviously a foreigner you are advised to avoid travelling in local trains late at night. A Berlin official responsible for foreign residents of the city is on record as cautioning non-Europeans against venturing into certain East German towns at any time. The vast majority of Germans are dismayed that the activities of a tiny, xenophobic minority make such warnings necessary. Equally, most east Germans are extremely hospitable, welcoming visitors with a warmth often found lacking in the more prosperous West. A whole generation grew up with Russian as their first foreign language, but English is now spoken by an increasing number of people.

Eastern Germany

Woodlands of Vogtland (see page 166)

Eastern Germany

Bernburg, which lies south of Magdeburg, has an imposing Renaissance castle surrounded by 15th-century ramparts

▶ **Bernburg**   *132B2*

Bernburg is interesting mainly for its huge Renaissance castle, with buildings of different styles and ages grouped around a large irregular courtyard. On one side, steep wooded slopes extend down to the River Saale and the lower town. Bernburg also boasts, in both the lower and upper towns, well-kept town walls and streets of 16th- to 18th-century town houses. The outskirts, though, are run-down and industrial.

There is another Renaissance palace situated at **Köthen**, 20km to the east. J S Bach worked for six years as *Kapellmeister* in the Ludwigsban part of the town and there is a small museum dedicated to him here (*Open* Tue–Sun, Sat pm only. *Closed* Mon). There are also some particularly fine aristocratic houses dotted about around the town centre.

In the other direction, 19km west of Bernburg, **Aschersleben** clusters below the 80m tower of St Stephen's, a fine 15th-century Gothic hall church. There are several attractive burghers' houses located in the ancient town centre.

▶▶ **Brandenburg**   *132B3*

Brandenburg is surrounded by numerous lakes along and around the River Havel, an area popular for excursions. Known as Havelland, it is famous for its birdlife – reed warblers, marsh harriers, bitterns, storks, herons, and cranes are to be observed in abundance.

Both town and *Land* take their name from the castle known as the Brandenburg, first mentioned in AD 948. It took 200 years before this seemingly impregnable fortress was finally overcome by a warrior prince with the delightful name of Albrecht the Bear. Both old and new towns remained separate members of the Hanseatic League until 1518, and only joined together in 1715. Huguenot settlers increased the town's prosperity. In the 20th century it became a major industrial centre and consequently heavily bombed during World War II.

Brandenburg's cathedral took seven centuries to complete. It has a 14th-century Bohemian altar, a 13th-century Saxon crucifix, and countless valuable manuscripts. The town hall (1480) has a 5m figure of Roland, a symbol of civic rights, dating from 1474.

►► Colditz 132B1

The old town of Colditz, on the River Mulde in central Saxony, has a picturesque town centre with an attractive town hall, marketplace and 13th-century parish church. The ancient castle on a hill overlooking the town achieved notoriety during World War II as a formidable prisoner-of-war camp, from where a number of British officers made escapes. Since the war the castle has been a hospital but is now being transformed into a museum and a restaurant. Mementos of escapees are kept in the town museum, including some false German uniforms, photographic material and a printing press (*Closed* Mon).

Dessau 132B2

Dessau is world-famous among architects and designers as the home of the Bauhaus movement (see panel). The building from which it gets its name was built by Walter Gropius in 1925–6 and still stands – restored in 1977 to something like its former glory – in a suburban avenue 2km northwest of the centre. There are occasional performances and lectures held here. There are also examples of

135

Bauhaus architecture on the outskirts, including a 300-dwelling housing project at Dessau-Törten to the south, but they are hard to find and the buildings themselves are not well preserved.

Much of the city centre – also famous as the site of the Junkers aircraft factory – was destroyed in the war and has been rebuilt in modern style. Fortunately, the city has three estates that provide relief from the general drabness of its post-Bauhaus architecture. Within the city limits is the neo-classical Schloss Georgian (1790), set in a fine park, and just outside Dessau are two fascinating estates. The nearest, Schloss Mosigkau, 9km southwest, was commissioned by Prince Leopold of Anhalt-Dessau, for his favourite daughter, Anna Wilhelmine. She lived there as a recluse and left the splendid property to an order of nuns. The palace has one of Germany's few baroque picture galleries and an impressive collection of furniture (*Closed* Mon). East of Dessau is Wörlitzer Park, beautifully landscaped gardens modelled on the 18th century English style, with lakes, canals and decorative pavilions.

Above: the White Bridge at Dessau
Top right: Colditz castle

THE BAUHAUS
The Bauhaus movement was founded by Walter Gropius in Weimar in 1919. His school of art became an experimental laboratory for architects, engineers, painters, sculptors and designers. The aim was to bring together aesthetics with the needs of an industrial civilisation. Thus the courses at the Bauhaus school were directed at the creation of forms suitable for mass production.

Semper Opera House, Dresden

1945 AIR RAID
On 13–14 February, 1945, in the most intensive air raid of the war in Europe, over 2,000 Allied bombers attacked Dresden in three giant waves. The city was packed with refugees from the advancing Red Army, and thousands of virtually unprotected families were among the 35,000 people who died in the raids and the resulting fire-storm, compared by some historians with the horrors of Hiroshima and Nagasaki. Sixty per cent of Dresden was destroyed. The aim was to break German morale. But many critics, even among the Allies, have since argued that so cruel a raid, so near the war's end, on a town of little strategic value, was simply not justified. Among the older generation of Dresden, memories are still very painful and some bitterness is still evident.

▶▶▶ Dresden   *132C1*

Dresden used to be one of the loveliest cities of central Europe – 'Florence on the Elbe', it was called. It never quite recovered from the great air raid of 1945 (see panel) and many of its fine baroque buildings still wear a stunned, blackened look (exacerbated by decades of neglect and industrial pollution). In the 1950s and 60s, much of the city was rebuilt in a blocky, Stalinist style, impressive in its scale and self-confidence, but not much fun to explore. Even today, many of the outlying areas are still grimy and derelict.

For all this, Dresden is not to be missed. Enough of its enormous cultural heritage remains, providing plenty of worthwhile sights and famous works of art. Most of them date back to the city's heyday as capital of Saxony, especially to the reign of the aptly named Augustus the Strong in the late 17th and early 18th centuries. Even at the height of the cold war, considerable efforts were made by the East German authorities to restore the most important of those monuments that were not smashed to pieces. Since unification, this process has accelerated. Encouraged by Dresden's revived status as capital of the state of Saxony, western investors have poured money into building projects, which have begun to transform the centre and give the city a renewed claim to its old reputation for culture, commerce and gracious living. Germany's second-largest bank, the Dresdner, is again proudly present in the city where it was born in 1872.

What to see The **Brühlsche Terrasse**, a gracious, elevated terrace on the south bank of the Elbe, and once known as 'Europe's balcony', lies at the heart of the historic part of Dresden, surrounded by gaunt, dignified buildings in a range of styles. Immediately behind it, the stark, windowless remains of the 18th-century **Stadtschloss▶** are a reminder of the reconstruction work yet to be done. The castle is due to reopen for Dresden's 800th anniversary in

2006. The neighbouring **Frauenkirche** (Church of Our Lady)▶ is Germany's largest baroque and Protestant church. Ever since 1944 it was kept as a ruin, in memory of the horrors of the bombing of World War II, but now at last it is to be expensively rebuilt in its old style. The **Hofkirche** (royal cathedral), which was built in 1739–55 in Italian baroque style contains a fine mid-18th-century organ by Silbermann.

Facing the cathedral across the square stands the **Semper Opera House▶▶**(Tours daily, at 2 and 3pm), built by Gottfried Semper in 1838–41 and subject to a huge restoration programme by the German Democratic Republic. It was eventually reopened in 1985, to reveal a very high standard of comfort and facilities as well as painstaking attention to period detail.

A few steps away is Dresden's most famous sight, the **Zwinger▶▶▶** (keep), a complex of baroque-style pavilions grouped around a graceful, relaxed courtyard. It gets its name from the ancient fortifications that used to occupy the site: the buildings themselves date from 1711

HELLERAU GARDEN CITY
A short tram ride into the Dresdner Heide, north of the city, brings you to Hellerau, site of Europe's first 'garden city', built along lines pioneered by Britain's Ebenezer Howard. The beautiful little settlement grew from a community of artisans, housed in idyllic surroundings, into a cultural citadel. World War I interrupted Hellerau's development and the Third Reich killed it completely. Restoration work is now under way, but even the idealists admit Hellerau will never recapture its earlier glory.

137

to 1728 but have been added to and altered over the years. They contain a treasure house of museums, including a world-famous porcelain collection (*Closed* Thu) and museums of science (*Closed* Thu) and zoology (*Closed* Mon). Now that restoration work has been completed, the Gemäldegalerie Alter Meister (Gallery of Old Masters) has returned from its temporary home in the **Albertinum** (see below) to the Semperbau at the Zwinger (*Open* Tue–Sun). The collection includes Raphael's *Sistine Madonna*, Giorgione's *Sleeping Venus*, and works by Canaletto (many of them scenes painted on his visits to Dresden), Rembrandt, Vermeer, and Titian.

Behind the Zwinger you will find the **Langer Gang** (long passage), a 16th-century arcade with Italian-style white pillars. On the outside, it bears a huge 19th-century porcelain frieze depicting Saxon princes. Nearby are two more museums, of geology and transport (*Closed* Mon).

Back by the Brühlsche Terrasse stands one of Dresden's most important galleries, the **Albertinum▶▶▶**, a 16th-century building that once served as an arsenal and which currently contains one of the world's most impressive art collections. One part houses the Gemäldegalerie Neuer Meister (Gallery of New Masters; *closed* Thu), which includes pictures by Dix, Liebermann, and several French Impressionists. Another, the Grünes Gewölbe (Green Vault; *closed* Thu), contains the royal collection of silver, gold and jewellery, as well as the star of the show, *The Court of Delhi on the Birthday of the Great Mogul*, a set of 132 gold, enamel, and bejewelled painted figures. Further exhibitions include one of the most valuable sculpture collections outside Italy, as well as over 200,000 coins, medals, notes, and royal seals.

Further away from the river, the scene becomes bleaker, marked by big blocks and wide open spaces. One of these, the **Altmarkt** (old market), was the bustling centre of a great city before it was razed in 1945; it has now recovered some of its bustle, but the charm will be harder to restore. In its southeast corner stands the **Kreuzkirche** (Church of the Holy Cross), which dates back to 1764–92 and is the oldest church within the boundary of the former city walls. It is home to Dresden's famous choir, the Kreuzchor, which performs here most Saturday afternoons. To the south of the Altmarkt, you can continue along modern, pedestrianised **Prager Strasse**, along

Detail from the Zwinger

PROUD SAXONY
One of Germany's main industrial regions, Saxony has an intense local patriotism, like Bavaria. It even retained its own king until 1918, within a united Germany. The centralised GDR then removed its separate identity. Today Saxony is again an autonomous *Land*, under its prime minister from the West, Kurt Biedenkopf. There is strong rivalry between Dresden, the historic capital, and the other big Saxon city, Leipzig.

The River Elbe at Dresden, heavily polluted in GDR days, has now been cleaned up

which stand the city's larger restaurants and hotels. There's a little more of the flavour of prewar Dresden across the Elbe in **Dresden-Neustadt**, which has many imposing 19th-century buildings and centres on a car-free main boulevard, the Hauptstrasse.

Excursions The best bet is to take a paddle steamer (the **Weisse Flotte** steamers leave from the landing platforms by Terrassenufer) along the Elbe to some of the worthwhile destinations just outside Dresden. One option is the old town of **Meissen** (see page 152).

A very pleasant alternative is to go upstream to **Schloss Pillnitz▶** (10km southeast), a charmingly relaxed grouping of summer palaces built in Chinese style and dating from 1723; it's set in a beautiful wooded section of the Elbe Valley and is surrounded by a small park. Farther upstream is **Pirna** (20km from Dresden), an ancient market town that straddles the river. Its market square boasts fine medieval houses, and the Marienkirche (St Mary's Church) is one of the finest late Gothic hall churches in Saxony. Pirna is known as the gateway to Saxon Switzerland (Sächsische Schweiz; see pages 155–6).

The **Dresdener Heide** (Dresden Heath) starts on the northeastern edge of town and is easily reached by public transportation. It's a relaxed area of open woodland, crossed with well-marked paths.

▶▶ **Eisenach**   *132A1*

Despite its small size, this city nestling in wooded hills at the northwest end of the Thüringer Wald has an enormous importance in the history of German civilisation. This is because of its position at the foot of the

THE GROSSER GARTEN
The Grosser Garten (or Volkspark), a large 17th-century park about 1.6km southeast of the centre of Dresden, includes a baroque pleasure palace and the city's zoo. The Parkeisenbahn, an enormous model railway with five stations and 6km of track, runs through the park. The Deutsches Hygiene Museum, built for the 2nd International Hygiene Exhibition (held in Dresden in 1930), is best known for its glass models of a woman, a cow, and a horse (*Open* Sat–Thu).

PROPERTY CLAIMS

Eisenach's big department store, Schwager, is back in the hands of its Schwager family owners. It was expropriated by the GDR in 1950, and they fled west: now they have reclaimed it, and it booms. But of the east's million or so property claims, few have been solved so easily: some are by Jewish former owners, dating from Nazi times. This huge and complex property problem has deterred investors and hampered renovation. If, in a street of neatly restored houses, one remains decrepit, it may be that the lawyers can't decide who owns it.

Old Wartburg models in Eisenach's car museum: GDR citizens often had to wait ten years to buy one

Wartburg▶▶, a spectacular hilltop castle (*Open* daily, Mon pm only) dating back to the 11th century. It became an early centre for music and poetry, hosting the traditional *Sängerkrieg*, a competition for singer-poets, in the early 13th century – subsequently immortalised by Richard Wagner in his opera *Tannhäuser*. Two centuries later the fortress achieved a place in world history when it sheltered Martin Luther, who had been outlawed by the Roman Catholic Church for his 'heretical' views. During the year Luther spent here (1521–2) he worked on his German translation of the Bible.

It is a half-hour uphill slog to the castle, but the footpath winds pleasantly through thick woods of ash, beech and elder. You can also drive to a car-park just below the castle, from where youngsters can hire a donkey for the last few hundred yards to the castle courtyard. Within the castle walls you will find a very romantic hotel, with snug bedrooms, deep-cushioned comforts, open fireplaces and a baronial dining room. A tour of the castle takes in Luther's study, the castle's art collection and various halls, including the enormous Festsaal (banqueting hall) which was decorated with murals by Moritz von Schwind in the 19th century.

Back down in the town, a major point of interest is the J S Bach house (*Open* daily), commemorating the birthplace of Eisenach's most famous son. As well as a collection of music and instruments, and a very pretty garden, the museum offers short recitals on some of the keyboard instruments. Nearby is the 15th-century house, prettily restored, where Luther stayed as a student: it too is now a museum, with details of his translation of the Bible. The composer Richard Wagner often visited Eisenach while staying with the Liszts in nearby Weimar. He is commemorated with the most comprehensive exhibition on his life and work outside Bayreuth, the Reuter-Wagner-Museum (*Closed* Mon). Eisenach also has an automobile museum, housed in a small pavilion close to the centre (*Closed* Mon). This contains examples of Wartburg cars, produced at Eisenach in GDR days in a huge factory with 8,000 workers. It is now run by Opel.

One of Eisenach's attractions is its big squares surrounded by graceful houses: in the centre of the largest (the Markt) stands St George's Church, which has an unusual galleried interior decorated with murals.

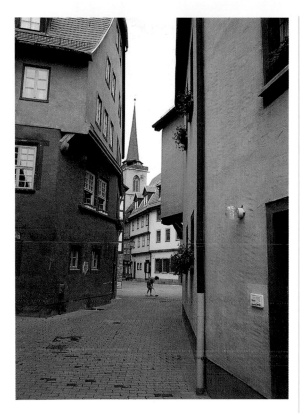

An old street of medieval Erfurt, neatly restored under the new regime

CITY OF FLOWERS AND TOWERS
Erfurt is known as the 'city of flowers and towers', because of its horticulture and its profusion of churches. The city is Europe's largest producer of seeds, and one of its most famous sons, the botanist Christian Reichart, pioneered seed research. Every summer the city hosts the huge Internationale Gartenbauaustellung, a horticulture, garden and landscaping exhibition.

141

▶▶ Erfurt   *132A1*

The capital and largest town of Thüringia, Erfurt has distinct charm despite some less attractive development. But at its core lies an extensive and, for the most part, well-preserved medieval town, crowned by its imposing cathedral and the neighbouring Gothic church of St Severin. The church's pointed spires loom over the large, irregularly shaped Domplatz (cathedral square), which is used for fun-fairs and markets of all sorts.

The **cathedral▶▶**, reached up a flight of 70 steps from the square, dates back to the mid-12th century and was built in the form of a Romanesque basilica, though it gained a Gothic choir in the mid-14th century. It contains some fine works of art, including a Romanesque altar, carved wooden stalls, and 14th- to 15th-century stained glass. The largest bell in eastern Germany, the 'Gloriosa', hangs in the middle tower. The 14th-century St Severin's boasts some of Germany's finest early Gothic architecture and an extraordinary 15th-century font.

Down in the town, there's a wealth of fine buildings and streets to see. Some of the ancient houses are still in poor shape, but many others have now been renovated, especially around the two pedestrianised main squares, the Anger and the Fischmarkt. Close by is the fascinating **Krämerbrücke▶** (Shopkeepers' bridge), spanning the wide and shallow River Gera. Lined with tall, narrow half-timbered houses, it is the only bridge of its kind north of the Alps. Nowadays, humbler trades in the narrow

*Many antiques shops fill
the St Andreas quarter
of old Erfurt*

cobbled street that passes between the houses have given
way to antiques shops. A few streets away you can see the
restored 13th-century Augustiner church and monastery
which once included Martin Luther among its novices
(*Open* Apr–Oct daily 11–12, 2–4; Nov–Mar by prior
appointment only).

A couple of kilometres southwest of the centre, the 15th-
century (but much altered) Cyriaksburg castle stands in
leafy grounds, part of which are given over to a large
permanent museum and exhibition devoted to all forms
of gardening and horticulture – a long-established
Thüringian local industry (*Open* daily).

► **Erzgebirge** *132C1*

The Erzgebirge is a range of mountains stretching for
140km along the Czech frontier from the Vogtland (see
page 166) to Saxon Switzerland (see pages 155–6). It
includes the highest point in eastern Germany, the
Fichtelberg (1,214m). The western part of the range is
characterised by steep-sided valleys and thick forests,
dotted with villages and small industrial towns; the eastern part, to the east of the River Flöha, consists mainly of
high plateaus and is more open in appearance. The whole
area gets its name (*Erz* means ore) from the mineral ores
that have been mined here since the 12th century, starting
with silver, tin and lignite. The area was one of the main
holiday resorts of the old GDR, despite the pollution
caused by open-cast lignite mining. The pollution is now
largely an evil of the past, and tourists now come for the
good skiing, hiking and walking.

As the mines became exhausted, people started a variety
of crafts, and the area is well known for its toy-making
industry. Look for the crafted and painted wooden Easter
eggs; you will find them only in the Erzgebirge.

Annaberg-Buchholz is the largest town in the area and has a spectacular hall church, the biggest in Saxony, dating from 1499–1525, with a fine main portal and several beautiful altars. The nearby town of **Frohnau** (2km west) has an unusual industrial museum, Frohnauer Hammer (*Open* daily), originally (1436) a corn mill but which was then converted to a silver and iron forge in 1621. To the south, **Ober-Wiesenthal** is a winter-sports resort at the foot of the Fichtelberg; the 1214m summit can be reached by cable car for a fine view.

In the eastern part of the Erzgebirge, **Seiffen▶** has been the centre of the Saxon toy industry since the 18th century. This remains active today, turning out hand-carved Christmas decorations, wooden nutcracker figures in local costume, and much else. You can watch the craftsmen at work, and see details of the industry and exhibits detailing its significance to social history, in the large Spielzeugmuseum (Toy Museum, *open* daily) which shows many of the traditional items made in the area. The Freilichtmuseum on the Deutscheinsiedel road out of town, shows furniture and exhibits on the folk history of the region (*Closed* Mon).

SCHWARZBIER
Small East German breweries experienced a welcome renaissance following reunification, and some are making inroads into areas previously dominated by the big West German companies. An East German speciality is Schwarzbier, literally 'black beer', and in reality a smooth, dark, stout-like brew. It is brewed according to the centuries-old German 'purity laws', with additional roasting of the barley malt giving the beer its rich colour. Try Eisenach's Schwarzer Drachen (Black Dragon) or the Köstriges Schwarzbier – both are quite delicious.

143

▶ ▶ **Görlitz** *132C2*

Görlitz is a large and extremely ancient city that once spread across both banks of the River Neisse but, following World War II, found itself straddling the German-Polish border.

The German part of town contains most of the old centre, which – though shabby in parts – has many crooked, narrow streets rich in medieval buildings, both secular and religious. The most interesting examples are grouped around the part-arcaded Untermarkt (lower market square), which has a fine collection of Renaissance and baroque town houses. Keep a lookout particularly for the house at No 22, which has an unusual portal.

In nearby Neissestrasse, look out for house No 29 (the 'Biblische-Haus') which dates from 1570 and bears bas-relief scenes from the Old and New Testaments. The Rathaus (town hall) has an unusual mixture of styles, dating mostly from the 14th and 16th centuries.

Görlitz on the Polish border, known for its optical and mechanical industries, has a fortified 14th-century gateway close to its upper market place

*The town hall clock
in Görlitz*

▶ Gotha   132A1

Gotha, which traces its beginnings back to the year 775, acquired European-wide significance when it became the residence of the princely house of Sachsen-Gotha-Altenburg. Later it shared with Coburg the title of 'residence city' of the historic house of Sachsen-Coburg und Gotha, often described as the 'stud farm' of the royal houses of Europe. Germany's version of the *Debrett* guide to the nobility, the *Almanach de Gotha*, was first published here.The centre of Gotha is dominated by the 360-room 17th-century baroque castle of Friedenstein, which stands on a hill above the main square. Ranged around a large, square courtyard, the massive white-painted, arcaded buildings incorporate a museum of local history and cartography, a theatre, and a library. Another highlight is the long, narrow Hauptmarkt (market square), which stretches down the hill. At the top of the square is a group of restored Renaissance buildings, and the neo-Renaissance red-and-white town hall.

Excursion
Friedrichroda is a small, relaxed resort on the edge of the Thüringian Forest: a 16km ride on the narrow-gauge Waldbahn (forest train) takes you through the fields and backyards of this pretty and unspoiled area.

▶ Greifswald and Usedom 132B4

Greifswald lies on the eastern side of Mecklenburg-Vorpommern, not far from the Greifswalder Bodden, a shallow, virtually tideless bay of the Baltic. In the 13th century, monks founded this settlement near their coastal monastery of Eldena. In 1278 the town became part of the Hanseatic League. In 1648, after the Thirty Years' War, Greifswald was granted to Sweden, only to return to Germany in 1815 under Prussian rule.

Greifswald has fine buildings, notably an originally Gothic town hall (rebuilt in the 18th century after a fire), the 13th-century Marienkirche, half-timbered St Spiritus Hospital, and town houses with elegant gabled façades. The painter Caspar David Friedrich was born in Greifswald in 1774 and spent much of his life here. His evocative paintings of coastal seascapes and the ruins of Eldena Monastery provide a record of the landscape as it was early in the last century. Some of his best work can be seen in the Charlottenburg Palace in Berlin.

Usedom Not far from Greifswald, across the straits of the Peene Strom, lies Usedom, a strangely shaped island that straddles the Polish–German border. Wollin, the eastern part of the island, is Polish territory. There are excellent beaches, with small seaside resorts at Bansin, Heringsdorf, Ahlbeck, and Zinnowitz (the last overlooked by a castle), and inland lakes such as the Gothenesee and the Schmollensee.

Eighty-five percent of the surface area of Usedom, mostly meadowland, woods, bays, and dunes, is protected landscape, much of it nature reserve. The area is peaceful and tranquil. In clear weather you can see the southeast tip of Rügen island, while the border crossing at Ahlbeck brings neighbouring Poland's Swinemünde within easy access.

PEENEMÜNDE

Peenemünde, on the northern extremity of Usedom, was the unlikely place where, during World War II, the physicist Werner von Braun and other German scientists developed and tested the notorious V1 and V2 rockets. This high technology was put to better use in postwar times when von Braun joined the U S space research team and helped to develop rockets for the US space programme and the successful first flight to the moon.

Greifswald is a handsome old university town on a flat plain close to the Baltic

LEFTISH SCULPTORS
Heiligenstadt was the home of the great 16th-century sculptor and wood-carver Tilman Riemenschneider, whose works can be seen today in Franconia. He was imprisoned for backing the Peasants' Revolt. In our own century, the radical humanist sculptor Ernst Barlach suffered under the Nazis. He came from Güstrow (near Rostock), where some of his work is on view.

Halle's Rathaus, itself no beauty, presides over an old town of fine buildings with a great musical and intellectual tradition

► **Halle**   *132B2*

Now a major industrial and cultural centre, Halle is one of eastern Germany's oldest cities and was the birthplace of the composer Handel (see opposite). A more recent son of Halle is the former German Foreign Minister, Hans Dietrich Genscher, who did much in 1990 to persuade the Russians to accept German unification. Halle's wealth came originally from the mining of salt. The city's Halloren and Saline Museum brings much of that past to life (*Closed* Mon). Halle's most striking landmark is the four-towered, 16th-century church of Unser Lieben Frauen in the market square.

The nearby Roter Turm (Red Tower), became a symbol to the people of Halle of their struggle against feudal domination. The Moritzburg, the city's art gallery, is a late 15th-century Gothic fortress, built as a stronghold for the powerful archbishops of Magdeburg against insurrection. In the Alter Markt don't miss the fountain of a boy with a donkey, the town's historic symbol.

► **Heiligenstadt**   *132A2*

A small, quiet resort on the River Leine, Heiligenstadt boasts a long, partly pedestrianised main street dominated by the parish church of St Martin. The town centre was partly destroyed by fire in 1759, but several half-timbered and Renaissance houses survive from earlier times, among them the 15th-century Mainzer house and the baroque Rathaus.

Set at the centre of the hilly and part-forested Eichsfeld region, Heiligenstadt has long been popular as a place for rest and recuperation.

Georg Friedrich Handel was born in 1685 (the same year as J S Bach) in the city of Halle, where his statue now surveys the market square. His complete mastery of composition is evident from the fact that he wrote 46 operas, over 30 oratorios and a large number of cantatas, concerti grossi, pieces of sacred music, and other instrumental and vocal works.

Against the wishes of his father, a noted barber-surgeon, Handel became organist at Halle Cathedral at the age of 17, while studying law. In 1706 he left for four years in Italy, where he became known as a virtuoso harpsichordist and violinist, earning himself the title of *il caro Sassone* ('the dear Saxon'). He also wrote his first operas – including *Almira* – in the Italian style.

On his return from Italy in 1710, Handel was appointed Kapellmeister (orchestra and choir conductor) at the court of the Elector of Hannover. Handel followed his master when the elector succeeded Queen Anne to the English throne as George I in 1714.

The *Water Music* may even have been written to appease his patron. If this was the composer's aim, he was certainly successful, since, on his succession to the monarchy, George I doubled Handel's pension.

In London Handel busied himself in the composition of more operas, but with mixed fortunes. This patchy operatic success caused him to experiment with a new musical form, the oratorio. In this new area of composition success was immediate and undoubted: Handel conducted no fewer than 15 separate oratorio concerts in 1735 alone.

In 1737 Handel suffered a stroke; nevertheless, the next five years saw him complete many of his finest works, including *Saul* (1739), *Israel in Egypt* (1739) and *Messiah* (1742). However, his health continued to deteriorate and in 1759 he died.

Georg Friedrich Handel is buried in Poet's Corner in London's Westminster Abbey.

147

Above: Handel's house in Halle, where the composer was born in 1685

Right: Georg Friedrich Handel, master of the oratorio

Old and new architecture in Jena

MUSEUMS AND MEMORIALS
There's a lot to see in Leipzig. The former Imperial Court of Justice, where Hitler set the phoney Reichstag fire trial, now holds a museum noted for its Dutch and German paintings (Cranach, Friedrich, etc.) (*Closed* Mon). You can see the farmhouse, now a museum, where Schiller wrote his *Ode to Freedom* (*Closed* Mon). Or inspect the huge, hideous Massacre of the People Memorial, completed in 1913 to mark the 1813 battle at Leipzig where the Prussians and allies defeated Napoleon – and 100,000 perished.

► **Jena**   *132B1*

The vast modern housing complex of Lobeda, which marches along the valley connecting the centre of Jena with the highway, makes a sad introduction to this ancient university town, famous also for its optical industry started by Carl Zeiss in the mid-19th century. Zeiss's name and work are commemorated in the planetarium (the world's oldest working one), which is located in the botanic garden just north of the centre. There is also an optical museum.

Jena has illustrious associations with some of the greatest figures in German culture: Hegel and Schiller taught at the university, and Goethe was a frequent visitor.

One end of the enormous market square, lined by the 14th-century town hall and Gothic St. Michael's Church, has some charm, but with most of the rest of the centre rebuilt in monumental modern style, topped by a 26-storey cylindrical university building, the city depends heavily on its past glories.

►►► **Leipzig**   *132B2*

Founded by Slavic settlers in the 7th and 8th centuries, Leipzig had become an important German stronghold by the 10th century and a flourishing centre where the great east–west and north–south trade routes intersected on the Thüringian-Saxon plain. Its name derives from Urbs Lizi, or 'the town of the lime trees'.

Today Leipzig is Saxony's largest city, a major industrial, shopping, cultural and administrative centre with 550,000 inhabitants, renowned for its long associations with trade, science, humanism, music and publishing, as well as for its twice-yearly trade fair.

Leipzig's university was founded in 1409. Martin Luther preached here many times and disputed passionately with his opponents. Books were printed for the first time in Leipzig in 1481, laying the foundations for the city's long publishing tradition. Music was first printed in Leipzig in 1754. Johann Sebastian Bach worked as cantor and director of music at the Thomaskirche for the last 27 years of his life until his death in the city in 1750. A bronze plaque in the church marks his grave. Richard Wagner was born in the city in 1813, but later had to flee for his life for supporting

Instant art: a street artist produces a portrait to order in Leipzig, where there are long-established links with many branches of the arts

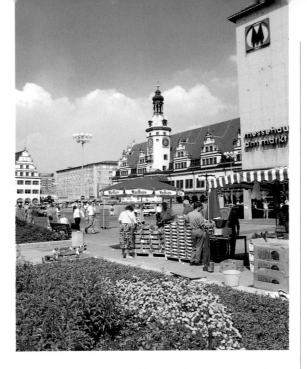

Looking towards Leipzig's Marktplatz and the Altes Rathaus

THE NIKOLAIKIRCHE

Protest against the 40-year-long Communist dictatorship in East Germany came to a head in the late 1980s in Leipzig in regular prayers for peace at the Nikolaikirche, led by Neues Forum – New Forum – an alliance of Christian and liberal-democratic protesters. Candles were lit and carried by thousands of people of the city as a potent symbol of peaceful protest, which helped to bring about the downfall of the hated Honecker regime. Prominent among dissidents was the celebrated Leipzig conductor Kurt Masur. The Nikolaikirche, built between the 13th and 16th centuries, has an inspiring 18th-century interior that symbolises hope – elegant white columns soaring upwards and bursting into delicate green palm fronds at their apex, crowned by a ceiling in shades of pink and green, complemented by stately white pews.

GOETHE IN LEIPZIG

Goethe studied law in Leipzig as a young man, and set a scene of *Faust* in Auerbach's Cellar, still to be found in the Mädlerpassage, where Mephistopheles is made to ride out on a barrel of wine. Goethe was also one of the celebrated visitors to the famous coffeehouse called the Kaffeebaum, in the Kleine Fleischergasse.

radical views. The world-famous Leipzig Gewandhaus orchestra is based in the city at the Neues Gewandhaus concert hall.

Much of the city centre is now traffic-free, with fine old squares, gardens, courtyards and shopping arcades opening out of the central pedestrianised areas. Despite some brutal rebuilding of office blocks, apartments and the university in modern concrete, many superb buildings remain. The richly decorated railway station is one of the most impressive in Germany.

The **Old Town Hall ▶** houses the Alte Börse, the old Stock Exchange, built between 1678 and 1687 and is one of the city's loveliest baroque buildings, newly restored. You can see many other fine baroque façades in the city centre, for example in the Katherinenstrasse.

Modern sculptures adorn Leipzig's trendy new shopping area

The medieval monastery of Our Lady in Magdeburg, a harmonious Romanesque ensemble

▶ Magdeburg

132B2

As early as AD 968, this archbishop's seat was the centre of the church's mission to Christianise the Slavic population. The city's original constitution of the same date became known as the Magdeburg Laws, and was used as a model for the establishment of numerous other towns in eastern Germany.

Magdeburg's 13th-century **cathedral▶▶** is the oldest great Gothic religious building in Germany, and its scale is a testimony to the power and influence of the city in the middle ages. Superb statues of the Wise and Foolish Virgins stand by the Paradise Doorway on the north side. Inside are remarkable seated statues (13th century) of Otto I and his wife Edith.

Though around 90 per cent of Magdeburg, including part of the cathedral itself, was destroyed by Allied bombing in World War II, its central areas have been rebuilt and elegantly laid out with boulevards and shops, and many of the historic buildings have been carefully reconstructed or restored.

The Monastery of Our Lady, north of the Domplatz, now houses a collection of medieval wood sculptures and also the national collection of contemporary small-scale sculptures (*Closed* Mon). A wine cellar in the Buttergasse dates from 1200 and was discovered only by chance during rebuilding operations.

In the old market square, which used to be the heart of the old city, there is a baroque town hall and the Eulenspiegel Fountain, a modern tribute to the famous medieval folk hero and prankster Till Eulenspiegel. The baroque composer Georg Philipp Telemann (1671–1767) was born in Magdeburg, and the present-day concert hall bears his name.

Germany's annual international garden and horticultural show was held in Magdeburg in 1999, and the park that was created for the event is being maintained, integrated into the city's urban landscape. The show's centrepiece, an extraordinary leaning tower, deliberately built at a greater angle than Pisa's famous campanile, is being kept as an unusual tourist attraction (*Open* daily).

THE MAGDEBURG HEMISPHERES
A 17th-century experiment by Magdeburg's scientific mayor, the physicist Otto von Guericke (1602–86), who wanted to prove the great strength of atmospheric pressure (the force exerted by the air around us), has ensured that Magdeburg's fame has spread worldwide. Von Guericke put together two metal hemispheres and removed the air from inside them, to form a vacuum. When 16 horses (eight tied to each hemisphere) failed to pull them apart, he conclusively proved his thesis.

►► The Mecklenburgische Seenplatte and Muritz National Park 132B4

The Mecklenburgische Seenplatte (Mecklenburg Lake Plateau) consists of over a thousand lakes. These are a residue from the last Ice Age, when retreating glaciers left great moraines – banks of sand and pebblelike detritus. The moving ice also carved out channels and basins through which the escaping water formed rivulets and waterfalls. Storms carried loose sand into hilly dunes, which, as the climate warmed, became carpeted with woodland to create an undulating landscape patterned with small lakes.

The 311-sq-km Müritz National Park was founded in October 1990 from Germany's largest nature reserve. It extends from Waren to beyond Neustrelitz and from the Müritzsee's eastern shore to the source of the Havel. Sixty-five per cent of the area is forest, 25 per cent moorland, and water, 6 per cent meadow and grazing land, and around 4 per cent is currently under cultivation. About 200 years ago the River Elbe was widened and deepened, causing the water level of the Müritzsee to sink by 2m, so that the low-lying eastern banks of the lake dried out, with consequent changes to the natural flora.

The Müritzsee, or Morcze (small sea) as it was known by the Slavs, is one of 117 lakes in the national park. It is 6m deep and 27km long and is Germany's second-largest lake. Conditions in the lake area can be very severe, particularly during February, when blocks of floating ice are a common occurrence; heavy thunderstorms and impenetrable mist can also be a hazard at other times of the year. Carpets of beautiful white water lilies cover stretches of water in the summer months.

RELICS OF THE PAST
Archaeological remains indicate that the Mecklenburgische Seenplatte was already settled by Mesolithic (Middle Stone Age) times. Neolithic stone graves, pottery and flint axes, Bronze Age jewellery, a Roman import of a richly decorated silver bowl in Iron Age times, and 7th-century evidence of Slavic settlement bear witness to the area's complex history of settlement and resettlement. Among especially attractive townships in the area, many of them of Slav origin, are Neustrelitz, Feldberg, Mirow and Weserberg.

151

NEUBRANDENBURG
This ancient fortified town is on the eastern edge of the lake district. Its Altstadt (Old Town) was largely destroyed in the war, but the 13th-century ramparts survive, with their four quaint brick Gothic gateways, nicely restored. One of these, the Treptower Tor, now houses a local history museum (*Closed* Mon). And tiny half-timbered houses are built into the ramparts at some points – one of them is now a bookshop.

The sculpted doorway of the Monastery of Our Lady, founded in 1015 by Augustinian monks. The cloister is superb

CHEMNITZ AND MARX
This big industrial city and working-class bastion was called Karl-Marx-Stadt by the GDR regime, but has now reverted to its true name. In its main square, the GDR in 1971 placed a titanic 12m-high Soviet-made bust of the bearded Marx himself, with his slogan, 'Workers of the world, unite!'. Attempts to remove this anachronistic monument – one of the few surviving official memorabilia from the Communist era – have foundered on stiff opposition by a left-wing lobby in the local council.

At Meissen's porcelain factory, visitors taking the guided tour can watch skilled craftsmen and women at work

MEISSEN WINE
Vineyards on the banks of the Elbe river around Meissen are among the northernmost in Europe and produce an excellent white wine. In the days of the old East German Communist regime Meissen wine was a rare and coveted drink, served at State banquets and other official occasions. The vineyard output is not high, so the wine is still relatively difficult to find and also quite expensive, but it is well worth hunting out.

The lake boasts 700 varieties of plants and grasses, 800 varieties of butterfly, and countless varieties of insects. It is noted particularly for its orchids, gentians, sundew, and rare grasses, especially in the area known as the Spukloch (the Ghost's Hole). Only Scandinavian Fjallrinder (white unhorned cattle), sheep, and horses are allowed to graze in this particularly vulnerable area. Rare birds such as cranes, white-tailed eagles, and black storks enjoy the strictly protected habitat. The shore woodland consists of alders, birches, oaks, beeches and firs. The wild deer that roam in the forest can at times cause problems by overgrazing.

Despite the emphasis on nature protection, there are plenty of well-marked paths for walkers, riders, and cyclists to enjoy. The lake is used for boating and sailing, though parts of the lake and its shore are restricted to exclude boats so that the breeding of the most vulnerable bird species is not disturbed.

►► Meissen   132C1
Meissen's castle – the Albrechtsburg, which stands on a rock rising above the broad River Elbe – was the birthplace in 1710 of the European porcelain industry, using local china clay deposits. Ever since, the town's name has been closely linked with the finest decorative tableware. The factory, at 9 Talstrasse, offers a demonstration of work (*Open* May–Oct daily; Nov–Apr Tue–Sun), but the main attractions are on and around the **Albrechtsburg►**.

The castle itself (*Closed* Mon) dates back to 929 and is a showpiece of late Gothic architecture. The rooms inside have richly decorated ceilings and vaulting. The neighbouring Dom (cathedral), which shares the triangular hilltop site, is older still, dating from the mid-12th century, though its soaring twin spires, which dominate the whole area, are early 20th century.

Down in the town centre, around the picturesque market square, you'll find numerous medieval town houses and a Renaissance brewery.

About 16km east, standing in pleasant informal parkland, is **Moritzburg Castle►** (*Closed* Mon), an outstandingly well-preserved 16th-century hunting lodge containing a collection of baroque furniture and exhibits on the history of hunting. Two rooms are devoted to the radical artist Käthe Kollwitz, who came here to escape the Nazis in 1944–5.

▶ Mühlhausen   132A2

Mühlhausen's old town is quiet and remarkably well preserved, encircled by town walls that you can still walk
around. They are punctuated by towers and gateways
leading to murky cobbled streets lined with ancient
houses. In the centre are several impressive churches,
including the enormous hall church of St Marien (the second largest in Thuringia, after Erfurt Cathedral), as well
as Renaissance mansions. The part-Gothic town hall has
an attractive inner courtyard and incorporates a 16th-
century church.

The town is associated with Thomas Müntzer, a leader
of the Peasants' Revolt that was organized from here in
1524–5; he was seen by the former East German regime as
an early revolutionary (though Martin Luther warned
against him!). The town has several monuments and
memorials, including one to Müntzer himself in the St
Marien church and one to the Peasants' Revolt in the
Barfüsser Monastery church.

Scholtheim (16km east) has half-timbered houses, a
baroque castle and a Romanesque church.

▶ Nordhausen   132A2

Nordhausen lies on a sloping site above the River Helme
and forms the southern terminus of the narrow-gauge
railway crossing the Harz (the Harzquerbahn), which is
partly operated by steam trains. Dating back over 1,000
years, the town centre is still partly encircled by walls.
The pleasant, irregularly shaped market square is lined
with half-timbered houses and overlooked by the twin
towers of St Basil's parish church, an imposing and spacious late 15th-century Gothic building. A few blocks
away, the modest Dom zum Heiligen Kreuz (Cathedral of
the Holy Cross) dates back to the 13th century, with a
Romanesque crypt and a 14th-century nave lined with
massive octagonal pillars.

Heavy air strikes late in World War II damaged parts of
the centre, but numerous half-timbered houses survive,
notably along the Barfüsser Strasse, at the top of which
stands the Flohburg, a large black-and-white structure
dating back to 1500. The large stone Renaissance town
hall bears a colourful figure of the knight Roland, a long-
established symbol of the town.

To the southeast of Nordhausen (about 20km) lies the
Kyffhäuser Nature Park, an area of modest but very striking wooded hills rising to 477m on the Kulpenberg,
topped with a TV transmitter. The slightly lower
Kyffhäuser (453m) bears a 80m monument to Kaiser
Wilhelm. Legend has it that one of his predecessors,
Friedrich I, dreamed of German unity on this site and
would sleep until the day it came – but there have so far
been no reports of his waking up. On the western edge of
Kyffhäuser, there's bathing at the Kelbra reservoir, and
the ruins of nearby Rothenburg castle lie in a secluded
woodland setting. To the south is the small town of **Bad
Frankenhausen**, which has mineral springs, a spectacularly leaning church (more precarious than the
Leaning Tower of Pisa) and a gigantic **mural▶** completed in 1990 by the Leipzig artist Werner Tübke.
Measuring 123m by 14m, it depicts the decisive battle of
the Peasants' Revolt in 1525.

153

DORA-MITTELBAU
Thousands of slave
labourers assembled V1
and V2 rockets in under-
ground bunkers at the
Dora-Mittelbau concentra-
tion camp outside
Nordhausen during World
War I. Twenty thousand
died or were executed for
not fulfilling work norms,
or for the slightest lapses
in discipline. The camp's
crematorium still stands
and has been made into a
memorial for the Dora-
Mittelbau victims.

RECYCLING
Rostock has found a novel way of recycling the rusty old ships that made up much of the merchant fleet of Communist-run East Germany. One decommissioned 40-year-old freighter has been converted into a youth hostel, with 85 beds. The 'Traditionschiff', tied up in the Rostock harbour suburb of Schmal, has cabins for two or four people, ideal for budget-minded couples or families. Although it's officially a youth hostel, there is no age limit on guests. The over-26s pay an extra few D-marks – in 1999 the cost of a berth in a four-person cabin ranged between DM 27.50 and DM 34, breakfast (and porthole view) included.

WARNEMÜNDE
This old fishing-port-cum-resort near Rostock has much appeal.The huge ex-GDR hotel on its broad sandy beach is not attractive, but at the east end of the promenade there is a lively old quarter of fishermen's cottages, now full of cafés. Fishing boats line the quay and car ferries arrive from Denmark and Poland.

▶▶ Rostock   132B4

The city of Rostock has a long history. Originally a Slavonic coastal fortress, after being sacked in 1161 by King Waldemar of Denmark, it was settled and developed in the 13th century by German merchants and soon became a prosperous port, part of the famous Hanseatic trading league. In 1419 one of the first universities in northern Europe was founded in Rostock, and the city became a centre for learning and culture, though from the 17th century onwards its economic importance declined compared with the rapidly growing rival ports of Hamburg and Kiel.

Sadly, much of the older part of this strategically situated Baltic port was destroyed in World War II – only four of the 22 former ancient city gateways remain, but these include the handsome 54m Kröpeliner Gate, dating from the 13th century. Several of the city's medieval churches have been restored, and there are some attractive gabled merchants' houses.

The city grew rapidly in importance during the postwar years, being developed into a major Eastern-bloc shipbuilding and industrial centre and becoming East Germany's main seaport. The port was particularly significant in terms of trade to and from the former Soviet Union. But this traffic has now almost vanished: the port is in decline, and some shipyards have closed. There are, however, impressive museums of shipbuilding and shipping, and a large zoological garden and botanic gardens (*Open* daily).

Excursions
Rostock is a conveniently situated base from which to visit a number of small but attractive seaside resorts along the Baltic coast. It's worth making the trip to the graceful old spa town of **Bad Doberan**, with its celebrated 14th-century Cistercian monastery, if only to take the narrow-gauge steam railway with the charming nickname of 'Molli'. This links Bad Doberan with **Ostseebad Heiligendamm**, Germany's oldest Baltic seaside resort, founded in 1793. It is celebrated for its charming period cottages, which resulted in it being known as 'the white town by the sea'. There is a lovely neo-classical spa building, or Kurhaus, in the centre of town, and nearby is the Conventer Lake Nature Reserve, a wildlife sanctuary.

Kühlungsborn, also linked to Bad Doberan by 'Molli', is a far newer seaside resort, developed from three villages which fused during the 1930s. As well as a heated seawater bathing pool, the town has a 4km sandy beach. Notable features are an early Gothic church with a wooden tower, and a 19th-century windmill.

▶▶ Rudolstadt   132A1

Rudolstadt nestles in the valley of the River Saale, on the eastern fringes of the Thüringian Forest. Its wide, pleasant main square, flanked on one side by an imposing medieval town hall and clock tower, is bypassed by the traffic that thunders through this town; from here it's a short, steep climb up to Schloss Heidecksburg, a graceful baroque hilltop palace ranged around three sides of a courtyard. It houses collections of furniture, painting and weapons, and hosts baroque music concerts in summer.

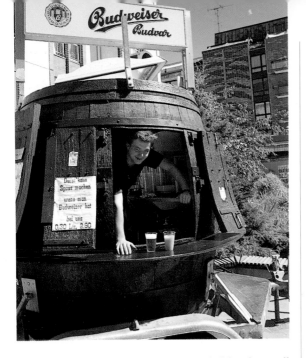

PRIVATISED HOTELS

In the old GDR, the state-run hotels were decent but dreary. New small privately run hotels of character, like those in the west, are now at last emerging in tourist areas such as Sächsische Schweiz. Many of them offer good Saxon cooking and a really friendly atmosphere. In the cities, the former giant state-run hotels have mostly been taken over by western chains such as Hilton and Maritim. In Dresden, one 18th-century baroque mansion is now a small luxury hotel. Another, medium price, is run by the Lutheran churches. There are several of these church-run hotels in eastern Germany, and they invariably offer excellent value for money.

Further cultural attractions are provided by the small Thüringian Landestheatre (provincial theatre), which was founded by Goethe, a frequent visitor to the town (as was Schiller, who met his wife, Charlotte, here).

Across the river from the castle and historic centre is the Thüringian Farm Museum (Volkskundemuseum), where two fine half-timbered farmhouses stand in an attractive parkland setting.

Excursions

About 8km to the northeast of Rudolstadt lies **Kochberg (Grosskochberg)** which has a castle owned by the von Stein family, whom Goethe often visited. Many of its rooms have been restored to what they were in Goethe's time. **Paulinzella** (23km west) has romantic 12th-century monastic ruins in a wooded setting.

▶ Sächsische Schweiz

Some of Germany's most dramatic scenery lies only a short way upstream along the Elbe, between the outskirts of Dresden and Czech border. Called the Saxon Switzerland National Park, it is also known as the Elbe Sandstone District.

High sandstone cliffs and crags form a deep gorge through which the River Elbe flows. They have been exposed, weathered and worn over millennia by frost, wind and rain into a series of fantastic sculptured shapes – pillars, towers, arches, and stacks towering nearly 300 m above the river. In places they are exposed as bleak, bare crags, a kind of Central European Grand Canyon. In other parts trees and shrubs twist out of cracks, cling to crevices, crowd onto summits and form the kind of fantastic landscape that inspired such painters as the great 19th-century Romantic Caspar David Friedrich. Ancient woodlands – pine, beech, oak, maple, fir – flourish

Eastern Germany

NAPOLEON'S DOWNFALL
The Festung Königstein, one of Germany's largest and most impressive fortresses, played a major role in the ultimate downfall of Napoleon. In an heroic defensive action in August 1813, 14,000 German and Russian troops garrisoned in the fortress turned back an offensive by 40,000 soldiers of Napoleon's elite Garde Française. The French were trying to block a retreat to Bohemia by Austrian forces after their defeat in the Battle of Dresden. The holding action by the German and Russian forces saved the Austrians from total decimation and strengthened the military alliance that was later to defeat Napoleon at Waterloo.

Schwerin lies on a lake that stretches to the gardens of its great castle

around and between the craggy rocks, forming a dense green backdrop to the sculptured formations.

Between the crags wind deep, narrow gorges, some of them barely a couple of metres wide, cool and shady on even the hottest summer day. Many of them are penetrated by winding footpaths that suddenly emerge into full daylight at thrilling viewpoints. Narrow tributary valleys of the Elbe, especially the Polenz, the Sebnitz, and the Kirnitz, also create dramatic features within this unique area of natural beauty.

At **Bastei▶** (road access and parking lot), a footbridge was built from stone in the 1850s, 194m above the Elbe, creating a remarkable viewpoint. It is linked to a series of pedestrian walkways across the crag summits, all with safety rails.

Across the river at Königstein, a massive crag has been used as the base of a great medieval fortress dating back to the 14th century. The Festung Königstein was strategically placed to defend the valley. Later the fortress played a major role in the ultimate downfall of Napoleon at Waterloo (see panel).

Although the area is now strictly protected as a national park and nature reserve, access is easy from Dresden by road along the B172 and by rail, either the local service or the Prague-bound express.

A series of ferries cross the river to such small riverside resorts as Stadt Wehlen, Kurort Rathen, Schmilka, and Bad Schandau. In the summer months, the Weisse Flotte boat services operate a regular passenger service along the river from Dresden.

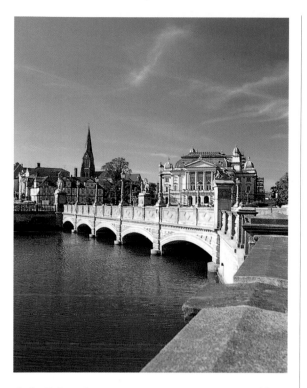

Across a bridge from the castle, Schwerin's state theatre lies in an old town that is now gracefully restored

WISMAR AND GÜSTROW
The old Hanseatic seaport of Wismar belonged to Sweden from 1648 to 1803 and retains traces of that influence. The finest of the old buildings around the market square is the 14th-century Alter Schwede (Old Swede), with a striking stepped-gable façade. To the east lies the ornate Gothic cathedral. In Güstrow there is a superb Renaissance palace.

►► Schwerin   *132A4*

The old city of Schwerin in Mecklenburg has some lovely half-timbered houses in its centre, and an imposing cathedral, founded in 1171. The town hall in the market square has a medieval core, though with a neo-Gothic façade of 1835. The early 18th-century Nikolaikirche, also called the Schelfkirche, is the finest of Mecklenburg's baroque churches. The imposing Kollegiengebäude in Schloss Strasse is the administrative headquarters of the state government. Boat trips operate from the town centre across the Schweriner See to Zippendorf, where the 138m television tower provides splendid panoramic views of lake, city, and countryside.

Schwerin's spectacularly beautiful **castle►** is set on an island, joined to the mainland by twin bridges. Reminiscent of a Loire château, it was built for the Dukes of Mecklenburg in the 1840s in a mix of mock-Gothic and mock-Renaissance styles, one of the architects being Gottfried Semper, who designed Dresden's Semper Opera House. The castle now houses the Mecklenburg-Vorpommern State Parliament. You can visit the restored throne room and other dark-panelled state rooms (*Closed* Mon). In the north wing there is a beautiful church. To the south of the castle are baroque pleasure gardens, with canals, groves, and paths in formal geometric patterning. To the northwest, in the former castle garden, is the state theatre and the art gallery, which has a collection of important Dutch and Flemish masters (*Closed* Mon). Muess, near Schwerin, has a Freilichtmuseum in the form of a reconstructed village.

Eastern Germany

158

▶ ▶ ▶ The Spreewald   *132C2*

The River Spree southeast of Berlin, between Berlin and
Cottbus, flows through an area of low-lying countryside,
splitting into countless minor tributaries and creating the
complex area of lakes, ponds, marsh, wetland and river-
ine woodland known as the Spreewald. There are also
areas of low-lying farmland that is drained by a network
of small canals and dikes.

This area has a unique beauty, due to the effects of light
both in early spring, when the birch trees lining its water
channels are reflected in the water, and again in late
summer and fall, when the luxurious vegetation and
vivid colours turn the shortest excursion into an adventure. Much of the area is now a Biosphere Reserve,
reflecting both the natural beauty and wildlife interest of
the area and its rich cultural associations, particularly
with the Sorbian settlements in the area. Ortenburg, a
castle in the 1,000-year-old town of Bautzen, is said to be
the place where the Sorbs tribal fortress used to stand.

Today Bautzen, with its baroque- and Renaissance-style
buildings, is the centre of Sorbian culture and tradition,
and the seat of the Sorbian national organization,
the Domowina.

The region is divided into the **Unterspreewald**, north of
Lübben, and the larger and better-known **Oberspreewald**,
north of Lübbenau. The whole of the Spreewald teems
with game, such as wild boar, deer, partridges and pheas-
ants. Here, too, are white storks and herons in abundance.

The area also had its own highly characteristic form of
local transportation – narrow barges or punts that carry
both people and goods along the myriad channels
between villages and outlying farms in the forest. A
favourite summer activity for visitors is to be punted

THE SORBS
The Sorbs are a Slavic
people who have kept
their own language and
culture in two regions of
Germany: in Lower
Lusatia, around the
Spreewald, and in Upper
Lusatia, in the southeast
of Saxony east of
Dresden. Signposts and
official notices in both
areas are in two
languages – German and
Sorbian – and Catholic
churches use the Sorbian
language in their liturgy.
There is also a Sorbian
publishing house, a regu-
lar newspaper, a school
and a Sorbian-German
folk theatre. Many
Sorbian customs are pre-
served, such as Easter
Riding, a mixture of the
pagan and the Christian.
During Lent young people
go from house to house
playing bagpipes and fid-
dles, asking for eggs and
bacon, and money. Straw
brooms are burned like
the witches of old, and
Easter eggs are decorated
with beautiful, intricate
designs. Sorbian national
costume is extremely
colourful with intricate
embroidery, now generally
worn only for festivals
and holidays.

along canals, canalised rivers and streams, though motors have replaced muscle power in most instances.

The Lower Spreewald, around the Lübben area, is a large enclosed forest region with alder, birch, and beech interspersed with areas of open, low-lying meadowland and water meadows. This provides an ideal habitat for numerous plants and animals, and biotopes for amphibians, water-loving insects, rare dragonflies, kingfishers, and cranes.

The attractive Sorbian township of **Lübben**, which was founded in 1150, has a history going back as far as mid-Stone Age times. Its castle, with richly decorated rooms, was built in the latter stages of the Renaissance and later became the seat and capital of the Lower Lusatian government. The town is the gateway to both the Upper and Lower areas of the Spreewald, with motorised punt services into the forest. From **Lübbenau**, a small tourist resort, there are splendid walks into the Oberspreewald along well-signposted paths over old canal-side dykes that go deep into the forest. In nearby **Lehde**, a fascinating open-air museum has traditional Sorbian farmhouses with their own distinctive waterside architecture – a kind of miniature Venice in the forest. In the summer months motorised barges link Lübbenau with Lehde. The soil for the pleasure grounds of Lübbenau's early 19th-century castle was brought by barge. Inside, look out for the old locomotive and carriage of the narrow-gauge train the Spreewaldguste, which ran for the last time in 1970.

The historic town of **Burg** is the eastern gateway of the Oberspreewald. There is another Biosphere Reserve here, of eels, pike, and flounder in abundance, woodruff (used to colour the Berlin Weissbier bright green) also flourishes. Labyrinths of water channels are crossed by high wooden bridges, at least 300 of them around the town of Burg and its satellite parishes alone. Water lilies bloom along quieter stretches of water and the whole area, with several nature reserves, is a naturalist's paradise. The town of **Cottbus**, near the Polish border, has a fine altarpiece of Jonah and the Whale in the Oberkirche.

Above and left: a favourite summer outing for Berliners is punting along the Spreewald canals

159

SPREEWALD PRODUCE
Market gardens in the area provide produce for nearby Berlin, Spreewald pickles being a much-prized delicacy. Plant extracts are also produced, and these are used in a variety of homeopathic remedies.

Eastern Germany

MARITIME GLORY
The sleepy little Baltic port of Barth was a busy ship-building centre just over a century ago, rivalling Rostock and even the North Sea cities of Bremen and Bremerhaven. In 1877, according to local records, Barth had no less than four shipbuilding yards and 18 shipping companies. Nearly 200 merchant sailing ships were registered in Barth. But then came the age of steam, and Barth was badly equipped to keep pace with the rapid changes. Today, only a museum (*Closed* Mon) reminds visitors of its short-lived maritime glory.

Stralsund is nearly completely surrounded by water and is an ideal centre from which to explore the Baltic coast

►► Stralsund   *132B4*

Stralsund occupies a defensive position on a small hillock between the Strelasund, the narrow strait that divides the Isle of Rügen from the mainland, and two attractive small lakes, the Knieper- and Frankenteichs.

Like Rostock, this was a Hanseatic town, but between 1648 and 1815 it became part of Sweden before being reclaimed by Prussia. The old town and small harbour boast particularly fine architecture, including impressive merchants' houses. There is a remarkable reddish-brick town hall in the Alt Markt dating from the 13th century, with a high elegant façade. The Marienkirche dates from 1298, and two surviving towers are both 15th century in origin. The town centre has an attractive pedestrianized market area, and scheduled passenger boats from the harbour link the mainland with the island of Hiddensee and with the Darss peninsula. The rail and road bridge linking Stralsund with the Isle of Rügen was built only in 1936.

Stralsund is a good base from which to explore the **Vorpommersche Boddenlandschaft National Park** – a national park consisting of a long, mainly wooded coastline along the Baltic, close to such small fishing villages and quiet seaside resorts as **Pramont**, **Prerow**, **Zingst**, and **Wiek**. This is an area of sand dunes, winding sandbanks, mudflats, and shallow seas, rich in birdlife, including many waders and coastal birds, and for that reason strictly protected. The area is a sanctuary for thousands of migratory birds, including some of the largest colonies of marine birds in northern Europe. The coast itself is famous for its ancient coastal woodlands, including rare shrubs and grasses.

Rügen► The whole of the Isle of Rügen is worth exploring. Putbus is a sleepy little inland resort deliberately planned by a local prince early last century to be like an English spa town, with elegant houses around a green 'circus' in the style of Bath. There is a fine neo-classical theatre, while the former Kurhaus in 'English' parkland is

ALONG THE COAST

There are fine stretches of virtually tideless beach with clean sand around the small Stralsund resorts. There are many attractive thatched cottages and farmhouses along the Darss peninsula and in many of the villages, that give the area an 'English feel', though the style is markedly different. The coastal road from Stralsund via Barth to Ribnitz Damgarten is a particularly attractive drive (there is also a bus service from Barth station). It follows the narrow peninsula between Darss and Fischland, the peninsula encloses areas of quiet inland sea and saltwater marsh known as Bodden, with their spectacular birdlife. There are well-signposted cycle paths and walkways along the coast, especially along the raised defensive embankments, partially enclosed by woodland.

the parish church. A narrow-gauge steam railway, known as 'Rasender Roland' (Rushing Roland), links Putbus with the seaside resort of Göhren. It puffs its way through an idyllic landscape of old meadows, scattered woodlands, small lakes, and storks' nests to the seaside resorts of Binz and Göhren, with their fine sandy beaches.

The narrow peninsula to the south, which is known as **Mönchgut**, is protected as a Biosphere Reserve and is safeguarded as much for its cultural qualities as for its landscape. There are old farmhouses and thatched fishermen's cottages, ancient meadows crowded with brilliant wildflowers, many of them rare, and low coastal cliffs and pebbly beaches overlooking a distant coastline stretching to Usedom and the Polish border. In the little museum in Göhren you'll find some examples of 19th-century Staffordshire ware, traded and brought back from England by sailors.

Sassnitz is an old port and ferry terminal on Rügen, where train and car ferries leave for Trelleborg in Sweden. Originally it was a small fishing port and quarry town, but it later became a holiday resort, and there are still some handsome 19th-century villas to be seen around the older part of the town. Immediately to the north of Sassnitz lies Jasmund National Park, which has some of the most impressive coastal scenery in Germany. High chalk cliffs crowned by dense beechwoods overlook the quiet Baltic Sea.

Though thousands of tourists crowd the Kaiserstuhl, a tall chalk cliff and impressive viewpoint, a few hundred yards away along the coastal path all is quiet, with impressive views. At Wissower Klinken, weather-carved chalk cliffs provide a dramatic feature that became the subject of one of the most famous of Caspar David Friedrich's Romantic paintings. The beechwoods, as well as the meadows and the heathland, provide a habitat for a rich flora, especially orchids. Fauna include small reptiles and rare butterflies.

►► Thüringer Wald (Thüringian Forest)   *132A1*

The Thüringer Wald covers an area of ancient hills stretching for about 100km southeastwards from Eisenach, and averaging about 30km wide. By German standards, the hills are not especially high – the highest point is the Grosser Beerberg at 982m – but the area is crossed by numerous narrow valleys and is quite densely settled with old-fashioned villages and small industrial towns. The area is heavily forested, as its name implies, mostly with fir and beech trees, but the woodlands are interspersed with meadows and orchards, and there's plenty of variety from one square kilometre to the next.

Because of its small scale and varied scenery, the Thüringer Wald is excellent walking country, and has long been popular for quiet country vacations and excursions, as well as for cross-country skiing in winter. A long-distance path – the Rennsteig – runs southeastwards from the Wartburg for 160km within the Thüringer Wald. Even for those not inclined to tackle its full length, it offers lots of opportunities to get into the countryside. Like many of the shorter paths that crisscross the area, it's well marked ('R' symbols on trees and signposts) and easy to follow.

Today the Thüringer Wald offers a reasonably good variety of accommodations. Proximity to western Germany has encouraged many local people to try their hand at catering for tourists, and you'll find plenty of

MODERN TROUBLES
Despite the Thüringer Wald's many charms, it also has its sad side. Emissions from nearby open-cast brown-coal mines have caused dreadful air pollution in many parts, and a survey in 1989 showed that more than half the trees were affected. A massive post-reunification clean-up programme has slowed down the rate at which trees are falling prey to pollution, but it's still a worrying problem as Germany enters the 21st century. It's not an exclusively east German problem, either – surveys of pine forests in southern Germany have produced alarming results, but here the major cause points to heavy motor traffic.

MEININGEN'S THEATRE
This little town in southern Thüringia is the home of one of Germany's grandest theatres, built in 1908 in the style of a Greek temple. Meiningen was the capital of a duchy in 1680–1918, and Duke Georg II, married to a famous actress, created its theatre. The theatre flourishes under a dynamic manager and draws top Euopean companies and orchestras that play to packed audiences from the larger nearby towns.

small pensions and *Zimmer frei* (rooms to let) signs even in the villages, together with family-run restaurants and bars. There's plenty of Thüringer bratwurst to go around, often purchased from roadside barbecues. Thüringia has many of its own folk songs and folk dances. These were discouraged under the centralised GDR regime, but are now being revived.

What to see The best of the forest scenery in the Thüringer Wald lies along a line fairly close to the Rennsteig, and you will have to come off the main roads to see it – see page 165 for a suggested route.

Of the smaller places towards the centre of the forest, it's worth making for **Schmalkalden** for its fine half-timbered houses grouped around an imposing irregular market square. Nearby Schloss Wilhelmsburg dates back to the 1580s and is one of Thüringia's most important Renaissance buildings. **Bad Liebenstein** has dignified spa buildings lining its leafy avenues and there are extensive views from the ruins of medieval Liebenstein castle, while nearby 18th-century Schloss Altenstein is set in an English-style park. **Wasungen**, set in the wooded Upper Werra Valley, has numerous half-timbered buildings (including a fine three-storey town hall dating from 1533) in its specially protected town centre. **Friedrichroda** (see also page 144) is a relaxed forest resort with parks, an open-air swimming pool, a lake and a large early

163

In the Thüringer Wald, the well-tended villages have red roofs and grey slate façades. In some parts there is skiing

Tanks used to patrol the Thüringer Wald, so close to the old border with West Germany

19th-century castle, Reihhardsbrunn, which was once reserved for high party officials and is now a hotel. The nearby Marienglashöhle caves (*Open* daily) have unusual gypsum crystal formations.

Oberhof is an important local winter-sports centre, dominated by the strikingly modern Hotel Panorama, built in the form of two ski jumps. A botanical garden, the Rennsteig Garten, contains 1,500 specimens collected from all over the world including many rare alpine plants (*Open* late Apr to Nov).

A number of larger towns of historical and architectural interest ring the edge of the main forest area. **Suhl** was the capital of the whole region when this was part of the GDR, and gained high-rises and an egg-box-style shopping precinct. Famous since medieval times as a home of gun making, the town also has a weapons museum (*Open* Tue to Sun) in the 17th-century malthouse building. The nearby old main street, the Steinweg, has been pedestrianised and has several fine 18th-century houses.

Ilmenau, a glass- and porcelain-making town, was a favourite retreat of Goethe's and has several places associated with him: the Amtshaus (official's house), the Gabelbach hunting lodge, and the Goethe hut and Kickelhahn – all linked by a footpath called Auf Goethes Spuren (in Goethe's footsteps).

Arnstadt gave J S Bach his first job as an organist, in the baroque church that now bears his name and a jaunty statue of the great man watches over the small market square of this very well preserved small town. The baroque Neues Palais has a remarkable collection of 400 dolls made locally in the 18th century. The surrounding landscape of lush, gentle hills is exceptionally pretty and is known for its botanical rarities, including German gentians. Lauscha, to the south, has long been a glassblowing centre, invented Christmas tree decorations in 1848 and still produces them.

Thüringer Wald

This 187km tour starts from Eisenach.

Travel out of Eisenach for 12km on the B19 Meiningen road, turn left at Etterwinden on an unmarked road to Ruhla and Brotterode. Here, turn left towards Tabarz. After 4km there is a parking lot on the right, and then climb the Grosser Inselberg (approximately half an hour each way, on an easy path) for the mountaintop café and a great view.

Continue to Tabarz, then right on the B88 road to Friedrichroda; leave by a minor road to Schmalkalden, then take minor roads to Steinbach-Hallenberg and Oberhof.

Turn right onto the B247; drive a kilometre south, then turn left on a minor road. This follows the Rennsteig and passes the Grosser Beerberg.

Continue to the main B4 road, turn left and return through Ilmenau and Arnstadt, to take the E40 highway back to Eisenach.

CITY OF CULTURE
Weimar was Europe's 'City of Culture' in 1999, and the year was celebrated with the reopening of a major German art gallery, the Neues Museum (New Museum). This imposing neo-Renaissance city palace, built in 1868, was plundered by the Nazis, who banished most of its modern works. It was then left to decay by the East German Communists. A West German gallery owner, Paul Maenz, breathed fresh life into the historic building by donating much of his private collection. Among the treasures of modern art, all dating from 1960, are works by the American minimalists Dan Flavin, Donald Judd, Carl Andre and Sol Lewitt. (*Closed* Mon *Admission charge.*)

The rich wheat fields of Vogtland. Many state collective farms are now becoming cooperatives

▶ Vogland

132B1

This hilly region of forests, steep-sided valleys, isolated rocks, lakes and dams extends along the southern frontier of the former GDR, to the Erzgebirge on the Czech border (see page 142). The area is dotted with small industrial towns – some of which are famous for making musical instruments – and with modest spas based on mineral-rich springs. The area's relaxed character and varied scenery make it a good choice for simple, open-air pursuits, notably walking on the many well-marked paths. There's some sailing on the lakes and reservoirs, too.

Some of the best scenery is around **Klingenthal**, a straggling semi-industrial village situated right up against the Czech frontier and famous for its manufacture of harmonicas. Five kilometres to the north of Klingenthal lies **Schneckenstein**, the only place in Europe where topaz can be found – there are still some isolated rock formations in the area.

Schoeneck, 12km northwest, marks the southern end of the dramatic, deeply cut valley of the Steinicht River. About 20km north of the town, around Schnarrtanne and Beerheide, you'll find some of the Vogtland's prettiest woodland scenery.

The biggest of the reservoirs is **Stausee Poehl**, near the region's main town, Plauen, but there are many attractive small lakes in the area stretching south from here to Markneukirchen and Bad Elster.

Markneukirchen, Germany's leading musical instrument producing town since the early 19th century, has a small baroque castle, the Paulusschloessel. A collection of 1,000 musical instruments is housed in the Musikinstrumentenmuseum, Biensgarten 2 (*Closed* Mon).

Bad Elster, in a quiet wooded valley off the main road, has spa buildings dating from the mid-19th century. At **Landwuest**, 6km to the east, there's a small open-air folk museum with farm implements and local history collections (*Closed* Mon). It is easy to make day excursions to the famous Czech spa towns of Karlovy Vary and Mariánské Lázn.

►►► Weimar   132A1

Although only a modest-sized town, Weimar is one of
Germany's greatest cultural treasures. With public buildings, parks, squares and boulevards, it feels like a small
capital city – which indeed it was, of Sachsen-Weimar
from 1547 to 1870. Following a meeting of the German
parliament in the city in 1919, it gave its name to the ill-
fated democratic republic that preceded the Hitler years,
and was capital of Thüringia from 1919 to 1949. The city
was lucky enough to be spared wartime destruction, and
for 40 years after World War II it escaped the effects of
mass international tourism. Now it is catching up fast,
and has acquired a Hilton hotel and a wide choice of bars
and restaurants. Many of the fine buildings have been
expensively restored.

Weimar's catalogue of cultural connections is almost
endless: Goethe spent most of his working life here, and
his influence on the life of the city was immense; the writers Friedrich von Schiller and Johann Gottfried von
Herder lived here; musical residents included Franz Liszt
and Richard Strauss; the writer Nietzsche spent his final
years here (his house contains a small museum); in the
20th century, Walter Gropius founded the Bauhaus
movement here.

*Weimar: the
Wittumspalais (top)
and a flower stall in
the market (above)*

There are lots of sights, many associated with Weimar's
famous residents. Despite the tourist crowds (particularly
in summer), it can be a relaxing city, helped by its man-
ageable size, neat squares, outdoor cafés, and above all by
the huge park that extends along the River Ilm almost to
the town centre.

The **Goethehaus►►** on the Frauenplan (*Closed* Mon)
will be at the top of most people's lists. This combines
Goethe's own family house – still complete with his
study, books, furniture and collections of coins, minerals
and art – with an imposing museum explaining the
writer's life and influence (most explanations in German

Map of WEIMAR with scale:
```
0    200    400    600 metres
0    200    400    600 yards
```

168

BUCHENWALD CAMP

On a hill near Weimar lies the largest Nazi concentration camp on German soil: 56,000 died here, many from torture or starvation. A memorial and museum (*Closed* Mon) movingly give the details. The number 6 bus runs from Weimar to the camp site. The GDR regime firmly put the accent on the sufferings of the German Communist and Russian prisoners, and ignored the Jews. This shocking bias has now been corrected, and there is a new Jewish memorial – also a new museum about the cruel Soviet prison camp on the site in 1945–9, where 7,000 died.

only). There's a charming small garden at the back. A few hundred metres away, in the Ilm Park, you can also visit **Goethe's Gartenhaus►** (*Closed* Tue), an idyllic rural retreat in which he lived for six years.

The renovated **Schillerhaus►** (*Closed* Tue), on Schillerstrasse, was lived in by Schiller for the last three years of his life and incorporates many of his and his family's possessions and a modern museum annex documents his work.

The **Liszthaus►** (*Closed* Mon), by the west entrance to the Ilm Park, was used by the composer as a summer residence for 17 years and sets out his living and working quarters with many of his possessions, documents, pictures and other mementos.

Of the city's many palaces and castles, the **Wittumspalais** stands on the Theatreplatz, immediately opposite the National Theatre, with its famous double statue of Goethe and Schiller holding hands. The small baroque palace (*Closed* Mon) was built for Duchess Anna Amalia in the 1770s when the main city palace burned down. It has been furnished in baroque style and has the atmosphere of a typical prosperous town house of the period. One room – the Tafelrundenzimmer (round-table room) – was a popular meeting point for artists who were friendly with the court. In one wing of the palace there's a museum commemorating another famous Weimar resident, the writer Herder. Beside the palace is a small new museum (*Closed* Mon) devoted to the Bauhaus.

The main **Weimar Castle** (*Closed* Mon), rebuilt in 1803, is an inspiring neo-baroque structure overlooking the Sternbrücke (Star Bridge) and River Ilm. It houses a collection of local paintings and fine arts.

The nearby **Herzogin Anna Amalia Bibliothek** (*Open* Apr–Oct daily. *Closed* Nov–Mar) houses the 900,000 volumes of the Library of the German Classics, many of which are extremely ancient. The best pieces are kept in the large Rococo Room, which is decorated with busts of Weimar's literary giants.

Out of Town It is a very pleasant 20-minute walk along the River Ilm to the south of the town, passing through a large relaxed park, to the '**Roman House**' (*Closed* Tue). This classical pavilion, which was built in the 1790s, enjoys a beautiful setting overlooking the river and inside there's a collection of local works of art.

A further 5km out of town in the same direction brings you to **Schloss Belvedere** (*Closed* Mon and Nov–Mar), a modest but charming country retreat and hunting lodge that was built in the 1730s. It is flanked by two delightful single-storey pavilions. The surrounding park was landscaped in the early 19th century, when it acquired a large exotic-plant collection that is kept in the Orangery and neighbouring greenhouses.

About 5km northeast of the town of Weimar, **Schloss Tiefurt** (*Closed* Mon), built in 1760, became a major cultural centre in the late 18th century. The castle contains interesting displays of furniture, busts, porcelain and a collection of paintings and fine arts of the period, and stands in a finely landscaped park stretching down towards the banks of the River Ilm.

GOETHE'S TOMB

In 1999 some reporters discovered that 30 years ago East Germany Communist Party officials and forensic experts secretly opened up Goethe's tomb in Weimar and had the remains 'cleaned up'. They went about the task with typical thoroughness, cleaning out the skull (in which they found just dust), reducing the remains to a clean skeleton and measuring the corpse. Goethe was not as large as some statues of him suggest – he was a mere 1.67m tall. The results of the examination and post-mortem can be seen (on prior request) in the National Museum in Weimar.

169

The Duchess Anna Amalia lived in this small yellow baroque palace (above) after the death of her husband in 1767. Here she held intellectual salons that were attended by, among others, Goethe, Schiller, Herder and Wieland

OLD AND NEW ALLIES
In 1346 a group of six towns from the Oberlausitz (Bautzen, Görlitz, Lobau, Laubau, Kamenz, and Zittau), with imperial permission. banded together. Their aim was to further the development of cloth making and linen weaving and to protect each other against attacks from robber knights and their followers. In the 1990s, following German reunification, the towns reconstituted this union as an aid to economic survival, an interesting example of history partly repeating itself.

▶▶ **Wernigerode**   *132A2*

Wernigerode, strategically situated on the northern fringe of the Harz Mountains, is famed for its richly coloured half-timbered houses and its elaborately carved, twin-spired, late Gothic town hall. Wernigerode was granted its town charter in 1229 and in 1449 became the seat of the powerful counts of Stolberg, and a prosperous trading centre. Its decline in later years perhaps helped to keep its medieval character. Inevitably the town suffered a number of fires in earlier periods, but miraculously its town hall, most of its charming streets and part of its defensive walls (with impressive gates) were spared. In the 18th century a number of baroque buildings were added.

Overlooking the town, Wernigerode's castle, which was largely rebuilt in the mid-19th century, stands on the site of a much older fortress that dates from 1121. It is rapidly being rediscovered as a tourist centre for the Harz, and there are several rebuilt and restored hotels. The town lies at the northern terminus of the Harzquerbahn narrow-gauge steam railway to Nordhausen, close to superb walking country.

It's worth traveling just 50km east of Wernigerode to **Quedlinburg**▶ (see also page 123), which has been designated a UNESCO World Heritage Site because of its astonishing wealth of half-timbered houses along narrow streets and courtyards, with groups dating from the late Gothic (15th century) period onwards. One example, in Wordgasse, dating from the first half of the 14th century, is the oldest house in central Germany. With its narrow windows and uneven floors, it has been beautifully restored as a museum.

The castle, which was built between the 16th and 17th centuries, also houses a museum. The Renaissance Town Hall, with a statue of Roland dating from 1426 symbolising citizens' rights, overlooks a handsome pedestrianised square fringed by old inns, cafés and attractive shops.

The countryside surrounding Wittenberg

▶ **Wittenberg**   *132B2*

'Lutherstadt' Wittenberg is forever associated with Martin Luther, the great Protestant reformer, and his criticism of contemporary clergy and particularly of the sale of indulgences or pardons. As was then customary, in 1517 his 95 theses were nailed up on the town's church door. His ideas gained further prominence at Wittenberg's university, which was founded in 1502, then spread throughout the whole of Europe. Luther's house is a museum (*Open* Apr–Sep daily, Oct–Mar Tue–Sun), and on the site of Luther's Oak, in front of which a Papal Bull condemning

THE BEER PUDDLE
Zittau's relationship with its neighbours wasn't always peaceful. In the 15th century the town went to war over beer when townsmen of nearby Görlitz spilled several barrels of Zittau's celebrated beer at a place still known as the Beer Puddle.

The Stadtkirche of St Mary in Wittenberg, where Martin Luther often preached

him was burned, a (later) oak tree stands. Close by is the Lutherhalle, the world's largest collection of exhibited material devoted to the Reformation. Local contemporaries of Luther included court painter Lucas Cranach the Elder and theologian Philipp Melanchthon, whose 16th-century dwelling is also a museum.

▶ Zittau   *132C1*

Zittau lies in the extreme southeast of Germany in the area known as Dreiländereck, where lakes and heather predominate. The town dates from the 13th century, when it became an important trade centre under the protection of the Bohemian kings.

The town's former fortifications have now been replaced with green spaces and a flower clock, which in winter is decorated with moss, pinecones and branches instead of flowering plants. The town has a market square with a Mars fountain dating from 1585 and an Italian-style town hall. The Marstall (stables) of 1511 dominates the Salzmarkt and the Dornsprachhaus is a lovely Renaissance building. The church of St Petri and St Pauli was originally an old Franciscan monastery church; the buildings now house the town's museum.

The 12km Zittauer narrow-gauge steam railway, was opened in 1890 to the spa towns of Oybin and Jonsdorf, It passes through beautiful rocky landscape in the Zittau Mountains – an area which is a paradise for walkers and climbers. Oybin has a medieval castle, churches and monastery ruins. Jonsdorf is a former weavers' village, and has fine examples of the typical Oberlausitz Umbindehaus, a characteristic style of vernacular architecture with wooden arches over the house front to support the weight of looms.

THE SACRED CLOTH
The citizens of Zittau were horrified to find that a centuries-old sacred cloth from their local church was being used by soldiers in a nearby Red Army garrison as a tent. The cloth – a *Fastentuch*, hung before the altar at Lent – had been missing for more that 200 years. Before the town could recover the cloth from the Red Army it disappeared again and was given up for lost when the Soviet Union disintegrated and pulled its troops out of East Germany. However, the cloth resurfaced in Switzerland and is now back in Zittau's Kreuzkirche (Church of the Holy Cross), where it can be viewed daily except Monday. The cloth, dating from 1542, measures 8m by 4m and is decorated with 90 paintings of biblical scenes.

SOUTHWEST GERMANY

172 F

The southwest is an appealing region for gentle rural exploration, with plenty of peace and quiet, charming countryside, deep forests, wooden farmhouses and smart spas. This is good walking country, and sports facilities are plentiful. A wide range of accommodation exists, offering higher standards than in other regions.

The region incorporates **Baden-Württemberg**, one of the youngest of the German *Länder* – it was formed only in 1952 and still has two distinct sides to its character.

The people of Baden, predominantly Catholic, are known for their friendly and relaxed dispositions, as opposed to their neighbours in Württemberg (or Swabia), who take life more seriously and are reputed to be careful how and when they spend their money. Other Germans call them *Häuslebauer* (House builders), believing them to spend most of their time and money on bourgeois home-tied pursuits.

The southwest is dominated by several upland masses, principally the **Schwarzwald** (Black Forest), which rises to over 1200m. The **Danube** rises in the Schwarzwald and follows a course east, forming a deep gorge as it approaches the **Schwäbische Alb** (Swabian Jura), a less elevated and far less well known area of limestone ridges with cliff-top castles, half-timbered villages and many gushing waterfalls.

The Rhine defines the western border with France. Germany's largest lake, the **Bodensee**, shared with Austria and Switzerland (and also known by its other name, Lake Constance), is like an inland sea and has a string of pretty resorts on its shores.

Another river, the **Neckar**, is Swabia's main waterway. Flowing through a country of vineyards and fruit trees in its upper course, and through wooded valleys in its lower course, it passes through the lovely university towns of **Tübingen** and **Heidelberg**.

More commercial and industrial centres, such as **Stuttgart**, **Mannheim** and **Karlsruhe**, constitute the modern face of Baden-Württemberg. The region's charms are well known – Heidelberg and the main resorts of the Black Forest and Bodensee are the principal draws.

►►Baden-Baden   172A3

Stylish in its woodland setting on the edge of the Upper Rhine plain, Baden-Baden draws visitors from all over the world to its renowned spa and its casino, Germany's oldest. Its position in the lush valley of the River Oos, on the western slopes of the northern part of the Black Forest, adds much to its attraction.Though its heyday may be over, it remains a handsome place, with elegant 19th-century hotels, a Jugendstil (art-nouveau) Trinkhalle (drink hall) where you can test the saline waters, a white neoclassical **Kurhaus►** (spa building) and a long park that looks as expensively groomed as most of the visitors.

Baden-Baden's mild climate makes it a pleasant place to visit all year round, but it is best known for its thermal springs, Europe's hottest, which gush out at 69°C. The Roman emperor Caracalla bathed here in AD 213 – you can view remains of the baths through a glass plate window in the basement of the 19th-century Friedrichsbad. The Lichtentaler Allee, Baden-Baden's lovely *corso*, most

Spectacular views from above Baden-Baden

Baden-Baden – still a fashionable and popular spa town

'BEAUTIFUL CASINO'
The casino at Baden-Baden can accommodate 2,500 gamblers at 35 tables. According to Marlene Dietrich, 'The most beautiful casino in the world is at Baden-Baden – and I have seen them all.' It was built in 1853 and in the decades that followed its portals welcomed many royal guests, including Kaiser Wilhelm I. The Russian novelist Dostoyevsky lost a fortune on its gaming tables.

of which is traffic-free, runs from the Kurgarten, site of both the Trinkhalle and the Kurhaus, to the old Cistercian monastery at Lichtental, passing on its way the Theatre, the International Club, and the Kunsthalle (art gallery).

Baden-Baden suffered a calamitous fire in 1689, which destroyed most of the old town. The Stiftskirche fortunately survived. Inside is the tomb of Margrave Ludwig Wilhelm and a huge sandstone crucifix, a masterpiece carved in 1467 by Nikolaus von Leyden. The Neues Schloss was built in the 19th century in a combination of Renaissance and baroque styles on medieval foundations. It is still the home of the original family, former Grand Dukes of Baden. The castle can't be visited, but there is a local history museum in the gatehouse (*Closed* Mon), and views over Baden-Baden and the Black Forest from the grounds. It's a steep climb to the viewpoint, but you could reward yourself with a plunge in the warm waters of the Friedrichsbad or the more modern Caracalla-Thermen.

Excursion
The town of **Rastatt**, north of Baden-Baden, was rebuilt on uniform lines in the 18th century by Margrave Ludwig Wilhelm of Baden (nicknamed Louis the Turk because of his role in the anti-Turkish wars). Its massive red sandstone Schloss is Germany's first example of a palace in the style of Louis XIV's Versailles. It houses both the national Army Museum (with many of Ludwig Wilhelm's war trophies) and the Museum of Liberation (with displays on the evolution of German Liberalism). (Both museums *Closed* Mon.) Ludwig's widow, Sibylla, was responsible for the Schloss Favorite, 5km outside of town.

▶ **The Bergstrasse (Mountain Road)** *172B4*
This long-established route (the Strata Montana of the Romans and today's B3) runs through the orchards at the foot of the forested Odenwald hills for 58km.

The fruit trees and almonds between **Darmstadt** and **Heidelberg** come into blossom earlier than anywhere else in Germany, and are spectacular in late March/mid-April, while a string of picturesque little towns offers a welcome at all seasons.

South of Darmstadt is half-timbered **Zwingenberg**, the oldest place along the route, with steep alleyways and a pretty little market square overlooked by the 13th-century church. Prettier still are the narrow streets of **Bensheim**, lined with half-timbered houses and leading to shady cobbled squares. For a magnificent view of the Rhine valley and the Odenwald forest, climb to the 13th-century **Schloss Auerbach**, one of several castles of this region captured by French armies in 17th century wars. Just east of Bensheim and Schloss Auerbach is the extraordinary **Felsenmeer (Stone Sea)**, a jumble of thousands of huge granite blocks, the site of a Roman quarry and weathered by time into an eerie landscape.

Fürstenlager Park was laid out in the 18th century with pavilions and garden monuments in the taste of the time. There is a trail laid out among the exotic trees that flourish in the mild climate.

Heppenheim is dominated by the ruins of Schloss Starkenberg. Within the ruins is an observatory and a youth hostel. The place has the cheerful air of a centre of wine production, with fine timber-framed buildings in the market square, including an ancient apothecary's shop. The square is overlooked by the massive neo-Gothic church, the 'Cathedral of the Bergstrasse'.

Weinheim has picturesque streets, an old tanners' quarter, and a marketplace. The town's attractive Schlosspark (castle park) has many rare trees, and nearby, up in the valley of the Weschnitz, is the castle of Wachenburg, with a fine panorama towards Mannheim and the Rhine.

PIONEERING CASINO

Baden-Baden has long been a playground for the rich and famous – Brahms, Dostoevsky and Queen Victoria were among its many visitors. Following the construction of the Kurhaus in the 1820s, the French impresario Jacques Benazet opened a casino, the first in Germany. The famous Iffezheim races began here in 1858, enhancing the town's prestige. The Lichtentaler Allee is the most glamourous thoroughfare, scene of many historic events.

ANCIENT TORHALLE

A great Benedictine abbey once stood at Lorsch. Of it there remains the delightful little arched and brickwork-decorated markethall-like structure known as the Torhalle, Germany's oldest intact building, dating from the late 8th century and probably erected as a triumphal gateway for the emperor Charlemagne.

Windeck Castle, on the Bergstrasse

175

▶▶ Bodensee (Lake Constance) 172C1

Fed by the Rhine and shared with Austria and Switzerland, the Bodensee is the second largest (after Lake Geneva) of the great Alpine lakes. Sometimes called the 'Swabian Ocean' for its sheer size (roughly 65 by 12km), it has of the character of an inland sea, which, together with the distant backdrop of the Alps and a mild climate that allows exotic vegetation to thrive, has made it a popular place for German holidaymakers, who flock to the chain of resorts along the north shore.

The historic town of **Konstanz▶** stands at the end of a peninsula astride the channel linking the main body of the lake – the Obersee – to the smaller Untersee, with its varied shoreline. The lakeside at Konstanz is attractive enough, with steamers tied up in the harbour, a verdant park (the Stadtgarten), old defensive towers, and the venerable warehouse of 1388 known as the Konzil. In summer the traffic-free Altstadt (old town) has a bustling, almost Mediterranean atmosphere; there is a cathedral – the Münster – and a fine Renaissance Rathaus. The Rosgarten Museum exhibits finds dating back to prehistoric times. It was being totally restored in 1999 and hoped to reopen by 2000. Now an elegant lakeside hotel, the town's 13th-century Dominican monastery was also the birthplace of Graf Zeppelin, the airship pioneer.

Mainau▶, reached by road and footbridge or by lake steamer, is a paradise island of tropical plants with a fairy-tale castle. Laid out by Grand Duke Friedrich I of Baden in the mid-19th century, it is now owned by the flamboyant Swedish count Bernadotte.

Reichenau Island▶ is accessible along its causeway or by boat. Less crowded than Mainau, it is of exceptional interest because of its three Romanesque churches – testimony to an important monastic past. Look particularly for the 10th-century frescos at Oberzell church. Mittelzell abbey dates from the 10th century and has Gothic reliquaries in its treasury. **Singen**, farther west, is dominated by Hohentwiel, the biggest castle ruin in Germany (*Open* daily). The castle was razed by the French in 1801 but the ruins still offer a terrific panorama of lake and Alps.

One-thousand-year-old **Meersburg▶**, easily reached by car ferry from Konstanz, is perhaps the prettiest place

176

LAKE WINE
Seewein (lake wine) is a good reason for visiting the Bodensee. On the shores of the lake, Meersburg holds a wine festival every September – a very good introduction to the region's wines.

along the lake, with a formidable feudal castle, the Altes Schloss, and a baroque palace, the Neues Schloss. Both castle and palace were built for the bishops of Konstanz, who fled here when that town turned Protestant. The clif-flike shoreline between the Oberstadt (upper town), with its delightful Marktplatz (market square) and the Unterstadt (lower town), with its busy lakeside prome-nade, provides excellent growing conditions for the vines that have made Meersburg the centre of the Bodensee wine trade.

North of Meersburg the shore of the Überlingersee, a northwest-reaching arm of the Bodensee, continues steep and rugged in places. At **Unteruhldingen** a prehistoric lake dwellers' village has been imaginatively recon-structed (*Open* Mar–Nov daily, weekends only, Dec Sun only). A short distance inland lies Schloss Salem, its Gothic church complemented by baroque abbey build-ings. Since 1922 this has been Germany's most famous

Konstanz, the main town on the Bodensee (Lake Constance), is popular with tourists but has not been spoiled by high-rise construction

boarding school, numbering among its alumni Britain's Duke of Edinburgh. One of the most appealing of all Germany's baroque buildings, the pilgrimage church at **Birnau▶** stands in a romantic setting among the vineyards overlooking the lake. Inside you can see a famous little figurine, a honey-stealing cherub licking his fingers.

Medieval **Überlingen**, clinging to its steep lakeside site, retains most of its fortifications and is dominated by its richly furnished, five-aisled late Gothic Münster.

From Meersburg to Lindau Southeast of Immenstaad the lakeside becomes flatter and the main points of interest are the lakeside settlements, such as **Friedrichshafen**, where Zeppelin based his great airships; little **Wasserburg** on its peninsula; and, above all, **Lindau▶**. Built on the lake's largest island and connected to the mainland by two bridges, this ancient city is the southernmost in Germany, priding itself on its mild climate, its spectacular setting against the backdrop of the Alps and its high reputation as a summer resort. The monumental harbour entrance is guarded by the Lion of Bavaria and a lighthouse, the quayside by another lighthouse, the 13th-century Mangturm. Behind its traffic-free promenades, the Altstadt is full of interest, not least because of its blend of architectural styles, medieval painted houses, 15th-century Rathaus, baroque Cavazzen House (with a fine local museum, *Closed* Mon) and Jugendstil train station.

178

Loved by yachtsmen, the big Bodensee is sometimes called 'the Swabian ocean'

▶ Donaueschingen   *172B1*

High up among the rich farmlands of the Baar plateau between the Black Forest and Swabian Jura, little Donaueschingen owes its name to its position at the source of the Danube – Europe's second largest river after the Volga. The great river's starting point, 2,859km from the Black Sea, is marked by the monumental fountain standing in Donaueschingen's Schlosspark (castle park), though the name Danube really only applies downstream from the confluence of two streams (the Breg and Brigach) just outside the town. From 1723 Donaueschingen was the seat of the princes of Fürstenberg. Their Schloss (*Open* Apr–Oct. *Closed* Tue) was rebuilt twice, first in 1772 and again in 1893. It houses a sumptuous collection of porcelain, gold and silver plate, as well as Brussels tapestries. The Fürstenberg princes' rich art collections can be viewed in the Karlsbau. They include paintings by both Cranachs and by the Master of Messkirch, as well as by a number of 15th- and 16th-century Swabian masters.

MUSIC FESTIVAL
Apart from brewing, Donaueschingen prides itself on its excellent annual music festival – the Donaueschinger Musiktage. It is held each year in October and features works by contemporary composers.

▶▶ Freiburg   172A1

Known as the capital of the Black Forest, Freiburg has a lovely setting surrounded by green hills and vineyards, and a sunny climate. It is a city where foreigners love to live. It is famous for its cathedral, and for many Germans it also conjures up images of youth: some 27,000 students are housed here, giving the town an unusually lively atmosphere all year round. The Albert Ludwig University was founded in 1457; the College of Education, State Music College, and the five technical colleges are more recent additions.

What to see A walk through the squares and arcaded streets of the old town is delightful, but the real glory of Freiburg is its red sandstone **Münster▶▶**, with a soaring tower that dominates the city. Colourful medieval and baroque-style houses (many of them careful postwar reconstructions) fringe the cathedral square.

Begun as a ducal burial place by Bertold V of Zähringen, whose family founded the city in 1118–20, the Münster passed into the hands of the citizenry after the last of the Zähringens died in 1218. To the late Romanesque east end were added the Gothic nave and the incomparable west tower. The desire of rich families for their own burial chapels determined the form of the late Gothic choir, begun in 1354. Its consecration in 1513 marked the completion of the minster. Since 1827 the Münster has been the seat of an archbishop. The rich interior bears witness to the generosity and civic pride of local families: stained-glass windows with coats of arms of patricians and guilds; the magnificent high altar triptych by Hans Baldung Grien; and the splendid furnishings of the choir chapels with their 16th-century windows and fine altars

Top: a street in Freiburg leading to the 13th-century Swabian gate, part of the old ramparts Above: the glorious Freiburg Münster

and monuments. The cathedral tower, with its splendid traceried spire, has been described as the most beautiful tower in Christendom (you can climb the tower any day except Monday).

Augustinermuseum▶ This owes its name to the former monastery of the Augustinian Hermits, going back to about 1300. Since 1923 the church and cloisters of the monastery buildings have housed the attractively displayed collections of the museum, which specialises in Upper Rhenish art from the Middle Ages to the baroque. Besides the medieval art treasures, there is a special section for southwest German baroque sculpture and a rich collection of objets d'art.

The Augustinermuseum also has a folk-art section holding a collection of clocks, local costumes and folk art of the Black Forest. In the 19th century, artists became aware of the beauty of the Freiburg area and the Black Forest, and some of their canvases can be seen in the section devoted to Baden painters (*Open* Tue–Sun).

Remnants of the medieval town walls can still be seen south of the Augustinermuseum, while the old fishermen's quarter, known as the Insel (Island), has sensitively restored old buildings.

Other sights The colourful Münsterplatz (cathedral square) is graced by the Gothic/Renaissance Kaufhaus (merchants' hall), with an arcaded façade that contains statues of Habsburg rulers; the baroque Erzbischöfliches Palais (Archbishop's Palace); the 18th-century Wenzingerhaus; and the restored 15th-century Kornhaus (the original was destroyed during World War II).

A short distance away is Rathausplatz (town hall square), pleasantly shaded by chestnut trees. It contains the Neues Rathaus (the present town hall), once the university's main building.

Excursions
If you have time, there are some worthwhile side trips to be made to nearby places, such as the fortified town of **Breisach**, which towers immediately above the Rhine and the French frontier. Other interesting places to visit are the **Kaiserstuhl**, a volcanic, vine-clad hill standing isolated in the plain, and the wine town of **Burkheim** – all three are less than 24km west of Freiburg.

▶▶ Haigerloch 172B2
This is one of southwestern Germany's most delightful small towns, a perfect synthesis of buildings and landscape at a point where the River Eyach has carved a deep double loop in the limestone of the Swabian Jura. The best panoramas of the town in its setting are seen from the Kapf viewpoint, from the rococo St Anne's pilgrimage church, and from the tower known as the Römerturm. The Hohenzollern Schloss dominates the place; its Gothic church has a resplendent rococo interior.

A curiosity in this remote place is the Atommuseum, where German scientists tinkered (unsuccessfully) with a nuclear reactor in the last stages of World War II. (*Open* May–Sep daily, Oct–Nov, Mar–Apr Sat–Sun. *Closed* Dec–Feb.)

180

WINE FESTIVALS
A showcase for Baden wines, the Freiburger Weintage (Freiburg Wine Festival) is held in Münsterplatz in late June. Another city celebration with wine associations is the Fastnet (carnival) in February, when masks traditionally ward off evil spirits from the vines.

SCHNAPPS
A sixth of all Germany's distilleries are in the Freiburg region, most of them on Black Forest farms. An ancient church edict gave Black Forest farmers the right to distil their own schnapps, and the ruling still applies. Farms with distillery rights are allowed to produce and sell locally 300 litres a year. If a distillery falls into disuse it cannot be revived and no further concessions are given. The best Black Forest schnapps are made from cherries (the famous Kirsch), but you can also find excellent ones produced from damsons (Pflümli) and Williams pears (Williams).

▶▶▶ Heidelberg 172B4

For people the world over, friendly Heidelberg is the very image of romantic Germany. The River Neckar flows through its deep wooded valley past ancient towers and bridges; the red sandstone castle ruin rises majestically over the roofs of the old town. This, and the sheer exuberance of the life led by the students of Germany's oldest and most tradition-bound university (immortalised in Sigmund Romberg's operetta *The Student Prince*), all combine to make the place quite irresistible to countless visitors. One big draw are the boisterous student pubs of the old town, former haunts of the exclusive Verbindungen (fraternities). Here giant mugs of beer, shaped like a boot or horn, are passed around the tables. There is also a vigorous cultural life, with more than ten museums, several theatres and an annual theatre festival in August.

There are good views of Heidelberg from the graceful Alte Brücke (old bridge) spanning the fast-flowing waters. The bridge's gateway, its twin towers topped by spiky helmets, has long been one of the city's landmarks. It has been a favourite inspiration for poets and painters, among them the English artist J M W Turner, who came in 1836 and left many oils and watercolours of the city in its changing moods. If time permits, there are breathtaking views from the **Philosophenweg▶** above the quayside, the 'philosophers' path' trod by many wishing to contemplate the incomparable panorama to the south.

SCIENTIFIC POWERS
Despite the romantic image of the city, Heidelberg is a major exporter of scientific know-how to countries throughout the world. Today 'Made in Heidelberg' is proof of excellent quality for a number of famous products. Research institutes include the European Molecular Biology Laboratory, the German Cancer Research Centre and the Max Planck Institutes.

181

Heidelberg's great 17th-century castle above the River Neckar

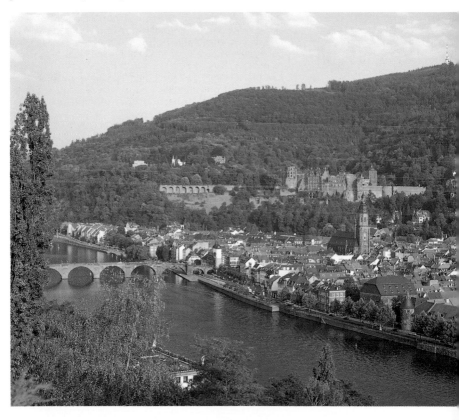

GIANT WINE VAT

The Grosses Fass (great vat) in the Fassbau in Heidelberg's castle is a wine barrel, with a capacity of 2,200 hectolitres, built in the 18th century to hold the tithe of Palatinate wines. On top of it is a platform that is used as a dance floor. *'Fill me the beaker! Now, Rhine and Nekkar, Health to ye both, ye noble streams! Yours is a power, To bring the hour High above Wisdom's heavy dreams'*. – Walter Savage Landor, 'Gardens at Heidelberg'

STUDENT DUELS

A generation or two ago, the caricature of a German male would show a reddened, almost bald pate with perhaps a few bristles adorning the roll of fat overlapping the collar, a monocle framing a glaring eye, and a scar or two adorning a cheek. Worn with pride, and known as a *Schmiss*, such a facial scar would have been acquired in the course of the fencing bouts that were a feature of upper-class student life in the more tradition-bound universities. The contestants, wearing goggles and padding to protect their vital parts, would face each other in the company of their supporters and attendant medics. The liberal-minded students of the postwar generation were eager to put such behaviour, with all its associations of fanaticism and militarism, behind them. But the tradition persisted among certain student associations and has recently come into prominence again.

The Schloss►►► High above the city's alleyways are the majestic ruins of the castle (guided tours daily), graced with fine terraced gardens, the creation of Friedrich V between 1616 and 1619. The princes of Pfalz (the Palatinate) lived here for 500 years; and included Friedrich V, who married the English princess Elizabeth Stuart, daughter of James I. It was for her that he built the Englischer Bau (English building), near the Dicker Turm (fat tower), and the Elisabethentor (Elizabeth Gate), in the form of a classical triumphal arch.

It was as a 17-year-old bride that Elizabeth came to the court over which she presided for five years before she was forced to flee to Prague when Friedrich V, who was a Protestant, failed in an attempt to oust the Catholic Habsburgs from their supreme position. He was eventually stripped of his titles, and his machinations contributed to the outbreak of the Thirty Years' War. Later, the Schloss, and the city itself, suffered badly when Louis XIV attacked the Palatinate, to which he laid claim, in 1689 (four years later, a disastrous fire destroyed the old town). The castle fabric was much restored in the 19th century by Count de Graimberg, but numerous earlier features survive.

The Well House contains Roman pillars brought from Charlemagne's palace at Ingelheim. Look, too, for the 16th-century Dicker Turm and the Glockenturm (bell tower), built for defense but with six subsequent residential floors added. The Deutsches Apotheken-Museum (German apothecary museum) (*Open* daily) within the castle complex provides a fascinating look into baroque and rococo workshops of German pharmacists from the early 17th century.

The University Heidelberg's is the oldest university in Germany, founded by Elector Ruprecht I von der Pfalz in 1386. It was badly neglected during the 18th century, but in 1803 Grand Duke Karl Friedrich declared it the first state university of Baden. One part of Universitätsplatz, dating back to the 18th century, is devoted to the Alte Universität (old university) while the rest of the square is taken up by university buildings of the 1930s.

The Studentenkarzer (students' jail; *Open* Apr–Oct Tue–Sun, Nov–Mar Tue–Sat), in use from 1712 to 1914, was built for unruly students, whose graffiti are still in evidence. In the library (*Open* Mon–Sat), the **Codex Manesse►**, a 14th-century collection of Middle High German poetry, is illuminated with 137 exquisite miniatures. Here, too, is *Des Knaben Wunderhorn* (*The Boy's Magic Horn*), a collection of folk poetry that inspired the German Romantic poets and the composer Gustav Mahler (*Open* Tue–Sat).

Excursion

About 13km west, **Schwetzingen** is known for its **Schlosspark►** (Guided tours of the Schloss Tue–Sun), a wonderfully fanciful 18th-century dreamland of romantic follies and eye-catching sites. Beyond the formal French garden lie a Temple of Apollo, a statue of Pan playing the flute in a grotto, mock ruins, tricks of perspective, and more. Mozart conducted an orchestral concert of his own works in the theatre here.

▶▶ Karlsruhe   *172B3*

Karlsruhe is the youngest of German cities. In 1715, tired of living in a medieval castle, in nearby Durlach, that had seen better days, Margrave Karl Wilhelm of Baden Durlach began building a new residence deep in the hunting forests of the Rhine plain. A city soon grew up, laid out in the shape of a fan, with the palace at its centre. This unusual pattern persists today, enhanced by the sober civic buildings in neoclassical style by Friedrich Weinbrenner. On his Marktplatz stands the famous pyramid where the town's founder is buried.

What to see Standing neatly in its formal gardens facing the city centre, the Schloss is now the home of the **Badisches Landesmuseum▶** (*Closed* Mon), where the rich and beautifully presented collections include the unique Türkenbeute, the booty won by Louis the Turk (see page 174) from his Ottoman opponents. Nearby are the excellent galleries of the Kunsthalle (an array of superb old masters, including Grünewald's intensely moving *Crucifixion*, together with fine examples of German 19th-century painting) and of the Orangery (*Closed* Mon). The latter has works by the 19th-century German artist Hans Thoma, who died in Karlsruhe, as well as German and French Impressionists (Monet, Cézanne, etc.) and Cubist-inspired pictures by Delaunay and Léger.

Excursions

There are superb views of the surrounding area from the **Turmberg**, high above the margrave's old castle at Durlach. Karlsruhe's sleek tramway system will whisk you out beyond the city to delightful half-timbered **Ettlingen**, also with a Schloss, or even farther into the Black Forest itself, to the upland resort of **Bad Herrenalb**.

HERTZ AND BENZ
Students of Karlsruhe's School of Technology (1825), have included such illustrious names as Hertz, the discoverer of electromagnetic waves; Benz, inventor of the car; and Karl von Drais, said to have invented the bicycle.

183

CONSTITUTIONAL COURT
Karlsruhe is no longer the capital of Baden, but its importance was confirmed by the siting here of Germany's Federal Constitutional Court.

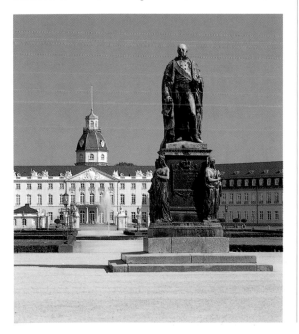

The Schloss (ducal palace) in Karlsruhe built by the Margave Karl Wilhelm

Intellectuals enjoy high status in Germany, and many universities boast hundreds of years of tradition. Before World War II they tended to be elitist, conservative bastions – many German students and professors supported Hitler's rise to power.

Students performing for passersby in Tübingen, an ancient university town with a lively cultural scene

The student movement and after Following the subdued period of the Wirtschaftswunder (economic miracle) in the 1950s, a generation of postwar German youth began questioning the establishment – and the university system – in the student movement that exploded in 1968. Student self-governing committees were formed and curricula opened to all qualified high-school graduates. Universities became vastly overcrowded, and the quality of teaching fell. In addition, students extend their studies well into their 30s – supported by generous government grants, although some universities are showing signs of growing impatience with their 'middle-aged undergraduates'. Munich University refused to admit 9,000 of them to the 1999 summer semester. Of the University's post-graduates studying for doctorates in 1999, 8,000 had exceeded the permitted three-year time limit for submitting their final theses.

In Germany students rarely live on campus as they do in Britain or the United States, although they eat together in a student *Mensa*, or cafeteria. Attendance is not compulsory, and many students are accused of not taking their studies very seriously. However, this may be changing – proposals for more rigourous, 'élite' universities are gaining ground, and a new generation of competitive Germans has appeared.

STASI SUSPECT Involvement by the west since unification has had some negative consequences. For example, in Berlin, western authorities dismissed the popular head of Humboldt University, the theologian Heinrich Fink, because of suspicions of secret police (Stasi) contacts under the Communist regime. This unleashed a storm of student protest, particularly since it was suspected that many western academics were after positions in the better-known universities of eastern Germany.

In the east Under the Communists, East German universities established their own traditions, with student admissions based on political criteria. The peaceful revolution in 1989 threw the universities into chaos, with large-scale firings of professors and restructuring of departments according to western standards.

▶ **Mannheim**   *172B4*

The second-largest river port in Europe and an important industrial centre, Mannheim is at the meeting point of the Rhine and the Neckar. Like Karlsruhe, it is an 18th-century planned town focused on its Schloss, a huge edifice that is now the seat of Mannheim's university. (Guided tours of the Schloss, Tue–Sat). Laid out on a grid pattern, the streets define 144 city blocks, each of which is designated by a letter and a number, a logical system without parallel in Germany.

Mannheim is proud of its former eminence in the world of music and theatre, but little of its original 18th-century architectural elegance survives. The most striking part of the town is the Jugendstil Friedrichsplatz, laid out around a monster water tower. Here is the **Kunsthalle**▶ (*Closed* Mon), with one of Germany's leading displays of 19th- and 20th-century art. In the Zeughaus (arsenal) is the Reiss Museum (*Closed* Mon), where the local collections evoke the look of the city before its industrialisation.

FRENCH ART
Mannheim's Städtische Kunsthalle has an excellent collection of 19th-century French art, including Manet's *Execution of the Emperor Maximilian of Mexico*, a work exemplifying the artist's realism and the influence of Spanish painting on his style.

▶ **Maulbronn**   *172B3*

Maulbronn has one of the earliest Cistercian monasteries (founded in 1147) to survive – a superb and almost untouched example. As the locals tell it, a group of monks stopped by here to let their mules drink (the name originally meant 'mule well'), and they stayed on forever. This story is depicted in sketches for a fresco on a wall of the Brunnenkapelle (well chapel) Romanesque with later Gothic additions. You can also see the cloisters with refectory and chapter house, early 15th-century chapels, and a crucifix of 1473.

▶▶ **Neckartal (Neckar Valley) and Odenwald**   *172B4*

The Neckar rises in the Black Forest and runs for nearly 400km before entering the Rhine at Mannheim. Downstream from **Bad Wimpfen** it flows through charming countryside of orchards and vineyards before cutting its way through the Odenwald uplands in a deep, narrow wooded valley. The best way of enjoying the Neckar's

185

The lovely Neckar River flows past numerous old castles and fortified medieval towns

Picturesque Bad Wimpfen (right) is not a spa town, but gets its name from the big local saltworks.
Odenwald natural park (below) is gently pastoral in some parts, forested in others

SIEGFRIED'S SPRING
Siegfried, hero of the medieval German *Nibelungenlied* and immortalised in Wagner's music, was treacherously killed by the evil Hagen while drinking from a spring in the Odenwald. Several springs in the forest bear the name *Siegfriedquelle* (Siegfried Spring).

varied landscapes, attractive towns and castles is from a steamer (the river has been 'improved' for shipping as far as Stuttgart), but the road (the signposted touring route called the Burgenstrasse) and railway closely follow its winding course.

To the east of Heidelberg the road passes beneath the 658m **Königstuhl** (King's Seat), crowned by a TV tower offering a panorama of the Neckar Valley and the Rhine Plain beyond. Equally dramatic views can be enjoyed from the castle ruins of **Dilsberg**, while Neckarsteinach is overlooked by no fewer than four castles. **Eberbach** has several quaint inns and pubs, including the Wirtshaus Kraabbenstein, as well as Germany's oldest bathhouse (the 13th-century Altes Badhaus). The little resort of **Zwingenberg** has a splendid medieval castle, and the Wolfsschlucht ravine provided the inspiration for Weber's opera *Der Freischütz*.

Just off the main valley, **Mosbach** is well known for its fine collection of half-timbered buildings. Back on the Neckar again, **Burg Hornberg** (*Open* daily) dates back to 1148, while **Burg Guttenberg** (*Open* Mar–Nov daily at 11 and 3) is famous today for its birds of prey, which are flown in public demonstrations.

Bad Wimpfen▶▶ is the highlight of the valley. This fortified medieval town was once the imperial residence of the Hohenstaufens and retains an appealing mixture of half-timbering, narrow streets, and stepped gables. The tall tower known as the Blauer Turm stands squarely among the steep-pitched roofs and gives the best views over town and river.

Odenwald Stretching northwards from the Neckar, this wooded upland of beech and spruce contrasts strongly with the fertile landscapes of the Bergstrasse, running along its western rim. It is traversed from west to east by the Niebelungenstrasse on its way from Worms to Würzburg, an attractive touring route that passes through delightful **Michelstadt**. The little town's Rathaus, with its stout oak columns and its corner turrets, is almost too picturesque to be true.

Michelstadt makes a good centre for visiting several of the Odenwald's other attractions: **Eulbach Park**, which has ornamental hunting grounds dating from the 18th century; Renaissance **Schloss Fürstenau**, in an attractive countryside setting; and **Erbach**, also with a Schloss, plus a unique museum of ivory carving (*Open* Apr–Oct daily. *Closed* Nov–Mar Mon). The nearby Einhardsbasilika – like the Torhalle at Lorsch, a striking example of Carolingian architecture – was completed in the year 827.

▶ **Ravensburg**   *172C1*

This old town thrived in the Middle Ages, with its position on a great trade route that connected northern Europe to Italy. Before the rise of the Fuggers of Augsburg, the Ravensburger Handelsgesellschaft was southern Germany's most important trading company.

Ravensburg grew up at the foot of the Veitsburg, the fortified hill where Henry the Lion was born. The town walls are still mostly intact, with several gates and towers, including the Mehlsack (flour-sack tower), originally erected so the citizens could keep an eye on the Veitsburg. The Marienplatz is full of character, with another tall tower, the Blaserturm; a 15th-century Rathaus; and the Waaghaus, the focus of trading activity. Its hall once rang with the cries of foreign merchants promoting their wares, while weights and measures were checked on the main floor.

▶ **Rottweil**   *172B2*

Rottweil enjoys a dramatic setting on a spur overlooking a bend in the upper Neckar. Its streets are a delightful collection of fine old houses, mostly Renaissance and baroque, with such features as elaborate oriel windows and exuberant carving. A further contribution to the townscape is made by four Renaissance fountains, of which the Marktbrunnen is the most splendid. The town's churches include the Kapellenkirche, which has been baroquified inside but has a richly decorated Gothic tower, and the Heiligkreuz Minster, which has a *Crucifixion* above its high altar attributed to Veit Stoss. The Lorenzkapelle houses a fine array of medieval sculpture.

The interesting local museum (Stadtmuseum) recalls the Roman presence here with a 2nd-century mosaic of Orpheus and also displays some of the weird and wonderful wooden masks worn at carnival time. Fastnet (carnival) spans six days; the climax is the Narrensprung (Fools' Dance) on the Monday before Shrove Tuesday and on Shrove Tuesday itself.

ROTTWEILER DOGS
The Rottweiler, a rugged cattle dog, is believed to have crossed the Alps from Italy with the Romans. Rottweilers were bred in the city as guard dogs. Their German name *Metzerhund* ('butcher's dog') derives from the local butchers' practice of training the dogs to pull their carts.

187

Ravensburg, once a bastion of the Guelph political dynasty (13th–17th centuries) is a fine old town of towers and painted gateways

BEURON MONASTERY
The village of Beuron, west of Sigmaringen, clusters around its huge abbey. Founded by the Augustinians in the 9th century, Kloster Beuron now belongs to the Benedictines. It is celebrated for the monks' singing of the Gregorian chant (which can be heard by visitors at high mass and vespers) and for the Nazarenes, an early 19th-century group of artists who came here and adopted an early Christian art style (later known as the Beuron School). Male visitors might find accommodation in the abbey.

▶ **Schwäbische Alb (Swabian Jura)** *172B2*

The Schwäbische Alb is a range of limestone hills located on the east side of the Black Forest. They are about 55km wide and 150km long. The young River Danube flows through part of the region in a landscape of wooded limestone cliffs, crag-top castles and lush green meadows. The southwest part of the Schwäbische Alb has been designated the Naturpark Obere Donau (Upper Danube Nature Park).

The name of Hohenzollern is closely associated with this part of Germany – forged by the marriage of the Zollerns, originally Swabian overlords, to the Burgraves of Nuremberg. From the early 1700s, the family, as rulers of Brandenburg and Prussia, fought to establish a German empire and finally achieved this in 1871 under Wilhelm I. In 1918, after defeat in World War I, Wilhelm II abdicated, but the family name and tradition continue. The present head of the family, who would have the title of Kaiser if the empire had continued, is Prince Ludwig Ferdinand of Prussia, grandson of Wilhelm II.

In **Sigmaringen**, at the mouth of the Upper Danube gap, the Swabian Catholic branch of the family managed to hold on to its **castle▶**, which today is the product of several periods, most prominently of 19th-century Romanticism. During the height of the tourist season there are vast crowds, but it is well worth the wait. For those with an avid interest in European royalty this is a treasure trove, and there is perhaps the largest collection of armoury and weapons in Europe, with more than 3,000 items in one hoard.

In the neo-Gothic hall a splendid collection of south German art of the 15th and 16th centuries includes works by the Master of Sigmaringen – actually two brothers, Hans and Jacob Strüb (*Open* Feb–Nov daily, Dec–Jan weekends and public holidays only). The Johanniskirche, on the castle rock, is decorated with elaborate rococo stucco work and houses the shrine of St Fidelio, who was a local martyr.

Between Sigmaringen and Tuttlingen the Danube flows through a superb gorge dominated by crags and lofty castles, including Burg Wildenstein (now a youth hostel), giving a spectacular view of the river, and the Knopfermacherfelsen, a magnificent viewpoint from a chaos of cliffs.

In a valley at the edge of the Schwäbische Alb lies **Zwiefalten**. The great Münster here rivals its Bavarian counterparts in splendour. The abbey church is largely the work of the south German 18th-century architect J M Fischer. Its spacious interior is lavishly decorated in a whirl of white and gold, with stucco masquerading as marble; the sculptures and large figures on the altar, set between pink and white columns, are by J J Christian. Among the many caves hollowed out in the soft limestone of the Alb, the **Wimsener Höhle** is perhaps the finest. It can be entered by boat.

The church at **Obermachtal**, built in 1686, displays stucco decoration and is an early example of wall-pillar construction, where a wall of internal buttresses represents a refinement to the medieval approach of using external flying buttresses.

CHERRY SPIRIT
Dettingen in the Schwäbisch Alb is famous for its Kirschgeist (cherry spirit). Selected cherries are cropped to make this strong, clear pick-me-up, which is drunk from thimble-size glasses.

BROOM-PUBS
Amid the vine-clad hills east of Stuttgart, you'll find delightful wine pubs in the cosy villages – Stetten and Kernen, Uhlbach with its wine museum, and Strumpfelbach with its tiny quaint Rathaus. One old tradition in this area is that of the *Besenwirtschaft* (broom pub): from November to March, many wine growers put a broom outside their houses to show that their new wine is ready, and they run an impromptu pub. You can sit among the locals in a chummy ambience, drinking the semi-fermented wine at below pub prices.

In Schwäbish Hall, St Michael's church is noted for its high vaulted ceiling and fine 16th-century altarpiece

JURASSIC FOSSILS
At Holzmaden, near Kirchheim, the remarkable Hauff museum displays fossilised skeletons of Ichthyosaurs 160–180 million years old. The Hauff family have long owned stone quarries here in the Swabian Jura, and they unearthed these crocodile-like Jurassic relics buried in the layered rock. Their museum has fossilised sea lilies looking like sea urchins, and a saurian mother with five embryos in her womb. (*Closed* Mon.)

HOHENSTAUFEN
Schwäbisch Gmünd was once the possession of the Hohenstaufen family, which ruled the Holy Roman Empire from 1138 to 1254. When they fell from power, Schwäbisch Gmünd became a Free Imperial City.

Burg Hohenzollern▶, the original seat of the Hohenzollern family, presents a spectacular outline, sited on a peak 850m above sea level near the town of Hechingen. There are daily guided tours and the castle is open all year round. The castle was largely rebuilt in neo-Gothic style in the mid-19th century, but the 12th-century Catholic chapel of St Michael, with beautiful stained glass, the oldest in Germany, remains. The Protestant chapel held the tomb of Frederick the Great until the mighty monarch's mortal remains were reburied at Potsdam in 1991 (see panel page 45). Many of his possessions, such as his uniforms and military decorations, can still be seen here.

Schloss Lichtenstein (*Open* daily, Nov weekends only. *Closed* Dec), a formidable 19th-century fortress, caps a craggy peak. Close by are several worthwhile caves, including the Nebelhöhle and the Bärenhöhle. Farther west, Rossberg (869m) gives a vast panorama of the region from its viewing tower.

Bad Urach is a pleasant small resort in a narrow valley and endowed with a pleasing half-timbered square. Out of town to the west, **Urach Waterfall** is found only a short walk away from the main road.

▶ Schwäbisch Gmünd   172C3
This attractive town set in good walking country, just north of the Schwäbische Alb, is famous for its jewellery and silver tableware. The 14th-century master builder Peter Parler was born here. One of the main works of the Parler family is the Heiligkreuzmünster (Cathedral of the Holy Cross). The decorative exterior includes fine tracery, pinnacles and a depiction of the Last Judgment in the south portal. The interior conforms to the Cistercian hall plan. Notice the magnificent vaulting, the Tree of Jesse altar in the Baptistery, and the carved choir stalls. The local museum (Johannisplatz 3) concentrates on late Gothic and baroque sculpture. The town maintains its craft traditions with its well-known college of gold- and silversmithing.

A short distance south of Schwäbisch Gmünd are the **Kaiserberge**, three wooded hills once topped by castles. One of these, Hohenstaufen, was the original seat of the great imperial family. There are wide-ranging views from ruined **Hohenrechberg**, where there is a baroque pilgrimage church.

▶▶ Schwäbisch Hall   172C3
One of the treasures of southwest Germany, this medieval town nestles in the heart of the Swabian forests, on the banks of the River Kocher, a tributary of the Neckar. Many of the houses and buildings are neatly arranged in tiers that overlook the ancient wooden bridges over the river. The site was already known for its saltwater springs in the 3rd century BC, and these encouraged a permanent Celtic settlement. During the Middle Ages, Schwäbisch Hall began to mint silver coins, first known as the Häller and then later renamed Heller (the name derives from Hall, meaning 'place of salt'). In the 13th century the town became a Free Imperial City.

Its charming, sloping **Marktplatz▶** is often reckoned to be among the most stunning in Germany. It is used for theatrical performances (Jun–Aug). The baroque **Rathaus▶**, built 1730–5, has a palatial appearance and is architecturally one of the most important buildings of its time. It was rebuilt after war damage. The roof proudly displays a decorative clock and imperial eagle. The central part of the square is dominated by the Marktbrunnen, a 16th-century fountain adorned with statues of St Michael with St George and Samson. The old pillory

Timbered buildings above the River Kocher in Schwäbisch Hall

HELLER UND PFENNIG
The word *Heller* in the German language means a very small monetary unit. If a German says he hasn't a *Heller*, he is flat broke. If he watches every *Heller und Pfennig*, then he is very careful with his money. This is a characteristic ascribed to the people of Schwäbisch Hall and other Wurttemberg towns. Significantly, Schwäbisch Hal – not exactly a financial metropolis – is the seat of one of the country's largest building societies.

forms part of the fountain's structure. The Pfarrkirche (St Michael's) adjoins the Marktplatz and you can reach it by mounting a wide flight of stairs. The church has hardly been touched since 1573, and besides the tombs in the chapels, there are interesting furnishings in the choir stalls, tabernacle, and altars.

The Keckenburg, once an aristocratic mansion, houses the Hällisch Fränkisches Museum (*Closed* Mon), explaining the town's history.

About 30km north, the quiet countryside between the Swabian Forest and the Tauber Valley is known as the Hohenloher Ebene, after the princely German family, the House of Hohenlohe; here the most common language is the Schwäbish (Swabian) dialect, which even other Germans often find difficult to understand.

At **Jagsthausen** is the much restored Götzenburg castle (now a hotel), and the birthplace in 1480 of the knight Götz von Berlichingen – the Knight with the Iron Hand. Goethe wrote a drama about him, and every summer a drama festival including Goethe's play is held in the courtyard of the castle.

About 6km on from Jagsthausen is the Cistercian abbey of **Schöntal** in the Jagst Valley (guided tours daily Apr–Oct). The church is famed for its 17th-century alabaster altarpieces.

At **Öhringen** the late Gothic Stiftskirche (dedicated to St Peter and St Paul), on the Marktplatz, contains tombs of members of the house of Hohenlohe. Note the monument to Philip of Hohenlohe, son-in-law of William the Silent, with detailed reliefs of battles from the Netherlands' War of Independence. Foremost among the furnishings is the high altar from around 1500.

The Schloss at **Neuenstein** (with an interesting collection of weapons) has been Hohenlohe family property since the 13th century and displays a variety of styles, including Renaissance, Romanesque and Gothic.

Waldenburg was once a fortified town, from which the princely family overlooked the plain and protected their empire against approaching enemies.

SALT HEROES
Schwäbisch Hall's annual pentecostal festival recalls an occasion when salt workers saved the town's mill from fire, and is called the Kuchen und Brunn en Fest de Haller Salzsiede – the Cake and Fountain Festival of the Salt Miners of Hall.

At Schwäbisch Hall in summer, a drama festival is held in the sloping Marktplatz

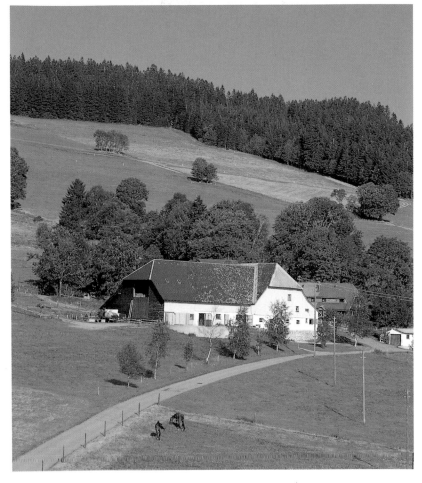

▶ ▶ ▶ Schwarzwald (Black Forest) 172A2

The highest land in southwest Germany, the Black Forest is a rewarding area for gentle exploration. Only in the gloom of its most inaccessible stands of spruce does the term 'black' seem appropriate, and by no means all of it is woodland. Picturesque wooden farmhouses and pleasantly unassuming villages nestling in green valleys are distinctive elements of the landscape; the terrain gets more open as you travel south into the orchards and farmlands of the Markgräfliches Land. The western slopes are dominated by vineyards; the **Badische Weinstrasse** (Baden Wine Road) winds through the Black Forest foothills. Development across the region is mostly low-key and small-scale, with few big resorts.

Beneath all this is a thriving and well-organised tourist industry, mostly catering to the Germans themselves, who come for short breaks and nonmedical 'cures'. Newish hotels in traditional style are found on the edges of many villages and are scattered around the country areas. Sports facilities (particularly tennis and squash) have been developed to an impressive degree, even in

The Schwarzwald is noted for its special rural architecture, as well as traditional industries and local costumes, still worn for Sunday church and festivals

Huge ornamental clocks are typical of the Schwarzwald. One cuckoo-clock at Schönach forms the entire side of a chalet

many smaller villages. The region excels as an area for outdoor pursuits, above all for walking. Marked paths of varying degrees of difficulty (including many very easy ones) abound and the signposting and tourist information are excellent. A useful tourist-board scheme is *Wandern ohne Gepäck* (walking without luggage), where you can walk from village to village, to prebooked guest houses, and have your luggage transported by car. In winter, there is skiing on moderately challenging runs and a network of specially-prepared cross-country ski trails.

There are many Black Forest specialities. Most famous are undoubtedly the Schwarzwälder Kirschtorte (of which the ubiquitous factory-made Black Forest cake is a bland imitation), and the cuckoo clocks on sale in every souvenir shop. Zwiebelkuchen (onion cake) is often served accompanied by a young white wine. Black Forest smoked ham is best eaten sliced thinly on locally baked bread. In season, white asparagus, plums, and cherries appear on the menu. Local drinks include the Baden wines and Kirschwasser, Schnapps made from cherries (see panel page 180).

The heart of Black Forest clock making is centred around the industrial town and spa of **Triberg** (see pages 196–7). **Furtwangen** is the home of the Deutsches Uhrenmuseum (German clock museum), a must even for non-enthusiasts (*Open* daily). There are also factories and workshops in the area, which will be only too pleased to give you a firsthand glimpse of local clock production in this region.

Southern Schwarzwald You will find this region one of the sunniest in Germany. The cherry trees display their blossoms in the early spring while the mountains are still topped with snow from the previous winter. Four of the region's tallest hills lie close to **Freiburg** – the **Feldberg**, **Schauinsland**, **Kandel** and the **Belchen**. All are easily reached from the road, but the Belchen has the best views; and just north of it is **Münstertal▶**, a deep and especially pretty valley, steep-sided and graced with the baroque church of St Trudpert. East of the Feldberg is one of the

CLOCK MAKING
The tradition of Black Forest clock making goes back to 1667, when the wooden clock with foliot (weighted arm) was made for the first time in Waldau. Metal for the mechanisms was imported until 1787, when Leopold Hofmayer set up his brass foundry in Neustadt. Since then numerous variations have been produced, among them musical clocks with trumpeters or flutes, clocks with painted or lacquered shields, clocks to control watchmen, and regulators, alarm clocks, even modern quartz-crystal clocks and radio clocks. As early as 1840, subsidiaries of the Black Forest clock traders existed in four continents and 23 countries. In 1845, 600,000 clocks were produced in the Black Forest – today the figure stands at 60 million a year!

main resort areas. Many visitors come for the two lakes, the **Titisee** and the **Schluchsee**. Of these, the Titisee, which is set among gentle woodlands, is the prettier, but the modern village on its northern side partly spoils the effect; the Schluchsee attracts older people and is less commercialised. More peaceful is **Hinterzarten**, which is an upmarket family resort.

The views are breathtaking in this area, whichever way you decide to travel. If it fits in with your plans, you might want to take a train ride from Freiburg to **Feldberg Bärental**, following a steep and winding route through the Höllental (Hell Valley) Gorge. The station at Feldberg Bärental is proud of its special location, which at 976m is the highest train station in Germany. If you prefer to put on your hiking boots, the nearby **Feldbergsee** lies at the end of an unspoiled romantic road that is available only to walkers.

Further south, the terrain is lower and less spectacular, but the country is more open – typically consisting of orchards, meadows and rounded hills of small-scale charm. There is less tourist development, and plenty of old-fashioned farmhouses have survived. Of the resorts, **Todtmoos** is especially pleasant, prettily placed amid gentle hills.

Not far from the Swiss border, halfway between Freiburg and Basel, is **Badenweiler▶**, a popular tourist attraction not only because of its spa, but also because of its fine views over the Rhine plain. The thermal springs here, which have been well preserved since their rediscovery in 1784, have been flowing since Roman times. Today's inhabitants are intent on keeping things as clean and intact as possible, and you have to leave your car on the edge of town and walk in. There are open-air pavilions where numerous musical events are held throughout the summer months.

About 8km to the south of Badenweiler is **Schloss Bürgeln**, built in 1764 on the orders of the abbot of the Benedictine abbey of St Blasien. From here you can obtain a spectacular view of the surroundings as far as the Swiss Alps.

Gutach and Kinzig valleys: the central Schwarzwald A journey north through some fine towns and villages will bring you into the Gutach and Kinzig valleys. Here you will see examples of the distinctive Black Forest farmhouses with their low-hanging roofs, deep eaves and animal quarters under the roof, usually approached by an earth ramp. This is the heartland of Black Forest folk costume, such as the wide-brimmed hats with red pom-poms worn on special occasions by local girls. The **Schwarzwaldbahn** (Black Forest railway), with its 45 tunnels, crosses this landscape.

The highest waterfall in Germany (162m) is at **Triberg▶** (the Gutach falls). Cuckoo-clock sceptics may be surprised that the business launched by Josef Weisser in 1824 in Triberg, called the 'Haus der 1000 Uhren' (House of 1,000 Clocks), is still thriving. Triberg is not just clocks, however. It is a year-round spa, a winter-sports resort and a relaxed sort of town. The forest at Triberg acts as a dust filter, and visitors to the spa and health resort often remark on the purity of the air. In Triberg's **Schwarzwald**

FRUIT CAKES
As well as Schwarzwälder Kirschtorte (cherry cake), Black Foresters have other delicacies to tempt the sweet tooth at coffee time. Zwetschenkuchen (blue plums on a pastry base), Käsesahnekuchen (a rich cheesecake) and Johannisbeerenkuchen (a sponge cake with red currants) are just a few.

197

Museum▶ (*Open* daily) you'll find a wide array of local costumes on display, as well as wood carvings, ceramics and – of course – clock-making memorabilia, which will give you an idea of the rural culture.

Gutach is known for the Vogtsbauernhof, an imaginatively arranged open-air museum with an absorbing collection of reconstructed and traditionally furnished thatched farmhouses, complete with farm implements; in its pretty country setting, the whole place has the feel of a real village.

Freudenstadt▶ was badly damaged in World War II and has little ancient character, but it has been carefully reconstructed and is now second only to Baden-Baden as a health resort. The town sits high on a plateau at the meeting point of all the main routes in the northern Schwarzwald. The arcaded market square, which is Germany's largest, has neatly laid out sidewalks and lawns. The unusual 17th-century Stadtkirche has aisles set at right-angles, each with its own green-domed tower, and a glorious 12th-century carved lectern.

To the south, **Schiltach** and **Wolfach**, both close to main roads, are among the prettiest Black Forest villages and boast half-timbered market squares.

The northern Schwarzwald The B500 Schwarzwald Hochstrasse linking Freudenstadt with Baden-Baden is a popular road. It runs along almost the entire spine of the

Dark green trees, reflected in dark water, give the 'Black' forest its name

DYING TREES
Dying and diseased trees with yellowing needles and peeling bark are widespread in the forests. Acid rain is thought to be the main culprit, and government pollution controls have been increased to curb the Waldsterben – Dying Forest Syndrome.

FROLICKING FOOLS
The folklore frivolity of winter carnival, known as Fastnacht in the Black Forest and Fasching in Bavaria, is eagerly pursued in Catholic areas. The fun starts on the 'Elfte Elfte Elfte Elfte' (11.11 am on 11 November), to reach a climax before Lent. At Elzach, masked fools clad in red scourge people with blown-up hogs' bladders; at Wolfach, fools scour the town in nightgowns and nightcaps; at Uberlingen they crack long whips.

Black Forest. There are numerous roadside stopping places that will enable you to picnic alfresco – if the weather allows – and to admire the view. Alternatively, there are plenty of villages or hamlets for a meal or perhaps an overnight stay. At romantic **Allerheiligen▶**, the ruins of a 13th-century church stand next to three 18th-century ornamental fishponds.

The drive along the Nagold Valley from Freudenstadt (part of the Schwarzwald Bäderstrasse) brings you to **Pforzheim**, at the northern extremity of the Schwarzwald, some 30km north of Calw, with its half-timbered houses. At Pforzheim, the River Nagold joins the River Enz. As a centre of the jewellery trade, the town likes to think of itself as wealthy and has christened itself 'Goldstadt' (town of gold). The Schmuckmuseum (jewellery museum) has a collection of valuable pieces spanning 17 centuries in the Reuchlinhaus in Jahnstrasse (*Closed* Mon). Pforzheim is also the starting point for hikes into the northern tip of the Schwarzwald (see **Walks**, below, for possible walking routes).

Walks

Black Forest footpaths

The Black Forest offers an excellent range of long-distance walks, taking in viewpoints, unspoiled farmland, villages and wetlands.

Signposting (look for diamond-shaped signs) and path maintenance are of a high standard; there is plenty of good-quality accommodation on the way, and there's no shortage of refreshment facilities.

Long tracks divide into Hohenwege (hill paths), which take north–south courses along the footpaths, and Querwege (linking paths), which lead west–east. Of the four Hohenwege, the longest is the 350 km Pforzheim-to-Basel Westweg. The Querwege range from the 164 kmFreiburg-to-Bodensee Querwege to short expeditions such as the 48 km Rheinfelden-to-Albbruck path.

Boats at Titisee

▶▶ Speyer   172B3

The **cathedral**▶▶ in the Rhine town of Speyer is one of Europe's great Romanesque churches. Founded in 1030, it was remodelled at the end of the 11th century with four towers and two domes. Located in front is the Domnapf (cathedral bowl) of 1490, where wine is traditionally poured at the induction of a new bishop or for other special occasions, such as the 2,000th anniversary of the city in 1990. At the entrance to the vault of the emperors, or **Kaisergruft**▶, the name given to the huge 11th-century crypt▶ (the largest of its period in Germany) where eight rulers were buried, is the 13th-century tomb of Rudolph of Habsburg.

From the cathedral's west front the broad Maximilianstrasse leads to the massive 13th-century Altpörtel, the only city gateway to have survived.

At the Historisches Museum der Pfalz (Palatinate Museum; *Closed* Mon) the Bronze Age 'Golden Hat' of Schifferstadt is the highlight of the collection, that includes paintings and porcelain from ancient through to modern times. The Weinmuseum (Wine Museum) (*Closed* Mon) in the same building houses wine-making equipment with, amazingly, a 3rd-century bottle of wine (complete with its contents).

The synagogue that once existed in Speyer has been destroyed, but 10m below ground level in Judenbadgasse is the Judenbad, a fine example of the ritual baths used by Jews for cleansing on important religious holidays and by brides prior to their wedding.

HEAVY DIET
Speyer hosted 50 imperial diets (assemblies) in the course of the Holy Roman Empire's history. As well as the emperor and the six electors, the diet was made up of 30 lay princes, 140 counts and lords, 120 bishops and archbishops, and the representatives of 200 cities.

199

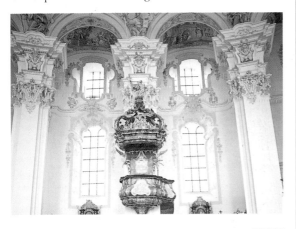

Of the baroque churches of upper Swabia, one of the finest is the Wallfahrtskirche in the village of Steinhausen, near Biberach

▶ Steinhausen   172C1

Steinhausen's Wallfahrtskirche (pilgrimage church), built between 1728 and 1733, is the work of Dominikus and Johann Baptist Zimmermann, who perfected the baroque style in their work. Dominikus designed the building and Johann was the painter; both were involved in the stucco work. The airy oval nave with an encircling gallery above has been left as the brothers decorated it. Stucco flowers, insects, birds, and squirrels form part of the composition. Not all the work originally intended was completed, as the building cost four times as much as was estimated in 1727. Work ceased in 1733. The church is popularly described as the world's most beautiful parish church.

In central Stuttgart, a café facing the elegant Schlossplatz

▶▶ Stuttgart

172B3

Capital of the *Land* of Baden-Württemberg, Stuttgart has an enviable valley setting among green hills. Home of charismatic names like Mercedes, Porsche, Bosch and Zeiss, the city is one of the most glittering jewels in the crown of industrial Germany, its standard of living one of the highest in the country. Cultural and environmental standards are high, too, with splendid galleries and a park system that is a model of its kind.

Stuttgart's evolution was closely tied to the fortunes of the house of Württemberg, who made the city their seat in the 14th century. Under Napoleon, who made Württemberg a kingdom, the city became a royal capital, and though this lasted only a century, something of the feeling of royal splendour has persisted to the present. Stuttgart takes its name from a stud farm (Stutengarten) established in the 10th century by the duke of Swabia, and a horse features in the city's coat of arms. In spite of being the focus of a metropolitan region of some 2 million people, the city has a relaxed air about it, possibly something to do with the abundance of vineyards within the municipal boundary; grapes grow within spitting distance of the central station.

CAR MUSEUM

The Porsche Museum and the splendid Daimler-Benz museum are outside Stuttgart centre but easily accessible by the S-Bahn rapid transit system. Porsche (*Closed* Mon. *Admission free*) features racing cars, Daimler-Benz (*Closed* Mon. *Admission free*) all kinds of stars from the Mercedes stable to the first 'Popemobile'.

A good way of starting your tour of Stuttgart is to ascend the 217m TV Tower (Fernsehturm), completed in 1956 and the first of its kind in Germany. It rises above the woods in the south of the city. The viewing platform offers a magnificent panorama.

What to see The traffic-free main street, Königstrasse, runs south from the monumental train station to the vast Schlossplatz. Here are some of Stuttgart's great civic buildings, such as the baroque Neues Schloss, last home of the Württemberg kings and now used for government purposes; the shop-lined neoclassical Königsbau; and the

STUTTGART

Hauptbahnhof · Mittlerer Schlossgarten · Planetarium · Landes-Pavillon · Kurpark · Mercedes-Benz Museum · Katharinenhospital · Linden-museum · Universität · Universitäts-hochhäuser · Bibliothek · Hoppenlau-Friedhof · Stadtgarten · Oberer Schlossgarten · Staats-Schauspiel · Staatsgalerie · Liederhalle · Landes-gewerbeamt · Dom-Kirche St.Eberhard · Kunstgebäude · Staatstheater · Neue Staatsgalerie · Königsbau · Staatsoper · Landtag · KLEINER SCHLOSS-PLATZ · SCHLOSS-PLATZ · Neues Schloss · Landes-bibliothek · Gerichte · Hospitalkirche · SCHILLER-PLATZ · Altes Schloss (Landesmuseum) · Akademie-garten · Stiftskirche · KARLS-PLATZ · Staatsarchiv · Markthalle · Wilhelmspalais (Städt.Bibl.) · Innen-ministerium · CHARLOTTEN-PLATZ · Rotebühlbau · RÖTEBÜHL-PLATZ · Rathaus · Fernsehturm · Leonhards-kirche · Engl.kirche · Schloss Solitude · Altes Schauspielhaus · Turmhaus · Siegle-Haus

0 100 200 metres
0 100 200 yards

201

City Art Gallery. Linking the much more atmospheric Schillerplatz is the **Altes Schloss▶**, part medieval castle, part Renaissance palace, home of the Landesmuseum (*Closed* Mon) with its memorabilia of the House of Württemberg as well as an excellent collection of Swabian religious sculpture. Beyond the expressway is one of Europe's great modern art galleries, the **Staats-galerie▶▶** (see page 202).

It is possible to walk from the city centre via parks and gardens to the far bank of the Neckar and Bad Cannstatt, Stuttgart's spa, with its Kurhaus. The Canstatter Volksfest in September is one of Germany's largest beer festivals.

A good 15km from Stuttgart is **Schloss Solitude▶**, a fine example of 18th-century rococo and a glimpse of life under the Württemberg rulers, who used it as a summer residence (*Open* Tue–Sun).

Several places of interest lie close to the Neckar and other rivers. To the north are **Ludwigsburg**, with one of Germany's largest baroque **palaces▶▶** former residence of the Württemberg rulers (guided tours daily), where mechanical figures act out fairy tales in the Märchen-garten (Fairy-tale Garden); **Marbach**, where Friedrich Schiller was born in 1759 – his house (*Open* daily) contains a few personal mementos – and where today the impressive **Schiller National Museum▶** (*Open* daily) attracts literary pilgrims; and **Besigheim**, with its walls and towers. Felsengärten Hessigheim, a natural rock 'garden', towers over a bend in the Neckar.

The Duke of Württemberg still inhabits Ludwigsburg's vast castle

The Staatsgalerie was founded by Wilhelm I of Württemberg in 1843. Its famous extension, inaugurated in March 1984, was designed by a British architect, the late James Stirling. This new building put Stuttgart on the map in the world of art and architecture. Its varied forms and bold use of different materials have made it one of the landmarks of Postmodernism – and it is surprisingly popular with the public. Some 25 per cent of the DM 70 million for its construction came from lottery funds collected since 1958.

202

Modern collection Without doubt the art is worthy of the building, with important works by Henri Matisse and Oskar Schlemmer, Joseph Beuys and Alberto Giacometti, Franz Marc and Giorgio de Chirico. Modern German art is particularly well represented. The gallery also houses the largest Picasso collection in Germany.

The old gallery The mainstream collection of the Staatsgalerie provides an overview of the history of western European painting, with works from medieval times to the 19th century, from early altarpieces to French Impressionists. There is a particularly fine collection of works from the local 15th-century Swabian school; other German works include Cranach's *Judith with the Head of Holofernes* and Hans Baldung Grien's *Man of Sorrows*. One of the most important works is the Herrenberg Altar, with vivid scenes of Christ's Passion painted by Jörg Ratgeb in 1518–19 for the Herrenberg collegiate church; it was brought to Stuttgart in 1892. Almost every major 19th-century French painter is represented – including Manet, Monet, and Cézanne. One of the best-known works of German Romantic painting, Caspar David Friedrich's *The Cross in the Woods*, is in the Staatsgalerie.

If you favour Romantic art, don't miss the eight scenes from *The Legend of Perseus* by English Pre-Raphaelite Edward Burne-Jones. The Dutch masters – Memling, Hals, Rubens and Rembrandt – are prominent, too. Some of the best treasures are displayed in the basement of the building – this is for security reasons *and* also to preserve the collection from environmental damage.

The gallery is located at Konrad Adenauerstrasse 30–32, tel: 0711 212 4050. *Open* Wed, Fri–Sun, 10–5, Tue and Thu, 10–8.

Outside Tubingen's old Rathaus, the farmers mix with students on market days

KÜNG DISMISSED
Founded on papal authority as a training centre for Protestant ministers in the Reformation, Tübingen University became the focus for religious controversy with the removal of Hans Küng, an academic theologian, for criticising church dogma.

▶▶ Tübingen   172B2

Situated on the tranquil upper reaches of the Neckar, Tübingen is one of Germany's oldest and most atmospheric university towns. Less plagued than Heidelberg by tourism, though quite its equal in charm, it has a castle, Hohentübingen, high above old colour-washed houses, their gables turned to the river. The university, founded in 1477, has always been strong on philosophy, theology and medicine. The philosopher Hegel was a student.

The best view of the town is from the Eberhardsbrücke over the Neckar. The bridge gives access to a long island between two arms of the river. The Platanenallee promenade, so called because it is lined with plane trees, is a favourite place for an evening stroll.

Schloss Hohentübingen is of Renaissance date, built on 11th-century foundations. Its entrance gateway bears the coat of arms of the house of Württemberg, together with the Order of the Garter awarded to one of the dukes by Queen Elizabeth I of England.

The Marktplatz, with its Neptune fountain, seems to be the hub of all the narrow winding streets and is still the focus of attention – particularly on market days (Monday, Wednesday and Friday). On one side of the square is the 15th-century (but much restored) **Rathaus▶**; a short distance east (in Münzgasse) is the Protestant collegiate church of St Georg, which contains late Gothic features, including notably the rood screen, vaulting and tracery.

Excursion

Reutlingen, 10km east of Tübingen, retains town walls and numerous fine buildings, despite war damage. In particular see the Marienkirche, a strikingly unified Gothic church of the 13th and 14th centuries. The Cistercian monastery at **Bebenhausen▶**, north of Tübingen, was founded 1185 and is encompassed by a double wall and centred on a late Gothic cloister (completed in 1496).

FAMOUS WRITERS
After the establishment of the 'Cotta' publishing house – which published works by Goethe and Schille – many distinguished writers and poets came to make their home in Tübingen. These included Friedrich Hölderlin, and the tower where he lived, insane, for 36 years is on the riverbank (it can be visited daily except Monday). The poets Eduard Mörike and Ludwig Uhland, as well as the philosophers Hegel and Schelling, also came to Tübingen.

FISHERMEN'S QUARTER
The Fischerviertel
(Fishermen's Quarter),
among tributaries of the
Danube, prompted writer
Herman Hesse to
describe Ulm as an
'extraordinary and
beautiful city'. Here, in
half-timbered houses,
artisans once lived.

*Ulm Münster (right)
boasts a set of 15th-
century carved choir
stalls (below)*

►► Ulm
172C2

Ulm's location at a significant crossing point of the
Danube made it an important trading centre in the late
Middle Ages. The city suffered severe damage in a bomb-
ing raid in 1944, which virtually destroyed the old centre,
but many of the ancient edifices have now been restored.
Ulm's famous son was Albert Einstein, born here in 1879.

The best general view is from the Tahn Ufer, on the far
side of the Danube. Look for the leaning gateway known
as the Metzgerturm (butchers' tower). The **Münster**►► is
one of the largest and most important religious buildings
in Europe, and it was fortunately little damaged by the
1944 bombs. Construction began in 1377, and was
completed, with the tower and steeple, in 1890. The latter,
the tallest in the world, soars 161m above the rest of the
city. You can climb almost to the top (768 steps) for a small
charge and take in a view stretching from the Danube
across the Black Forest to the Swiss Alps, if the weather is
on your side. Details of the Book of Genesis are carved
above the doorway under the tower, as well as figures of
Mary and the Apostles. There is much to be seen in the
massive interior, including a magnificent set of 15th-
century carved choir stalls and a display of architectural
plans by the various designers of the cathedral. The huge
Ulmer Museum has 50 exhibition rooms, with a heavy
accent on Gothic art in Upper Swabia, plus works by 20th-
century artists (*Open* Tue to Sun 11–5, Thu 11–8. *Admission
charge*, Fri *free*). The baroque monastery at Ulm-Wiblingen
is famous for its rococo library (*Open* Apr–Oct Tue–Sun
10–noon, 2–5; Nov–Mar Sat–Sun, public holidays 2–4.
Admission charge).

West of Ulm, the former abbey church at **Blaubeuren**►
(*Open* daily, winter pm only) is charmingly reflected in a
deep blue pool. The building contains an exceptional
15th-century late Gothic altarpiece, the work of a group of
local craftsmen.

▶ Wertheim
172C4

At the meeting point of the Main and Tauber rivers, Wertheim is a town of delightful half-timbered houses neatly erected along narrow streets amid a setting of wooded hills. The ruined Altes Schloss, towering over the town, was built by the counts of Wertheim in the 12th century. There are wonderful views from here. A glass museum in Mühlenstrasse has collections of historic glass, while the 16th-century Rathaus contains an historical museum. The impressive Stiftskirche was built in the 14th century, and the Kilianscapelle (St Kilian's chapel) in the 15th: its basement served as an ossuary. In the Marktplatz you will see half-timbered houses and the Engelsbrunnen (Angels' Well), dating from 1574, named for the stone angels bearing the Wertheim coat of arms. From the left bank of the Tauber there is a stunning view.

▶ Worms
172B4

This cathedral city on the banks of the Rhine, one of the oldest in Germany, has a particularly eventful past. There was a Celtic settlement here, then a Roman garrison. A Bergundian tribe, the Nibelungen, established itself in Worms in the 5th century and provided the material which gave rise to the famous legend which bore its name and so inspired the composer Richard Wagner. Worms has a Nibelungen bridge, built near the spot in the river Rhine where the evil Hagen, the treacherous slayer of Siegfried, is said to have thrown treasure he captured from the defeated Bergundians. In medieval times over 100 imperial diets, or assemblies, were held in Worms, the most noted being the Reichstag of 1521 (Diet of Worms), which summoned Luther to stand before it. He refused to retract his doctrines and was banned from the empire.

Besides industry, Worms has a flourishing wine trade. The famous Liebfraumilch comes from here, taking its name from the Liebfrauenkirche (Church of Our Lady), standing in the midst of a vineyard to the north of the city. It contains a 15th-century Madonna and tabernacle.

One of the best examples of Romanesque architecture in Germany is **Worms's cathedral** ▶ ▶, the Kaiserdom, with two domes and four corner towers. St Martins Kirche, also Romanesque, has the same design as the cathedral.

JEWISH CEMETERY
The synagogue of Worms – the oldest in Germany – and the Jewish cemetery date back to the 11th century. There was a large Jewish community here up to the 1930s. The Alte Synagoge was rebuilt in 1961, and the cemetery contains over 1,000 gravestones and pillars carved in Hebrew, amazingly untouched by the Nazis. After Prague, this is the second-largest Jewish cemetery in Europe.

205

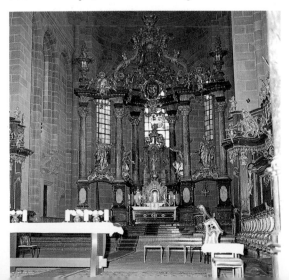

Worms's superb cathedral is Catholic, although the city itself is two-thirds Protestant

Stretching from Aschaffenburg in the northwest to Passau on the Austrian border far to the southeast, this region offers some of Germany's most fascinating historical cities, including **Nürnberg**, **Regensburg**, and **Würzburg**, and stretches of unspoiled countryside. The world-famous **Romantische Strasse** (Romantic Road) links medieval towns, while backwaters of the Bavarian Forest are explored by the **Bayerische Ostmarkstrasse**.

The region's cultural riches are unsurpassed. In the late Middle Ages and Early Renaissance, some of the most characteristically German contributions to the arts were made by painters (Altdorfer, Cranach and Dürer) or by master craftsmen (Veit Stoss and Tilman Riemenschneider). Their work can be seen in museums such as the outstanding Germanisches Nationalmuseum at Nürnberg, or sometimes in the original settings see

NORTHERN BAVARIA

0   20   40   60 km
0   10   20   30 miles

CZ

A72
Plauen
Oberwiesenthal
Klingenthal
Markneukirchen
Bad · ▲661m
ster
Bad Brambach
Selb
Kappel ■
Waldsassen
Mitterteich
Tirschenreuth
Oberpfälzer
Weiden
Leuchtenberg
Wald
Nabburg
Naab
Schwandorf
A93
Furth im Wald
Cham
Regen
Kötzting
1293m ▲ Osser
1456m Gr-Arber
Bayerischer
Viechtach
Regen
Zwiesel
1452m Gr-Rachel
allmünz
Walhalla ■
Regensburg
A3
Metten
Grafenau
1370m Lusen
Straubing
Natternberg
Deggendorf
Wald
Gr-Laaber
Geiselhöring
Kloster Niederalteich
Ils
Tittling
Rohr
Ergoldsbach
A92
Landau
Osterhofen
Donau
Vilshofen
Wegscheid
Jochenstein
Isar
Aldersbach
Aidenbach
Passau
Ortenburg
Neuburg
Furstenzell
Vornbach
Landshut
Vils
burg
Vilsbiburg
Massing
Rott
Triftern
Asbach
Bad Füssing
A
Taufkirchen
Rotthalmünster
Ering
Inn
D
E

Riemenschneider's *Madonna in a Rose Garland* in the little church at Volkach. Architecture particularly worth noting includes a number of sumptuous 18th-century baroque and rococo edifices.

National parks offer unparallelled opportunities for exploring, on foot, by cycling or by canoe along the rivers. Rural scenery ranges from the romantic **Altmühl Valley** to the mysterious depths of Europe's last remaining fragments of virgin forest in the **Bayerischer Wald**.

Enjoy the region for its food and drink. Hearty game dishes or spicy sausages from Nürnberg are complemented by famous beers (the world's oldest brewery is at **Freising**, near Munich) or wines from Franconia, where Main Valley vineyards rival those of the Rhine and Mosel. This is a favourite holiday area, with bargains to be had in remoter places along the border with the Czech Republic.

CONTROVERSIAL CANAL
The lower reaches of the Ahltmül have become part of the new Main–Danube Canal. Completed in 1992, this gigantic and bitterly controversial project connects the waterways of western and central Europe, enabling large vessels to ply between the Rhine and the Black Sea. Nowhere else has a river landscape been so transformed nor so conscientiously restored, a process best seen at Essing, just downstream from Prunn. Here the idyllic riverside scene of village, barbican, and ancient timber bridge seems completely untouched by time.

The Befreiungshalle (Liberation hall), built to celebrate 'liberation' from Napoleon's rule

▶▶ **Altmühltal (Altmühl Valley)**   *206C1*

This is one of Germany's most attractive river valleys, with unspoiled towns and villages, dramatic crags topped by castles, and the nation's largest nature park, **Altmühltal**. The river rises in the Frankenhöhe (Franconian Heights), near Rothenburg-ob-der-Tauber; crosses gently rolling countryside to the small spa town of Treuchtlingen; then twists deeply through the limestone of the Fränkische Alb (Franconian Jura), joining the Danube at Kelheim.

The meadowlands, rock pinnacles, and juniper-studded slopes are enjoyed by walkers and by cyclists on the riverside bike path.

Downstream is **Eichstatt▶**, a superior little episcopal city of classic elegance, an architectural showpiece. Its 14th-century cathedral, a mix of Romanesque, Gothic and baroque, contains the famous Pappenheim Altar, an arresting late medieval depiction of the Crucifixion. Rococo mansions, neatly painted pale blue or yellow, line the Residenzplatz, crowned by a gilded statue of the Virgin. All is aesthetically impressive, but almost too much like a stage set, with the Willibald fortress looming on a hill above. The town has a small private Catholic university. There are fine views from the Frauenberg pilgrimage chapel crowning a hilltop or from the chunky, chalk-white Willibaldsburg overlooking the river.

The valley's most extraordinary castle is 11th-century Prunn, perched precariously over the river.

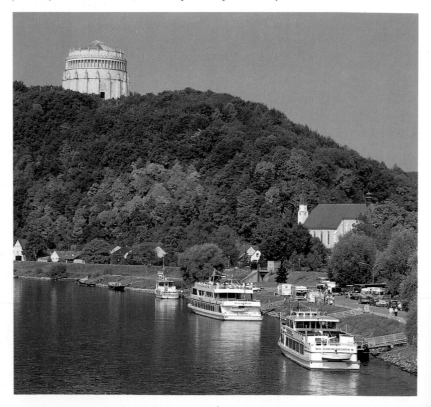

▶ Amberg 206C2

Untouched by wars and heavy industry, Amberg has within its medieval walls a variety of buildings from its prosperous past, including four fine gateways and the ancient bridge – the Stadtbrille (City Spectacles – note the reflection of its twin arches in the waters of the River Vils).

The gabled and arcaded Gothic Rathaus, one of the finest town halls in Germany, dominates the market square. The churches include the stately St Martin's (1421), St George's, given a Baroque interior in the late 17th century, and the Deutsche Schulkirche, a rococo gem. Stations of the Cross lead uphill to the late Renaissance pilgrimage church of Mariahilf, with its fine views over the town and the countryside of the Oberpfalz (Upper Palatinate). Amberg holds its Altstadtfest in June and its Bergfest in July, though the products of its 10 breweries can be sampled at any time!

▶ Ansbach 206B2

Administrative and cultural centre of central Franconia, Ansbach is one of Germany's finest 'Residenz towns', its history and townscape fashioned by its role as the seat of its rulers, the margraves of Brandenburg-Ansbach. Streets and squares feature many attractive buildings, from high-gabled medieval burghers' houses to the three-towered church of St Gumbertus, redesigned in the 18th century to become an ideal 'preaching church', dominated by the pulpit rather than the altar.

The **Residenz▶** itself is a splendid Renaissance structure, incorporating parts of the original medieval moated stronghold. Its rococo interior contains the Bavarian state collection of Ansbach ceramics. Beyond is the palace's park, the Hofgarten, with stately avenues of lime trees, an impressive orangery, and a memorial to the enigmatic foundling Kaspar Hauser, mysteriously murdered here in 1833 and the subject of fascinated speculation ever since and of various books and films.

▶ Aschaffenburg 206A3

The first Bavarian town for visitors coming from the Frankfurt direction, Aschaffenburg is dominated by the huge red sandstone **Schloss▶** standing foursquare on a bluff overlooking the River Main. Known as the Johannisburg, it was erected at the start of the 17th century by the bishop of Mainz, Aschaffenburg's overlord. The interior includes state apartments, fine paintings (including pictures by Cranach), and a range of glass and ceramics (*Open* Apr–Oct Tue–Sun 9–12, 1–5; Nov–Mar Tue–Sun 11–4. *Admission charge*). Other master works including another Cranach and a Grünewald can be found in the town centre's Stiftskirche, a church incorporating a variety of architectural styles from the Romanesque onwards. Treasures of a different kind feature in the Automuseum, with its 200-odd classic racing cars and collection of automobile art (Obernauerstrasse 125. *Open* Apr–Oct Tue–Sun 10–6, Nov–Mar Sun and public holidays 10–6. *Admission charge*).

The town's two parks, Schöntal (in the centre) and Schönbusch (on the far bank of the Main), are excellent examples of German landscapers' attempts to imitate the 'English Style' in garden design.

209

A golden baroque statue-fountain adorns Ansbach, which was once a royal town with a brilliant court

Aschaffenburg's Schloss above the River Main. Next door is a quiet quarter of old Fachwerk (half-timbered) houses down narrow alleys

Excursions

The Spessart East of Aschaffenburg the River Main swings south then north again in a great bend, forming the southern boundary of the Spessart, one of Germany's finest areas of unspoiled uplands. Here are some of the country's most extensive woodlands, magnificent stands of beech and oak stretching away to distant horizons – an awesome prospect even when viewed from the great scenic highway, the Frankfurt–Nuremberg autobahn.

In the romantic setting of a deep forest valley lies **Schloss Mespelbrunn** (*Open* mid-Mar–mid-Nov Mon–Sat 9–noon, 1–5; Sun 9–5. *Admission charge*), its picturesque silhouette reflected in the calm surface of its moat. Still inhabited, the castle's furnished interior is pleasingly evocative of the life of the provincial nobility.

The stretch of the Main upstream from Aschaffenburg forms part of the Franconian wine-growing area. It is a landscape of orchards, south-facing vineyards and pleasant little towns and villages, among them half-timbered **Miltenberg** – 'the very essence of medieval Germany'.

▶▶ Augsburg   *206B1*

With a population of 250,000, Augsburg is Bavaria's third-largest city, as well as its oldest, founded in Roman times and named after Emperor Augustus. Commanding the Alpine trade routes linking northern Europe to Italy, Augsburg enjoyed its heyday in the 15th and 16th centuries. Second then only to London as a banking centre, it became the base of great financial dynasties, such as the immensely rich Fuggers. The former family home, the **Fuggerhaus**, sits majestically on busy Maximilianstrasse, busts of two Fugger patrons adorn the entrance to the 16th century building, and a restaurant, crowded with today's local businessmen, is in the cellar. The socal welfare settlement founded by the Fuggers, the **Fuggerei**, a picturesque quarter of tiny houses, is still home to more than 100 Augsburg elderly people, who have to pray daily for the Fugger family in return for a peppercorn rent. Later names associated with Augsburg include Mozart's father, whose birthplace, Frauentorstrasse 30, is now a Mozart museum (*Open* Wed–Sun 10–4. *Admission charge*); Rudolf Diesel (who invented his engine at the MAN works); Willy Messerschmitt (famous for his fighter planes); and the playwright Brecht (who was born here).

What to see Augsburg has a big city centre, focussed on the Ludwigplatz. Here the imposing Renaissance Rathaus (1620) has a glorious Goldener Saal (golden hall), once Germany's largest city hall (*Open* Mon to Sat 10–6. *Admission charge*). The landmark tower, the Perlachturm, offers good city views from its top (*Open* May to mid-Oct, daily 10–4, weekends noon–7. *Admission free*). To the north stands Augsburg's Cathedral, the Domkirche St Maria, originally Romanesque but much altered and added to subsequently. Augsburg has a number of fine fountains. The Augustusbrunnen (1594), with its majestic figures of the emperor and river gods, stands in the Ludwigplatz, the Herkulesbrunnen (1596–1602) in the broad Maximilian-strasse to the south. This stately city artery is lined with many splendid residences, including

the Fuggerhaus and the rococo Schaezlerpalais, which has art collections and a Festsaal (banqueting hall) (*Open* Wed to Sun 10–4. *Admission charge*).

The Rathaus and Perlachturm in the Ludwigplatz at Augsburg

Excursion

Just east of Augsburg is the small town of **Friedberg**. Its notable features include a castle dating from 1150, a Renaissance Rathaus, and above all Herrgottsruh, a pilgrimage church with an exuberant rococo interior.

▶ Bad Kissingen   206B4

Located among parks and gardens along the banks of the River Saale, this is Bavaria's most popular spa.

The spa buildings include an 1838 arcade and the monumental 1913 Regentenbau, a complex of halls and public rooms linked to the Wandelhalle, a covered promenade. The Theatre, completed in 1904, has a fine Jugendstil interior. On the far bank of the Saale from the Wandelhalle is the immaculate Kurpark with buildings housing a spa and a casino.

Crowning a hilltop south of town are the ruins of Bodenlauben Castle, once the residence of the medieval poet and keen crusader Otto von der Bodenlauben whose statue forms part of the fountain on the Rathausplatz.

The Rhön Bad Kissingen is one of the main 'gateways' to this area of varied upland scenery that stretches northwards to **Fulda**. Rising in places to over 900m, the rounded summits carry a covering of moorland and pasture rather than forest. This splendid walking country is also much favoured by gliding enthusiasts. The most extensive views, both involving a short hike of half an hour or so, are from the **Wasserkuppe** (950m) and the **Kreuzberg** (928m). In the valleys are attractive little towns such as **Gersfeld**, with its three castles, and

An elegant Kurpark and Kurgarten are features of Bad Kissingen

Bad Brückenau, a spa with classical buildings inspired by the ubiquitous King Ludwig. **Bad Neustadt** has kept intact its ring of medieval fortifications. Within the walls stands the former church of the Carmelites, dating from the 14th century but with an exceptionally fine baroque interior. On the far bank of the Saale are the spa facilities, including a Kurhotel comfortably installed within an 18th-century castle.

Münnerstadt, too, has retained its walls, but its greatest treasure is the high altar by the great Riemenschneider in the parish church.

A favourite short excursion from Bad Kissingen is to **Bad Bocklet**, on the historic mail coach that plies between the two spas, passing the Renaissance castle at **Aschach**, its rooms filled with fine furniture and paintings and a collection of oriental art.

▶ Bad Mergentheim 206A2

Pleasantly situated in the picturesque valley of the River Tauber, this is an important stopping place along the Romantische Strasse, as well as a spa. In contrast to the newer spa town, the old town has a picturesque market square, churches, high-gabled Rathaus and an ancient fountain. The most prominent structure is the ochre mid-16th-century Deutschordensschloss (*Closed* Mon; see also Ellingen, page 222). The castle is a fascinating assembly of high walls, gables, towers, and turrets. Inside there is a splendid Renaissance staircase. The baroque castle church has a light-filled interior with a magnificent ceiling painting; in the crypt are the tombs of long-dead grand masters.

Excursion

The parish church at **Stuppach**, about 7km southwest, has a famous *Madonna and Child* by the great Grünewald, one of this tormented master's more spiritual paintings (see panel page 214).

▶▶▶ Bamberg 206B3

Bamberg is perhaps the most perfect of all Germany's ancient cities, a wonderful synthesis of architecture of all periods in a harmonious setting of river vale and gentle hills. Since 1994 it has been named as part of UNESCO's World Cultural Heritage.

Founded in AD 973, the city was made a bishopric by King Henry II, and its division into two distinct districts is still apparent: the Bürgerstadt, or merchants' town, by the River Regnitz, and the Bischofsstadt, or ecclesiastical quarter, on the slopes above. Linking the two is the extraordinarily picturesque old **town hall▶**, an incongruous mixture of rustic half-timbering and rococo elegance perched on a tiny island in the Regnitz. Downstream is Bamburg's Little Venice, once the home of fishermen.

Higher up is the **Kaiserdom▶▶**, the city's great cathedral, with its four tall towers finding their echo in those of St Michael's Church, crowning the hilltop in the middle distance. The cathedral is a triumph of the transitional period between late Romanesque and early Gothic. Its

213

Northern Bavaria

Bamberg's quaint old Rathaus was built on an island in the river, so as to serve the city's two rival parts

STUPPACHER MADONNA

The little parish church of Stuppach, 11km south of Bad Mergentheim on the B-19, found itself in possession of one of the greatest German Renaissance paintings in 1908 when a dark, grimy altar picture of the Virgin Mary was identified as the work of the early 16th-century master Matthias Grünewald. Later repainting of the picture had given it a flat and undistinguished surface. Now the restored Stuppacher Madonna can be seen in all its original glory. (The church is open daily from 9 until dusk.)

CITY OF SCULPTURE

Bamberg is making a name for itself as a 'city of sculpture'. After a highly successful city-wide exhibition of 14 large sculptures by the South American artist Fernando Bottero, Bamberg citizens organised an initiative to keep at least one of the works. Bottero's sculptures command very high prices, but that did not daunt the good burgers of Bamberg, who raised more than $500,000 to buy a symbolic statue of a typical Bottero fat lady, Europa, riding a bull. It stands on one of the squares in Bamberg's pedestrian shopping zone.

interior is enlivened by some of the most remarkable sculpture to be found in Germany. The **Bamberger Reiter▶** (Bamberg Knight) on his stone steed has come to represent the essence of medieval chivalry, while the **tomb of Henry II▶** and his Queen Kunigunde is one of the masterpieces of the great Tilman Riemenschneider (*c* 1513). The royal pair appear again in the elaborately carved choir stalls, while the Marienaltar (1523) is by the Nürnberg wood-carver Veit Stoss.

The Domplatz (cathedral square) is overlooked on one side by the Neue Residenz, with its splendid baroque interior, and on the other by the Alte Hofhaltung. Beyond the Renaissance gateway the undulating cobbled courtyard is enclosed by a delightfully irregular sequence of late Gothic galleried buildings.

Bamberg offers much to the unhurried explorer, including churches (from Gothic St Jakob to the rococo interior of St Gangolf), splendid town residences (the richly decorated Böttingerhaus or the riverside Concordiahaus) and museums – the Diocesan Museum, off the cathedral cloister (*Open* May–Oct Tue–Sun. *Closed* Nov–Apr), or the exemplary local history museum, in the Alte Hofhaltung (*Closed* Mon). A close-up of the city can be seen from the Vierkirchenblick (four-church view), south of the cathedral, a more distant prospect from the old Bishops' castle, the Altenburg, 3km southwest.

Excursions

In **Pommersfelden**, 20km south, is Schloss Weissen-stein, one of Germany's most grandiose baroque palaces, built by Prince-Bishop Schönborn of Bamberg in 1711–18. There is a sumptuous interior and an English-style park beyond (Palace *Open* Apr–Oct Tue–Sun). The **River Main** joins the Regnitz downstream from Bamberg. Along its course lie a number of pretty little places: Zeil-am-Main, half-timbered Königsberg (north of the river), and Hassfurt, graced by a parish church (with a Riemenschneider carving) and the Ritterkapelle (Knights' Chapel), a minor masterpiece of late Gothic.

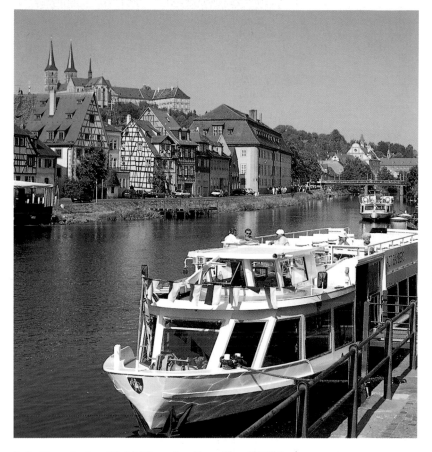

►► Bayerischer Wald (Bavarian Forest) 207D2

Between the Danube and the Czech border stretch 6,000 sq km of upland country, forming, with the Sumava (Bohemian Forest) on the far side of the frontier, 'Europe's Green Roof'. Rising to 1,456m at the Grosser Arber, the area contains traces of primeval forest and ancient stands of spruce carefully preserved as part of Germany's first national park. Woodland is continuous on the higher land, interspersed elsewhere with attractive farming countryside and meticulously modernised villages. Churches with onion domes pierce the skyline and little streams channel through steeply sloping meadows to tributaries of the Danube.

Though there are no large towns, impeccably engineered roads stitch the whole area together, and the occasional two-coach train still trundles the single tracks of the surviving branch lines. With an abundant variety of accommodation, this is one of the areas favoured by Germans for their holidays. Attractions are plentiful, from relics of the metalworking industries that flourished until recently to castle ruins perched on rocks, or little medieval towns. Many places have their Heimatmuseum (local-history museum), and there are curiosities like the snuff museum at Grafenau.

So-called Klein Venedig (Little Venice) is a charming area of Bamberg, on the Regnitz River

WINTER SPORTS
Long winters provide the perfect conditions for winter sports in the Bayerischer Wald. As well as some provision for downhill skiing, there are altogether more than 2,000km of cross-country trails.

Drive

Passau to Cham

Climbing from the Danube, the B85 (the Bayerische Ostmarkstrasse) is a splendid scenic highway linking Passau on the Austrian border with Bayreuth.

Near **Tittling**, look around the Museumsdorf Bayerischer Wald, where old buildings have been renovated (*Open* mid-Mar–Oct daily 8–5. *Admission charge*).

Continue on the Ostmarkstrasse to Cham via Regen, located on the Schwarzer Regen, and Viechtach with its 17th-century Rathaus, or detour around the Grosser Arber. Just north of Neuschönau, the Hans-Eisenmann-Haus, the visitor centre run by the Bavarian Forest National Park, has displays, leaflets (in English) and self-guided trails that tell you all about the origins of the forest and its wildlife (*Open* daily 9–5).

The road northwest to the Arber goes through towns where the glass industry flourishes, though Spiegelau, Frauenau, and Zwiesel are more like resorts than manufacturing centres. Some glassworks can be visited, while Frauenau has a superb Glasmuseum. **Bodenmais**, in the Bavarian Forest,

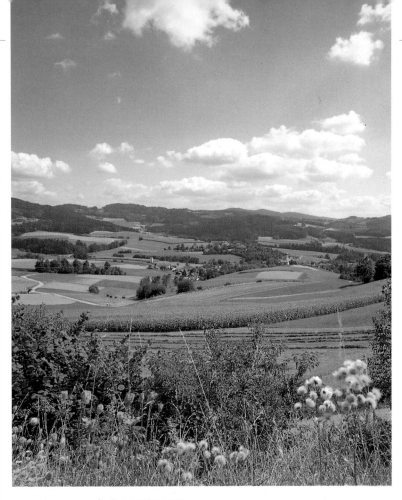

Open views across the Bayerischer Wald

deals in glass, but outside the town is the **Silberberg**, mined for its copper, tin and silver and now open to visitors (though no longer in production). (*Open* Apr–mid-Jun and Oct daily 10–4; mid-Jun–mid-Sep daily 9–5; Dec 1–3; Jan–Mar Tue, Wed, Fri, Sat. *Closed* Nov.)

To the north rises the Arber, with remnants of the inaccessible primeval forest. This is one of the most inhospitable areas in Germany. Frost occurs on 200 or more days a year, and deep snow lies well into spring. Solitude can be enjoyed here, though not around the chalets on the banks of the **Arbersee**.

An arduous ascent on foot (3½ hours there and back) will take you to the summit of the **Grosser Arber** –

more easily reached by the skilift on the highway to **Lam**. This ridge-top road gives panoramic views of the mountains (notably from the Hindenburg viewpoint) before descending into gentler countryside around Lam.

The Ostmarkstrasse is rejoined at **Cham**, with its fine market square, via either Kötzting, rebuilt after a great fire in 1867, or Furth im Wald. Kötzting has a flamboyant Whit Monday procession (*Pfingstritt*) and Furth has the *Drachenstich*, a pageant in which an 18m animated dragon is slain, with much jollity. Situated on the Regensburg–Plzen (Pilsen) road, Furth is a frontier town: the Skoda cars of Czech shoppers can be seen parked among the local cars on its little market square.

WAGNER'S THEATRE
Wagner's real monument is the bulky Festspiel-haus, on rising ground north of the city centre. Designed by Semper, but aesthetically no rival to the Markgräfliches Opern-haus, it provides the optimum setting for the master's works. At inter-mission time during the festival the grounds fill with up to 1,800 people recovering from the oper-atic onslaught. Admire the massive bust of Wagner by Arno Breker, one of the Third Reich's most suc-cessful sculptors, as well as the representations of Cosima and of Liszt, who died during the 1886 festival.

*Modern Bayreuth,
much rebuilt since
Wagner's day*

►► Bayreuth   206C3

Founded as long ago as the 11th century, Bayreuth first came into its own in the 18th century under the rule of Margrave Friedrich and his energetic and talented spouse, Wilhelmina, sister of Frederick the Great. A second flowering occurred in the late 19th century, when Richard Wagner made it the showcase for his innovative operas (see page 237). The operatic tradition persists, attracting fans in their thousands to the Bayreuth Festival, held annually in July and August.

Traces of Bayreuth's medieval past can still be seen, for example in narrow alleyways and the typically Bavarian elongated market square, as well as the Gothic Stadt-kirche (city church). The original residence of the margraves, the Altes Schloss (old palace) (*Closed* Mon) goes back to the 14th century and its present appearance is due to 17th-century rebuilding.

The baroque age contributed most to Bayreuth's archi-tectural character, again largely because of the energetic Wilhelmina. The Neues Schloss (new palace, 1754) has lighthearted rococo interiors, including grotto and garden rooms, and houses some of the town's museums (*Closed* Mon). The grounds of the Hofgarten are an early example of Romantic landscape design.

To the north is the 18th-century Markgräfliches Opernhaus. Undistinguished outside, it has a galleried interior that shows the baroque style at its most theatrical.

Connected to the Hofgarten by a gateway, erected in 1874 to celebrate the composer's 61st birthday, is Wagner's Bayreuth residence, the classical Villa Wahnfried, now the National Wagner Museum (*Open* daily). In the gardens stands the grave of the great man. His wife Cosima, daughter of Franz Liszt, is buried beside him, his faithful hound Russ a short distance away.

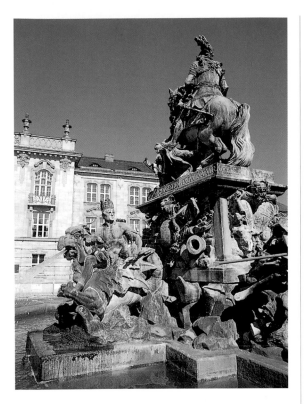

Marking the eastern extremity of the great limestone outcrop that begins far away in the Jura Mountains, Bayreuth is one of Germany's most romantically picturesque regions. The porous rock has been eroded to form some two dozen deep and narrow valleys through which flow clear trout streams that once powered ancient mills. Medieval castles cap many crags; look for the one perched above the tiny town of Pottenstein. Nearby Tüchersfeld has an even more bizarre setting, with fairy-tale houses wedged among the rock pinnacles. Below ground, equally strange landscapes can be seen in the caves known as the Teufelshöhle, where there are weirdly shaped concretions and the bones of prehistoric animals.

Excursions

The beautiful grounds of the **Schloss Eremitage** (Hermitage Castle), 4km northeast of Bayreuth, go back to the 17th century, when the margraves would come here to escape court life in town. The original hermitage, the Altes Schloss, was built by the ruling margrave in 1715.

The **Fichtelgebirge** (Fichtel Mountains), ancient granite-littered uplands, form a horseshoe-shaped massif enclosing eastwards-facing lowlands, and are named after the extensive forests of *Fichte* (spruce) that clad their slopes. The area's abundant rainfall feeds rivers flowing to all points of the compass, the Eger east to the Elbe in the Czech Republic, the Naab south to the Danube, the Weisser Main west to the Rhine.

The Ochsenkopf summit (1024m), with its TV tower (chairlift from Bishofsgrün), gives majestic views. In contrast the tranquil scene by the banks of the little Fichtelsee, set deep among the dark conifers, or the Luisenberg labyrinth, a chaos of granite blocks eroded into strange shapes and was much admired by Goethe. Here is Germany's oldest open-air theatre, still the venue for summertime performances.

The towns in the sheltered lowland include the area's little capital, **Wunsiedel**, with the Fichtelgebirge museum, and busy **Marktredwitz**, on the route leading to the north-western Czech Republic.

The **Frankenwald** (Franconian Forest) is Germany's smallest upland, with peaceful valleys, remote hamlets, deep forest, and wild areas of heath bog. The highest point

Above: Baroque sculptures reflect the golden age of 18th-century Bayreuth under Princess Wilhelmina

SANSPAREIL GARDEN

The picturesque potential of rocky outcrop and eerie forest was appreciated by Margravine Wilhelmina. Around the crag-top ruin of Zwernitz Castle she laid out a romantic landscape to tickle the refined sensibilities of her contemporaries and called it Sanspareil, in the Francophile fashion. Beyond Morgenländischer Bau (an Asian hermitage), winding paths lead past strange rock formations to fanciful features like the theatre conceived as a ruin and set in a grotto. The castle itself forms part of the artful composition and from its keep you can see a wonderful panorama reaching far away to the Frankenwald and the Fichtelgebirge.

THE STRONGEST BEER

The picturesque little market town of Kulmbach lays claim to the largest per capita production of beer in Germany: 4,250 litres per man, woman and child. More than an quarter of Kulmbach households earn a living directly or indirectly from the town's six breweries. One of them, the Erste Kulmbacher Union, produces the strongest beer in the world – the Doppelbock Kulminator 28. With an alcoholic content of more than 11 percent, it has the kick of a mule. At the end of July and start of August, Kulmbach has a nine-day beer festival that rivals Munich's Oktoberfest – the beer, at any rate, is stronger!

is the Döbraberg (794m) with a tower giving panoramic views to the Fichtelgebirge to the south and the Thüringian heights to the north. North from Bayreuth is **Kulmbach**, whose large breweries are known for their bitter dark beers and strong, sharp Pils (see panel). They lie below the **Plassenburg▶**, a splendid stronghold with a fine Renaissance courtyard.

Once a prison, the castle now houses the Zinnfigurenmuseum, the national collection of 300,000 tin figurines. Kronach has beautifully preserved medieval houses, including the birthplace of Cranach (1472–1553), painter of rugged landscapes and courtly nudes. Above the town rises its great fortress, the Rosenberg. With its triple ring of walls pierced by a single entrance above ground, this is Germany's most extensive medieval stronghold to remain intact. Its picture gallery includes works by Cranach.

The River Wiesent runs through one of the prettiest valleys in **Fränkische Schweiz** (Franconian Switzerland) and is best seen from the viewpoints in the little market town and resort of Gössweinstein, which is also famous for its pilgrimage church.

▶▶ Coburg
206B4

During Germany's division, Coburg was on the edge of things, situated in a cul-de-sac ending at the East German border. Its name, which is linked to half the dynasties that once ruled Europe, never lost its fame, and the place, busier now with the disappearance of the frontier, is still dominated by its two, very different, ducal castles.

High above the town, and visible from far across Coburg's attractive rural surroundings, broods the majestic **Veste▶** (fortress) (*Closed* Mon), called 'the Crown of Franconia' because of its tower-studded outline. Founded in the 11th century and much rebuilt in Renaissance times by the vigorous Duke Johann Casimir, it ranks among the country's most splendid strongholds. Within its double ring of defensive walls there are many treasures, including the 300,000-plus items of its print collection, paintings by a number of German masters (among them Cranach), arms, armour, furniture, and Johann Casimir's State Carriage (1560). Martin Luther stayed here in 1530, and his visit is commemorated by the room named after him.

Linking the Veste to town is the Hofgarten, its verdant slopes embracing a notable Natural History Museum (see panel). In the 16th century, the dukes moved down the hill into their new castle, the Ehrenburg. Remodelled externally to suit the 19th-century taste for the Gothic, the palace retains much of its original interior, including its resplendent chapel and the Riesensaal (Giants' Hall), so called because of the 28 plaster heavies holding up the painted ceiling. You can also see the bedroom where the British Queen Victoria stayed while visiting Ehrenberg.

While the burghers built their fine half-timbered and high-gabled town houses, the dukes gave the town a Renaissance touch. Johann Casimir was responsible for the academy known as the Casimirianum and for the Stadthaus, facing the rococo town hall across the cobbled market square. The ducal imprint can be seen, too, in the Gothic Church of St Moriz, with its incredibly elaborate 13m-high (five-storey) memorial to Duke Johann Friedrich (d 1598).

THE SAXE-COBURGS
The influence of this aristocratic family was out of all proportion to its possessions or power. Comely rather than rich, its children were married off judiciously and, by the 19th century, were well established in many of the courts of Europe. Most famous of them was Albert – consort to the British Queen Victoria – born at Rosenau Castle, near Coburg, and brought up in the Ehrenburg. His statue stands in the market square. Coburg blood ran in Victoria's own veins and after Albert's death in 1861 she stayed here several times. One of her grandsons, Carl Eduard, ruled the duchy until its abolition in 1919. In the same year, Ferdinand von Coburg-Kohary returned here after his abdication as Czar of Bulgaria, devoting the rest of his life to ornithology. The birds he stuffed form the basis of the collection in the town's Natural History Museum (*Closed* Mon).

221

Coburg's massive Veste fortress, above the town, has a stark exterior but a pretty inner courtyard

CHILDREN'S APPEAL
Dinkelsbühl has escaped the ravages of wars, though there was a close shave in the course of the Thirty Years' War, when the fury of the besieging Swedes was mollified by an appeal made to their commander by the town's children. The event is marked by the Kinderzeche, a colourful 10-day festival held annually in July.

Oxcarts for tourists keep the medieval touch alive in Dinkelsbühl, a town that still has watch-towers and ramparts

▶▶▶ Dinkelsbühl   206B2

More compact than Rothenburg-ob-der-Tauber, further up the Romantische Strasse (Romantic Road – see page 230), Dinkelsbühl is one of Germany's most delightful medieval towns, perfectly preserved within its ring of walls, bastions and 16 towers.

The best approach is across the causeway leading to the late 14th-century gateway known as the Rothenburger Tor. From the gate the broad Martin Luther Strasse curves down to the market square with its splendid early Renaissance town houses, among them the Deutsches Haus, with seven projecting storeys reaching up into its high gable. The nearby Hezelhof has tiered flowerladen balconies in its lovely inner courtyard. The church of St George still has its Romanesque tower; it is one of the grandest hall churches in southern Germany, with fan vaulting spanning the lofty interior, carving and statuary.

Dinkelsbühl has many more delights that you can discover on your own by wandering the narrow streets, or take the guided tour (in German) on foot that starts at St George's. A walk around the ramparts at night is an atmospheric experience, especially in the company of the town's nightwatchman as he does his rounds (Apr–Oct and Dec, 9 pm).

A BAROQUE GEM
Ellingen was rebuilt following its destruction in the Thirty Years' War and is a little gem of baroque town planning, with a pretty Rathaus and several churches.

▶ Ellingen   206B2

Ellingen was for many years the headquarters of the Deutscher Orden (the Order of Teutonic Knights), a militant brotherhood of priests and soldiers founded around 1190 during the First Crusade but best remembered for their vigorous conversion to Christianity of the pagan population of the Baltic seaboard. Their sombre castle, built 1708–21, rears clifflike over the town and is awkwardly approached from the side. It is enlivened by its main façade, a splendid staircase, rococo interiors, and an elaborately decorated church. The corridors are hung with portraits of the Hochund Deutschmeister, the order's leaders.

▶ Freising   206C1

Easily reached from the centre of Munich by S-Bahn suburban train, Freising is a city in its own right, a bishopric
from as early as 739. The dominant feature of the town is
the Domberg, a bluff of higher land looking out over the
interminable flatlands stretching southwards to Munich.
The chalk-white cathedral rises over a cluster of churches
and other ecclesiastical buildings, including the Prince-
Bishop's Residenz, now a museum (*Closed* Mon), and the
Gothic Johannes-Kapelle, with its baroque interior. The
cathedral interior exults in baroque splendour, but a more
somber era is evoked in the crypt, with its capitals and
columns bearing strange figures of men and beasts.

▶ Ingolstadt   206C1

Strategically located on the upper reaches of the Danube,
Ingolstadt is one of Bavaria's great cities, with a long history and a thriving present (oil refineries, Audi works).
First mentioned in 806, Ingolstadt blossomed in the
Middle Ages. Come into town via the brick Kreuztor gateway of 1385. Beyond is the minster, dedicated to Our
Lady, its high west gable flanked by asymmetrical towers.
There are fine old houses, including the Ickstatt-Haus of
1740, a rococo confection in yellow with white stucco
icing. The interior of the church of Maria de Victoria is
from the same period. Note its painted ceiling, which is a
masterpiece of perspective effects.

Excursions
Weltenburg Abbey (45km east via Neustadt) is sited on
the Danube at the entrance to the Donaudurchbruch, a
spectacular gorge cut by the river en route to its confluence with the Altmühl at Kelheim. 'The Danube in
Flames', a floodlit lighting of the gorge, takes place on the
first Saturday in July. A high point of German 18th-
century baroque, the abbey church's oval interior verges
on high kitsch, with a tableau of St George smiting the
dragon and cherubs flying around in chunky clouds. It
certainly draws the crowds, whom you can join for beer
(the abbey's own) in the courtyard.

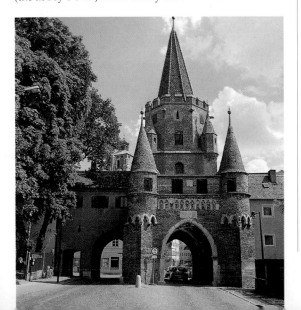

WEIHENSTEPHAN
On a wooded bluff to the
west of Friesing is
Weihenstephan, famous
for beer (the world's
oldest brewery – 1040)
and the prestigious
Technical University of
Munich.

MILITARY MUSEUM
Ingolstadt's importance
as a fortress and garrison
town was enhanced in the
19th century with the
construction of massive
fortifications. Most have
been razed, but some
severely classical gate-
ways remain, including the
Kavalier Heydeck. The
Gothic Nenes Schloss, a
relic of earlier defences,
is an appropriate setting
for the Bavarian Military
Museum (*Closed* Mon).

**NEUBURG AN DER
DONAU**
Neuburg an der Donau is
an old Residenz town 16
miles up the Danube from
Ingolstadt. The place is
dominated by the
Renaissance palace built
by Protestant Prince
Ottheinrich, whose hope
of making the town's
Hofkirche a beacon of
Protestantism in Catholic
Bavaria was frustrated by
the Counter-Reformation.

*The 14th-century
Kreuztor gateway,
hexagonal, with six
pointed turrets, stands
at the entrance to
Ingolstadt's old town*

LAVISH PAGEANT

In 1475, at the peak of its prosperity and prestige, Landshut marked the wedding of its Prince George to a Polish princess with lavish celebrations which became a byword all over Europe. These great days are recalled every three years by contemporary Germany's most extravagant pageant, the Landshuter Fürstenhochzeit, when revellers in period costume perform against the splendid stage set of Landshut's historic townscape. The next pageant is in 2001.

'DANIEL' TOWER

Nördlingen's massive grey stone parish church of St George has a lofty white interior and a 89m tower nicknamed 'Daniel'. It is worth the climb for the view over the red roofs of the oval-shaped town. From here, an inner oval of streets can clearly be picked out, marking the course of an older ring of fortifications, long since demolished.

► **Landshut**   *207D1*

On the banks of the River Isar at the foot of Trausnitz Castle, Landshut has kept much of the appearance and atmosphere of the provincial capital it once was. This old city is centred on two fine market streets lined with late medieval town houses, many with stepped gables and arcaded courtyards. The gently curving Altstadt (old town) dates to the founding of the city in 1204, and the Neustadt (new town) was laid out a century later.

The Altstadt is closed off by the church of St Martin, a bold Gothic brick building. Its slender tower rises to 133m, higher than the castle behind it and the tallest structure of its kind in the world. Among the treasures of the light and airy interior is a huge Madonna and Child, carved in 1520 by a local man, Hans Leinberger.

In 1543, Duke Ludwig X moved from the castle into the Stadtresidenz, which has a splendidly decorated interior, part of which houses Landshut's museum (*Open Apr–Sep daily 9–noon, 1-5; Oct–Mar daily 10–noon, 1–4. Admission charge*). Not long afterwards, the castle itself (same opening hours as museum) was refurbished as a base for the lavish court life of Prince William of Bavaria. He kept the 13th-century chapel, with its superb Romanesque statuary, adding a fine galleried courtyard in Renaissance style, and had the famous Narrentreppe staircase painted with robust figures from the Italian comic theatre. The castle terrace gives a spectacular panorama over the town.

Excursion

A sixth of the world's hops are grown in the **Hallertau** area around Mainburg. This is pretty, hilly countryside, with hops standing out against dark woodlands. Pickers no longer camp in the fields, but the season is still celebrated by the election of a Hop Queen in the village of Wolnzach.

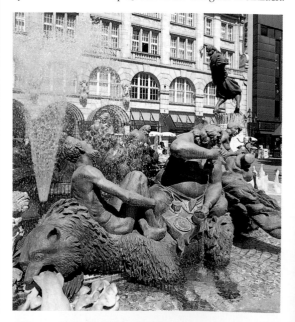

Nürnberg's huge Schöner Brunnen (beautiful fountain) contains 40 different figures arranged in a pyramid

▶ Nördlingen 206B1

Nördlingen's heyday came between the 14th and 16th centuries, when its great Whitsun Fair drew traders from all over Germany. Its subsequent stagnation has helped preserve its townscape, much to the delight of today's many visitors. It is now one of the principal stops along the Romantische Strasse. The ramparts, intact after 500 years, have 16 towers and five gateways, from which five main streets converge on the Marktplatz with its 13th-century Rathaus.

Excursions

Two fine churches are close to Nördlingen. In spite of its baroque furnishings, the former abbey church at **Kaisheim** (6km northeast of Donauworth) evokes the severe lives of its 14th-century Cistercian founders.

Neresheim (19km southwest) has a fine abbey church, too. The last work of Balthasar Neumann, it is a fitting conclusion to the career of this foremost architect of the South German baroque. Under its three domes, the interior is unusually light and spacious, with fine ceiling paintings by the Tirolean Martin Knoller.

▶▶▶ Nürnberg (Nuremberg) 206C2

Crowning the outcrop of warm red sandstone from which much of Nürnberg is built, the **Kaiserburg▶** (*Open* Apr–Sep daily 9–12, 12.45–5; Oct–Mar daily 9.30–12, 12.45–4. *Closed* 1 Nov, 24–25, 31 Dec, 1 Jan. *Admission charge*), or imperial castle, goes back to the city's founding years in the 11th century. Kings and emperors resided here for 500 years, and the sprawling complex of buildings was added to, demolished and rebuilt throughout this time. Thus the tall five-sided tower dates from 1040, the two-tier Imperial Chapel from the 12th century and the stables (now the youth hostel) from the late 15th century.

Nürnberg's Hauptmarkt, the site of Germany's biggest pre-Christmas market, the Christkindelsmarkt

MEDIEVAL HEYDAY
Before the devastation wrought by the terrible air raids of 1945, Nürnberg was Germany's greatest surviving medieval city. The destruction was not total, and sensitive rebuilding has respected the ancient street pattern, enabling the visitor to recapture the atmosphere of the city's heyday, in the 15th and 16th centuries, when it was the principal focus of Germany's politics, culture, trade, science and technology.

TOY FAIR

In view of Nürnberg's long-standing role as the toy-manufacturing capital of Europe, it is fitting that the annual Toy Fair, the most important of its kind, is held here.

'THE NASTY GIRL'

Passau was confronted with an ugly chapter from its Nazi past in a film which achieved international success. It was based on research in the 1980s by a local girl, Anja Rosmum, who courageously examined the past of many respected burghers: she found that some had once been active Nazis, but had kept it hidden. For this she was victimised and physically attacked locally. But nationally she became a heroine. The famous film *The Nasty Girl* told her story. The film is still frequently shown on German TV.

These decorated steins (beer mugs) are typical of Passau, which is famous for its beer

NAZI RALLIES

The huge parade ground outside Nürnberg where Hitler held his biggest rallies (filmed by Leni Riefenstahl) is now a weed-covered expanse of crumbling concrete echoing with memories. The tribune from where Hitler harangued the Nazi hordes still stands, and contains a small exhibition of contemporary photographs and documents to be replaced in the year 2000 by a permanent museum in the nearby Congresshalle (modeled on the Colosseum in Rome). You can get there on tram line 9 (Luitpoldhain stop). The Palace of Justice where the Nürnberg war crimes trials were held is still Nürnberg's main law court (Furtherstrasse 212).

Directly below the castle timber-framed and gabled houses are crammed up against the ramparts. Albrecht Dürer lived here from 1509 until his death in 1528. The Dürer-Haus (Albrecht-Dürer-Strasse 39. *Open* Tue–Sun 10–5, Thu 10–8. *Admission charge*) has good interiors and displays, though there are more copies than original works In the Burgstrasse is the 16th-century Fenbohaus, now the city museum (reopening late 1999, after renovation). Beyond it is the Rathausplatz, with the Altes Rathaus and, opposite it, the twin towers of the early Gothic St Sebald's Church, with outstanding artwork in the interior by Kraft (*Christ Carrying the Cross*), Vischer (*Shrine of St Sebald*), and Stoss (*Passion and Crucifixion*).

South is the Hauptmarkt – a daily market and site of the pre-Christmas Christkindelsmarkt. The Schöner Brunnen fountain competes with the gabled façade of the Gothic Frauenkirche (Church of Our Lady) and its 16th-century mechanical clock with automata that perform at noon.

Nürnberg's Altstadt is divided into roughly equal halves by the River Pegnitz. One arm of the river is bridged by the Heiliggeist-Spital, a 14th-century almshouse, now a restaurant; downstream is the Weinstadl, a venerable wine store that, together with an old water tower, covered bridge, and weeping willows, makes the most idyllic scene.

Although the southern half of the Altstadt has a more modern air, it contains much of interest. The Gothic church of St Lawrence has a cathedral-like west front. Inside are splendid works: Stoss's multicoloured carving of the Annunciation is suspended from the vaulting; the tall tabernacle is carried by the sculpted figures of Adam

Kraft and his apprentices. The nearby Mauthalle of 1502 was built to store corn; its six-storey roof is pierced by sinister hooded dormers, so characteristic of the city.

Nürnberg has a fine choice of museums. Among the Verkehrsmuseum (Transport Museum) (*Open* Tue–Sun 9–5. *Admission charge*) exhibits is the gleaming Adler, the locomotive that hauled the first-ever German train. The Spielzeugmuseum (*Open* Tue–Sun 10–5, Wed 10–9 pm. *Admission charge*) holds the largest and most varied toy collection in the world. At the outstanding **Germanisches Nationalmuseum ▶ ▶** (*Open* Tue–Sun 10–5, Wed 10–9 pm. *Admission charge, free* Wed 6–9 pm), founded in the 19th century, exhaustion is only avoided by concentrating on a fraction of the exhibits. Don't miss the works of the great painters who spanned the transition from Middle Ages to Renaissance (Altdorfer, Cranach, Dürer) or the carvings and sculptures of their contemporaries, including Kraft, Riemenschneider, and Stoss.

▶▶ Passau 207E1

On a long tongue of land at the confluence of the rivers Danube, Inn and Ilz, Passau has one of the most spectacular settings of any German city. Wooded heights hem in the rivers and provide splendid sites for the pilgrimage church of Maria Hilf to the south and for the Veste to the north, the great fortress built by the city's prince-bishops to keep unruly townsfolk firmly under control.

Passau is still one of Germany's main gateways to Austria; steamers sail from here to Vienna and beyond, to Budapest and the Black Sea. Inland, the web of narrow streets leads to the **cathedral▶**, with its trio of helmeted towers. Founded in the 8th century, it owes much of its present appearance to a thoroughgoing baroque rebuilding (1680). Inside is the world's biggest church organ, installed in the 1920s and with a total of 17,388 pipes. It is played daily at noon and at 7.30pm on Thu in summer. Reconstruction spared the flamboyant Gothic east end of the cathedral, best viewed from the Residenzplatz, an irregular square flanked by fine Renaissance mansions. Opposite the 14th-century Rathaus is a large museum of glass, in the Hotel Wilder Mann (*Open* Mar–Sep, daily 10–4, Oct–Feb, daily 1–4. *Admission charge*).

The city's splendid roofscape is best appreciated from the lofty tower of the Veste. The bishops began building the fortress in 1219 and added to it over the centuries, creating an extraordinary mixture of Gothic, Renaissance, and baroque architecture. It now houses a medley of museums and galleries, including a folk museum (*Open* Tue–Fri 9–5, weekends 10–6. *Admission charge*).

BAROQUE MONASTERIES
To the west of Passau are delightful landscapes between the rivers Vils, Rott and Inn. Visit the baroque monasteries (Vornbach, Aldersbach and Fürstenzell, the last with a particularly splendid library), castles (Neuburg, looming over the Inn; Ortenburg, with one of the finest carved ceilings in Germany) and attractive small towns (Vilshofen, Aidenbach, and Rotthalmünster, with a fine parish church and pilgrimage chapel).

227

Passau, on the Danube, has a legacy of glorious buildings from its past as a Free Imperial City

ROMAN GATE
Regensburg's history
goes back further than
the Middle Ages. The
Celtic name, Radaspona,
survives in the French
name of Ratisbonne. As
Castra Regina, it guarded
the frontier of the Roman
empire at the northern-
point of the Danube. The
remains of the Roman
Praetorian Gate still stand
in the strangely named
street Unter den
Schwibbögen (Under the
Flying Buttress).

HAPPY ANGEL
Regensburg cathedral's
rich sculptural decoration
includes the famous
Angel of the Annunciation,
positively bursting with
enthusiasm at the good
news he has to tell, while
another note is struck by
the figures popularly
known as *The Devil and
His Grandma*, housed in
niches in the main portal.

▶▶▶ Regensburg   207D2

The capital of eastern Bavaria, this historic cathedral city
on the Danube was one of the largest in Germany to
escape wartime destruction. Its narrow cobbled streets
and intimate squares evoke its medieval heyday, when its
merchants were among the most prosperous in Europe.

Near the remains of the Roman Praetorian Gate rise the
lacelike **cathedral**▶▶ spires, added as late as 1869 to the
great edifice begun in the 13th century. This is one of
Germany's finest Gothic churches and has lovely cloisters
and 14th-century stained glass. (Guided tours May–Oct,
Mon–Sat 10, 11, 12; Sun and public holidays 12, 2;
Nov–Apr, Mon–Sat, 11; Sun and public holidays 12.) The
squares around the cathedral form the kernel of the city.

The cathedral's parish church, the Nieder-
münsterkirche, is a mid-12th-century basilica built over
the remains of three previous churches. The oldest (700)
goes back to the Merovingian Age and was erected on top
of Roman remains. Across the Alter Kornmarkt is the
ancient Liebfraukirche (Church of Our Lady). Its interior
was remodelled in rococo style to suit 18th-century tastes.

Whole days could be spent wandering Regensburg's
labyrinth of streets and alleyways lined by venerable
houses in a style as much Italian as German. Like their
counterparts in various Italian towns, the city's leading
families built towers in competition with each other and in
the 13th century there were 60 such structures, of which 20
survive to give the city its unique skyline. Among them is
the Baumburger Turm, with its gallery, and the Goldener
Turm in the Wahlenstrasse, the city's oldest street.

The broad Danube makes a pleasing contrast to this
medieval inner city, best appreciated from the upper
arches of the Steinerne Brücke (Old Stone Bridge), built in
the 12th century and for 800 years the only river crossing
hereabouts. To the left of the towered gateway guarding
the bridgehead is the immense roof of the 17th-century
salt store and at its side, Regensburg's oldest restaurant,
the Historische Wurstküche.

The mostly 19th-century palace of the princes of Thurn
und Taxis presides over the far side of the city centre. The
palace incorporates the cloisters of the church of
St Emmeran, famous for its tombs. Among them is that of
poor Queen Emma, who died in 876 and whose tomb
bears a mournful expression. (Guided tours of the palace
and cloisters: Apr–Oct daily 11, 2, 3, 4; Nov–Mar Sat–Sun
and public holidays 11, 12, 2, 3.)

The aristocratic air of an earlier era is captured in the
Gothic Altes Rathaus, with splendid interiors redolent of
the Imperial Diet which used to assemble here.

The Stadtmuseum (city museum), in the buildings of an
old monastery, displays a wonderful scale model of the
city as it used to be, and the works of members of the
Danube School, including Albrecht Altdorfer.

Excursions

Kallmünz, about 27km northwest, is a self-conscious little
place and a favourite subject for painters. The old stone
bridge near the confluence of the contrastingly coloured
waters of the rivers Vils and Naab is overlooked by the
castle, ruined in the Thirty Years' War but still a wonderful lookout point.

Walhalla▶, a gleaming white copy of the Parthenon, sits in an un-Grecian setting of wooded slopes running down to the Danube. Inspired by Ludwig I of Bavaria and completed in 1841, it houses busts of the great and good of Germanic history. River boats from Regensburg and Kelheim make the journey to Walhalla, but be warned – you have to climb 358 steps to the temple. The easiest way to reach it is by road. At the top is a view over the Danube and the ruins of Donaustauf castle. (*Open* Apr–Sep daily 9–5.45; Oct daily 9–5.45; Nov–Mar daily 10–11.45 and 1–3.45. *Admission charge*. Boat trips to Walhalla start from Regensburg Apr–mid-Oct at 10.30 and 2.)

A view over the River Danube at Regensburg

THURN AND TAXIS

Schloss Emmeram, the Thurn and Taxis ancestral home, has seen many high dramas over the centuries, and in more recent times some wild parties thrown by its high-living young *maitresse*, Princess Gloria – until her husband, Prince Johannes, died. His death left crippling taxes to pay, and she was reduced to selling much of her jewellery and even family furniture before the Bavarian State relented and allowed her to keep the bulk of the palace's other treasures on condition she open her home to visitors. It was the final humiliation in the decline of a family whose fortune was built on Germany's early postal system.

ALBRECHT ALTDORFER

Altdorfer raised landscape painting to a high pitch of emotional intensity – and also found time to serve his native Regensburg as city architect.

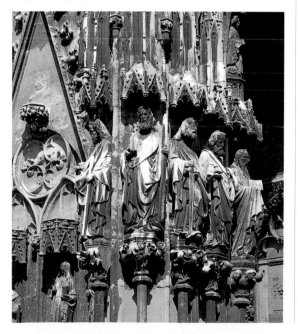

The statues on the main doorway are typical of the elaborate decoration of St Peter's cathedral

RIES VALLEY
Both Nördlingen and the little Residenz town of Wallerstein lie in the vast (20km across) fertile depression known as the Ries. Its origin was long a subject of controversy, but it is now known to have been created by the impact of a meteorite some 15 million years ago. The Apollo 7 astronauts studied the region in preparation for their moon landing. The history of the Ries valley and its continuing significance for terrestrial and space research is described in Nördlingen's Ries Museum (*Closed* Mon).

Würzburg, on the Main, lies amid vineyards. The people are jovial and open-minded, as so often in wine-producing areas

▶▶ Romantische Strasse 206A3
Germany's renowned Romantische Strasse is the most popular of all the named tourist highways spanning the country. Linking Würzburg in the wine country of Franconia with the Alps at Füssen, and some 350km long, it is less remarkable for the tranquil scenery it traverses than for the string of historic towns through which it passes. Between them they encapsulate the essence of the country's past, from medieval *Gemütlichkeit*, or coziness (Rothenburg-ob-der-Tauber, Dinkelsbühl, Nördlingen), via the mercantile magnificence of the early Renaissance (Augsburg), to the splendours of the baroque (Würzburg). The major destinations on the way are described under their own headings, but others mentioned here should also be seen if possible.

The route strikes southwest from **Würzburg** (see page 235) to join the pretty valley of the Tauber at **Tauberbischofsheim**, an unspoiled medieval town with timber-framed buildings and a good local history museum in the old princely palace. Beyond **Bad Mergentheim** (see page 213) is **Weikersheim**, the home of the Hohenlohe family (with a splendid Knights Hall and formal park).

Creglingen and **Detwang** have churches that feature fine altarpieces by Tilman Riemenschneider, while **Feuchtwangen** boasts Romanesque cloisters that serve as an open-air theatre in summer.

On the far side of the Ries (see panel), boldly standing out above the countryside, **Harburg Castle** no longer bars the way since the road tunnels straight under it.

On either side of **Augsburg** (see page 210) the road runs across the broad Bavarian plain. To the south of the city is the **Lechfeld** – today it is a NATO base and it is redolent of military memories. In 955 it was the site of one of the most decisive battles in European history, when Otto the Great finally put an end to the heathen Hungarians' incursions into western Europe and drove them back down the Danube.

Beyond **Landsberg** (see page 251) lie the Alps, a spectacular barrier when seen from the town walls of **Schongau** on a clear day. Easily reached from the Romantische Strasse as it nears its end at **Füssen** (see page 245) are some of Bavaria's greatest architectural treasures, the rococo church at **Wies** (see page 265) and the royal castles at **Hohenschwangau** and **Neuschwanstein** (see page 246).

▶▶▶ Rothenburg-ob-der-Tauber 206B2

Rothenburg is among Germany's best-preserved and most picturesque medieval towns, but *very* touristy. Once more important than Nürnberg, Rothenburg stagnated after the Thirty Years' War before being discovered by Romantic artists and writers in the 19th century as the 'epitome of Germanic medievalism'.

Completely ringed by ramparts, the town overlooks the winding valley of the Tauber. A succession of charming pictures unfolds as you stroll the cobbled streets or pace the sentry walk along the walls. A sea of red roofs rises above the half-timbered, high-gabled houses, no two quite alike, crowded together along the crooked streets. The highest roof is the Gothic St Jakobs-Kirche. Its cool interior holds a meticulously carved 1505 altarpiece by the great Riemenschneider. The focal point of the town is the Marktplatz, dominated by the **Rathaus▶**, half Gothic, half

BIBULOUS SAVIOUR
Rothenburg's perfect state of preservation is in part due to its having survived the Thirty Years' War intact. The threat by General Tilly to raze the town was averted when Mayor Nusch accepted, and won, a challenge to drain a six-pint-plus measure of wine in one go. This feat – the so-called *Meistertrunk* – is commemorated by the mechanical figures on the clock attached to the Ratstrinkstube and also by a colourful pageant.

Renaissance, with a splendid Imperial Hall inside. Enjoy the view from the top of the 60m bell tower.

Another excellent viewpoint is from the Burggarten, the little park on the promontory once occupied by the castle of the Hohenstaufens. Spanning the river below is the strange Doppelbrücke (Double Bridge), and not far away the even stranger Topplerschlösschen, a defensive tower on which an ordinary little house is perched.

Picturesque highlights of Rothenburg's townscape include the Plönlein, where changing street levels enhance the scene around the 1385 Siebersturm gateway; the patrician mansions along the Herrengasse; the Rodertor gateway, flanked by twin little tollhouses; or the Gerlach Schmiede (smithy) nearby, with its impossibly exaggerated gable.

Rothenburg-ob-der Tauber retains its old-world quaintness

CHAM'S FAMOUS SON
The French national anthem, the *Marseillaise*, rings out from a *Glockenspiel* (carillon) in the town hall tower of Cham, on the northwest edge of the Bavarian Forest, every day at five minutes past noon, in tribute to the little town's most famous son, Nikolaus Graf von Luckner. Luckner was a professional soldier who rose to the rank of Marshal in the French Army in 1791. The newly composed Marseillaise was dedicated to him in Strasbourg in 1792. Luckner's luck ran out during the French Revolution, however, and he died on the guillotine scaffold in 1794.

232

▶ **Staffelstein**   *206B3*

Staffelstein, with its fine Rathaus, is one of a number of half-timbered small towns and villages on the fertile floor of the broad and tranquil valley of the Main, north of Bamberg. Lichtenfels, the country's basket-making centre, is just upstream. Attractive enough in themselves, these places are visited less for their own sake than for their proximity to two great works of baroque architecture facing each other across the tranquil vale.

Crowning the wooded height to the west is the massive **Kloster Banz▶** (*Closed* Mon; guided tour Thu 2pm), a monastery founded by the Benedictines in 1069 and rebuilt between 1695 and 1768. The domestic buildings (with collections that include an ichthyosaurus) are dominated by the twin spires of the church, the work of Johann Dientzenhofer. The interior is outstanding, with splendid stuccos, colourful frescoes, and vigourous altarpieces. From the terrace are sweeping views across the valley towards the pilgrimage church of Vierzehnheiligen.

Vierzehnheiligen Pilgrimage Church▶▶ (*Open* daily) is one of the key buildings of the 18th century in Germany. It is a place of pilgrimage not only for the faithful but for anyone prepared to be persuaded that the German spirit is capable of the most sublime flights of fancy.

The Benedictine monastery of Kloster Banz, not far from Staffelstein

A stiff uphill walk from the large parking lot leads to a bevy of booths selling every kind of souvenir. The church's conventional exterior, in rough-looking ochre sandstone, is grand enough, with two tall towers, but gives little hint of the delights that lie beyond. Inside, the mood changes; all semblance of convention disappears in the abundant light that illuminates an extravagant interior in a froth of pink, gold and white decoration.

The focal point is less the main altar at the east end than the central confection, 'half coral reef, half fairy sedan chair' (Nikolaus Pevsner), adorned with figures of the 14 saints who gave the church its name. This ecstatic creation is the work of the great Balthasar Neumann. His patron was the ambitious prince-bishop of Bamberg, Friedrich Carl von Schönborn.

▶ Straubing 207D1

Once one of Bavaria's most important cities, Straubing is still the centre for the rich arable region known as the Gäuboden and has kept much of the air of a prosperous provincial city of the late Middle Ages.

The Romans built a fort here to guard their Danube frontier; spectacular evidence of their presence is provided by the rich hoard of gold masks and other objects that is the pride of the Gäuboden Museum (*Closed* Mon). The wealth of a later age is expressed in a heritage of fine buildings, including such churches as Romanesque St Peter's, with its atmospheric walled graveyard; the tall-towered Jakobskirche; and the little baroque jewel of the Ursuline church. Straubing's main landmark, however, is its 14th-century tower dividing the elongated market square into two parts; its corner turrets enabled an all-around watch to be kept for intruders or for the fires that could easily devastate the timber-built towns of the time.

Straubing's main festival, the biggest in Bavaria after Munich's Bierfest, is the annual Gäuboden Fair, which is held annually in August.

Excursions

Deggendorf, some 34km southeast, resembles Straubing on a smaller scale, with a fine market square dominated by the town tower.

Nearby are two splendid baroque monasteries: **Metten**, with a particularly fine library (tours daily at 10 and 3), and **Niederalteich**, the first foundation of its kind in Bavaria. Built as a Gothic hall church, it was remodelled in baroque style. The unusual lantern windows in the galleries offer a good view of the vaulting.

The rich agricultural land around Straubing was settled at an early date and is well endowed with old churches, including the picturesquely sited Romanesque church at **Rankam**. Of later date are the Benedictine buildings of the monastery at **Oberalteich**, completed in 1630, though the interior had to wait another 100 years before being decorated with its spectacular frescoes.

AGNES BERNAUER

Straubing's most famous figure was Agnes Bernauer, a barber's daughter whose beauty so impressed Duke Ernst's son that he married her in spite of her humble origins. This so enraged the duke that in 1435 he had Agnes tried on a trumped-up charge of witchcraft, then executed by drowning in the Danube. The tragic tale is reenacted in the courtyard of the ducal castle every four years.

233

Straubing, always lively, is at its most boisterous during the Gäuboden festival in August

▶▶ Waldsassen *207D3*

In the Middle Ages, many monasteries were established in the densely wooded uplands along the ancient border between Bavaria and Bohemia. Monks toiled to convert the forest to farmland and bring Christianity to the few inhabitants. Waldsassen (1133) is one of the greatest of these centres of medieval civilisation. It stood alone for centuries until the little town to which it gave its name began to develop in the early 17th century.

The monastery buildings date from 1681 to 1704. The long, narrow church is one of the masterpieces of the great Bavarian baroque architect Georg Dientzenhofer, who worked with a cosmopolitan team including the Italian Carleone, who embellished the interior with 200 stucco angels. Attracting special reverence is a battered figure of Christ, found hanging on the border barrier with Czechoslovakia in 1951 at the height of the cold war.

In the monastery itself is the library. Karl Stopl, the master carver responsible for this extraordinary interior, took as his theme everything that goes into the production of a book; the sequence of 10 figures supporting the upper level includes the humble rag collector (gathering raw materials for paper), the author, the critic (his bound hands symbolising his unproductive vocation), and the reader (a portrait of the artist).

Excursions

The gentle hills and vales of Waldsassen have always attracted admirers, including Goethe. **Tirscheneuth**, to the south, is the area's market centre. The Renaissance Rathaus survived a great fire in 1814. All around are pools and ponds, breeding carp and trout.

On a hill to the northwest of Waldsassen stands one of the most unusual buildings in Bavaria, the pilgrimage church of **Kappel**. Commissioned by the abbot of Waldsassen, Dientzenhofer designed a church to honour the Holy Trinity, linking together three rounded apses, each topped with a bulbous tower. Seen across the fields, the church's exotic outline is more reminiscent of Orthodox Russia than Catholic Bavaria.

THE SUDETENLAND
On the Czechs' side of their frontier with northern Bavaria and Saxony is the much-contested Sudetenland. Because of its large German minority, Hitler seized it in 1938: then the Czechs won it back in 1945, and in reprisal expelled most of the Germans. Many of them settled in Bavaria, and during the Communist era felt deeply bitter. Even with today's open borders, hard feelings linger.

Waldsassen dates from the early 17th century

▶▶▶ Würzburg 206A3

This university city, the ancient seat of powerful prince-bishops, is situated among vineyards on the steep banks of the River Main. Celtic tribesmen first fortified the strategic height occupied by the massive Marienberg fortress, but Würzburg's history really begins with the martyrdom here in 689 of an Irish missionary, St Kilian, whose mission was to convert the locals to Christianity. His gravestone is in the cathedral named after him, in the centre of the old city on the eastern bank of the river.

Würzburg is notable for its many churches. One of the oldest is the round, thick-walled Marienkirche, in the courtyard of the **Marienberg fortress▶**. The fortress was rebuilt and extended over the years to become a most formidable stronghold. Occupied for nearly 500 years by the prince-bishops, it now houses the splendid collections of the regional **museum▶** (Mainfränkisches Museum) (*Closed* Mon); its greatest treasures are the tenderly sculpted sandstone figures of Adam and Eve, by the great Tilman Riemenschneider (1460–1531), who was both artist and mayor.

By the 18th century, the Marienberg had become too cramped for the bishops' lifestyle, and the bishop's quarters moved to purpose-built quarters on the far side of the city. Their new address, the **Würzburg Residenz▶▶**, designed by Balthasar Neumann, is the greatest baroque building of its kind in Germany, dominating the vast cobbled square linking it to the town. Its interior spaces are staggering, in both sheer size and lavishness of decoration. They include the grand staircase, covered by the largest ceiling painting in the world (by the Venetian

The Marienberg fortress overlooks the river at Würzburg

AUGSBURG'S ALMSHOUSES
One of Bavaria's major oddities is the Fuggerei in Augsburg, a collection of neat almshouses built in 1519 by Jakob Fugger 'the Rich', a philanthropic banker. Here he housed some of the city's poor families, virtually for free. The snug kitchens must have seemed ultramodern then. Some 300 poorer people still live there, and the Fugger family still runs the place.

Tiepolo), the oval Kaisersaal (with *trompe-l'oeil* painting, also by Tiepolo) and the sumptuous Gartensaal, the great ground-floor room linking the palace to the gardens beyond. These form a perfect example of rococo garden art and make an ideal backdrop for the summer Mozart Festival that is held here. Neumann's palace chapel, the gorgeous Hofkirche (Residenz, *Closed* Mon), is a favourite place for weddings.

Würzburg suffered almost as grievously as Dresden in World War II, when an air raid left most of the city centre in ruins. Bravely rebuilt, it is a cheerful and lively place, with plenty of wine taverns and a buzz of student life. Its restored churches include the splendidly severe Romanesque **Cathedral▶**, with the gravestones of the prince-bishops – among them are two wonderful examples by Riemenschneider.

Opposite the cathedral is the Neumünster, built over St Kilian's grave and given a fine baroque façade in the early 18th century. It also has a garden with the grave of Germany's medieval troubadour Walter von der Vogelweide. In the market square stands the Gothic Marienkapelle, with Neumann's tombstone at its portal. Nearby is the fine rococo façade of the Haus zum Falken, meticulously restored after the bombing (and now the city tourist office). Spared destruction were the two great charitable institutions founded to house the city's senior citizens, the Bürgerspital of 1319 and the Johannesspital of 1576. Both derive part of their income from their vineyards; their produce is dispensed in their atmospheric wine taverns.

Würzburg's only church to survive the war unscathed was the Kappelle pilgrimage chapel. Owing its good fortune to its isolated position above the wooded ravine separating it from the Marienberg, it is yet another dazzling display of baroque virtuosity by Neumann.

Excursions

On either side of Würzburg, the deep valley of the Main forms one of Germany's most distinctive wine-growing regions. Its excellent wines are relatively dry and come in bulbous flasks, Bochsbeutel, quite different from the elegant bottles of Rhine and Mosel vintages.

Upstream from the city, one delightful little place succeeds another: **Sommerhausen**, favoured by artists; half-timbered **Ochsenfurt** ('Oxford') within its ramparts; **Frickenhausen**, accessible only through one of its four gateways; **Marktbreit**; **Sulzfeld**... Walled **Volkach** has many picturesque houses, a 16th-century Rathaus, and a local museum in the baroque Schelfenhaus. Crowning the hilly vineyards outside the town is Maria im Weingarten (Our Lady of the Vineyard), a late Gothic pilgrimage church, housing one of Riemenschneider's most delicate works, *Madonna in a Rose Garland.*

The summer palace of the prince-bishops of Würzburg, **Veitschöhheim** (7km northwest. *Closed* Mon), has an exquisite rococo garden, a delight of hedged enclosures, playful statuary, and the Grosser See, an artificial lake with an even more artificial Mt Parnassus rising from it. This jewel of landscape architecture was rescued from neglect by the indefatigable King Ludwig I of Bavaria, who restored it to its former glory.

236

Würtzburg's splendid Residenz was intended to symbolise the wealth and power of the ruling prince bishops

Revolutionary, exile, focus of scandal, writer and composer – Richard Wagner led a life that at times matched the more dramatic passages of his titanic operas. Certainly, in works such as **Tristan und Isolde,** *the themes of his own eventful career found their most eloquent musical expression.*

In 1834, at the age of 21, Wagner was appointed director of the Magdeburg opera. Here he wrote his first operas, and married a singer, Minna Plater, with whom he lived for 25 years in a largely unhappy marriage. To escape his private life he composed increasingly, including *Rienzi* (1840) and *Der fliegende Holländer* (*The Flying Dutchman*, 1842). In the latter, the romantic idea of redemption through love – a theme recurring in Wagner's operas but absent from his marriage – is first expressed. Mixed receptions of his next, less conventional, works, including *Tannhäuser*, reinforced his belief in his own ability; this period of musical innovation even saw him as a political revolutionary, manning barricades during the Dresden uprising.

New rules Wagner abandoned the traditional 'rules' of recitative and aria for a continuous musical dialogue, and used the leitmotiv, a representation of symbols and characters in musical terms, to perfection. With the help of his friend Liszt, *Lohengrin* (1850) was triumphantly performed in Weimar – despite Wagner's enforced exile in Zürich due to the failure of the uprising. In Zürich he began a passionate affair with the wife of a Swiss benefactor and conceived the idea for *Tristan und Isolde*, while also working on his masterwork, *Der Ring des Nibelungen*, a cycle of four epic operas based on German mythology.

Scandal erupted again when Cosima, Liszt's daughter and the wife of composer Hans von Bülow, bore Wagner a child. She obtained a divorce and, after Minna's death in 1866, Cosima married Wagner in 1870.

In his later years, Richard Wagner turned his attention to the foundation of the ideal opera house. In 1876 the Bayreuth Festspielhaus was opened with a complete performance of Wagner's *Ring* cycle. (The opera house is now the venue for the annual Bayreuth Festival.)

After a very full life, which among other things saw him writing on a variety of subjects, including vegetarianism and hygiene, Wagner died in 1883. He is buried at Wahnfried, his Bayreuth villa.

Above: Spy's impression of Wagner, from Vanity Fair, *1877*
Top: Richard and Cosima Wagner

The panorama from Munich's Olympic tower makes this region appear remarkably compact. The easygoing, cosmopolitan Bavarian capital lies on a fertile plain that extends southwards towards the snowy peaks of the Alps, Germany's highest and most dramatic mountains. In between are neat, clustered villages, pine forests, sparkling lakes and gently rolling pastures.

This is a rewarding area for exploration, with a host of entertainment and cultural offerings in Munich, magnificent scenic variety and (particularly away from the Alps) a number of historic small towns. All over the area are examples of Bavarian baroque churches and castles, many of them spectacular compositions with ornate stuccowork and frescoed ceilings.

While the German Alps comprise only a thin strip (the bulk of the great range lies in Italy, Austria, Switzerland and France), the mountains form a backdrop that is the key to much of the charm of the low-lying hinterland. The scenery immediately around Munich is rather flat, but farther south are several lakes, popular for walks, boat trips and sailing. The Alps themselves can be enjoyed by driving along the **Deutsche Alpenstrasse** (German Alpine Road), a scenic theme road threading its way from **Lindau** to **Berchtesgaden** and passing close to the four remarkable 19th-century castles of Ludwig II, Bavaria's mad king, whose extravagant fantasies now provide Bavaria with its

Munich and the Alps

top tourist attractions. Tourism is big business, with numerous resorts geared to winter sports and medical and nonmedical 'cures'.

For most of the year, many Alpine summits can be reached by cable cars and chairlifts; at the top there's often a strategically placed restaurant. Walking is by no means confined to arduous mountain ascents; easy paths, meticulously signposted, give gentle strolls through woods, along gorges, around lakes and up to viewpoints. The mountain resort towns are not especially interesting, however.

Southern Bavaria – with the notable exception of liberal Munich – is staunchly conservative, both politically and in general outlook. You will see men wearing Bavarian hats and *Lederhosen* (leather trousers), and women in embroidered dirndl dresses. Festivals are celebrated with gusto, particularly May Day, when huge maypoles are erected and decorated. The tradition of painting murals (and the family name in old Gothic lettering) on house exteriors is widespread. Food is hearty and traditional – pork, dumplings, potatoes and sauerkraut are *de rigueur* in country areas. The region is strongly Catholic: '*Grüss Gott*' (God's greeting) is the standard greeting (never '*Guten Tag*' – good day), and churches have a prosperous look. Much of the region is accessible within a day trip from Munich, but beware of crowds and traffic jams at peak times at the main sights and resorts.

▶ **Ammersee and Andechs**   *238C2*

Ammersee, a 35km lake situated west of Munich, is a popular weekend retreat, with small, quiet resorts, reedy shores and pleasant, low hills. Boat trips and yacht rentals are offered, and swimming is quite feasible in the warmer months. The west side is more congested, but Herrsching, the main resort, is on the east shore, a starting point for gentle lakeside walks.

The pilgrimage church of the Benedictine monastery of **Andechs▶**, close to Herrsching, is one of the rococo masterpieces of Bavaria, with frescoes and stuccowork by J B Zimmermann. Carl Orff (1895–1982), the composer best known for his *Carmina Burana*, is buried here. The tower offers a good view of the lake.

Next door, the monastery *Bräustüberl* (beer hall) does a roaring trade in the excellent beer produced by the monks and dispensed straight from the barrel. The monastery shop sells a Klosterlikör (monastery liqueur) and its own bottled beer.

Höher Peissenberg, southwest of the lake and accessible by road from Höhenpeissenberg village, has been a place of pilgrimage since the 16th century, when peasants erected a chapel on this lofty site, with its magnificent panorama of the German Alps (on a clear day you can even discern the restaurant on top of the Zugspitze). The church has been expanded and given the ubiquitous rococo treatment; note in particular the organ loft's elaborate parquetry.

Railings on the roof of the adjacent house mark the site of the world's first weather station (1781). Observations were made first by Augustinian monks and then by priests and teachers; in 1937 an official weather station was set up here.

The huge satellite dishes at **Raisting**, just south of the Ammersee, that dominate the area constitute the world's largest telecommunications centre. A visitor centre (*Open* Mon–Fri 8.30–noon, 1.45–5; Sat–Sun noon–4. *Admission free*) is located within the huge white sphere.

240

WESSOBRUNN ABBEY
Wessobrunn Abbey, west of the Ammersee, is famous for the 'Wessobrunner Gebet' (Wessobrunn Prayer), a poetic fragment of nine lines that dates from the last 30 years of the 8th century. Although written in a Bavarian dialect, the 'Wessobrunn Prayer' is often considered the oldest-known text written in the German language.

Ammersee is popular with weekenders

▶▶ Berchtesgadener Land   *239E2*

Jutting into Austria, Germany's southeastern corner offers glorious Alpine scenery; **Salzburg** is within close reach just across the border. The vicinity of **Schonau** and **Berchtesgaden** is ideal as a base for exploration.

Berchtesgaden▶▶ is a comfortable medium-sized resort with an active town centre; turn-of-the-century villas full of character perch on the hillside. The menacing form of the Watzmann (2,713m) looms high to the south; not surprisingly, the mountain inspired many artists and is the subject of local legends.

The town is the place to visit on bad-weather days. Particularly interesting are the still-functioning **Salt Mines▶** (*Open* May–mid-Oct daily 8.30–5, mid-Oct–Apr Mon–Sat 12.30–3.30), where visitors don miners' clothes and travel on the mine wagons. You can even slide down a slope (heavy-duty trousers are issued for the purpose) and raft across a subterranean lake. The guides, who are experienced miners, are very knowledgeable and will explain the salt-extraction process.

In the town centre are the Heimatmuseum (*Open* daily 10–6), which has a display of local wood crafts, and the Residenz (*Open* Tue–Sun 10–6), which was formerly an Augustinian priory, then from 1810 a Wittelsbach palace, and today it is a museum housing a collection of weapons and paintings.

For details of guided walks (May–Oct) visit the national park offices in Berchtesgaden (tel: 08652-64343) or Königsee (tel: 08652-62222).

As with much of Bavaria, the area has many baroque churches. The most photographed are probably **Ramsau** and the idyllically sited **Maria Gern**.

Tables with a view at a Berchtesgaden mountaintop café

Berchtesgaden, an active resort set on the hillside, and an ideal base for exploring the Berchtesgadener Land mountains

Berchtesgaden won additional fame during the Third Reich because of its popularity as a retreat for top Nazi leaders, most notably Hitler and his deputy Martin Bormann. They built villas on a slice of mountaintop, the Obersalzberg, and a guesthouse, the Kehlsteinhaus, at the summit (see page 244). Hitler built a road from the valley below in 1937–9 – a winding route that climbs 600m in about 6km.

From mid-May to mid-October, special buses make the journey from Berchtesgaden to a parking lot 150m below the summit. From there a lift built inside the mountain takes visitors to the Kehlsteinhaus, where there is a restaurant and a staggering view that led one diplomat guest of Hitler's to give the building its abiding nickname, the 'Eagle's Nest' (or 'Adlerhorst', as Hitler himself knew it).

Often likened to a Norwegian fjord, the much-visited **Königsee▶▶** stretches over 8km below the mighty slopes of the Watzmann, its depths plummeting over 190m. At the lake's northern end, from the village of Königsee (a tourist trap of kitschy souvenir shops, fortunately invisible from the lake itself), boat trips are available over the length of the water, with breathtaking vistas all the way. The round-trip takes an hour and three quarters and operates all year, weather permitting. Attractions near the far end include short walks to the chapels of St Johann and St Paul, and a more ambitious ascent to an ice 'chapel', which even the summer heat fails to melt (allow an hour each way).

A pleasant 75-minute circular walk, the Malerwinkel Rundweg, starts to the left of the main boat pier (at the lake's north end), taking an easily managed gravel track up into the trees. The crowds disappear and you are soon rewarded with views over the Königsee.

Also from Königsee you can take the cable lift up the **Jenner** (1874m), where the mountaintop restaurant gives views of the lake on one side and of nearby Austria on the other.

The Almbachklamm, a gloomy chasm with dramatic rock overhangs and swirling waterfalls, can be explored between May and October by a gently rising path (admission charge), which can be followed for an hour and a half to the Theresienklause Dam; the best of the gorge is seen at the beginning. The parking lot is signposted from highway 305, northeast of Berchtesgaden at the 5.5km post.

Bad Reichenhall is a spa that is reputed to have the most powerful saline springs in Europe. Look for the Quellenbau: King Ludwig I gave it his royal seal of patronage in the early 19th century, commissioning an elaborate salt works and ornate spa pavillion, the Alte Saline and Quellenhaus. They now house a museum with displays describing the history of the salt trade and a glass foundry (*Open* Apr–Oct daily 10–11.30, 2–4; Nov–Mar Tue and Thur 2–4). You can sample the saline waters in the attractive spa gardens.

The Hintersee

This small lake nestles beneath the wooded lower slopes of the Schottmalhorn (2,045m) and the Hochkalter (2,607m). The walk around takes about 45 minutes, with an optional climb of the Wartstein (15 minutes).

Start at the Seeklause car park at the 25km post on the Ramsau–Weissbach road, west of Berchtesgaden. Turn left out of the car park and walk along the road, which soon crosses a stream; immediately turn right along a broad path bordered with wooden railings. Ignore turns to the right, and walk through the **Zauberwald** (magic wood). After following the shore, reach an intersection and turn left, signposted Fussweg am See.

After 30m or so, detour right to the **Wartstein** (signposted), keeping right at subsequent intersections until the summit, with its fine view and tiny cave shrine. Return the same way to the bottom, turn right and continue the signposted Fussweg am See, which passes in front of the hotels and branches off left. The final section leads left along the path by the road.

The Wimbachtal

The **Wimbachklamm**, west of Berchtesgaden on highway 305 at the 19km post, is a pretty gorge and a good starting point for walks along the Wimbachtal (the Wimbach River valley).

Start at the car park, and take the rising road (closed to cars) called Wimbachweg. After the road becomes unsurfaced, fork left into the gorge. A gentle 2½-hour ascent leads you to the Wimbachgrieshütte, sited in a post-glacial valley below the Watzmann and the Hochkalter. There is a restaurant (Wimbach Schloss) midway along. Return the same way.

FRAUENINSEL
On the intimate little Fraueninsel (women's island on the Chiemsee), Benedictines have had a monastery since AD 780, and their nuns still live there (hence the name). They run a girls' boarding school, and still brew their *Klostergeist* liqueur ('convent spirit'), which can be tasted in their Klostercafé. Behind the altar of the tiny 13th-century church are charmingly naive ex-votos, some done by local fishermen giving thanks to the island's saint.

The landing stage of Fraueninsel, a lushly fertile little island, full of apple trees, birdsong and religious peace

HITLER'S EYRIE
On the Obersalzberg heights above Berchtesgaden (see page 242) Hitler built a grandiose mountain retreat, where he welcomed many top-rank visitors. It was razed to the ground in 1945 (only some stone slabs now remain); and it is not signposted, so as to deter Neo-Nazi pilgrims from using it as a shrine. A museum documenting the area's Nazi past and the history of the Third Reich opened there in 1999.

▶▶ **Chiemsee**   *239D2*

Bavaria's largest lake looks best from the northern side, particularly from the little resort of Gstadt; the Alpine foothills form part of a distinguished backdrop. It makes a good base for hiking, with easy routes in the vicinity of the lake itself and more energetic rambles in the hills to the south.

Boating is the other main attraction, with yachts for rent in many of the resorts, and a passenger boat service making stops around the lake. Try to see both of the principal islands.

On **Herreninsel**, the larger, stands Herrenchiemsee, an unfinished palace of Ludwig II (*Open* Apr–Sep daily 9–5; Oct–Mar daily 10–4. English language tours daily 11.45 and 2.45. *Admission charge*). The king decided to make a replica of Versailles, but only built the central portion before funds ran out. What exists is impressive, with formal French gardens, a hall of mirrors, and a state room where classical concerts are held by candlelight. This would have been the largest of Ludwig's castles.

Nearby is lovely Fraueninsel (see left). From Prien, on the west side of the lake, a steam train pulls 19th-century wooden carriages 2km to the pier for boats to the islands. The old village of Breitbrunn is a haunt of writers and artists from Munich. Local tourist offices stock booklets detailing the annual classical music festival held in several venues in the area between May and July.

To the south lie the Alpine foothills, which are an excellent area for medium to energetic walks without the daunting scale of the Alps proper. The **Kampenwand** (1,664m) is a popular objective and has cable lifts to get you up to the high ground. **Reit im Winkl** is an Alpine resort of much charm.

▶▶ **Dachau**   *238C3*

There are a few places in the world that cause a frisson at the mention of their very names. Dachau, a small commuter town near Munich, is one of them. It was the site of the Third Reich's notorious first concentration camp, established in 1933 in a former munitions factory. The camp has now become a memorial museum (*Open* Tue–Sun, 9–5. *Admission free*).

Although Dachau was not an extermination camp, torture, disease and death were commonplace. The barracks have gone, but accurate reconstructions give an idea of the cramped conditions prisoners had to endure. Around the perimeter fence, watchtowers still stand. The Jourhaus (guardhouse), formerly the camp entrance, still displays the chillingly inappropriate legend *Arbeit macht frei* (work makes freedom). The gas chambers, which were disguised as shower rooms, were never used for extermination, but hanging by the stake, a common punishment, was carried out within them; adjacent are the cremation ovens, which were kept burning day and night. A museum now occupies one side of the site, which has a disturbing account of the camp and a half-hour film (in English at 11.30 and 3.30).

As an antidote to the bleakness of the visit to the camp, walk into **Dachau town**, perched above the River Amper. Despite its proximity to Munich, its centre has an unspoiled small-town atmosphere, with a pretty Hofgarten (castle garden), a nicely laid out local museum and a Gemäldegalerie (picture gallery) of works by a colony of artists who were attracted to the area because of the unique light of the Dachauer Moos, an area of heathland. Both the museum and the gallery are open Wed and Fri 10–4, Thu 2–6, Sat, 11–5 and Sun 1–5.

Dachau camp is easily visited from Munich; take the S-Bahn 2 (direction Petershausen) to Dachau, from where, outside the station, bus 724 or 726 takes you to the Konzentrationslager (KZ) Gedenkstätte (concentration camp memorial).

▶▶▶ Füssen, Neuschwanstein and Hohenschwangau   238B1

Füssen abuts the Forggensee, a popular sailing area, and has its back to the Alps. Among several scenes of picturesque charm is the cobbled main street, the Reichenstrasse, with a trio of the town's most distinguished buildings at its far end – church, abbey, and towering about it, the castle, the Hohes Schloss. Close by, an archway gives onto a riverside park by the Lech.

The Benedictine abbey of St Mang now operates as a local museum (*Open* daily 11–4, Nov–Mar 2–4; *Closed* Mon. *Admission charge*), and there is a violin maker's workshop included among the displays. Above all, the abbey is an enjoyable place to just wander around and appreciate the host of well-preserved baroque rooms, including a very attractive oval library. Within the Höhes Schloss (*Open* Tue–Sun 11–4, Dec–Mar Tue–Sun 2–4 only) there is an exhibition of medieval religious art from the Allgäu and Swabia.

Königschlösser (royal castles) Despite unavoidable tourist crowds for most of the year, the wonderfully spectacular castles of Ludwig II – Linderhof (see page 261), Herrenchiemsee (see page 244), Hohenschwangau, and Neuschwanstein – are very seldom disappointing. Fair-weather timing assists an appreciation of the mountain setting, but may also bring out the crowds.

There is quite a lot of walking involved, particularly a fairly steep haul up from the car park by Hohenschwangau to Neuschwanstein; alternatively, you may prefer to make use of the horse-and-carriage service. It is probably best to make Hohenschwangau your first stop in order to avoid a sense of anticlimax (see also **Walk** on page 248).

245

Linderhof, one of Ludwig II's castles, was built in a mix of baroque and Renaissance styles. The gardens include a Moorish pavilion with bronze peacocks

Hohenschwangau►, on a forested hill, is the older of the two castles, built in the 12th century, but destroyed by Napoleon and restored by Crown Prince Maximilian (later Maximilian II) in the 1830s. Ludwig spent his early years here. The decor is troubadour style, with wall paintings of Bavarian knights and folk heroes; Ludwig's bedroom is decorated with stars that were illuminated in the evening. The music room evokes his love of Wagner.

Neuschwanstein►► stands high and mighty, bristling with turrets and mock-medievalism, its interior styles ranging from Byzantine through Romanesque to Gothic. This fairy-tale fantasy come true was built between 1869 and 1886 for Ludwig II but the king spent less than six months here before being certified insane and drowning mysteriously in the Starnberger See. Only about a third of the building was actually completed and the unfinished feeling is manifest everywhere – the second floor is a mere shell, doorways lead to nothing but suicidal drops, and steps in the throne room lead to a throneless stage. The 15 rooms you do see on the tour show astonishing craftsmanship and richness of detail, which extend to the lamp fittings and elaborate central heating system. The wood carving in Ludwig's bedroom took 14 carpenters four and a half years to complete. Wagner's operas are referred to everywhere, in murals and even in a mini-grotto recalling the Venusberg in *Tannhäuser*.

The best view of the castle is from the **Marienbrücke** (Mary's Bridge), which spans a deep gorge. On the path between here and the castle is a vista of Hohenschwangau and the Alpsee lake (Schloss Neuschwanstein *Open* Apr–Sep daily 8.30–5.30; Oct–Mar daily 10–4. *Closed* 1 Nov, 24, 25, 31 Dec, 1 Jan. Schloss Hohenschwangau, *Open* mid-Mar–mid-Oct daily 8.30–5.30, mid-Oct–mid-Mar daily 9.30–4.30. *Closed* 24 Dec; *Admission charge*.)

A recommended extra is the cable-car up the **Tegelberg** (1,720m), signposted between Hohenschwangau and Schwangau. It operates all year (until 5 in summer and 4.30 in winter) and there is a summit restaurant.

Drive

The Deutsche Alpenstrasse

A tour around and into the heart of the German Alps, using the Alpine Road for much of the way.

From the pretty town of Füssen, the road heads northeast past the turning for Höhenschwangau and Neuschwanstein – the famous fairy-tale castles built by Ludwig II – and skirts the Bannwaldsee before reaching Steingaden. At Steingaden head east.

Detour south at the signpost for the sumptuous baroque **Wieskirche**. Between the low-lying lakes, the **Staffelsee** and **Kochelsee**, is the turnoff for the **Glentleiten Freilichtmuseum** (open-air museum), which is worth a visit.

From Kochel, the road climbs into the Alps, passing the prettily set Walchensee, best seen by taking the cable car up the Wendelstein.

Detour to the village of **Mittenwald** before continuing to **Ettal Abbey** and past **Linderhof**, a Ludwig II castle.

Cross the Austrian border to reach Reutte and continue on to arrive back at Füssen.

The deep-blue Walchensee, one of the loveliest Bavarian lakes

Walk

Höhenschwangau and Neuschwanstein

A good way of seeing castles and the Marienbrücke, and avoiding the crowds. Allow one hour for walking and at least two for sight-seeing.

Park at either of the first two car parks (on the left) for the castles. Cross the road and take the steps to the left of the information centre to **Höhenschwangau**. After seeing the castle, retrace your steps for a few yards, then, just after the end of the castle building, take the right fork, to drop down to hotels and restaurants.

Cross the road and take steps to the left of the Schloss Hotel, and carry on up to reach the road. Cross over and take the stony path opposite, which ascends steadily. At the top, there is a surfaced track near a wooden shelter. Here you can detour right and immediately left to the **Marienbrücke** then return to the shelter and turn right to **Neuschwanstein** (don't miss the viewpoint over Hohenschwangau that shortly appears on the left). After leaving the castle, follow the main driveway down, forking right after 500m down steps (signposted Cafe Kainz) to reach the car parks.

Schwangau, the village close to Hohenschwangau, is famed for its Colomansfest, on 13 October, when the thanksgiving for horses and cattle takes place. With a grand procession of horse-drawn carriages, the festival marks the return of the cattle from the summer pastures and of the workhorses from the forests.

Hohenschwangau, set high among the mountain crags

FORGGENSEE THEATRE
In 1999 a theatre opened on the shores of the Forggensee, just outside Füssen, with a world-premiere performance of a musical based on the life and times of King Ludwig II. The musical forms a permanent feature of the theatre programme, with year-round, daily performances. The music, written by a pupil of the composer Richard Strauss, blends together folk themes, traditional musical harmonies and Wagnerian elements.

As well as ski resort, Garmisch is a centre of Bavarian folklore, with a major Heimatmuseum

249

▶▶ Garmisch Partenkirchen   238C1

Garmisch Partenkirchen is really two towns, joined together but different in character. Garmisch has village origins and retains some old-world rusticity in Frühlingstrasse (in the northern outskirts) and surroundings, with quaint whitewashed, gabled houses and the village fountain. Partenkirchen has been a town for much longer, and has lively, narrow main streets. Both towns have expanded for tourism, above all for the winter-sports industry, together becoming the largest German Alpine resort. As the site of the 1936 Winter Olympics and the 1978 alpine skiing world championships, the town is endowed with an Olympic ice stadium and ski jump. It is not a very good place to get away from the crowds, but nearby villages make good bases.

The towering **Zugspitze▶▶▶** (2,962m), Germany's highest mountain, dominates the area and can be reached effortlessly by rack railway from Garmisch; clear-weather views justify the substantial fee, and there is a restaurant at the top. A quicker but less exciting way up is to take the

Germany's leading ski resort is quite a glamorous place. It lies beneath Germany's highest mountain, the Zugspitzee

Zugspitze, towering over Garmisch Partenkirchen

BADERSEE
Near the peaceful village of Grainau, west of Garmisch, the tiny Badersee is sited secretively among the trees. For a few marks you can rent a boat and view an endearingly ludicrous statue of Nixe, a nymph, placed at the bottom of the lake by Ludwig II.

cable-car from the **Eibsee**, itself a lovely lake encircled by a 7km footpath. Other mountains where you can ascend by chairlift from town and walk down gently graded paths include the **Wank** (1,780m) and the **Eckbauer** (1,237m); both have summit restaurants.

Whatever the weather, be sure to visit the famous **Partnachklamm▶▶**. From the Olympic ski stadium, walk or take a horse and carriage along a traffic-free road to the entrance to the gorge.

The path is one of the wonders of the Alps, snaking near the bottom of the very deep chasm past spraying water and remarkable rock formations. A cable-car runs from the gorge entrance to the Hotel Graseck. From here follow the track up the valley, enter the gorge at its far end, and walk back down.

Less crowded, owing to its relative inaccessibility, is the **Höllentalklamm** sandwiched between the bases of the Alpspitze and the Waxenstein; allow at least two hours to travel each way; starting from Hammersbach, southwest of Garmisch.

Walk

Eckbauer and the Partnachklamm

This route takes the chairlift up the Eckbauer, where there is a viewing platform, with close-ups of the Alpspitze.

An easy ascent zigzags into a valley of Alpine meadows before the finale along the Partnachklamm, a magnificent gorge. The Gasthof on the summit serves excellent buttermilk. Take the Eckbauerbahn (chairlift) from the ski stadium in **Garmisch**. At the top, walk past the Berg Gasthof Eckbauer and follow signs for the Partnachklamm, down through woods, later forking right to reach a track near the Hotel Graseck.

Turn left (a detour is possible to Hohe Brücke, a high bridge over the gorge), return to the main route to reach the top entrance to the gorge, and follow it downstream. If this is closed, follow the track the other way, past the Graseck to the bottom entrance.

From there, you either walk along the traffic-free road or take a horse and carriage.

▶ Kaufbeuren
238B2

The unspoiled town centre, with its twisting, cobbled streets, merits exploration; the tourist information office (in the Rathaus) publishes a walk about town, in English. A walk along the town walls to Kaufbeuren's northwest corner leads past the Fünfknopfturm (five-spired tower) to the 15th-century church of St Blasien. The church's greatly treasured high altar by the master Bavarian woodcarver Jörg Lederer (1518) features golden-robed figures of the Virgin and Child, St John the Baptist, and St Anne. The Stadtmuseum in Kaisergässchen (*Open* Tue–Sat 9–12, 2–5, Sun 9–12) features an impressive collection of crucifixes. In Ludwigstrasse, the Puppenmuseum (*Open* Tue–Sat 9–12, 2–5, Sun 9–12) displays puppets from Europe and the Far East.

The town's big annual event is in July, when the Tänzelfest takes place. This medieval-style pageant is played out by as many as 1,600 children and is accompanied by processions and re-enactments of scenes from the town's history.

▶ Kempten
238A2

A busy commercial centre rather than a tourist destination, Kempten nevertheless has some good museums (*Open* Tue to Sun, 10–4; *Closed* at Christmas). These are the Alpenländische Galerie (Alpine arts gallery), Alpinmuseum (museum of the people and mountains of the Alps), the Allgäu Museum für Kunst und Kulturgeschichte (regional art), the Allgäuer Heimatmuseum (regional museum for the Allgäu), and the Römisches Museum (Roman museum).

East of the town centre, across the River Iller, the Archäologischer Park (*Open* Tue–Sun 10–5, Nov–Apr, 10–4.30. Guided tours Sun at 11. *Closed* Jan–Feb) occupies the former site of the Roman town of Cambodunum. The complex includes a partial reconstruction of a Roman-Celtic temple as well as many archaeological finds from the vicinity.

▶ Landsberg-am-Lech
238B2

On the Romantische Strasse (Romantic Road, see page 230) and quickly reached by train from Munich, the hillside town of Landsberg has retained an authentic old-world atmosphere without losing its workaday spirit. The signposted Stadtrundgang (circular town walk) takes in the best of Landsberg, weaving down crooked alleys and beneath arches, and climbing onto the largely intact town ramparts, with its series of gateways and views of red roofs huddled by the River Lech. Since the route is complicated, collect a free town map showing the walk from the tourist office in the Rathaus, whose rich stucco exterior by Dominikus Zimmermann graces the Hauptplatz. Zimmermann was also responsible for the Johanniskirche, which he designed using the plans for the more famous Wieskirche (see page 265).

Of the town's towers and gateways, the Bayertor is the most renowned and is one of the largest Gothic fortifications in southern Germany.

The Neues Stadtmuseum has a fair miscellany, including medieval religious art (*Closed* Mon). In Hintere Salzgasse, between the Rathaus and the river, you will

Kaufbeuren is an old-world town of narrow streets and tall churches

251

High rocky peaks, the Karwendel and Wetterstein, rise high above Mittenwald

find the more modest Puppenstuben Museum (*Open Sat–Sun, 2–5. Admission charge*), which displays a fun collection of antique toys.

►► Mittenwald   *238C1*

In a beautiful Alpine setting close to the Austrian border, the village has expanded as a tourist resort but retains much of its charm and numerous corners of old-world rusticity, with a photogenic array of houses with white-washed walls, wooden balconies, and green or brown shutters. The best houses are in the Obermarkt and the Gries quarter.

The baroque church has fine frescoes. Outside stands a statue of violin maker Matthias Klotz (see panel). The craft continues to be carried out here by such veteran masters as Anton Maller at his workshop in Stainegasse 14., and souvenir spin-offs include miniature violins and liqueurs sold in violin-shaped bottles. The Geigenbau Museum close by (*Open* 10–11.45, 2–4.45; Sat–Sun and feast days am only. *Closed* 1 Nov–20 Dec. *Admission charge*) has a collection of old violins and other string instruments, and exhibits detailing their history and manufacture.

Excursions

Cable-car and chairlift excursions include the **Karwendel** (2,384m) by Mittenwald and, farther north, the **Herzogstand** (1,731m), majestically placed above the attractive **Walchensee**.

KLOTZ'S VIOLINS
Matthias Klotz (1653–1743) brought the violin-making tradition to Mittenwald. He is thought to have been a pupil of the great Amati of Cremona. This industry may have saved Mittenwald from economic oblivion after Venetian merchants, who brought prosperity to the village, returned to Italy. Mittenwald violins are highly regarded by musicians and fetch good prices.

Monument to a music maker: the statue of violin maker Matthias Klotz, in Mittenwald

▶▶▶ München (Munich)   238C3

Germany's third-largest city contrasts sharply with the cosy conformism of much of the rest of southern Bavaria. With its exuberant atmosphere and vitality, it is one of the great cultural centres of Europe. Despite wartime devastation the city has a seductive flavour – blue-and-cream trams, tree-lined boulevards, fountains, parks, pavement cafés, beer halls and beer gardens. Its array of museums is unrivalled in the country.

Central Munich is easy to see on foot. From the main railroad station, you literally enter the city through one of its historic gateways, **Karlstor**. Ahead of you are nearly 2km of busy shopping centres, leading to the **Marienplatz▶** at the heart of Munich; the square is dominated by the somewhat sinister-looking, neo-Gothic Neues Rathaus, its exterior jollified by the famous carillon whose mechanical musicians, jousting knights and dancing coopers perform at 11am and at other times posted below the clock. Close by are the **Frauenkirche▶**, the symbol of Munich, with huge twin onion-domed towers that dominate views from all around, and the Renaissance **St Michael's Church**, with Wittelsbach tombs (see page 258) in the crypt. Immediately south of the Marienplatz, the **Viktualienmarkt▶** is a cheerful food market, excellent for regional cheeses and prepared hams in particular; the high quality is matched by the high prices.

A short distance southwest are two of the finest churches, the **Damenstiftskirche**, high baroque and thick with incense, and the astonishing **Asamkirche**, the ultimate statement in rococo, with no square centimetre unadorned in its dark, compact interior.

In the north-central area lie some of Munich's most impressive streetscapes. **Max-Joseph Platz** is presided over by the massive Corinthian columns of the National

The tower of the neo-Gothic Neues Rathaus (1867–1908) offers a good view over the town

MÜNCHEN

Theatre and the southern end of the huge Residenz, which marks the western end of **Maximilianstrasse▶**. This is a tree-lined thoroughfare known for its expensive boutiques and galleries and dominated at its far end by the towering Maximilaneum (1874), the Bavarian parliament and senate.

Odeonsplatz▶, full of students on bicycles, has a reconstructed look, but the regularity of the composition is pleasing. Adjacent is the massive dome of the baroque Theatinerkirche, whose bright yellow façade contrasts with an intricate grey stone interior. Across the road, the former royal gardens, Hofgarten, offers a peaceful retreat from the city bustle.

The Odeonsplatz looks northwards to the Siegestor,
a triumphal gateway close to the university; beyond it lies
Leopoldstrasse, which is the main axis of the district
of **Schwabing▶**, with numerous bars, outdoor cafés, theatres, cabarets, and other entertainment venues. Around
Münchener Freiheit, at the junction of Leopoldstrasse
and Ungererstrasse, is good territory for browsing in
secondhand shops.

Northwest of the centre are two adjacent squares,
Leubachplatz and Maximilianplatz, with pricey antiques
shops, and the main **museum quarter**.

The **Englischer Garten▶▶** (English garden) extends
along the banks of the River Isar for roughly 7km and is

QUICK HISTORY OF MUNICH

- The city's name means 'monks', a reminder of a monastic settlement established here in the 9th century. The Münchener Kindl (little monk) is the city's emblem even today.

- Munich became the ducal residence of the Wittelsbachs in 1255, and the Bavarian capital in 1503. During the Thirty Years' War (1618–48) the city was a stronghold of German Catholicism.

- The city was enriched by the Wittelsbachs in the 18th century, when churches and two palaces were built. In the 19th century, Ludwig I endowed the city with its university and its great collections of art and antiquities.

- In 1920 Adolf Hitler launched his National Socialist Party's programme at a meeting at the Hofbräuhaus.

- Postwar years have brought great prosperity. BMW is among the many companies with headquarters here.

one of the largest city parks in the world. The 'garden' resembles parkland landscaped in the English manner, with informal areas of grass and mature woodlands, and is the haunt of strollers, cyclists, joggers, picnickers, sunbathers, and the occasional nudist (one southern section is specially designated for nude sun-bathing). The Chinesischer Turm (Chinese tower), with its beer garden, is a popular rendezvous.

Less countrified in character, but equally popular, is the **Olympia Park▶**, north of the centre, the site of the ill-fated 1972 Olympic games, when Israeli athletes were taken hostage and died in a tragic shoot-out. Today people come for walking, jogging and boating, and for the range of sports facilities, which include the Olympic swimming pool. You can walk into the strange tentlike structure of the Olympic stadium and also take part in 'virtual reality' reconstructions of Olympic sports in the newly-opened 'Olympic Spirit' exhibition centre and fun park (*Open daily 10–6. Admission charge*). On clear days thousands take the lift up to the top of the Olympic Tower for a panorama of Munich and the Alps. The tower is open daily until midnight.

City tours in English Panorama Tours (tel: 089/5502-8995) runs various bus tours around the city; **Radius Touristik** (tel: 089/596113) offers personal guided tours by tram or on a bicycle.

Museums and galleries
Alte Pinakothek▶▶▶ (Barerstrasse 27; *Open* Tue–Sun daily 10–5, Tue and Thu until 8). This great art museum specialises in paintings up to the 18th century and is famed for works by Dürer (*Self Portrait, The Four Apostles, The Baumgärtner Altar,* etc) and for its Spanish, Dutch and Italian collections. The Neue Pinakothek exhibits late 18th- and 19th-century art, from Turner and Friedrich to the French and German Impressionists.

Street musicians are a familiar sight in this cosmopolitan, university city

TRAINS AND BUSES

Munich's public transport system works admirably well but can confuse the newcomer. You can buy tickets individually or in blue strips (which works out cheaper); if choosing the latter, you need to use one strip for short journeys (five bus or tram stops, or three train or subway stops) or two strips for longer journeys. You are allowed to transfer among different modes of transport as long as you don't double back on your direction of travel; short journeys must be completed within one hour, long journeys within two hours. If you are doing a lot of travelling or are in a group, buy a *Tageskarte* (day pass). Validate your ticket in one of the automatic stamping machines. Day passes must be validated only the first time you travel. Travellers without validated tickets may be fined on the spot.

Munich's Marienplatz

Antikensammlungen (Königsplatz 1; *Open* Tue–Sun 10–5, Wed until 8. *Admission charge. Free* Sun) Adjacent to the Glyptothek (see page 258), this state collection of classical art owes its origins to the collecting endeavours of Ludwig I. Amongst the exhibits, it boasts some superb Etruscan gold jewellery and a renowned set of Greek decorated vases.

Bavaria Film Studio▶ (Bavariafilmplatz; *Open* Mar–Oct daily. *Admission charge*) Guided tours (lasting 1½ hours) of the one of the largest film studios in Europe.

Bayerisches Nationalmuseum▶ (Prinzregentenstrasse 3; *Open* Tue–Sat 9.30–5. *Admission charge. Free* Sun) Three floors of Bavarian arts and crafts. Highlights include wooden sculptures by Tilman Riemenschneider and a wonderful collection (the world's largest) of nativity tableaux.

Deutsches Museum▶▶▶ (Museumsinsel 1; *Open* daily 9–5 *Admission charge*) Rated the world's foremost museum of science and technology, this has everything from do-it-yourself chemistry experiments and complicated models of hydraulics and bridges, to areas of more mainstream appeal, such as historic cars, locomotives, musical instruments, space travel and aircraft.

PLAYS AND MUSIC
Munich is well endowed with theatres and concert halls. The Münchener Kammerspiel is one of the most famous theatrical companies; the Cuilliés-Theatre makes an evening out just for the architecture. The Nationaltheater in Max-Joseph Platz is a venue for opera and ballet. Munich has a number of resident orchestras, including the Bayerisches Rundfunk Sinfonie Orchester and the Münchener Philharmonie. For details of events contact the tourist offices at the train station or in the Rathaus building.

Glyptothek (Königsplatz 3; *Open* daily except Mon, 10–5; Thu, 10–8. *Admission charge*) Greek and Roman statuary, nearly all collected by Ludwig I, housed in an aptly classical building designed by Leo von Klenze.

Lenbachhaus▶ (Luisenstrasse 33; *Open* daily except Mon, 10–6. *Admission charge*) Of interest for the Italianate villa, complete with 19th-century furnishings, and for the Kandinsky collection of works by the Blauer Reiter group of Expressionist painters.

Neue Pinakothek (Barerstrasse 29; *Open* Wed to Sun 10–5, Tue 10–8. *Admission charge*, Sun *free*) Munich's 'new' art gallery has a very fine collection of 18th- and 19th-century work, from German Romantics such as Caspar David Friedrich to the French Impressionists (Manet, Degas and Monet are particularly well represented).

Nymphenburg▶▶ In the western suburbs stands this great summer residence of the Wittelsbachs, former rulers of Bavaria. Although built and added to over many centuries, the palace has a strikingly unified symmetry. The best-known feature of its splendid baroque interior is

Some beer houses take pride in their collection of decorated beer mugs

the Schönheitsgalerie, 36 beauties of the day painted between 1827 and 1850 for the pleasure of Ludwig I. Adjacent to the house is the Marstallmuseum, with a grand array of royal carriages and sleighs, and rooms of Nymphenburg porcelain.

Behind the palace lies perhaps its chief glory: a park with canals, a lake, and a series of whimsical hunting lodges and pavilions. Of these, the Amalienburg steals the show, a neat essay in rococo, with a hall of shimmering mirrors: from the centre you see yourself reflected in all 10 of these. The Magdelenklause was built as a mock-hermitage, complete with a bizarre grotto chamber.

Next door, the fine Botanical Garden has an alpinum, rhododendrons, and greenhouses. (*Open* palace, daily except Mon, 9–12.30, 1.30–5; Oct–Mar, 10–12.30, 1.30–4. Botanical Garden, daily, 9–6; greenhouses are *closed* between 11.45 and 1.)

Pinakothek der Moderne (Corner Türkenstrasse and Gabelsbergerstrasse; *Open* Wed–Sun 10–5, Tue 10–8. *Admission charge*, Sun *free*.) This latest addition to Munich's museum scene, which opened in late 1999, brings together five important collections that were until now distributed in various galleries and storage cellars: modern, 20th century art and sculpture, graphic art and design, objets d'art, as well as the Technical University's architectural exhibits.

Residenzmuseum▶ (Max-Joseph Platz 3; *Open* Tue–Sun 10–4.30. Theatre *open* Mon–Sat 2–5, Sun and feast days, 10–5. *Admission charge.*) The vast baroque palace of the Wittelsbachs has been painstakingly restored after extensive wartime damage. Different parts of the building are open in the morning and evening, because there is far too much to see at once. In addition to the state rooms, do not miss the magnificent vaulted Antiquarium (begun in 1568), housing statues collected from the classical world, a dazzling treasury of pristine jewel-encrusted riches dating from the 11th century onwards, and the enchanting Cuvilliés-Theater (separate admission), a rococo creation by François de Cuvilliés, still used for performances.

Within the same complex, but requiring separate admission, are museums of coins and Egyptian art.

Spielzeug Museum (Marienplatz; *Open* daily 10–5.30. *Admission charge.*) In the tower of the old town hall is this most appealing (and nostalgic) treasure trove of toys, including retired dolls, vintage model cars, and some pre-war teddy bears. There are also toys from as long ago as the 2nd century.

Stadtmuseum (Sankt-Jakobs-Platzl; *Open* Tue–Sun 10–5, Wed until 8.30. *Admission charge.*) In a former arsenal, this is more than just the city local history museum, with floors devoted to brewing, the early days of photography, a film museum, a worldwide collection of musical instruments, and a splendidly entertaining puppet and fairground museum.

ZAM (41 Westenriedstrasse; *Open* daily 10–6. *Admission charge.*) Seven quaintly unrelated museums in one: pedal cars, memorabilia relating to Empress Elisabeth of Austria, *bourdalous* (fancy china chamber pots), corkscrews, padlocks, chamber pots, and even Easter bunnies.

HERE FOR THE BEER
Munich is one of Europe's foremost beer-producing cities, famous for its annual Oktoberfest (lasting 16 days up to the first Sunday in October) on the Theresienwiese fairground on the west side of the city. Munich's more than 100 beer-gardens are a central feature of social life in summer. Families pack picnics for evening suppers at wooden tables groaning under the weight of litre mugs of beer. The Hofbräuhaus beerhall is world famous – the Bavarian regulars dress up in green Loden and feathered hats for their evenings out.

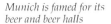
Munich is famed for its beer and beer halls

259

THE PASSION PLAY AT OBERAMMERGAU

The Passion play was first performed in 1633, after villagers had been spared the ravages of the plague; the play now takes place every 10 years, the next occasion being in 2000. Some 100 daylong performances are given to aggregate audiences of over 500,000 by a cast of 1,700. Tickets are difficult to obtain unless you book through a tour operator. Competition among the locals for the major parts is keen. Men grow long hair and beards for the event. The 1674 text mentions the use of trumpets, but this music has been lost. The music now used is by Rochus Dedler (1779–1822).

Painted buildings at Oberammergau, internationally known for its Passion play

▶▶ Oberammergau and area   *238C1*

Known the world over for its Passion play (see panel), Oberammergau is physically dominated by a rock pinnacle known as the Ettaler Mandl. The village has a number of painted houses and a baroque church, but gets completely overridden with visitors at peak times. Its main streets cater to the mass tourist trade, notably with its plethora of shops selling locally produced wood carvings (mostly on religious themes). The Heimatsmuseum has a display of antique wooden artifacts.

The Passion Play theatre, is the Passionspielhaus, is closed during 2000, for rehearsals and then the performances themselves. From the year 2001 it will be open again daily for visitors.

Ettal, the next village to the south, has two claims to fame. One is Ettaler, a sweet herbal liqueur originally made by monks. The other is the great Benedictine **abbey church▶**, with an unusual 12-sided nave beneath a huge dome, modelled on the Church of the Holy Sepulcher in Jerusalem. Though the foundation is 14th century, the church interior is high baroque, with a painted ceiling by Johann-Jakob Zeiller.

The road west from Ettal is a very pretty route, leading deep into the fir-clad mountains, hugging a rushing stream and crossing the Ammergebirge range, over the 1,200m high Ammer pass into Austria and the Austrian border town of Reutte. Except for cross-country skiers, it is not to be recommended in winter, when this corner of Germany can be snowed in for weeks on end, but

Born in 1845 in Nymphenburg Castle, near Munich, Ludwig II was a member of the Wittelsbach dynasty and became king of Bavaria at the age of 18. Within two years of his accession to the throne he became involved in a war with Prince Otto von Bismarck of Prussia; Bavaria was defeated, and the Prussians took over the Bavarian army.

In 1870, under Bismarck's influence, Bavaria was drawn into the war between Prussia and France that was to be the catalyst in the formation of the German Empire, of which Bavaria became a part. Bismarck now had Ludwig under his thumb and ordered the Bavarian king to send a letter naming Wilhelm I of Prussia as the emperor of Germany. Disillusioned, Ludwig lost interest in politics and became increasingly eccentric. He built a trio of castles – Linderhof, Neuschwanstein, and Herrenchiemsee – at huge expense. A stage-set designer drew the first sketches for Neuschwanstein, the most theatrical of the three; Ludwig watched the progress of building through his telescope from Höhenschwangau. Linderhof, the only one of Ludwig's royal castles to be completed, was his favourite. Louis XIV became Ludwig's inspiration: his dream was of absolute rule. He gave financial aid to Richard Wagner, whose operas fired his imagination. But the funds ran out; Ludwig's extravagance, homosexuality and near or actual insanity worried the Bavarian government, which colluded with Luitpold (his uncle and successor) to depose him. Ludwig was certified insane in his bedroom at Neuschwanstein; a few days later, on 13 June, 1886, he and his physician were found drowned in the Starnberger See. It has never been ascertained whether this was an accident or an assassination.

throughout the year the road is kept open as far as Linderhof, which is the site of perhaps the most appealing of King Ludwig's castles, **Schloss Linderhof▶** (*Open* daily except Christmas and New Year's Day, summer 9–12.15, 12.45–5.30, winter 10–12.15, 12.45–4; guided tours in English).

Schloss Linderhof was completed in 1878 for Ludwig II and modelled on the Petit Trianon at Versailles. Its interior, though nothing as spectacularly bizarre as Neuschwanstein (see page 246), is characteristically lavish, full of mirrors, painted ceilings and gilded cherubs, in a mixture of Renaissance and baroque styles.

The grounds have some wonderfully offbeat features, including a grand cascade, a water jet that shoots higher than the Schloss itself, a grotto modelled on the Venusberg of Wagner's opera *Tannhäusser*, and a Moorish kiosk resplendent with a 'peacock throne'.

Local wood carvings

OBERSTDORF

Stiefenhofen
Simmerberg
Alpsee
Kranzegg
Wertach
Pfronten
Falkenstein
1268m
Rettenberg
Grünten
▲ 1738m
Vils
Deutsche
Alpenstrasse
Oberstaufen
Immenstadt
Blaichach
Burgberg
Steibis
Weissach
Sonthofen
Hindelang
Jochstrasse
Oberjoch
Oberjochpass
Hochgrat
1832m
Ofterschwang
Deutsche
Alpenstrasse
Altstädten
Bad Oberdorf
Balderschwang
Riedbergborn
1786m
Hinterstein
Obermaiselstein
Fischen
Oberstdorf
Nebelborn
2224m
Breitachklamm
Stillach
Hochvogel
2593m
Freibergsee
Himmelschrofen
▲ 1790m
Mädelegabel
2645m ▲
Einödsbach
Spielmannsau
Allgäuer
Alpen

0   5   10 km
0   5 miles

A

There's good walking and challenging rock climbing in the Oberstdorf valley

▶ Oberstdorf and area   238A1

Oberstdorf is a busy valley resort, excellently placed for exploring the Allgäuer Alps; it flourishes as a winter-sports (top-class skiing and skating facilities), climbing and hiking centre. More peaceful bases include **Fischen**, on the valley floor but bypassed by the road, remote **Balderschwang**, high up a lonely side valley, **Oberstaufen**, large and neatly tended, **Altestädten**, with its characteristic wooden Allgäuer houses, and **Hindelang**, nestling in green countryside.

From Oberstdorf, horse-drawn carriages leave every day for the **Stillachtal**, the southernmost valley in Germany, with Einödsbach as its southernmost village. The road is closed to motor traffic and affords magnificent mountain views.

Southwest of Oberstdorf, the **Kleines Walsertal▶**, an enclave of Austria, can only be reached from Germany and has typical wooden farms and modest family hotels within a dramatic Alpine setting. The walk along the **Brietachklamm**, west of Oberstdorf, squeezes through a magnificent gorge and beneath unlikely looking over-hangs (closed during the spring thaw). Cable cars from the east side of town whisk you up to the **Nebelhorn** upper station for a chairlift to the summit (2,224m), which is graced with a summit restaurant and a superb panoramic view.

▶▶ Ottobeuren   238A2

The mighty Benedictine abbey church of Ottobeuren (*Open* daily 9–5. *Admission charge*) dwarfs the adjacent town. Founded in 764, the abbey prospered under the patronage of Charlemagne, and the complex was rebuilt in the 18th century by Johann-Michael Fischer. It is Germany's largest baroque church, and the proportions are quite cathedral-like, with a nave 90m long and a transept 60m across. Its interior is wonderfully light, and

Ottobeuren's abbey has a superb organ and choir stalls

adorned with frescos by Amigoni, Zimmermann, and J J Zeiller, and stuccowork by J M Feuchtmayr.

The Trinity organ, built by K J Riepp, is one of the most splendid in Europe.

▶ Starnberger See   238C2

The largest lake close to Munich is served by a suburban train service, which makes it a good out-of-town base for the Bavarian capital. It is well suited for yachting (boat rental available), strolls and relaxation; the scenery is undramatic but pleasant.

A boat sails around the lakes; stops include the Votive Chapel at Berg, erected in memory of Ludwig II, who drowned here in 1886. The best views are to be had from the Bismarckturm (Bismarck tower), south of Berg, and from Ilkahöhe, a modest hill southwest of Tutzing, the main resort.

Just to the south lies the peaceful and unspoiled **Ostersee**, part of a complex of over 20 small lakes, with reedy shores and wooded isles. The 8km Rundweg Ostersee, a circular path, is an easy two-hour walk; the parking lot is between Seeshaupt and Penzburg.

At **Kochel**, the Franz Marc Museum (*Open* Tue–Sun, 2–6) exhibits a collection of work by the great 20th-century Bavarian artist.

MEMMINGEN
Northwest of Ottobeuren, Memmingen has an attractive town centre of arcaded buildings and patrician houses, with the irregular Marktplatz dominated by the Gothic tower of the Nikolaikirche (fine murals and stalls within). Parishaus, a pink-and-white building north of the Rathaus, houses the tourist office, which issues a leaflet detailing a walk around town. The Hermansbau (1766) is the town's finest house, and now contains the local museum (*open* daily except Sat and Mon, 10–noon, 2–4), worth a look for its oak staircase and stucco ceilings; exhibits include porcelain, dolls' houses, clocks, medieval religious art, and an 1825 model of Memmingen itself.

263

The Heini-Klopfer Ski Jump and the Freibergsee

A varied walk (1–2 hours) that begins with a gentle riverside path. You can either ascend on foot or take the ski lift. The routes conjoin at the Eibersee, a small lake circled by wooded slopes, before you reach the final descent.

Start at the car park northeast of the Freibergsee, in the Stillachtal. From the west side of Oberstdorf, drive southwards (signposted Fellhornbarn and Schiflugschanze). The car park can be seen in the trees after 4km.

Walk to the rear of the car park and cross the footbridge; turn left, and follow the river 1.5km to reach the ski jump. Either take the ski lift to the top and turn right at the path above the lift; or continue forwards, on a rising traffic-free road, forking right at the top and following signs to Freibergsee, past Gasthof Schwand, then forking right just before the ski jump.

At the next major fork bear right downhill, then right again (signposted Parkplatz) to the river. Turn right to cross the footbridge into the car park.

The Schliersee (above) is one of the loveliest Alpine lakes

Wangen's Rathaus rules over a town of painted gateways and modern sculptures

▶ **Tegernsee, Schliersee and Spitzingsee** *239D2*
These three mountain-ringed lakes are an hour's train ride or drive southeast of Munich and at weekends are crowded with winter-sports enthusiasts, walkers and (in summer) with picnicking families. Tegernsee is the most popular and interesting of the three. A Benedictine monastery was founded here in the 8th century. The Bavarian King Maximilian I used it as a summer retreat following secularisation in the early 19th century. A very fine beer is brewed within its ancient walls and it's served up in one of Bavaria's most original beerhalls, the **Braüstüberl**, directly adjoining the monastery church in lakeside Tegernsee town. Pleasure boats ply the lake, linking Tegernsee with three other resorts, fashionable Rottach-Egern, the expensive spa Bad Wiessee and ancient Gmund. Schliersee is quieter and less showy, while tiny Spitzingsee is tucked in the mountains between the two other lakes, at the end of a serpentine drive from the valley floor. There are moderately challenging ski slopes above Spitzingsee, and very fine hikes in the mountains which rise to around 1,600m.

▶ **Wangen im Allgäu** *238A1*
An appealing Swabian town with a wealth of painted houses. Its old town is a simple crossroads, centred on the Marktplatz and entered by two frescoed gateways, the Frauentor (Ravensburg Gate) of 1608, the symbol of Wangen, and the St Martin Tor (Lindau Gate), with its pyramidal roof and intriguing array of gargoyles. A local museum within a half-timbered building devotes itself to cheese making and folk art in the Allgäu.

Isny, to the east, is another unspoiled old town, with 13th-century ramparts, a pretty corner by the church of St Jakob and St Georg, and 17th-century monastery buildings (now a hospital).

▶ Wasserburg am Inn

239D2

Wasserburg occupies a naturally fortified site all but surrounded by a tight meander of the turbulent Inn River, itself lined with white cliffs. This was one of the most prosperous towns in Bavaria during the Middle Ages, when it became a river port for Munich on a salt trading route and was allowed to levy tax on the salt that passed through town. Wasserburg's fortunes slumped after 1504, when the salt trade route was moved, and later suffered the ravages of war and plague. Its heyday gone, Wasserburg nevertheless retains a legacy of old merchants' houses and characterful winding streets.

Opposite the Rathaus, the façade of the Kernhaus displays outstanding 18th-century stucco work by J B Zimmermann. Behind the Rathaus, the local museum (*Closed* Mon) has a fine collection of ancient farm furniture, implements and carriages.

The main town gateway dates from 1374 and displays wall paintings of two warriors bearing the banners of Wasserburg and Bavaria; within it, the Erstes Imaginäres Museum houses a collection of old masters from all over the world, with a difference: all of them are fakes (*Closed* Mon). Through the gateway, continue on over the bridge over the Inn River, then turn left into Kellerstrasse for a path up to a fine viewpoint over the town.

At Wasserburg even some of the modern buildings by the Inn River have stepped gable façades

265

▶ Wieskirche

238B2

Set amid quiet, green meadows, the famous Wieskirche stands almost by itself. It was built as a pilgrimage church to house a figure of the Scourging of Christ, which had allegedly shed miraculous tears. The architect, Dominikus Zimmermann, gave it a wonderfully light, frothy interior, with an outstanding frescoed dome depicting the Gate to Paradise. His composition was a personal masterpiece (so much so that he spent the rest of his life in a house close by) and is one of the great rococo buildings of Europe.

Arriving and departing

To enter Germany you need a valid passport, or an identity card in the case of EU and some other countries. Visitors from 40 other countries, including Australia, Canada, New Zealand and the USA, do not need a visa for business or tourist visits of up to three months, provided they are not looking for work in Germany. British citizens can use a UK Visitors' Passport, which is valid for one year.

It is advisable to check entry regulations with the appropriate German Embassy before departure (addresses under Embassies).

Channel Tunnel Eurotunnel operate frequent Le Shuttle drive-on car and passenger carrying services between Folkestone and Calais. Booking is not essential outside peak times. For information telephone 0990 353535.

By air The main international airports are Frankfurt, Düsseldorf, Cologne, Stuttgart, Munich and Berlin. Internal air services connect these and other airports within Germany. Lufthansa (German Airlines) will arrange onward train connections between main cities, for its passengers (see Public transport). There is a regular airport bus transfer between Berlin's Tegel and Schönefeld airports.

All German airports connect efficiently with the local urban transport network. In some cases there is a connecting coach service; other airports tie in with the metro system.

By boat

To Germany: Scandinavian Seaways (tel: 01255 240240) operates the only direct sailings to Germany from the UK, out of Newcastle and Harwich, Essex, to Hamburg (from mid-March to end December). The crossing takes 20-plus hours.

To Holland: Crossing to Holland from the UK means a shorter sea journey and unless you specifically want to visit the north of Germany, it is an alternative jumping off point. Stena Sealink (tel: 01255 243333) operates from Harwich to the Hook

of Holland – a crossing which takes roughly seven hours.

To Belgium: Another option is to arrive at a Belgian port. P&O European Ferries (tel: 01304 203388) sail from Dover to Ostend, crossing time around 4 hours. P&O also operate from Felixstowe to Zeebrugge, with five-and-three-quarter-hour day-sailings.

North Sea Ferries (tel: 01482 377177) also sail from Hull to Zeebrugge; the crossing takes fourteen-and-a-half-hours.

To France: It could be that if you're heading for central and southern Germany a quick sea crossing to Dunkerque , Boulogne or Calais works out best for you. Work out if there will be savings in time and petrol.

Driving times from Channel ports to German destinations vary from four hours to Cologne, to 10 hours down to Munich.

Ferry companies which serve these ports from the UK include Sealink, P&O and Sally Line (tel: 0800 636465).

All ferry companies offer special deals of one sort or another, for instance concessions for family groups, senior citizens, special sailings and so on. It's advisable to read their brochures very carefully or to ask what kind of offers are available before booking.

By coach Eurolines (tel: 070-2730 8235) have frequent coach departures from London Victoria to Frankfurt, Hamburg, Munich, Berlin, Leipzig, Dresden and other destinations. Sample travel times are fourteen hours to Cologne, 23 hours to Berlin, and 25 hours to Dresden. Special children's fares operate on all routes.

For travellers going to Germany from parts of the UK outside London, Transline coaches (tel: 080-2998 7791) depart from most of the major UK cities.

By rail Eurostar trains go via the Channel Tunnel from London Waterloo (and also Ashford in Kent) to Brussels Midi (3¼ hours), with connections to Cologne (a further

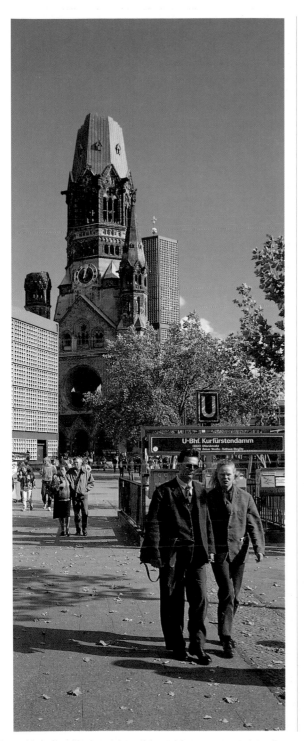

U-Bhf. Kurfürstendamm
(BRE) Uhlandstraße
Oskar Straße · Rathaus Steglitz

Travel Facts

3 hours) and on into Germany. Ring Eurostar telesales (0990 186186). By rail-sea-rail, there are services from London-Victoria via Ramsgate (boat or jetfoil) to Ostend and on into Germany. Check with International Rail Centre Victoria (tel: 070-2834 2345). There are also services from London Liverpool Street via Harwich to Hook of Holland (7 hours' crossing, day and overnight) and on into Germany.

Travel times vary, depending on what Channel crossing and route is taken. Holders of rail tickets to the German border can purchase Euro Domino tickets for 3–10 days unlimited travel on German Rail, and also a variety of Regional Rail Passes; all are valid on days of the user's choosing within the period of validity, and offer unrestricted travel on rail and certain bus and boat services within Germany.

Also available are Rail Europe Senior Citizen Rail Cards for holders of UK Senior Citizen Railcards offering a third off rail ticket prices, and the Inter-Rail Pass for under 26-year olds, valid for one month on most northern European rail networks. ·

Camping
Germany abounds in campsites – there are about 2,500 sprinkled liberally around the country. The standard is high: even the most basic have toilet and washing facilities plus on-site shop. Top class campsites feature swimming pools, supermarkets, discos and all the trimmings.

Campsites are located by a blue sign carrying the international camping symbol: a black tent on a white background, Most are open from Easter to October, with around 400 staying open all year. June to September is the busiest season and as reservations are usually made on site, you must get there early to avoid disappointment, especially in popular places; better still, book in advance.

A list of campsites can be obtained free from the German National Tourist Office (address under Tourist Offices). The German Camping Club (DCC) publishes a complete guide,

available from 28 Mandlstrasse, D-80802 Munich , while the German motoring organisation ADAC also produces a guide to over 1,000 sites (address 8, Am Westpark, D-81373 Munich).

If you prefer to pitch your tent outside official campsites, you must first ask the permission of the landowner or local police.

Most of the major car rental firms will also rent out a camper van.

Children
If you're in need of a baby-sitter, enquire first at your hotel reception – they may well offer this service. Tourist offices in most towns and cities keep updated lists of recommended baby-sitters and details of local crèche facilities.

Under-fours travel free on public transport and children aged four to 11 go half price. Reduced rates are usually offered in hotels and guest houses for children, and it is the norm for attractions such as museums and historic buildings to offer discounts for younger visitors.

Germanic theme parks tend to take the form of fairy-tale tableaux lands, such as the Märchenwald, with its adventure playground, at Wolfratshausen near Bad Tölz in the Bavarian Alps, the Grimm 'fairy tale park' at Ludwigsburg, near Stuttgart, and the Taunus Wonderland at Wiesbaden. Attractions at Phantasieland at Brühl (halfway between Bonn and Cologne) include re-creations of the Wild West, ancient China and pre-war Berlin, a massive roller coaster and overhead monorail. Zoos and puppet theatre are popular features throughout the country.

Climate
Generally speaking the weather in Germany is rather similar to that in Britain: changeable, neither extremely hot nor cold, and sprinkled with rain.

The climate does not get dramatically warmer the further south you go. Berlin has an average July temperature of between 15° and 24°C, more southerly Munich of between 13° and 24°C. This city also has an above average summer rainfall.

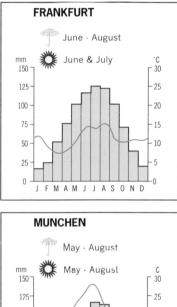

However, Hamburg in the north is consistently several degrees cooler than, for instance, Frankfurt in the centre. Berlin has long been famous for its bracing air – the Berliner Luft – while South Bavaria has its Föhn. This mountain wind can spring up at

any season, causing a sudden change in temperature as it brings very warm conditions and a cloudless sky.

Summers are usually pleasantly hot and dry throughout the country. Towards the Alps they get shorter, starting around May, and ending in warm autumns. May or October are good times to visit Germany; the popular haunts can get crowded in the peak tourist months of June to September. Later, snows start around November, and winter can be very cold: the January temperature in Berlin and Munich, for example, can hit a minimum of –5°C.

Crime

Crime figures have risen sharply since unification, but violent crime remains less common in Germany than in many countries. Trouble spots, as in any other nation, are large cities such as Hamburg, Frankfurt, and Berlin, where the usual car theft and house robberies are a hazard of urban life. Late at night in eastern Berlin, travellers should be wary of empty areas or being alone in train carriages.

As a tourist, it makes sense to avoid attracting unwanted attention: do not flaunt expensive jewellery or camera equipment, or leave baggage unattended, valuables on show in your car or your vehicle unlocked. Wear a shoulder bag on the side away from the street, or use a money belt for cash and travellers' cheques. It is a good idea to have photocopies of important documents, including passport, driving licence and travellers' cheques, and to remember to keep them in a safe, separate place from the originals.

If you are unlucky enough to fall foul of thieves, register the theft straightaway with the police (Polizei). This is necessary if you wish to claim on your travel insurance. In an emergency, dial 110. When arriving at the police station, make sure you have some form of identification (one instance where your photocopies could be useful). Do not inadvertently commit an offence yourself by, for instance, crossing the road before the green light for pedestrians shows. This may

CONVERSION CHARTS

FROM	TO	MULTIPLY BY
Inches	Centimetres	2.54
Centimetres	Inches	0.3937
Feet	Metres	0.3048
Metres	Feet	3.2810
Yards	Metres	0.9144
Metres	Yards	1.0940
Miles	Kilometres	1.6090
Kilometres	Miles	0.6214
Acres	Hectares	0.4047
Hectares	Acres	2.4710
Gallons	Litres	4.5460
Litres	Gallons	0.2200
Ounces	Grams	28.35
Grams	Ounces	0.0353
Pounds	Grams	453.6
Grams	Pounds	0.0022
Pounds	Kilograms	0.4536
Kilograms	Pounds	2.205
Tons	Tonnes	1.0160
Tonnes	Tons	0.9842

MEN'S SUITS

UK	36	38	40	42	44	46	48
Rest of Europe	46	48	50	52	54	56	58
US	36	38	40	42	44	46	48

DRESS SIZES

UK	8	10	12	14	16	18
France	36	38	40	42	44	46
Italy	38	40	42	44	46	48
Rest of Europe	34	36	38	40	42	44
US	6	8	10	12	14	16

MEN'S SHIRTS

UK	14	14.5	15	15.5	16	16.5	17
Rest of Europe	36	37	38	39/40	41	42	43
US	14	14.5	15	15.5	16	16.5	17

MEN'S SHOES

UK	7	7.5	8.5	9.5	10.5	11
Rest of Europe	41	42	43	44	45	46
US	8	8.5	9.5	10.5	11.5	12

WOMEN'S SHOES

UK	4.5	5	5.5	6	6.5	7
Rest of Europe	38	38	39	39	40	41
US	6	6.5	7	7.5	8	8.5

be acceptable behaviour at home, but is illegal in Germany. Far more serious is being caught in possession of drugs, of any sort – imprisonment or deportation is the penalty.

Customs

There are no restrictions on the import or export of German Marks (DM) or any other foreign currency.

Your private car is exempt from duty (subject to re-exportation) as are personal travel requisites.

Since July 1999 people travelling within the European Union are no longer entitled to import duty-free goods. However, travellers from outside the EU can bring in duty-free goods up to the current EU allowances:

Alcohol (over 22° vol): 1 litre or
Alcohol (not over 22° vol) 2 litres and
Still talbe wine: 2 litres
Cigarettes: 200 or
Cigars: 50 or
Tobacco: 250g
Perfume: 60ml
Toilet water: 250ml

If you are bringing expensive items such as computers, it may be worth carrying receipts.

Travellers with disabilities

The German government agency involved in assisting disabled people has details of hotels with special facilities to meet their requirements. Write to Hilfe für Behinderte Kirchfeldstrasse 11492 40215-Düsseldorf (tel: 0211 310060).

The wheelchair symbol (a wheelchair set in a box) indicates access for disabled tourists. Airports and rest stops on the autobahns are all equipped with toilet facilities, and at major railway stations staff are specially briefed to help passengers in wheelchairs, etc.

Access guides produced in Germany by social services departments or groups of residents list hotels, restaurants, buses, etc accessible to disabled visitors. RADAR 250 City Road, London EC1V 8AS, tel: 070-2250 3222) can give callers an idea which towns offer the best facilities. RADAR also publishes its own guide to holidays and travel which lists useful contact organisations.

Driving

The condition of autobahns, major and minor roads is excellent in the former West Germany, and has now greatly improved in former East Germany. Autobahns are toll-free.

Foreign motorists may drive a vehicle for up to one year in Germany with a national or international driving licence. Holders of Australian and US licences must carry an official translation. (Contact your Embassy or a German National Tourist Office.) Third party insurance is compulsory. Check with your insurers and they will issue a Green Card to show that they have extended your cover to allow driving abroad.

Even if you come from outside the EU you do not need an international car registration document, though you should ensure that you always have your ordinary registration documents with you.

Germans drive on the right side of the road; traffic coming from the right normally has right of way.

Children under 12 are not allowed to travel in a front seat unless they are using special seats or safety belts suitable for children or unless the rear seats are occupied by other children. It is compulsory for driver and passengers to wear seat belts if they are fitted.

Some drivers go very fast on autobahns, even up to 200kph. On these roads there is no official speed limit, though 130kph is a recommended maximum (100kph in some places: watch for the signs). There is a countrywide official limit on country roads of 100kph and in built-up areas of 50kph.

On-the-spot fines are levied for speeding, and other road offences such as using abusive language, making offensive and derogatory signs and for running out of petrol on the motorway!

The rule for drinking and driving is that the level of alcohol in the bloodstream must be under 80mg/100ml, although it is, of course, wisest and safest not to drink and drive at all. Motorists are sometimes given breathalyser tests if they seem to be driving incautiously, or after an accident, regardless of its cause.

Mozart's house, Augsburg

271

In the case of a breakdown, contact the ADAC (Allgemeiner Deutscher Automobil Club). On autobahns emergency orange telephones are sited at regular intervals (follow the yellow marker arrows). Ask for 'Strassenwachthilfe'. The ADAC breakdown number, country-wide, is 01802/222222. The ADAC do not charge you for their labour, but only for materials (unless it's a serious problem, so check that your insurance covers this).

Filling stations are regularly sited along autobahns and in urban areas off the main roads. Lead free – Bleifrei – is available almost everywhere. Petrol prices vary, tending to be higher on autobahns, cheaper at self-service – SB-Tanken – stations.

Car hire: Pre-booking a hired car from home can save time and using a major company means you can pick up at one place and drop off at another for no extra charge. Most airports, railways stations and larger towns have booking offices if you prefer to arrange car hire (Autovermietung) in Germany. International firms include Hertz, Avis and Sixt Budget. Ask at the local tourist office for German companies. The minimum age at which you can rent a car is 21 and you need to have held a full driving licence for 1 year.

Electricity

The current in Germany is 220 volts, 50 cycles. Sockets are for the two-pin type of plug. You will find adapters are widely available.

Embassies/Consulates*

Of other countries in Germany:

Australia: Godesberger Allee 105–107 53175 Bonn 2; tel: 0228 81030*
Canada: Friedrich Wilhelmstr. 18, 53113 Bonn 1; tel: 0228 9680*
Eire: Godesberger Allee 19, 53175 Bonn; tel: 0228 6937-39
New Zealand: Bunderskanzlerplatz 2–10, 53113 Bonn; tel: 0228 228070
UK: Unter den Linden 32-4, Berlin; D-10117; tel: 2202431
US: Neustädtische Kirchstrasse 4–5, D-10117, Berlin; tel: 2385174

Of Germany in other countries:

Australia: 119 Empire Circuit, Yarralumla AC, Canberra, 2600; tel: 2701911
Canada: PO Box 379, Postal Station A, Ottawa, Ontario KN8V4; tel: 613 23 21101
Eire: 31 Trimelston Ave, Booterstown, Blackrock, Co Dublin; tel: 1. 2693011
New Zealand: 90-92 Hobson St, Wellington; tel:473 6063
UK: 23 Belgrave Square, London SW1X 8PZ; tel: 070-2235 5033.
USA: 4645 Reservoir Road NW, Washington DC 20007 – 1998; tel: 202 298 4000

Emergency telephone numbers

Police: 110
Fire Department: 112
DZT (Deutsche Zentrale für Tourismus – German National Tourist Board), Frankfurt (tel: 069 75720)
ADAC – Allgemeiner Deutscher Automobil Club (Germany's leading motoring organisation) – emergency breakdown number: 01802 222222

Etiquette

In Germany, never, but never, call anyone by their first name unless you are invited to do so. Germans tend to be formal in business and in their private lives, too, though the younger generation takes a more relaxed attitude to this rule. Always use either Herr or Frau; it is considered an insult to address a woman as Fräulein, until you know for sure that she is a Miss rather than a Mrs. You should also say, 'Guten Morgen, meine Dame', as opposed to 'meine Frau'. When speaking to a professional person, eg a doctor, address him/her as Herr or Frau Doktor or with whatever other job title is appropriate. Holders of non-medical doctorates are also often addressed as Herr or Fran Doktor.

The distinction between 'Sie' and 'Du' – both meaning you – is comparable to the difference between the French 'vous' and 'tu'. You must wait to be told to use the familiar 'Du', though it's always safe to use it with children and animals.

Germans shake hands whenever they meet, even if it's only a casual encounter between neighbours on the stairs. Expect to offer to kiss a woman on both cheeks when greetings are conducted.

Another German custom is to bring a gift when invited to someone's home. The safest and most welcome item to take is a bunch of flowers.

As you will pick up pretty quickly if asked to a meal, Germans use their cutlery in a manner which may seem unusual to foreign visitors.

Health

Currently, no immunisations are required for entry into Germany. Health care is privatised, all Germans belonging to a health insurance scheme. EU citizens are entitled to free medical treatment in Germany, on production of Form E111. Get hold of one in advance of your holiday, from post offices.

In addition you should take out travel insurance to cover expenses connected with illness – such as a special flight home or longer hotel stay – that are not covered by E111. And to be able to make a claim, remember to keep receipts of all medical treatment, prescriptions and other expenses to give your insurers once home. The number for emergency/weekend doctors and dentists can be found in local telephone directories for German cities. If you want to ensure that you will be treated by English-speaking medical staff, contact the local consulate, which should hold details.

Doctors' consulting hours are usually 7am–8pm in hospital outpatients' departments; doctors' surgeries about 10–noon, 4–6 (times vary); closed Wed pm. (Hospital outpatients' provide an emergency service outside these hours, too.) Dispensing chemists are open during normal shop hours; in larger towns they display a list of late night and Sunday opening pharmacies (see Pharmacies).

Hitch-hiking
Hitch-hiking is not illegal, except on the autobahns and their feeder roads, although it is not encouraged. However, since the recent increase in crime, motorists have generally become more suspicious and therefore they are more reluctant to pick people up.

Every major city has a Mitfahrerzentrale, which provides a useful alternative. Drivers inform this office when and where they are travelling and those wanting a lift – and willing to share the cost of petrol – pay a fee to the office to get the driver's name and telephone number. This is by far the cheapest way of travelling around the country by car, but again, not without hazards.

Lone travellers should always be aware of the inherent dangers of taking lifts with strangers. Some cities have women-only Frauenmitfahrerzentrale.

Insurance
Make sure you take out travel insurance. It should cover you for accident or illness in the areas of motoring and health, and also for the loss or theft of valuables while on holiday.

This insurance is best taken out at home before departure. Speak to your insurers, travel agent or motoring organisation, when planning your trip.

Language
There is one official standard German language, Hochdeutsch, which all the children are taught in school and which everyone in the country should be able to understand. However, regional dialects, with strong local accents, are widely spoken in many areas. Some cities, notably Berlin and Cologne, retain their own dialects which a visitor from a village even 20 miles away may find hard to follow; and the Plattdeutsch of Friesia is a distinct language with its own literature. Saxony, Bavaria and Swabia are regions with pronounced local dialects, which vary greatly. For example, 'We have seen it' is 'Wir haben es angesehen' in Hochdeutsch, 'Mir hens a guckt' in Bavarian, 'Mr hannct gesäh' in Swabian, and 'Wir haben's angekiekt' in Berlin!

Pronunciation guide
Vowels (in Hochdeutsch)
a (short) as in hat, e.g., *Hand* (hand)
a (long) as in father, e.g., *sagen* (say)
e (short) as in bet, e.g., *Wetter* (weather)
e (long) as in day, e.g., *geben* (give)
i as in fit, e.g., *bitte* (please)
o (short) as in lost, e.g., *voll* (full)
o (long) as in coach, e.g., *Mond* (moon)
u as in boot, e.g., *gut* (good)
ä (short) as in wet, e.g., *Äpfel* (apple)
ä (long) as in wait, e.g., *spät* (late)
ö as in fur, e.g., *schön* (beautiful)
ü as in blue, e.g., *über* (over)
ai as in spy, e.g., the River *Main*
ei as in spy, e.g., *ein* (one)
au as in how, e.g., *Maus* (mouse)
ie as in tree, e.g., *Lied* (song)

eu as in boy, e.g., *treu* (true)
äu as in boy, e.g., *Fräulein* (miss)

Consonants
Most are pronounced as written. The
following are exceptions.
ch is either a throaty sound as in
Scottish *loch*, e.g., *Nacht* (night), or
an unvoiced sh sound, e.g., *nicht*
(not)
j is as y in yacht, e.g., *ja* (yes)
r is rolled
s is as z in zip, e.g., *sein* (his)
sch is as sh in shut, e.g., *scheinen* (to
seem)
sp/st are pronounced shp/sht, e.g.,
sprechen (speak), *Stadt* (town)
v is as f in fit, e.g., *Vater* (father)
w is as v in very, e.g., *Wand* (wall)
z is as ts in bits, e.g., *Zeit* (time)

Words and phrases
Days of the week
Sunday	*Sonntag*
Monday	*Montag*
Tuesday	*Dienstag*
Wednesday	*Mittwoch*
Thursday	*Donnerstag*
Friday	*Freitag*
Saturday	*Samstag*
	or *Sonnabend*

Months of the year
Januar	*Juli*
Februar	*August*
März	*September*
April	*Oktober*
Mai	*November*
Juni	*Dezember*

Basics
yes/no	*ja/nein*
please	*bitte*
thank you	*danke*
	(can also mean "no, thank you")
hello	*Guten Tag; Grüss Gott* (in the south)
goodbye	*Auf Wiedersehen*
Do you speak English?	*Sprechen Sie Englisch?*
I don't understand	*Ich verstehe nicht*
Help!	*Zu Hilfe!*

Questions
Where is/are	*Wo ist/sind*
the bank?	*die Bank?*
the station?	*der Bahnhof?*

the airport?	*der lughafen?*
the bus stop?	*die Bushaltestelle?*
the police station?	*as Polizeirevier?*
the nearest toilets?	*die nächsten Toiletten?*
right	*rechts*
left	*links*
straight ahead	*geradeaus*
How much is...	*Wieviel kostet...*
the fare?	*der Fahrpreis?*
the entrance fee?	*der Eintritt?*
When...	*Wann...*
does the museum open?	*wird das Museum geöffnet?*
does the train leave?	*fährt der Zug ab?*
at 10 o'clock	*um zehn Uhr*
at half past 10	*um halb elf*

Staying and eating
I'd like...	*Ich hätte gern...*
a single room	*ein Einzelzimmer*
a double room	*ein Doppelzimmer*
with bath	*mit Bad*
open	*Geöffnet*
closed	*Geschlossen*
Waiter!	*Herr Ober!*
May I see the menu, please?	*Die Speisekarte bitte?*
breakfast	*das Frühstück*
lunch	*das Mittagessen*
dinner	*das Abendessen*
bread	*das Brot*
butter	*die Butter*
egg	*das Ei*
cheese	*der Käse*
vegetables	*das Gemüse*
fruit	*das Obst*
coffee	*der Kaffee*
tea	*der Tee*
beer	*das Bier*
wine	*der Wein*

Numbers
0	*null*	18	*achtzehn*
1	*eins*	19	*neunzehn*
2	*zwei*	20	*zwanzig*
3	*drei*	21	*einund-*
4	*vier*		*zwanzig*
5	*fünf*	30	*dreissig*
6	*sechs*	32	*zweiund-*
7	*sieben*		*dreissig*
8	*acht*	40	*vierzig*
9	*neun*	50	*fünfzig*
10	*zehn*	60	*sechzig*
11	*elf*	70	*siebzig*

12	*zwölf*	80	*achtzig*
13	*dreizehn*	90	*neunzig*
14	*vierzehn*	100	*hundert*
15	*fünfzehn*	101	*hunderteins*
16	*sechzehn*	500	*fünfhundert*
17	*siebzehn*	1,000	*tausend*

Laundry

Most towns of any size in former West Germany have a launderette –'Waschsalon' – with prices from DM5 for a wash (usually including soap). Camp sites have their own washing facilities.

Lost property

All bus and railway stations have lost property offices, look in the telephone directory or enquire at the station for the Fundbüro.

It is very important to read carefully the instructions for loss issued with your travellers' cheques. Make a separate note of the serial numbers of all cheques (or take photocopies) and of the telephone number to call in case of emergencies. Major issuing companies will have refund facilities available. Contact their nearest office or, failing that, the nearest bank. Register loss of cheques with the police, and if you are stranded without money, contact the local consulate.

Follow similar procedure for the loss or theft of Eurocheques and cheque cards. Lost passports should be reported to the police station and contact your consulate if you need emergency travel papers.

Maps

Road atlases: The *Grosse Shaell Atlas* has good, detailed road maps of Germany (scale 1:400,000) with scenic routes, plus city plans, maps of the rest of Europe too, and a full index.

If you take the short ferry crossing the Automobile Association's 1:1,000,000 double-sided map of the whole of Germany could be useful as its coverage extends to the Channel ports from Dieppe.

Hallwag's three 1:500,000 maps of north, east and south Germany include plans showing approach and through roads in all big cities.

Hostelling: The Youth Hostels Map of Germany (Mairs) shows the location of hostels on the map plus a full list with the addresses and phone numbers for the former West Germany (East Berlin only is covered in the East).

Walking: Special tourist maps of West Germany –'Sonderkarte' – showing footpaths and cycling routes in popular destinations are compiled by the German Topographic Society. A full list can be obtained from Stanford's, 12 Longacre, London WC2E 9LP (tel: 070-2836 1321).

Media

The leading German quality daily papers are the conservative *Frankfurter Allgemeine Zeitung* and the more liberal *Süddeutsche Zeitung* (Munich). In addition, nearly every main city or area has its own daily, usually a morning paper. *Die Welt* and the mass-selling tabloid *Bild*, which tends to be sensational, are the two main dailies of the right-wing Springer group.

Some weeklies are also influential: the news magazines *Spiegel*, *Stern* and *Focus*, and women's weeklies such as *Brigitte*. In many towns, local publications will give you a run-down on what's on where: in Berlin, for instance, the best are *Tip*, *Zitty* and the English-language *Checkpoint*.

The main German TV channels, run on a regional basis, are ARD and ZDF. There are also satellite and cable channels, and many radio networks. In many hotels, TV sets can get CNN, Super or Sky with news and other English-language programmes.

Money matters

The Deutschmark (DM) is the official currency. 1 DM equals 100 Pfennigs (pf). Coins are: 1, 2, 5, 10 and 50 pfennig; 1, 2 and 5 DM.

Notes come in denominations of 10, 20, 50, 100, 200, 500 and 1,000 DM.

There are money exchanges – Wechselstuben – at airports, border crossings and major rail stations, that generally stay open from 6am–10pm daily.

Branches of the Deutsche Verkehrs-Kredit Bank, situated in railway

275

stations, can also be used for changing money, and they usually also stay open until 6 pm.

Otherwise, normal banking hours are Mon–Fri 8.30 or 9am to 12.30 or 1pm, then 2.30–4 (5.30 on Thu). Banks are closed Sat–Sun.

You can also change money at post offices, which are open Mon–Sat 8–6 (Sat until midday). Money exchange is usually available in larger branches in main towns only.

Travellers' cheques can be cashed in banks, currency exchanges and post offices, but used directly only in smarter shops in main cities.

Eurocheques, backed by the appropriate card, can be cashed in banks and exchanges and also used in some shops and restaurants, but always take the precaution of checking first. Credit cards are less widely used in Germany than in some countries so it is sensible to check that they are acceptable before eating a meal or making a purchase.

National holidays
1 Jan: New Year's Day
6 Jan: Epiphany (only in Baden-Württemberg and Bavaria)
Good Friday
Easter Sunday/Easter Monday
1 May: Labour Day
Ascension Day (in May)
Whit Sunday and **Whit Monday** (May)
18 June: Corpus Christi (honoured only in certain areas)
15 August: Maria Himmelfahrt (Assumption of the Blessed Virgin Mary, only in Bavaria and Saarland)
3 October: Day of German Unity
1 November: All Saints' Day (honoured only in certain areas)
Day of Prayer and Repentance (in November, changes annually)
25–26 December: Christmas

Opening hours
Legislation liberalising Germany's traditionally strict shopping hours now permits shops to remain open until 8pm from Monday to Friday and until 4pm on Saturday. Very few shops open on Sundays.

Although most large department stores take advantage of the new hours, many smaller stores still close around 6pm. If you're really caught short of supplies at the weekend make for the nearest railway station, where bakeries and grocery shops can stay open especially for travellers. The modest shopping areas near petrol stations also tend to stay open later and at weekends.

Time your arrival carefully at smaller out-of-the-way restaurants. They often serve meals only between noon and 2pm, then from 5 to 8pm.

Business people are usually at their desks by 9am, often earlier, and government offices close punctually at 4pm, or 2pm on Fridays.

For doctors' hours, see above under Health.

Evening entertainments – theatre, concerts and so on – usually start at 8pm, and last about two hours.

Organised tours
Deutsche Touring runs a variety of coach tours, such as the Romantic Road trip from Würzburg to Füssen, or vice versa. A variety of packages lasting from two to seven days is on offer; details from the company at Am Römerhof 17, 60486-Frankfurt am Main.

See the German countryside afloat, on a river trip. The Köln–Düsseldorfer (KD) Line offers trips on the Rhine, Mosel and Elbe. Trips range from five hours to five days and concessions for children and senior citizens are a regular feature. KD Lines is at Frankenwerf 15, 50667 Köln 1 (tel: 0221 208 80). Their UK representative is KD German Rhine Line, 28 South Street, Epsom, Surrey KT18 7PF (tel: 01372 742033).

Sächsische Dampfschiff Gesellschaft Weisse Flotte boat company makes tourist trips on the Havel, Elbe, Oder and Saale rivers, and the Baltic Sea. Contact them at Terrassenufer 1–2, 01067 Dresden.

Hiking is very popular and the Jugendherbergswerk (German Youth Hostel Federation) publishes a list of guided walks, from two-day trips to cross-country treks. Contact them at Hauptverband, Bismarckstrasse 8, D-32754 Detmold.

In addition, the local tourist offices will be happy to suggest local tour opportunities.

Pharmacies

German chemists or their assistants are usually able to speak some English.

If you are taking a course of drugs and need to have a prescription filled while staying in Germany, get your doctor at home to write out a prescription using the generic rather than brand name. It's a good idea to have a letter from him or her to the effect that you need the drug for health purposes.

Check before leaving home that what you are taking with you is not illegal in Germany.

In larger towns, pharmacies – Apotheken – display late-night or 24 hour rota lists. Or, ask at your hotel reception or local police station where to find one open.

Apotheken trade in pharmaceuticals only – cosmetics must be purchased at a Drogerie.

Police

German police – Polizei – are well-mannered and expect members of the public to be equally correct.

Post offices

The main post office – Hauptpostamt – in any large town is usually located near the railway station. Mail reaches the UK in about three days. Stamps for letters to EU countries cost DM1.10, post cards DM1.

To send a letter Poste Restante mark it Postlagernde Briefe/Sendungen and Bitte Halten. As it will be filed alphabetically, according to surname, write that first on the address. Mail is kept, free of charge, for two weeks. When collecting it, take along some ID.

Telegrams can be sent from post offices, or by telephone (see Telephones).

Public transport

Domestic air services between cities are frequent and fast. Within Germany, check with Lufthansa's central reservation service (tel: 01803 803 803) for advice on the many special ticket deals available.

A smaller German airline, LTU, also offers intercity services, as does British Airways.

The Air Travel Advisory Bureau, 41–45 Goswell Road, London EC5 7DN (tel: 070-2636 5000) can give advice on agents who specialise in discount flights.

If you arrive at one airport and want to transfer to another, check with Lufthansa for onward train connections linking major cities.

German Railways (the Deutsche Bahn, or DB) operates a nationwide network that links even the smallest villages with the outside world. It achieves this with a flexible variety of services: the high-speed InterCity Express (ICE) trains linking Berlin, Hamburg, Munich, Frankfurt and many other important towns in between; the InterCity (IC) trains connecting all major towns and cities at hourly intervals (and, as EuroCity trains, with cities in neighbouring countries); the InterRegio (IR) trains concentrating on fast travel between the German regions; and long-distance trains (FD) travelling specifically to holiday destinations (mostly in the Alps). Completing the network are three types of metropolitan and short-distance trains: the RegionalExpress (RE), RegionalBahn (RB) and StadtExpress (SE).

If you think that's a complicated compilation, then the fare structure will really flummox you. It takes nearly 20 pages of a DB brochure to cover all the various offers, most of which change from year to year. Yet you can save enormously by taking advantage of the flexible fare structure – a family of five, for instance, can travel the length and breadth of Bavaria for a whole weekend for DM 35. Never just buy a ticket from A to B but lay your travel plan in front of a (usually) helpful station counter clerk and ask for advice on the cheapest way to make the journey.

A new BahnCard, for the frequent traveller to Germany, offers a 50 per cent discount on standard fares for a year: details from European Rail, Tavistock House North, Tavistock Square, London WC1H 9HR.

If you are under 26 you may be eligible for a Eurail Youthpass. This lasts for one or two months, and offers unlimited second-class travel in Europe.

Coaches

Coaches link rural areas that railways cannot reach. Many are owned by the DB and are timed and routed to complement the train service. German towns operate their own local buses, and one ticket will often be transferable between these and other forms of city transportation, such as the S-Bahn, the Strassenbahn (trams), and the U-Bahn (underground). On entering the bus, train or tram, passengers insert their tickets into a machine that validates them for that trip. Inspectors make frequent rounds to check that tickets are valid – and they are tough on fare dodgers.

Long-distance buses are operated by Deutsche Touring, Am Römerhof 17, 60486 Frankfurt am Main (tel: 069/790–3240) and Berlin-based BerlinienBus, Mannheimer–strasse 33/34, 10713 Berlin-Wilmersdorf (tel: 0800–6666–999). Fares are much cheaper than rail, and buses are comfortable, many with hostess-service and on-board refreshments.

Taxis

It is possible to hail a taxi in the street or pick one up from the many ranks at train stations, hotels, and so on.

They carry an illuminated roof sign, and fares are made up of a basic charge plus payment per kilometre travelled. This varies from place to place, as do surcharges for carrying items of luggage, though this is usually somewhere in the region of 50pf per item.

Student and youth travel

There are over 600 youth hostels in Germany which accept members of all associations affiliated with the International Youth Hostel Federation, based at 9 Guessens Road, Welwyn Garden City, Herts, AL8 6QW (tel: 01707 332487).

Residents of the UK can obtain membership of the Youth Hostel Association from their office at 14 Southampton Street, London WC2 (tel: 070-2836 8541).

Deutsches Jugendherbergswerk Hauptverband (the German youth hostel association) publishes a complete list of hostels; it is on sale at tourist offices and hostels themselves.

It's wise, particularly in the high season, to pre-book accommodation in hostels; officially, there's a three-day limit to your stay, though if the hostel is not full you may be able to remain longer. It is worth noting that in Bavaria priority is given to under-27s. The DJH is at Bismarckstrasse 8, Post-fach 1455, D-32704 Detmold, Germany (tel: 5231 74010).

If you are under 23, or a student under 27, enquire about the Tramper Monats Ticket, entitling holders to one month's unlimited travel on the DB system (except the ICE) and DB buses. Prices start around DM290 (300 + ICE). Ask at railway stations for details (taking along some ID to prove your age).

Telephones

A few public call boxes take 10pf, DM1 and DM5 coins. Most only take phone cards – Kartentelefone – which you buy at the post or tourist office, price DM12 or DM50. You can make international calls except from booths marked 'National'. You can also go to a post office where the connection will be made for you: you pay after the call.

Directory enquiries is on 11834 or, for Europe, 11833. The operator is on 010 (for Germany) and 0010 (for abroad). Call rates are lower after 6pm and at weekends. To dial Britain the code is 0044; Eire, 00353; USA and Canada, 001; Australia 0061; New Zealand 0064.

Time

German time is one hour ahead of British time nearly all the year except for a few weeks in the autumn when the times are the same: this is because the Continent changes its clocks sooner than Britain. German time is normally six hours ahead of Toronto and New York time, nine hours behind Eastern Australian time and 11 hours behind New Zealand.

Tourist offices

Staff are normally very helpful and will provide, often free, maps and literature on attractions in the area, plus a list of local hotels.

Germany's main tourist organisation is the Deutscher Tourismus-verband e.v., Bertha-von-Suttner-Platz 13, D–53111 Bonn (tel: 0228 985–220).
In the **United States** the German National Tourist Office is at 122 East 42nd Street, New York, NY 10168–0072 (tel: 212/661 7200).
Canada has the German National Tourist Office at 175 Bloor Street East, North Tower, 6th Floor, Toronto, Ontario, M4W 3R8 (tel: 416/968 1570). In the **UK** the GNTO is at 65 Curzon Street, London W1Y 7PE (tel: 020-7495–3990). In **Australia**, the office is at Lufthansa House, 9th Floor, 143 Macquarie Street, Sydney 2000 (tel: 00612 3673890). There is no office in **Ireland**. Enquiries can be dealt with by the London office. For **New Zealand**, the nearest tourist office is based in Australia.
Tourist offices in major cities :
Berlin
Europa-Center Budapester Strasse, 10787 Berlin (tel: 030 262 6031)
Bonn
Munsterstrasse 20, 53111 Bonn (tel: 0228 77 34 66)
Hamburg
Am Hauptbahnhof, 20095 Hamburg (tel: 040/3005–1200)
Köln
Verkehrsamt Am Dom, 50667 Köln (tel: 0221/2213–340)

Taking in the fantastic view from Jenna Mountain, Berchtesgaden

Munich
Sendlinger Strasse 1, 80331 Munich (tel: 089 2330 300)

Walking and hiking
There are more than 132,000km of walks in Germany. Detailed information can be obtained from the Verband Deutscher Gebirgs- und Wanderverein, Reichsstrasse 4, D-66111 Saarbrücken 3. The Deutsches Alpenverein, Praterinsel 5, D-80538 Munich 2, can advise on hiking in the Alps and organises a number of mountaineering courses.

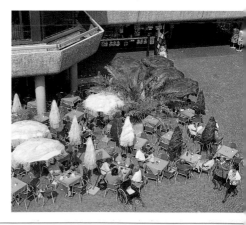

Hotels and Restaurants

HOTELS

These recommended hotels are divided into three price brackets, for a double bedroom with breakfast for two:
(£) = budget: up to DM160
(££) = moderate: from DM160 to DM280
(£££) = expensive: over DM280

BERLIN

Adlon (£££)
Unter den Linden 77, D-10117 Berlin
tel: 030/22610
This hotel is extremely expensive, but even a brief stay at Berlin's historic Adlon is the kind of once-in-a-lifetime experience that can't be measured in terms of money. All-embracing luxury and comforts.

Charlottenburger Hof (£)
Stuttgarter Platz 14, D-10627 Berlin
tel: 030/329-070
In a very convenient location (opposite the Charlottenburg S-Bahn station), basic but perfectly adequate facilities and the friendly staff make this an excellent budget hotel choice.

Residenz (££)
Meinekestrasse 9, D-10719 Berlin
tel: 030/884-430
The high-ceilinged rooms within this elegant turn-of-the-century building give guests a sense of Berlin's prewar beauty. Many art nouveau decorative features, particularly in the highly-regarded restaurant 'Grand Cru'.

NORTHWEST GERMANY

Benther Berg (££)
Vogelsangstrasse 18, D-30952 Ronneberg-Benthe, Hannover tel: 05108/64060
Friendly, comfortable country-house hotel (with motel extension). The extensive grounds of the hotel spill over into pleasant woodland. Bus and tram bring you rapidly into central Hannover.

Kastens Luisenhof (££–£££)
Luisenstrasse 1-3, D-30159 Hannover
tel. 0511/30440
Hannover's oldest hotel is also one of its best-managed and most stylish, furnished with antiques. Its restaurant is also one of Hannover's best.

Kronprinz (££)
Kirchenallee 46, D-20099 Hamburg
tel: 040/243-258
Well placed for sights, theatres, museums, galleries and shopping. The plushly comfortable rooms are sound-proofed.

Mittelweg (££)
Mittelweg 59, D-20149 Hamburg
tel: 040/414-1010
An elegant turn-of-the-century city mansion which has been tastefully converted into a charming hotel, with modern comforts and old-fashioned touches.

Ringhotel Jensen (££)
An der Obertrave 4-5, D-23552 Lübeck
tel: 0451/71646
One of Lübeck's old city mansions, a fine stepped-gable building directly overlooking the Trave river, has now been converted into a very comfortable hotel and restaurant. Most of the city's historic sights are a short walk away.

Romantik-Hotel Altes Gymnasium (££)
Süderstrasse 6, 25831 Husum
tel: 04841/8330
The Romantik is one of the most luxurious hotels on this stretch of Germany's North Sea coast. The red-brick exterior may be somewhat forbidding, but inside the building, discipline ends at the reception desk, and from then on it's all hedonism.

Strandhotel Blankenese (££)
Strandweg 13, D-22587 Hamburg
tel: 040/861-344
A beautiful, fussily-façaded art nouveau (Jugendstil) villa. Insist on a room overlooking the Elbe – if you can back your claim with a maritime connection it'll help.

Waldhotel am Schloss Gottorf (££)
Stampfmühle 1, D-24837 Schleswig
tel: 04621/23288
The hotel is situated in the grounds of the Gottorf Palace (Schloss) and on the edge of a thick wood (Wald). It is a very attractive Jugendstil (1908) villa, with large rooms which have been furnished in north German country-house style.

Rhineland

Burghotel Reichenstein (££)
Burg Reichenstein, D-55413 Trechtingshausen
tel: 06721/6117
This isn't the most luxurious of the castle hotels of the Rhine but it's unbeatable value for money – and includes a resident headless ghost if you're lucky. The rooms are large to immense in size, some with four-poster beds, and furnished in eccentric fashion. In good weather you can dine on a terrace above the Rhine.

Dom (£££)
Domkloster 2A, D-50667 Köln
tel: 0221/20240
A stately, unpretentiously luxurious mansion. The bedrooms have all been furnished with antiques.

Rheinhotel Dreesen (£££)
Rheinstrasse 45-49, Bad Godesberg, D-53179 Bonn tel: 0228/82020
The gardens of this hotel extend down to the river and there's a delightful 'chestnut-tree garden' with sliding roof for all-weather summer dining. Insist on a room with Rhine views.

Ringhotel Central (££)
Kirchstrasse 6, D-65385 Rüdesheim/Rheingau
tel: 06722/9120
An attractive house, with steep eaves, dormer and oriel windows. Within, modern comforts blend with traditional touches. The restaurant serves Rhineland specialities.

Residenz Domus (££)
Erzbergerstrasse 1-5, D-34117 Kassel
tel: 0561/ 72960
A stylish, comfortable hotel, retaining most of
its original art nouveau features. It has a glass-
domed winter garden and a French-influenced
restaurant that are among the best in
Hannover.

Dornröschenschloss Sababurg (££)
D-34369 Hofgeismar tel: 05671/8080
This hotel is said to have inspired the Grimm
brothers' story of the Sleeping Beauty. It's a
trifle self-consciously romantic but snugly
comfortable. The surrounding forest provides
in-season game for the (romantic, of course)
restaurant.

Kaiserworth (££)
Markt 3, D-38640 Goslar/Harz
tel: 05321/21111
A 15th-century guildhall which has been
converted into a hotel. Some rooms have four-
posters. In fine weather, you can dine on the
arcaded terrace.

Kempinski Hotel Gravenbruch (£££)
D-63263 Neu Isenburg, Frankfurt-am-Main
tel: 06102/5050
One of Germany's finest countryhouse hotels,
set in its own 12-hectare park. It also has an
extremely fine restaurant, beauty farm and
health centre, making it a favourite weekend
break destination.

Mozart (££)
Parkstrasse 17, D-60322 Frankfurt-am-Main
tel: 069/550-831
Mozart and his music are the motif of this
suitably harmonious city hotel. Rooms are
decorated and furnished throughout in
exquisite taste.

Zur Krone (££)
Osterstrasse 30, D-31785 Hameln
tel: 05151/9070
Request a room in the main building of this
fine old half-timbered Hameln hotel. Central
location and a very good restaurant.

EASTERN GERMANY

Arte Schwerin (f–ff)
Dorfstrasse 6, D-19061 Schwerin-Krebsförden
tel: 0385/63450
This hotel is situated in beautifully restored old
farmhouse; one of Schwerin's lovely lakes is a
short walk away and the city centre is easily
accessible by bus.

Balance (£–££)
Wasserturmstrasse 33, D-04299 Leipzig
tel: 0341/86790).
A smart, functional city hotel. It offers special
rates at the weekend which places this
otherwise middle bracket hotel in the 'budget'
category.

Haus Hainstein (f.f.)
Am Hainstain 16, 99817 Eisenach
tel: 03691/2420
Magnificent views of the Wartburg castle and
the surrounding countryside can be enjoyed
from many of the rooms and the garden-terrace
of this turn-of-the-century mansion.

**Ibis Dresden (Hotels Bastei, Königstein and
Lilienstein)** (£–££)
Prager Strasse, D-01069 Dresden
tel: 0351/4856-6661
These three Ibis chain hotels former a high-rise
complex on Dresden's main pedestrian
shopping mall. Clean and comfortable, they
are outstanding value.

Parkhotel Pannonia (££)
Hafenstrasse 27-31, 01662 Meissen
tel: 03521/72250
One of Meissen's few elegant villas, converted
into a stylish hotel, with a superb restaurant.
Porcelain tiles smother the fussy façade, and
elegant Jugendstil touches are in evidence
everywhere.

Russischer Hof (££)
Goetheplatz 2, 99423 Weimar
tel: 03643/7740
Now nearly 200 years old, this centrally-located
luxury hotel was once an early centre of
cultural life in Weimar. It was here that the
composer Franz Liszt founded his 'Neu-Weimar
Verein' in 1854. Heinrich Heine, Clara and
Robert Schumann, Hector Berlioz, Ivan
Turgenev and Richard Wagner all stayed at
one time.

Kempinski Hotel Taschenbergpalais (£££)
Taschenberg 3, D-01067 Dresden
tel: 0351/49120
This is one of eastern Germany's finest hotels.
It is located in a reconstructed city palace that
once housed members of the Saxon royal family. Everything at the Kempinski is palatial –
from the extensive rooms and suites to the
two restaurants.

SOUTHWEST GERMANY

Alter Fritz (££)
Feuerbacher Weg 101, D-70192 Stuttgart
tel: 0711/135 650
This delightful small hotel offers a peaceful
and quiet place to stay, but is still an easy
stroll to the city centre. Rooms are smartly
furnished and the restaurant has a very good
reputation.

Burg Hornberg (££)
D-74865 Neckarzimmern tel: 06261/92460
Ask for a room with a view overlooking the river
and book a window-table in the restaurant,
where wines from the castle's own vineyard
are served.

Der Kleine Prinz (£££)
Lichtentalerstrasse 36, D-76530 Baden-Baden
tel: 07221/3464
The city's most original and friendliest hotel.
Each room is decorated in an individual style,
ranging from baroque and Biedermeier to
American modern (one even has a Manhattan
skyline).

Insel-Hotel (£££)
Friedrich-Ebert-Brücke, D-7100 Heilbronn
tel: 07131/6300
The 'Insel' stands on an island of the river
Neckar in the centre of Heilbronn. Two restau-
rants and a sunny terrace serve excellent
Swabian fare. Modern, comfortable rooms.

281

Hotels and Restaurants

Romantik Hotel Zum Ritter St. Georg (£££)
Hauptstrasse 178, D-69117 Heidelberg
tel: 06221/1350
This is Heidelberg's most famous hotel. The distinctive Renaissance façade sets the style for the delightfully snug interior, which qualifies this hotel in every sense for that description 'Romantik'.

Schloss Wasserburg (££)
Halbinselstrasse 78, D-88142 Wasserburg
tel: 08382/98670
Of all the Bodensee castles this is unquestioably one of the loveliest – and it's also a comfortable and reasonably-priced hotel. Most rooms have views of the lake and all are furnished individually. Freshly-caught lake fish is on the menu.

Zum roten Bären (££–£££)
Oberlinden 12, D-79098 Freiburg
tel: 0761/21060
Germany's oldest hostelry (dating from 1311), the 'Red Bear' is now an impressive baroque-style luxury hotel, although a beer tavern still nestles within its ancient walls.

MUNICH AND THE ALPS

Munich

Admiral (££)
Kohlstrasse 9, 80469 München
tel: 089 216-350
Grand hotel touches are found here within an intimate, homely scale. The hotel does not have its own restaurant but snacks can be ordered at the snug bar.

Am Siegestor (£)
Akademiestrasse 5, München
tel: 089 399-550
These modest but comfortable bed-and-breakfast lodgings are perfectly located on the edge of the university quarter, which makes it very convenient for both the city centre and Schwabing.

Rafael (£££)
Neuturmstrasse 2, D-80331 Munich
tel: 089/290-980
The Rafael (a converted city palace) has made an international impression with the quality of its service and its range of comforts. The hotel restaurant is considered to be among the best on offer in Munich.

The Alps

Bayern (£££)
Neureuthstrasse 23, 83684 Tegernsee
tel: 08022/1820
Stunning views of the mountain-ringed water from the terrace, pretty pink-toned restaurant and bedrooms in the main house.

Stolls Hotel Alpine (££)
Ulmenweg 14-16, 83471 Schönau am Königsee tel: 08652/65090
A comfortable alpine hotel, set in spacious grounds. There are indoor and outdoor swimming pools, and the Königsee lake is just a short walk away.

Wittelsbach (££)
Von-Brug-Strasse 24, 82467 Garmisch-Partenkirchen tel: 08821/53096
There are fine views of the Zugspitze from this hotel. The restaurant serves cuisine with a Bavarian touch.

Zur Linde (££)
Fraueninsel im Chiemsee 1, 83256 Chiemsee tel: 08054/90366
You have to catch a boat to this delightful hotel, situated on a tiny island. Just the place to be marooned in.

NORTHERN BAVARIA

Bischofshof (££–£££)
Krautermarkt 3, 93047 Regensburg
tel: 0941/59086
This hotel is a former bishop's palace with spacious rooms and a central cobbled courtyard. One of the suites incorporates part of a Roman gateway.

Eisenhut (£££)
Herrngasse 3-7, D-91541 Rothenburg ob der Tauber tel: 09861/7050
This centrally-located hotel has a restaurant of note, a piano bar and a leafy beer-garden. A luxurious retreat from the crowds of tourists.

Goldener Anker (££)
Opernstrasse 6, D-95444 Bayreuth
tel: 0921/65051
Throughout the opera season you will have difficulty booking a room. The central location and a very good restaurant are strong recommendations.

Goldener Hirsch (££)
Untere Schmiedgasse 16-15, D-91541 Rothenburg ob der Tauber tel: 09861/7080
Once a 15th-century city mansion, now converted into a comfortable hotel. There are antiques in most rooms.

Hotel-Weinhaus Steichele (££)
Knorrstrasse 2 – 8, D-90402 Nürnberg
tel: 0911/202280
A 19th-century wine merchant's warehouse transformed into a very comfortable hotel. The hotel restaurant and wine tavern serve authentic Franconian fare, including Nürnberg sausages.

Wilder Mann (££–£££)
Am Rathausplatz, D-94032 Passau
tel: 0851/35071
The guests' register of this historic hotel reads like an historical Who's Who. Rooms range from 'comfortable' to unashamedly luxurious.

RESTAURANTS

BERLIN

Rockendorf's (£££)
Dusterhauptstrasse 1 tel: 030/402-3099
A Berlin institution that offers only set menus, assembled with artistry and imagination; classic German dishes with a nouvelle touch.

Marjellchen (££)
Mommsenstrasse 9 tel: 030/883-2676
Specialises in East Prussian cuisine: the
Königsberger Klopse (small dumplings in caper
sauce) are unbeatable. Try a Danzig Schnaps
to finish.
Zur Nolle (£)
*Georgenstrasse –S-Bahnbogen 203
tel: 030/208-2655*
Many features still survive from Berlin's
swinging 1920s, one of which is a backlit
ceiling.

Bars/cafés

Cafe Adler (£)
Friedrichstrasse 206 tel: 030/251-8965
This typical Berlin café once nestled right up
against Checkpoint Charlie.
Eierschale (£)
*Landhaus Dahlem, Podbielskiallee 50
tel: 030/832-7097) and Alt-Treptow-Strasse
14-17 tel: 030/533-7370).*
The two Eierschale café-restaurants have live
music daily and a Sunday jazz-brunch.
Friedrichstadtpalais (££)
Friedrichstrasse 107 tel: 030/2326 2474
A historic Berlin variety and revue theatre; it is
the biggest in Europe, and has world-class acts
performing here.

NORTHWEST GERMANY

Fischereihafen-Restaurant Hamburg (££)
*Grosse Elbstrasse 143, Hamburg
tel: 040/381-816*
The morning's catch lands on the lunch-time
menu. The experience is not cheap (try the
Fischerhaus at the Fish Market, Fischmarkt 14,
if budget-dining) but it's memorable.
Georgenhof (££)
*Herrenhäuser Kirchweg 20, Hannover
tel: 0511/202-244*
In fine weather, tables are laid on the shady
terrace, overlooking a pool and fountains.
The excellent menu is urbane and
international.
Landhaus Amman (£££)
*Hildesheimer Strasse 185, Hannover
tel: 0511/830-818*
Hannover's best restaurant (one Michelin star)
is in the skilful hands of one of Germany's
finest chefs, Helmut Amman. He insists on the
freshest produce and grows his own herbs.
Landhaus Scherrer (£££)
*Elbchaussee 130, Hamburg
tel: 040/880-1325*
A select restaurant, where you'll dine with the
city's élite (publishers, mostly).

Rhineland

Bodo-La Poele d'Or (£££)
*Komödienstrasse 50-52, Köln
tel: 0221/134-100*
Köln's top restaurant, where Rhineland French
influence meets German tradition. Service,
ambience and the wine list are all impeccable.

Hotellerie Hubertus (££)
*Metzger Strasse 1, Tholey-Saar
tel: 06853/2404*
The imaginative dishes (Franco-German with an
international touch) are served either in a
splendid, vaulted dining room or in the rustic
Marktstube ('Market tavern').
Schlosshotel Kommende Ramersdorf (££)
*Oberkasseler Strasse 10, Bonn
tel: 0228/440734*
The menu is Italian but the setting is noble
German: the restaurant is located in an
elegantly-converted wing of a half-timbered,
turreted Schloss.
Stapelhäuschen (£)
Fischmarkt 1-3, Köln tel: 0211/257-7862
The Stapelhäusen is a quaint and traditional
tavern-restaurant. The cooking is no-frills
Rhineland – try the Sauerbraten with bread
dumplings.
Zum Schiffchen (£)
*Hafenstrasse 5, Düsseldorf
tel: 0221/132-422*
The tavern, which has been in business since
1628, still brews its own beer, served with
solid homecookcd Rhineland fare such as
grilled marinated beef.

CENTRAL GERMANY

Brückenkeller (£££)
*Schützenstrasse 6, Frankfurt-am-Main
tel: 069/298-0070*
This is Frankfurt's best restaurant,and is
located in a 17th-century vaulted cellar. The
menu is German-international, and the wine list
is cosmic.
Der Achtermann (££)
*Rosentorstrasse 20, D-38640 Goslar
tel: 05321/21001*
A 'restaurant in the round' embraced by the
circular walls of an historic defence tower.
Venison is highly recommended.
Goldener Karpfen (££)
Simpliciusbrunnen 1, Fulda tel: 0661/86800
This elegant and inviting restaurant is fitted out
with snugly comfortable furnishings and dis-
creet lighting.
Hotel Gude (££)
*Frankfurterstrasse 299, Kassel tel:
0561/48050*
The Hotel Gude's 'Pfeffermühle' (Pepper Pot)
restaurant serves a range of international and
traditional German dishes.
Schloss Bevern (££)
Am Schloss, Bevern tel: 05531/8783
Meals are served in a baronial-style, pillared
and panelled dining room. Pheasant and
partridge from the surrounding countryside are
on the menu.
Zum Gemalten Haus (£)
*Schweizerstr. 67, Frankfurt-am-Main
tel: 069/614-559*
This is the most attractive of the countless
cider taverns of Frankfurt's Sachsenhausen
district. It is noisy and friendly and excellent
value for money.

Hotels and Restaurants

EASTERN GERMANY

Auerbachs Keller (££)
Mädlerpassage, Leipzig tel: 0341/216-100
Famous as the setting for part of Goethe's 'Faust'. The cuisine, solidly Saxon (lots of roast meat, rich sauces and dumplings), is excellent value and they serve interesting east German wines.

Caroussel (££–£££)
Rähnitzgasse 19, Dresden tel: 0351/80030
You will need to reserve well in advance for this excellent restaurant in the Hotel Bülow Residenz, with Baroque-style furnishings and a delightful interior courtyard.

Glockenhof (££)
Grimmelgasse 4, 99817 Eisenach tel: 03691/2340
The Glockenhof is among Germany's leading 500 restaurants. The imaginative menu is basically Thuringian, with international flourishes. The venison stew with dumplings is a classic.

Italienisches Dörfchen (£–££)
Theaterplatz 3, Dresden tel: 0351/498-160
An attractive, historic complex of restaurant, tavern, café and beer garden, centrally located on the banks of the Elbe.

Weinhaus Uhle (££)
Schusterstrasse 13-15, Schwerin tel: 0385/562956
Dine in style beneath a beautifully-frescoed, chandelier-hung vaulted ceiling. The excellent menu includes a variety of memorable duck dishes.

SOUTHWEST GERMANY

Bareiss (£££)
Gärtenbühlweg 14, Mitteltal/Baiersbronn tel: 07442/470
The menu at this restaurant features international cuisine with a Franco-German touch; this is a rare (and expensive) dining experience.

Grimm's Märchen (££–£££)
G7, 17, Mannheim tel: 0621/103636
Grimm's Märchen is one of Mannheim's most affordable and interesting restaurants. On chilly evenings a welcoming fire blazes in the hearth.

Rappen (£)
Münsterplatz 13, Freiburg im Briesgau tel: 0761/31353
This restaurant has a wood-panelled interior dining room and also a small terrace which looks out onto Freiburg's market square and famous Münster. The wine list includes some interesting Black Forest wines, and the beer is also local.

Roter Ochsen (£)
Hauptstrasse 217, Heidelberg tel: 06221/20977
Of all Heidelberg's celebrated student taverns this is one of the best, a judgment confirmed by the parade of world dignitaries who have left their names on autographed photos or in the visitors' book.

Stuttgarter Stäffele (££)
Buschlestrasse 2A/B (cnr. Augustenstrasse) (tel: 0711/61-276
You won't find better Swabian cooking than at this three-restaurant address. Take your pick between the large restaurant, the small restaurant and the wine-cellar, where more than 250 Württemberg varieties of wine are stored.

MUNICH AND THE ALPS

Munich

Nürnberger Bratwurst Glöckl am Dom (£)
Frauenplatz 9, Munich tel: 089/220-385
The sausages served at this historic old restaurant are absolutely delicious 'Nürnberg Bratwurst', but otherwise it is quintessential Munich.

Tantris (£££)
Johann-Fichter-Strasse 7, Munich tel: 089/362-061
The Tantris is considered to be Munich's top restaurant. The décor is smart international, the food good enough to attract the admiration of French and American critics.

Weinhaus Neuner (££)
Herzogspitalstrasse 8, Munich tel: 089/260-3954
Munich's oldest wine tavern, panelled in dark oak and lit by slightly tipsy chandeliers. Venison is always an excellent bet and the steak, with Swiss-style roast potatoes, is unbeatable.

The Alps

Reindl's Partenkirchner Hof (££–£££)
Bahnhofstrasse 15, Garmisch-Partenkirchen tel: 08821/58025)
Chef Marianne Reindl's menu combines Bavarian traditional excellence (particularly the sauces) with international flair. Situated just beneath the Zugspitze.

Residenz Heinz Winkler (£££)
Kirchplatz 1, 83229 Aschau tel: 08052/17990
Winkler, one of Germany's top chefs, runs this superb country restaurant in part of a 300-year-old coaching inn.

NORTHERN BAVARIA

Säumerhof (£££)
Steinberg 32, Grafenau tel: 08552/408-990
An excellent gourmet restaurant; book well ahead, particularly if your visit is during the hunting season, when venison and game-birds feature prominently on the menu.

Schenkerla (£–££)
Beim Tiergärtnertor 3, Nürnberg tel: 0911/225-474
A good place to eat delicious Nürnberg sausages, made daily on the premises. The Franconian smoked beer, straight from the barrel, is home-brewed, and it comes with a home-made cheese.

285

Index

Index/Acknowledgements

Acknowledgements

The Automobile Association would like to thank the following photographers, libraries and associations for their assistance in the preparation of this book.

ALLSPORT UK LTD 17, 23 Boris Becker **MARY EVANS PICTURE LIBRARY** 14 Beethoven, 24/5 French royalty, 25 French ruler, 26 German patricians, 27 Peasants co–opt leader, 27 Paul Rieth, 28/9 Nazi rally, 28 Treaty of Versailles, 29 Nazi Parteitag, Nürnberg, 32 Baccalaureate lecture, Luther 33 Friedrich Wilhelm Nietzsche, Hansel and Gretel, 75 Danzig, Ships – Hanseatic League, 120 Grimm's Red Riding Hood, 121 The Valiant Tailor, The Goose Girl, 147 Händel, 237a Wagner with Cosima, 237b Wagner, 261 Ludwig II **GERMAN NATIONAL TOURIST OFFICE** 15 Berlin Philharmonic, 17 Skiing, 18 Courthouse, Bonn **JAMES DAVIS TRAVEL PHOTOGRAPHY** Back cover Brass bandsmen **PICTOR INTERNATIONAL, LONDON** Spine Oberayern, Munich Steins **POWERSTOCK/ZEFA** Front cover c Rothenburg at night **REX FEATURES LTD** 23 Helmut Schmidt, Helmut Kohl **RICHARD BRYANT/ARCADE** Front cover b Reichstag, Berlin, 45 **SPECTRUM COLOUR LIBRARY LTD** 14 Munich Oktoberfest, 20 Smoking chimneys, 21 BMW Black Forest, Car scrapyard, 259 Munich Oktoberfest **THE BRIDGEMAN ART LIBRARY** 35 People by the Pool, The Garden Café (Kirchner) **THE KOBAL COLLECTION** 22 Wings of Desire **TOPHAM PICTURE SOURCE** 30 Breaking down the Berlin Wall **ZEFA PICTURES LTD** Front cover a Bavarian dress, 19 Money, Hintergrund.
All remaining pictures are held in the AA's own photo library (© AA Photolibrary) with contributions from:
A BAKER 3, 4, 6,8, 9, 12, 16a, 20/1, 27c, 31b, 34, 38, 39, 42, 43, 44, 46, 47, 49, 50, 79, 80, 81, 82, 84, 88, 89, 90, 91, 92, 93, 95, 96, 98, 99, 100, 101, 106, 107, 112, 113, 114, 131, 133, 166, 173, 174, 175, 177, 178, 179, 181, 183, 184b, 185, 186, 187, 189, 191, 192, 193, 195, 196/7, 198, 199, 200, 201, 202, 203, 204, 205, 208, 209, 210, 211, 212, 213, 214, 215, 217, 218, 219, 221, 222, 223, 224, 225, 226, 227, 228/9, 229, 230, 231, 232, 233, 234, 235, 236, 240, 241, 242, 244, 246, 247, 248, 249a, 250, 251, 252, 253, 256, 257, 258, 260, 261, 262, 263, 264, 265, 267, 271, 279 **P ENTICKNAP** 13a, 83 **C SAWYER** 5, 7a, 7b **R STRANGE** 240b **D TRAVERSO** 10, 13b, 15b, 31a, 35c, 40, 48, 51, 54, 55, 56, 57, 60, 61, 62, 63, 64, 65, 67, 68, 69, 70, 71, 73, 74, 75, 77, 105, 109, 110, 111, 117, 118, 119, 122, 123, 124, 125, 126, 127, 128, 129, 130, 134, 136, 138, 139, 140, 141, 142, 143, 144, 145, 146, 147, 148, 149, 150, 151, 152, 155, 156, 157, 158, 159, 160, 161, 162/3, 164, 165, 167, 169, 170, 171, 184a, 270, 272

Contributors

Revision copy editor: Grapevine Publishing Services
Original copy editor: Joan Miller Verifier: Robert Tilley